Sylv

Memoirs
of
William Miller

Adventist Pioneer Library

A Service of
Light Bearers Ministry
37457 Jasper Lowell Rd
Jasper, OR, 97438, USA
(877) 585-1111
www.LightBearers.org
www.APLib.org

Originally published by Joshua Himes, Boston, 1853.

Original page numbers are in brackets.

Published in the USA

Updated May, 2015

ISBN: 978-1-61455-024-2

MEMOIRS

OF

WILLIAM MILLER

Generally Known as

A LECTURER ON THE PROPHECIES, AND THE
SECOND COMING OF CHRIST.

By
SYLVESTER BLISS,
Author of "Analysis of sacred chronology," "A brief
commentary on the apocalypse," etc.

Boston:
Published by Joshua V. Himes,
S Chardon Street.
1853.

William Miller (1782-1849)

I remain yours affectionately
Wm Miller

CONTENTS

DAGUERREOTYPE VIEW OF MR. MILLER'S LATE RESIDENCE.

PREFACE

The name of William Miller, of Low Hampton, N. Y., is too well known to require an extended introduction; but, while well known, few men have been more diversely regarded than he. Those who have only heard his name associated with all that is hateful in fanaticism, have necessarily formed opinions respecting him anything but complimentary to his intelligence and sanity; but those who knew him better, esteemed him as a man of more than ordinary mental power, – a cool, sagacious, and honest reasoner, an humble and devout Christian, a kind and affectionate friend, and a man of great moral and social worth. That the impartial reader may be able to form a just estimate of one who has occupied so conspicuous a position before the public, the following pages are compiled.

To see a man as he is, it is necessary to accompany him through the walks of his daily life; to trace the manner in which he has arrived at his conclusions; to follow him into his closet and places of retirement; to learn the various workings of his mind through a long series of years, and to scan closely his motives. A knowledge of these can be arrived at only by a simple collection of facts and documents illustrative of his history. By full extracts from his unstudied correspondence, by his published writings, by narrations of interviews with him, by the free use of his papers and memorandums, and by the testimony of impartial witnesses respecting his labors in various places, in addition to a long personal acquaintance, his biographer has been enabled to embody much important information respecting him. It has not been deemed necessary to eulogize him, nor to apologize for him. His acts and life are permitted to stand forth, divested of the veil of partiality, or of prejudice. His opinions on all subjects are expressed in his own language, – having himself narrated the workings of his own mind, at the various periods of his life. His [iv] biographer has not felt warranted to omit opinions on any prominent question, or to modify the phraseology in which they are expressed, to meet the views of those who dissented from him. Such a course would have been unjust to Mr. Miller.

However his public labors may be regarded by a majority of the community, it will be seen, by a perusal of his life, that these were by no means unproductive of great good. The revivals of religion which attended his labors are testified to by those who participated in them; and hundreds of souls will ever refer to him as a means, under God, of their awakening and conversion.

His erroneous calculation of the prophetic periods he frankly confessed; and those who regarded his views of prophecy as dependent on that, may be surprised to learn that he distinguished between the manner and the era of their fulfillment.

It is believed that the influence exerted by Mr. Miller will not prove evanescent in its results. The attention which was given to his arguments caused many minds entirely to change their preconceived opinions respecting the millennial state, who have since remained devoted Christians, ardently looking for the Nobleman who has gone into a far country to receive for himself a kingdom, and to return. – Luke 19:12. As the public learn to discriminate between the actual position of Mr. Miller and that which prejudice has conceived that he occupied, his conservativeness and disapprobation of every fanatical practice will be admitted, and a much more just estimate will be had of him.

These Memoirs were commenced by Elder Apollos Hale, who prepared the first three chapters. Other duties having interfered with his progress in the work, its completion has devolved on another. No labor or expense has been spared to give a full and impartial history of his life, the principal incidents of which, as here recorded, were originally related by him. Desiring "nothing to extenuate, nor to set down aught in malice," these incidents of his history, and this embodiment of his views, I here present to the *Christian* public as an act of justice to Mr. Miller.

JOSHUA V. HIMES.

Boston, *January*, 1853. [v]

ORIGINAL TABLE OF CONTENTS

[The page numbers of the original table of contents reflect the original publication's layout. They are found **in brackets** throughout the text.]

CHAPTER 1

Ancestry and Early Life

About a mile west from the centre of Pittsfield village, one of the most pleasant in western Massachusetts, there is a noble and fertile swell of land, which rises from the west bank of Pontousooc river – the western branch of the head-waters of the Housatonic – and is of sufficient extent to constitute several large farms. The summit of this fine elevation embraces what is familiarly known in the neighborhood as "the Miller farm." It takes its name from a family by the name of Miller, who came from the vicinity of Connecticut river, in or near Springfield, Massachusetts, about a hundred years ago.[1] [2]

Family tradition uniformly connects this branch of the Miller family with Obadiah and Thomas Miller, of a previous generation; undoubtedly the persons of these names who are mentioned in the history of Springfield and Westfield, two hundred years since.

The surrounding country, as seen from the Miller farm, furnishes one of the most interesting prospects afforded by the natural scenery of New England. On the north, Saddle Mountain, the highest elevation of land in the state, towers far above all the other barriers of the valley; and while its "Gray Lock" will ever cause it to be regarded as the venerable and natural guardian of the adjacent portion of the world, it is pointed out as the site of Fort Massachusetts, so memorable for the scenes connected with its history during the French and Indian wars. The Washington Mountains

---

[1] We take the following extract from a manuscript copy of a letter addressed to one of the Miller family, in Georgeville, Lower Canada, dated September 27, 1830. It was written by William Miller, in answer to a request for information on his family history; and is a curious but characteristic production:

"My grandfather, William Miller, married a respectable girl, by the name of Hannah Leonard, in West Springfield; and moved into Pittsfield, then called Ponthoosoc, about 1747, and there had three sons and one daughter. One son died young; the daughter about middle age, after being married, and having a son and daughter, by Nathaniel Spring, named William and Hannah. The other two sons, named Elihu and William, married and had large families, many of whom are yet alive. I sprung from the youngest brother, William."

form the strong background of the view on the east; the Hancock Mountains, a section of the Green Mountain range, of which Saddle Mountain is the climax, bound the view on the west; and some isolated mountainous elevations, through which the branches of the Housatonic river and railroad pass, are the prominent items in the prospect to the south.

On this commanding spot, the family of early adventurers erected their primitive dwelling; and, although their history is unknown to the world, the strong features of their character, as preserved in the memory of their descendants, were, the most daring contempt of danger, great love of independence, great capability of endurance, and whole-souled patriotism. The head of this family was the grandfather of William Miller, whose life these pages record. The name of the grandfather was William; his son, who was born and resided here, was named William; and here also was born the one who has just passed away, and whose world-wide fame demands that his history should now be written. This William Miller was born February 15th, A. D. 1782. He was the eldest of sixteen children, five of whom were sons and eleven were daughters.

The lot of ground on which the ancient dwelling stood is designated, on the new map of Pittsfield, by the name of "Dr. J. Leland Miller." The building itself is [3] no more. The remains of the cellar are still visible; and the ruins are marked by an ancient gooseberry bush, a hardy specimen of the wild thorn, and an elm of the age, perhaps, of twenty years.

The period immediately preceding his birth was the most critical of any period in the history of our country; and was, probably, the most distinguished by its perils, the sublimity of its events, the noble development of character it furnished, and its commanding interpositions of Providence, of any period since the departure of Israel from the land of Egypt. If the English colonies were the only ones that were capable of bettering their condition, and that of the world, by asserting and obtaining their liberty, the colonies of our country, now the United States, furnish the only instance of successful rebellion against the power of the English throne.

What effect the events of this period had on the fortune, the character, and the history of the subject of this memoir, we may be unable fully to determine; but it will be readily seen, that the most fondly cherished memorials of his family, as of his country, could not fail of making a deep impression on his mind, at an early age. That the embarrassed condition of his early life was the direct result of the great sacrifices made by his progenitors, in the struggles and sufferings which they nobly shared with their contemporaries, is equally evident.

William's father, Captain William Miller, was in the army of the Revolution. At the time of the evacuation of New York by order of Washington, on the invasion of that city by Lord Howe, in August, 1776, he was confined, sick with fever, in the hospital. By rallying all his strength, and the assistance he obtained from his fellow-soldiers, he succeeded in leaving the city with the continental troops. The effort, however, proved almost fatal. When his companions, in the retiring movement, sought shelter in a barn, during a storm, he was left helpless under the drippings from its roof, until his sad condition moved the compassion of a fellow-soldier, in better health than himself, to come to his relief. This true soldier entered the barn; he crowded together those who filled the already crowded floor, and thus made room for his almost dying comrade, Miller; and then [4] he bore him gently to the rude place of repose he had prepared for him. Under such circumstances, the poorest accommodations are enjoyed with a soul-inspiring sense of comfort, of which those who are in health, among friends, secure from danger, and surrounded with the luxuries of life, can form no conception.

With our suffering soldier the point of danger appears to have been passed, by this timely assistance of his friend. How much he was afterwards indebted to the same, or some other generous heart, we have no recorded or traditionary testimony to inform us. He returned to Pittsfield, and was married to Miss Paulina Phelps, on the 22nd day of March, 1781. The family records inform us that he was born December 15th, 1757; and that Miss Phelps was born May 1st, 1764.

Five years after their marriage, they removed to Hampton, in the State of New York, where the survivor of the dangers and hardships of the revolutionary struggle was promoted to the office of captain in the militia of that state. In the last war with England, he was a member of the company called the Silver Grays, a volunteer body, to whose protection the public stores and other property at Whitehall were intrusted, on the approach of the British army along the shores, and of the British fleet on the waters of Lake Champlain. As a citizen, the character of Captain Miller was irreproachable. He never made a public profession of religion; but his house was often the place to which the neighbors gathered to hear the preaching of the gospel. He was taken away suddenly, with one of his daughters, by the pestilence which broke out in the army at Burlington, Vermont, and swept over a considerable portion of the country, with the most terrible fatality. He died December 30th, 1812, three days after his daughter.

Captain Miller's wife was the daughter of Elder Elnathan Phelps, a minister of the Baptist church, and well known, in his day, for the plain, scriptural character of his preaching, through the whole section of country extending from western Massachusetts, along the line of Vermont and New York, to Lake Champlain. She was one of the earliest members of the Baptist church formed at Low Hampton, then a branch of the church at Orwell, [5] Vermont, where Elder Phelps resided. We have the most convincing evidence of the sterling character of her piety; and shall find, as we progress, another instance to add to the long list, which the church of God keeps among her choicest memorials, to illustrate the power of a Christian mother's deportment and prayers, in recovering a gifted son from a dangerous position, and bringing him where his powerful natural energies, after being renewed by the spirit of God, would be devoted to the defense of the faith, and the edification of the church. Her death will be noticed in another place.

Thus were blended in the parents of William, as their strongest traits of character, the highest virtues which heaven and earth can confer on man – piety and patriotism. If patriotism became most conspicuous to the public eye, by its exhibition on the field of danger and suffering, where the husband moved, its claims on the comfort of the wife, in her retirement, were felt to be sufficiently heavy. And if the mother, by her public but appropriate profession of faith, made her piety the most noticeable, the father yielded, at least, his assent and respect to that name and service which had won the heart and added to the graces of William's mother. The soldier of the Revolution was to lead his son into scenes, and bring him under a worldly discipline, which would add to his efficiency; and the camp, for a time, would feel as sure of his permanent attachment as it was to be proud of his soldierly honor; but the disciple of the cross would, at last, see that son enlisted under a different banner, to become a leader of other ranks to a different warfare, and a different kind of glory!

The calling of William's grandfathers was entirely different; but there was a remarkable similarity in their end. Elder Phelps was suddenly attacked, while on a journey from Orwell to Pittsfield, by the army epidemic; he was found in a dying state by the wayside, in Pownal, Vermont, where he soon after died, and was buried by the side of their pastor's grave, all unknown to his friends at home, till these last acts of respect and affection had been completed. He is mentioned in "Benedict's History of the Baptists," (p. 485,) among "the first Baptist ministers who settled in Vermont." This [6] took place "about the year 1780." He died in peace January 2nd, 1813. Of his grandfather Miller, but little more is recollected than his escape from death at the hands of the Indians, almost by miracle, to find a grave among strangers, on his return from the wars of our colonial history; probably from some one of the ill-advised and unsuccessful attempts on Canada, at the commencement of the Revolutionary War.

The traditionary form of his Indian adventures is to this effect:- Somewhere in the western part of Massachusetts, when every exposed white settlement was protected by a rude fort, the grandfather and several companions were going to one of them, probably to strengthen the garrison, and must travel several miles by the road, or take a nearer route through the wilderness. Mr. Miller chose to take the shorter route, alone. He had come within hearing of the fort without harm, when a sudden stirring of the bushes awakened his fears, and he started to run. At the same instant the Indians fired their muskets, and several balls passed through the skirts of his heavy coat. He had proceeded but a few steps before he stumbled and fell to the ground; but his fall saved his life, for the hatchets of the Indians passed at the instant directly over his head. His self-command now returned; he arose to his feet, took aim at the spot where the savages were concealed, fired, turned and fled. The report brought some of the garrison, including several friendly Indians, to the spot. These Indians had already decided that the last gun heard was that of a white man, and that he had killed an Indian, for they heard his death-yell. On repairing to the spot, marks of blood were seen; and these were traced to a pond near by, into which it was supposed the dead Indian was thrown by his brethren.

It is thought by Deacon Samuel D. Colt, an aged, highly intelligent, and respected gentleman of Pittsfield, where he has resided since he was a child, that this incident is connected with the history of "Hutchinson's Fort," so called from the man who built it, during "the second French war." It was located about two miles west of the village. Its site is now covered by a brick dwelling-house. None of the other forts were then occupied. [7] The few inhabitants of Pittsfield nearly all left the place at the time, on which account there is an omission in the town records for several years. Deacon Colt remarked, on referring to the adventure, that "this Miller was a courageous fellow." Mr. Miller afterwards fell a victim to the small-pox, as before stated.

Such, then, were the family recollections and public events which were to make the first and deepest impression on the strong intellect and generous heart of the subject of this memoir.

When William's parents removed from Pittsfield, in 1786, the section which embraced what is now known as Low Hampton was an almost uninhabited wilderness. [2] The village of Fairhaven did not then exist. And the town of Whitehall, now one of the familiar and important centres of trade and travel, was marked only by a few rude dwellings, the inhabitants of which were in danger of being crushed by the trees impending from the mountain sides over their heads. Half a dozen, or possibly half a score, of farm-houses were scattered over the country, between the southern extremity of Lake Champlain and Poultney, Vermont. But it was naturally a much more fertile and inviting country than the western part of Massachusetts. William was then about four years of age.

The farm selected by Mr. Miller consisted of about a hundred acres. It was taken on a lease, for which twenty bushels of wheat were to be paid

---

[2] The name then applied to this section was "Skeenesborough;" though its extent or boundaries do not appear to have been very definite.

annually. The farm was located near the bank of Poultney river, about six miles from the lake. After a suitable clearing had been effected, the logs of the felled trees were converted into a dwelling, and farming life in the wilderness, with its toils, privations, and hardships, was fairly begun. This was the condition of things to which young William's lot consigned him. The difficulties with which he had to contend need not all be enumerated.

In his early childhood, marks of more than ordinary intellectual strength and activity were manifested. A [8] few years made these marks more and more noticeable to all who fell into his society. But where were the powers of the inner man to find the nutriment to satisfy their cravings, and the field for their exercise?

Besides the natural elements of education, the objects, the scenes, and the changes of the natural world, which have ever furnished to all truly great minds their noblest aliment, the inspiring historical recollections associated with well-known localities of the neighboring country, and the society of domestic life, there was nothing within William's reach but the Bible, the psalter, and prayer-book, till he had resided at Low Hampton several years. But were ever such natural scenery and such historical associations before blended together in so confined a circle?

A few rods behind and west of the log house, the level which began at the bank of the river was broken by one of those natural terraces which mark so often the long slopes of the outspread valleys of our country. From this beautiful elevation, a forest scene might be witnessed, at the return of every autumn, that was so rich in its variegated beauties, and covered so extended a field, that it could not fail to entrance the soul of even an ordinary lover of nature, on beholding it.

From the summit of the sharp mountainous ridge, half a mile further west, there was spread out before the eye a view as captivating by its grandeur as that from the lowlier position was by its beauty. The extent of country seen from this higher point was not less than fifty miles from north to south, while it stretched away easterly to the Green Mountains, the distant outline of which, including some of the higher peaks, seemed to rest against the sky.

Sometimes a dense, motionless sea of vapor spread over the low plain, through which the hill-tops rose up like islands, and to which the neighboring mountain sides seemed to form the coast. From the wide-spread surface of this mimic sea, the smoke of the scattered farm-houses arose, and, as it became chilled in the air above, turned and sunk into the vapory bed, very much in the form, but not with the force, of the water spouted by a whale in the ocean. Again, the rising smoke from [9] the farm-house, the coal-pit, and from masses of burning wood, when it reached an atmospheric line the temperature or density of which refused it an upward passage, slowly formed itself into an upper cloudy stratum, which connected the higher hill-tops as by an extended magic bridge. And sometimes the storm clouds swept along these mountain sides in their wildest and most imposing grandeur, the sure precursors of a sudden squall or tempest; and perhaps the spell-bound observer would not have time to reach the warm but rude cabin-door before the descending rain or snow would shut out every object but the ground beneath his feet.

Bears, wolves, and other dangerous wild animals, which had formerly abounded through the whole region, at this time usually kept among the unfrequented recesses of the mountains. But occasionally, during the severity of winter, when the wolves were pressed by hunger, their howlings disturbed the repose of the settler, if they did not inflict a more serious injury, by the destruction of his flock. And, one night, William's mother was out near their residence, and seeing what she supposed was one of their domestic animals, she approached it, and, as she was about extending her hand towards it, was very soon informed of her mistake, by the frightful growl of a bear.

From the earliest times reached by history or tradition, Lake Champlain, and the natural landing-places which open into the country on its southern extremity, seem to have been the chosen thoroughfare for the native savages in their migrations, for the savages and the French in their warlike expeditions against the English colonists on the Atlantic, and afterwards for the British in their wars with the revolutionary colonies and the United States. The scenes of savage cruelty, of patriotic daring and ordinary war, which have marked the face of the earth along that chosen highway, had well-nigh ended when William was born. But nearly every mile between Quebec and Albany had been a battle-ground; and many a spot, from Canada along the mountain passes of northern New York, Vermont, and western Massachusetts, was known as the scene of some terrible Indian tragedy. [10]

Only about two miles below his father's residence, on the river near the banks of which it stood, are "Carver's Falls," one of the most romantic localities in our country. Directly below the falls is a broad, oblong basin, which connects with the lake, the precipitous sides of which were formerly hung with a thick growth of hemlocks. Some of the most fatal expeditions of the savages, against the frontier settlements of New England, were carried on by parties who ascended the river from the lake to this basin, there secreting their canoes under the dark evergreen branches of the hemlock trees; and then, threading their way secretly to the dwellings of the English, would seize their captives, or take the scalps of the murdered inhabitants, and return to their canoes. Here, in this secluded hiding-place, the danger was all over.

Just across the lake were Ticonderoga, Crown Point, and Lake George. Within the limits of the view before mentioned, to the south, were Fort Edward and Fort William Henry; and, a little further distant, were Saratoga and Bennington. Of these names we need not speak.

This is the scenery, and these are the recollections, which entered largely into William's early education. He was not, however, entirely destitute of other resources.

In a newly settled country, the public means of education must necessarily be very limited. This was the case, at the time here referred to, in a much greater degree than it usually is with the new settlements of the present day. The schoolhouse was not erected in season to afford the children of Low Hampton but three months' schooling in winter, during William's schoolboy days. His mother had taught him to read, so that he soon mastered the few books belonging to the family; and this prepared him to enter the "senior class" when the district school opened. But if the terms were short, the winter nights were long. Pine knots could be made to supply the want of candles, lamps, or gas. And the spacious fireplace in the log house was ample enough as a substitute for the schoolhouse and lecture-room. But even the enjoyment of these literary advantages subjected the zealous student to a somewhat severe discipline. [11]

The settlers generally on our frontiers are under the necessity of exercising the most stringent economy in the use of everything which takes money out, or brings money in. The most moderate liberality in the scale of living is often as ruinous to their prospects as indolence, intemperance, disease or death, could be. Many a hardy farmer, or his widow and children, have been compelled to give up their claim to the spot on which they had settled, just as it began to afford a comfortable subsistence, simply because they had not the means at command to lift the mortgage. There are always human sharks enough to devour all they can. And woe be to those who are at the mercy of the common mortgage-holder! Such were the circumstances of William's parents that they had a plain question to settle: with health, hard labor, sobriety and economy, the farm they had cleared might become their own, to leave to their children; the absence of any one of these items in the condition of success, was sure to make it otherwise. It was on this view of the case that William's parents declined to provide him with candles to read by; and this led to the expedient of the pine knots.

There is an amusing and truly affecting incident connected with his application of this means for getting light, which shows how deeply his soul was bound up in his books, since an offence on that interest only could arouse his combativeness to commit an overt act. He was accustomed to select pine stumps of the proper quality for his candle-wood, chop them into a size and shape convenient for use, and then put these pieces into a place he had appropriated for that purpose, so that, when his hours for reading came, he would have nothing to do but light up. One day, when a sister of his, who is now living, had some of her little friends to visit her, she had some difficulty in kindling the fire, and, as William's pitch-wood was handy, she made use of that. The trespass was soon discovered by him; and so great was the provocation, he lost all self-command, and gave her a smart blow. It was the only one that sister ever received from him.

Another difficulty called for another expedient. As soon as William's age and strength rendered him able [12] to assist his father about the farm, it was feared that his reading by night might interfere with his efficiency in the work of the day. His father insisted, therefore, that he should retire to bed when he retired himself. But the boy could not be kept in bed. When the other members of the family were all asleep, William would leave his bed, then find his way to the pitch-wood, go to the fireplace, cast himself down flat on the hearth, with his book before him, thrust his pitch-wood into the embers till it blazed well, and there spend the hours of midnight in reading. If the blaze grew dim, he would hold the stick in the embers till the heat fried the pitch out of the wood, which renewed the blaze. And when he had read as long as he dared to, or finished his book, he would find his way back to bed again, with as little noise as possible.

But he came near losing even this privilege. His father awoke one night, and seeing the light of William's burning stick, he supposed the house was on fire. He hurried from his bed, and when he saw his son's position and employment, he seized the whip, and pursuing his flying son, cried out, in a manner which made it effectual for some time, "Bill, if you don't go to bed, I'll horsewhip you!"

The reader may wish to be informed where the books were obtained under such embarrassments. The first addition made to those belonging to the family, already named, was *the History of Crusoe!* The remains of this volume are still preserved. Its title-page reads as follows:-

> "The Wonderful Life and Surprising Adventures of the Renowned Hero, Robinson Crusoe, who lived twenty-eight years on an uninhabited island, which he afterwards colonized. Albany: Published by C. R. and G. Webster, State Street. MDCCXC."

It is evidently an imitation or abridgment of Defoe. But how many longings of soul, how many plans, and entreaties, on the part of the boy, preceded the possession of that book! At length, his father granted him permission to purchase the book, if he would earn the money by chopping wood during his leisure hours. The prize was soon in his hands. The second book he [13] possessed was *The Adventures of Robert Boyle*. Other books were loaned him by gentlemen in the vicinity, who had become interested in his improvement; among whom were Dr. Witherill [3] and Col. Lyon, [4] of Fairhaven, and Esquire Cruikshanks, [5] of Whitehall.

All this, however, only afforded a partial gratification to the inward desire for knowledge. But what could he do? His father could render him but little aid if he had been disposed to aid him. And, if he felt that his son must be denied even the trifling accommodations we have noticed, it must be seen that he would not readily favor a more liberal outlay for that son's benefit. There were then no amply endowed literary institutions, or zealous educational societies, standing with open doors and open arms to receive every promising or unpromising young man who might aspire to the honors, or the substantial benefits, of a liberal education. Was there any source then from which help might come? Some, no doubt, would consider it a cause of grief that more ample means were not within the reach of young William Miller. Viewing the case in some of its bearings, we could sympathize with them. In another view, we might not. Nothing could have been more gratifying to him than the attainment of means for an education; and his gratification, or that of any other, in itself, we should approve. And certain it is, that a more promising or worthy subject of the most generous appropriations could rarely be found.

He possessed a strong physical constitution, an active and naturally well-developed intellect, and an irreproachable moral character. He had appropriated to his use and amusement the small stock of literature afforded by the family, while a child. He had enjoyed the limited advantages of the district school but a few years, before it was generally admitted that his attainments exceeded those of the teachers usually employed. He had drunk in the inspiration of the natural world around him, and [14] of the most exciting events in his country's history. His imagination had been quickened, and his heart warmed, by the adventures and gallantries of fiction, and his intellect enriched by history. And some of his earliest efforts with the pen, as well as the testimony of his associates, show that

---

[3] *James Witherill.* After this time, referred to in the text, he was Judge of Michigan Territory.

[4] *Hon. Matthew Lyon.* Member of Congress from Vermont, from 1794 to 1798.

[5] *Alexander Cruikshanks, Esq.* He was formerly from Scotland.

his mind and heart were ennobled by the lessons, if not by the spirit and power, of religion.

What, now, would have been the effect of what is called a regular course of education? Would it have perverted him, as it has thousands? or would it have made him instrumental of greater good in the cause of God? Would it have performed its appropriate work, that of disciplining, enlarging, and furnishing the mind, leaving unimpaired by the process its natural energies, its sense of self-dependence as to man, and its sense of dependence and accountability as to God? or would it have placed him in the crowded ranks of those who are content to share in the honor of repeating the twaddle, true or false, which passes for truth in the school or sect which has "made them what they are"? We think it would have been difficult to pervert him; but where so many who have been regarded as highly promising have been marred by the operation, he would have been in great danger. He might have become externally a better subject for the artist; but we doubt if he would have been a better subject to be used as an instrument of Providence. There are those who survive the regular course uninjured. There are those who are benefited by it so far as to be raised to a level with people of ordinary capacity, which they never could attain without special aid. And there is a third class, who are a stereotype representation of what the course makes them: if they raise a fellow-man out of the mire, they never get him nearer to heaven than the school where they were educated.

Whatever might have been the result of any established course of education, in the case of William Miller, such a course was beyond his reach: he was deprived of the benefit, he has escaped the perversion. Let us be satisfied. But still we must record the fact, that it would have been extremely gratifying, if something of the kind could have been placed at his command. [15] He desired it. He longed for it with an intensity of feeling that approached to agony. He pondered the question over and over, whether it was possible to accomplish what appeared to him to be not only a desirable gratification and honor, but almost essential to his existence.

It should be noticed, however, that his circumstances became somewhat relieved as he advanced in years. The log house had given place to a comfortable frame house; and, in this, William had a room he was permitted to call his own. He had means to provide himself with a new book, occasionally, and with candles to read at night, so that he could enjoy his chosen luxury, during his leisure hours, in comparative comfort.

It was on one of those times of leisure that an incident occurred which marked a new era in his history, though it did not introduce fully such an era as he desired.

There was a medical gentleman in the vicinity of his residence, by the name of Smith, who possessed an ample fortune, and was known to be very liberal. In the plans which had passed through the mind of William, to secure the means of maturing his education, he had thought of Dr. Smith. At any rate, it could do no harm to apply to him. The plan was carried so far as to write a letter, setting forth to that gentleman his intense desires, his want of means to gratify them, his hopes and his prospects, if successful.

The letter was nearly ready to be sent to its destination, when William's father entered the room, which we may properly call his son's study. Perhaps it had not occurred to the son to consult his father in the matter; and to have it come to his notice in so unexpected a manner somewhat disturbed him for the moment. But there was the letter in his father's presence. He took it, and read it. It affected him deeply. For the first time, he seemed to feel his worldly condition to be uncomfortable, on his son's account. He wanted to be rich then, for the gratification of his son, more than for any other human being. There were the irrepressible yearnings of his first-born, which he had treated in their childish development as an annoyance, now spread out in manly [16] but impassioned pleadings to a comparative stranger to afford him help. There were plans and hopes for the future, marked by an exhibition of judgment and honor that could not fail of commanding attention! All that was tender in that father's heart, all that was generous in the soldier, and all that could make him ambitious of a worthy successor, was moved by that letter. The tears fell, and words of sympathy were spoken; but the plan was impossible.

The letter of William was never sent. It had the effect, however, of changing his father's course towards him, so that he was rather encouraged than hindered in his favorite pursuits.

By this time, the natural genius and attainments of young William Miller had distinguished him among his associates. To the young folks, he became a sort of scribbler-general. If any one wanted "verses made," a letter to send, some ornamental and symbolic design to be interpreted by "the tender passion," or anything which required extra taste and fancy in the use of the pen, it was pretty sure to be planned, if not executed by him.

Some of these first-fruits of his genius are still in existence; and, although it requires no critic to discover that he had never received lessons of any of the "great masters," still these productions would compare very favorably with similar efforts by those whose advantages have been far superior to his.

The facts connected with the early life of Mr. William Miller, and the incidents in his personal history, now spread before the readers of this work, will enable them to see, in the boy, a type of the future man. The most embarrassing circumstances of his condition could not master his perseverance. And if he could not accomplish all he desired to, the success which attended his efforts, in spite of great discouragements, was truly surprising. The position he had won opened to him a fairer prospect, though still surrounded with serious dangers. But the features of the next step in his history must be the subject of another chapter. [17]

CHAPTER 2

Marriage and Public Life

The successful military operations in behalf of the northern colonies of our country resulted, at the close of the Revolutionary War, in opening the whole territory along the northern frontier of the New England States and New York, for the occupancy of the immigrant; and gave security in prosecuting the business of peaceful life. The desire of possessing a home in this new, healthy, and fertile region, which led so many families from western Massachusetts – the Miller family among them – induced other families from the Atlantic settlements, particularly in Rhode Island and Connecticut, to try their fortunes in the same region.

Among the families which came from Connecticut about the time that the Miller family came from Pittsfield, there was one by the name of Smith. This family settled in Poultney, Vermont, some half a dozen miles from the residence of Mr. Miller. The Smiths were related to families in the Miller neighborhood, and this brought the members of the two families into each other's society. It was in this way that the subject of this memoir first met with Miss Lucy Smith, a young woman of about his own age, who afterwards became his wife.

There certainly is no relation which two human beings can sustain to each other, on which their mutual welfare so much depends, as that of husband and wife. To a great extent, their history, and that of their children, are determined by the fitness of the parties for each other, and the manner in which the relation is sustained. If the wisdom and goodness of God are seen in the institution of marriage, these attributes are quite as manifest in the philosophical, inartificial, and religious manner in which he requires the institution to be honored. We [18] shall see, by and by, that the importance of the duties growing out of this relation was a principal consideration in fixing Mr. Miller's purpose to become a Christian.

As Mrs. Lucy Miller is now living, all that might be said to her praise may not be said here. It is sufficient to state, that she was remarkably endowed, by nature and by her industrial and economical habits, to make domestic life highly agreeable, and to favor Mr. Miller's promotion and success in the departments of public life in which he was called to move. And few men could be better adapted to enjoy, or better qualified to honor, the office of a husband, than Mr. Miller. His warm-hearted and tireless sociability gave itself full play in the domestic circle; and his confidence was unbounded towards those whom he had decided to be worthy of it. The discernment which led Miss Smith to accept the offer of his hand was never called in question by a disappointment of her expectations. They were united in marriage June 29th, 1803.

By comparing dates, it will be seen that the subject of this memoir had passed his minority but a few months when this important change in his condition in life took place. Shortly afterwards, the new-made family settled in Poultney, Vermont, where the young wife's parents resided.

To the population generally, Mr. Miller was a stranger; and to those who knew him as the fortunate husband of one of the promising young ladies of the village, nothing very remarkable appeared in him, to attract their attention. In fact, he does not appear to have been, at that time, or during his subsequent life, either moved by external show in others, or led to make the least show to produce an effect on others. What was solid and unaffectedly natural and true was all he valued, or wished others to value, as worthy of their attention. He had been distinguished by no other public honors, we believe, prior to his leaving Low Hampton, but that of being promoted to the always dignified office of sergeant in the militia. However, he continued in Poultney but a short time before it began to be perceived that his natural genius would make itself felt, if it did not seek to make itself seen. [19]

One of the first objects of his interest, after he had become settled, was the village library. His constant use of its volumes brought him into the society of a superior class of men. His wife took a deep interest in his improvement and promotion; and made it her pleasure and business to relieve him as much as possible from all the family cares which might call him away from his books. She felt very sure that it would not be lost time on his part, or lost labor on her own part. Still, the time he could devote to books, on the best possible arrangement, was not so much as he desired;

for he had been trained to the farming business, and he made that his employment, for some years, in Poultney.

One effort of genius, though trifling in itself, which attracted towards him the public attention of the village and its vicinity, was a poetic effusion, the inspiration of his patriotic ardor. Preparations were going on, at the time, for the public celebration of the anniversary of our national independence; and the inspiration of that memorable day seized Mr. Miller while he was hoeing corn in the field. He had written poetry before; and so, after the labor of the field was done, he put his thoughts into a written form, to be adapted to the familiar old tune, called "Delight."

The appointed marshal, or manager, of the services of the day, was Esquire Ashley, who was then a neighbor of Mr. Miller, and afterwards became an intimate friend. But the poet of the day, as he became, was too reserved to offer his tribute, though there is reason to believe it would have been thankfully accepted; for the business of the manager hardly afforded him time to write poetry for the occasion, if he had the ability, or even to select it. Mr. Miller was willing to have his piece seen and used, if it was thought to be suitable, but he could not announce himself as its author. So he took the manuscript, and walked as usual to Esquire Ashley's house. He seated himself leisurely below the chamber window, where that gentleman was making his preparations for the great celebration. Then, taking an opportunity to place it near where Mrs. Ashley was at work, he shortly after withdrew. As soon as Mrs. Ashley discovered the paper, she took it to her husband, [20] supposing it was one of his papers which had fallen from the window. He took it, and read the hymn: it struck him as being just what was wanted; but he knew nothing of its origin. It was carried to several others, who were thought of, as its author, but no author or owner of it could be found. "Perhaps an angel from heaven had sent it!" So they talked, at any rate.

However, the hymn was copied with the pen, and the sheets multiplied to supply all who wished for one. The day came, and the hymn was sung, with the greatest enthusiasm, to the favorite old tune, "Delight"!

But among those who distributed the copies, there was a worthy Baptist minister, by the name of Kendrick, who had taken a warm interest in Mr. Miller. His suspicions had pointed him to the author of the piece; and when Mr. Miller came, with others, to get a copy, his appearance and manner confirmed Elder Kendrick's suspicions. Further inquiry brought forth a confession of authorship. To use the phrase of the old folks, "it was a great feather in his cap." He had touched the right chord in the right way. The pious and patriotic emotions of the aged were revived; the ardent responses of the young to these parental emotions found expression in the new hymn; and nothing more was needed, to make its author the popular favorite!

It is not known that an entire copy of the hymn is now in existence. A sister of its author has repeated to us a few of the stanzas, which we give, more for the purpose of exhibiting his religious and patriotic sentiments than from an expectation that our readers will be affected as were those who first heard it. Its style and metre were strictly in accordance with the standard contained in the hymn-book used on Sundays, doubtless the only standard the writer of it was familiar with; and the effect arose from the natural force and simplicity of the versified thoughts, and the perfect ease of the musical execution. But to the fragments of the hymn:-

* * * * *

"Our Independence dear,
Bought with the price of blood,
Let us receive with care,
And trust our Maker, God. [21]

For he's the tower
To which we fly;
His grace is nigh
In every hour!

"Nor shall Columbia's sons
Forget the price it cost,
As long as water runs,
Or leaves are nipped by frost.
Freedom is thine;
Let millions rise,
Defend the prize
Through rolling time!

*   *   *   *   *

"There was a Washington,
A man of noble fame,
Who led Columbia's sons
To battle on the plain;
With skill they fought;
The British host,
With all their boast,
Soon came to naught!
*   *   *   *   *

"Let traitors hide their heads,
And party quarrels cease;
Our foes are struck with dread.
When we declare for peace,
Firm let us be,
And rally round
The glorious sound
Of liberty!"

The reader will see that the piece was designed for home consumption. It was exactly suited to the occasion; and was marked throughout, in spirit, style, and thought, with the elements of his education. And this production, with others in prose and poetry, made him at once a notable in the community; secured to him a wide circle of friends, and opened the way for his promotion to office and honor. The old men were all ready to give him a lift, almost without distinction of "party." The young folks made his house a place of common resort, to which they gathered to spend their leisure hours; while himself and wife became the central unit which drew them together, and kept all in motion.

It was here that Mr. Miller became a member of the Masonic fraternity, in which his perseverance, if nothing else, was manifested; for he advanced to the highest [22] degree which the lodges then in the country, or in that region, could confer.

In his political sentiments, he was decidedly democratic. But he had intelligence enough to see that the practical patriotism of men did not depend so much on the party name they took as on their common sense and integrity. He knew that there were bad men enough in either party to ruin the country, if they had the power to do it; and good men enough in the same parties to promote the public prosperity to the best of their ability. His position, therefore, was taken in view of the tendency of different political principles and public measures, in their ultimate bearing on the established institutions of the country. He enjoyed, in a remarkable degree, the confidence of both the political parties of the day.

The first public office of a civil character to which he was elected or appointed was that of constable. His appointment to the office of sheriff took place in 1809. The first entry of "writs served," and of "executions levied, as sheriff's deputy," is dated "December 6th, 1809." A long list of writs and executions is still preserved, in good condition, in a book used for that purpose. The last writ in this list is dated 1811; [6] the last execution is closed up in "May, 1813." The names of the attorneys which occur the most frequently, in the issuing of these writs, are "R. C. Mallory, Esq." and "Chauncy Langdon, Esq." One of these was the "republican," and the other the "federal," lawyer of the place. So much business from the lawyer of the party opposed to Mr. M. corroborates the statement we have heard as having been made by that official, that "Mr. Miller was the only honest democrat he knew!" Indeed, in the various civil offices he was called to fill – constable, sheriff, and justice of the peace – he appears to have sustained an unimpeachable character, and to have given the highest satisfaction.

As an illustration of his standing in the confidence of the community, it may be stated that, when he was called on to furnish bondsmen for his fidelity in the office [23] of sheriff, responsible persons voluntarily offered their names, so that several times the amount required was at his command. He had good reason to expect promotion to the office of high sheriff, if he would restrain his military ardor, and decline entering the army.

In the case of most men of the world, with the avenues to honor, wealth, and domestic happiness wide open before them, it is not often that a public station so commanding would be voluntarily left for the hardships, privations and dangers, of the camp. What strong impulses could have turned him off in that direction? Already the business of his

---

[6] The time in the year is doubtless indicated by the capitals "M. T.," signifying the *March term* of the Court.

office had placed him in easy circumstances. Such was the amount of his business that he kept two horses, one of which he drove, while the other was kept up to rest, week by week, alternately. He enjoyed the respect and unbounded confidence of the public; and he only needed to make himself still as worthy of public favor as he had been hitherto, and then, with life and health, all that this world could afford was within his reach. His preference for the army, so far as we know, sprang from these two motives: First, he desired to participate in the glory which rested on the memory of those he held the most dear, in the history of his country and of his family. Second, he hoped to enjoy a more inviting exhibition of human nature in the scenes of military life than experience or books had afforded in civil life. His desire for something noble in character was greater than that for wealth or unsubstantial fame. He was satisfied with the trial of what was around him, and wished to try a new field. This is stated by himself in his published memoir:- "In the mean time, I continued my studies, storing my mind with historical knowledge. The more I read, the more dreadfully corrupt did the character of man appear. I could discern no bright spot in the history of the past. Those conquerors of the world, and heroes of history, were apparently but demons in human form. All the sorrow, suffering, and misery in the world, seemed to be increased in proportion to the power they obtained over their fellows. I began to feel very distrustful of all men. In this state of mind, I entered the service of my country. I fondly cherished the idea, that I should find one [24] bright spot at least in the human character, as a star of hope: *a love of country* – PATRIOTISM." His military life must be given at length, in another place.

Happy, indeed, should we consider ourselves, if there were no drawback to this apparent prosperity to be noted. Rarely is it the case that the honor of God and the honor of man are coincident. If Mr. Miller was not puffed up by the latter, he had lost much of his regard for the former. In his worldly advancement, there was a serious and dangerous departure from the Christian sentiments which were instilled into his mind during his early life. Still there was no defect in his character which the most rigid worldly standard of external morality could detect. He was perfectly upright and honorable in all his dealings. He was generous, almost to a fault, with his friends; compassionate and liberal to the poor, and he held in the highest contempt every act that could tarnish a man's personal and private honor. He was not profane, even to the extent that too many are who pass for gentlemen. He was not intemperate, although he was very much exposed to this ruinous habit, from the example of those into whose company his business called him – a habit which had broken down some of his predecessors in office, by rendering them incapable of attending to their business. He escaped from it without the least stain.

It could be shown, from sentiments embodied in some of his essays, in addresses delivered before societies existing at the time, and in his poetic effusions, that his moral and religious views were of a type that would pass with the world as philosophical, pure, and sublime. But the men with whom he associated from the time of his removal to Poultney, and to whom he was considerably indebted for his worldly favors, were deeply affected with skeptical principles and deistical theories. They were not immoral men; but, as a class, were good citizens, and generally of serious deportment, humane and benevolent. However, they rejected the Bible as the standard of religious truth, and endeavored to make its rejection plausible by such aid as could be obtained from the writings of Voltaire, Hume, Volney, Paine, Ethan Allen, and others. Mr. Miller studied these works [25] closely, and at length avowed himself a deist. As he has stated the period of his deistical life to have been twelve years, that period must have begun in 1804; for he embraced or returned to the Christian faith in 1816. It may fairly be doubted, however, notwithstanding his known thoroughness and consistency, whether Mr. Miller ever was fully settled in that form of deism which reduces man to a level with the brutes, as to the supposed duration of their existence. And the question is worthy of a little inquiry, to what extent was he a deist?

Robert Hall, with his usual comprehensiveness and truth, has remarked that "infidelity is the offspring of corrupt Christianity." It is much more successful in the discovery of supposed arguments against the existence of the Deity of the Scriptures, in the perversion of that which is divine, than in its institution and appointed use. Voltaire chose the ruins of human nature, in their most perverted and blighted condition, and

Volney chose the "ruins" of human habitations, for the theatre on which to display their mighty but evil genius. And they conjured forth the same evil spirit which had instigated or caused the ruin, in each case, to utter a false testimony, in reference both to ruined man and his ruined habitations. These men became the oracles of that falsehood to the world! But it was never the intention of God, that man, or the world fitted up for his habitation, should be in this ruined condition: it is the work of rebellion and sin! – of sin against the greatest displays of love and goodness that were possible, and against the purest and most reasonable law that could be given; of rebellion that was marked by contempt of the universal Sovereign, and of authority enforced by the lightest test of submission. And God has spoken to us, to inform us that he has made provision for the restoration of all men, and that it is his purpose to restore all who become interested in that provision, with the world now in ruins, to a condition which no history but the Bible has made known.

Paine could rail and belie the supernaturalism of the Bible, like an incarnate demon, and then endorse all the supernaturalism of the most stupid pagan mythology, in [26] his patriotic and poetic productions, which he published to the world. And that mind must be strangely out of balance naturally, or wretchedly perverted, which could bow to the authority of Volney's "spectre," or Paine's paganism, – the pure creations of fiction and superstition, – and then reject the Bible because it demands faith in that which is not familiar to the senses.

It is generally true, that those who become decided skeptics take that most hopeless position, because they have become so depraved or perverted that they feel the want of an infidel theory to afford them a license and quiet, in their chosen course. It was not so with Mr. Miller. In the days of his greatest devotion to deistical sentiments, he desired something better. He had his difficulties with the Bible under its current interpretations, and he tells us what these difficulties were. But a man like him could never be made to believe it consistent or safe to abandon the Bible, unless something more worthy of his trust were first put in its place. And such a condition must secure to that matchless book a certain and permanent supremacy. This was Mr. Miller's safety.

But if the poison which had infused its taint into the system did not appear as a loathsome blotch upon the surface, its victim was not only kept away from the sole remedy, but that remedy was treated by him with an afflicting and dangerous levity. This was now the painful feature of his case. Once it was not so. When he was a mere boy – "between the years of seven and ten" – as he tells us, a sense of the plague of his heart and of his lost condition caused the deepest concern in reference to his future prospects. He spent much time in trying to invent some plan whereby he might find acceptance with God. He tried the common and most natural course, in such a state of mind, that of being "very good." "I will do nothing wrong, tell no lies, and obey my parents," he thought. But his mind was still unsettled and unhappy. Good works are very proper, but they can never be accepted as the price of pardon and redemption. He thought, too, as all do in the same state of feeling, that something might be effected by sacrifice. "I will give up the most cherished objects I [27] possess." But this also failed. There is only "one offering" that can avail. In that, every sinner must rest his hope and plea, or remain without peace with God. The experience of Mr. Miller's childhood made him thoughtful and serious, if it did not result in the attainment of this inward sense of peace. Under his inward conflicts and apprehensions of worldly sorrow, when a young man, (in 1803,) he poured out his soul to "religion" in this touching strain:-

> "Come, blest Religion, with thy angel's face,
> Dispel this gloom, and brighten all the place;
> Drive this destructive passion from my breast;
> Compose my sorrows, and restore my rest;
> Show me the path that Christian heroes trod,
> Wean me from earth, and raise my soul to God!"

Two things, says D'Aubigné, are essential to sound Christian experience. The first is a knowledge of our condition as sinners; the second is a knowledge of the grace of God, in its manifestations to the soul. Mr. Miller, like most if not all others, had learned the first in his early life; but he had evidently not then attained the second of these elements of a true religious life. And, by not attaining that important position in the process of deliverance from our fallen condition, he became wearied of a sense of his need, if he did not lose it entirely. In the chosen employment of his intellect, with a more ample supply of books at command; in the midst of an admiring and merry social circle; in receiving the honors of the world from the hand of his superiors, and in reaping an honorable portion of the treasures of the world, why should he desire any other source of enjoyment – and one altogether unknown, unappreciated and unpopular, in the circle where he moved? What use had he for that religion he had seen verified, and felt the need of, in the less cultivated family circle at Low Hampton?

If those who never become acquainted with the lessons of truth may be satisfied without the consolation of which its lessons speak, with those who are made familiar with these lessons, it is generally very different. They can seldom feel satisfied with themselves without making a hearty surrender of life, and all God has given [28] them, to his service. As they know this is their reasonable service, anything short of this, they know, must be unreasonable. But how few take this narrow path! How many turn away to join the multitude! The talent, however, is in their hands. They must dispose of that, if they will not submit themselves to the disposal of its Giver. Some make it the reason for entertaining and venting a more malignant and blasphemous form of hatred against everything which bears the name of God. This quiets all fear of being reproached as religious, and it is the awful snare into which many are led by the fear of man. Another class of these unfaithful recipients of the talent of truth try to get along with a popular external expression of respect for its claims; and thus they escape the dreaded reproach.

A third class, naturally too frank even to appear to venerate what they do not heartily respect, and too deeply impressed with the goodness of the Deity to become blasphemers, but still too fearful of man to encounter his frown, seek to save themselves from it by making the defects of the humble but unpopular representatives of truth a subject of merriment. This course was taken by Mr. Miller. This is the class to which he then belonged. He banished from his memory the impressions of his early life, and must silence all fear of reproach on account of them; so he gave to his skeptical associates an assurance that he had mastered his superstition, as they deemed it, by performing, for their sport, the devotions of the worship to which he had been accustomed, and especially by mimicking the devotional peculiarities of some of his own family relatives.

Among these pious relatives there were two, in particular, whose presence or name was calculated to remind him of his repudiated obligations, and whose influence over him he labored to repel, by making them the theme of his mirth. One of these was his grandfather Phelps, pastor of the Baptist church at Orwell; the other was his uncle, Elihu Miller, who was settled as pastor of the Baptist church at Low Hampton, in 1812. These were men of unpolished exterior, but of decided character, strong voice, and ardent devotion. Men whose features were so strongly marked would make fine subjects [29] for striking portraits; and if all their traits could be brought out, there would be found a large bestowment of the treasure of heavenly wisdom and virtue in the earthen vessels. It was the excellence of the heavenly traits, and the roughness of the earthly, which made them so desirable and so ready subjects of caricature.

These humble ambassadors of Christ, and other pious relatives, often visited Mr. Miller's house at Poultney; and, although he received them with affection and respect, and entertained them in the most generous manner, he was in the habit of imitating, with the most ludicrous gravity, their words, tones of voice, gestures, fervency, and even the grief they might manifest for such as himself, to afford a kind of entertainment for his skeptical associates, which they seemed to enjoy with a particular relish.

Little did he then think, that he was measuring to these faithful men what was to be measured to him again, pressed down, shaken together, and running over. And probably it was not known to him, that these praying men had already expressed the hope – almost a prophecy – that their prayers would be answered, and that he would some day be engaged in perpetuating the work they were endeavoring to advance.

There was more than one heart that was almost inconsolably afflicted by this conduct of Mr. Miller. His mother knew of it, and it was as the bitterness of death to her. Some of his pious sisters witnessed, with tears, his improprieties. And when his mother spoke of the affliction to her father Phelps, he would console her by saying, "Don't afflict yourself too deeply about William. There is something for him to do yet, in the cause of God!"

Although Mr. Miller avowed himself a deist, and was recognized as such by deists, this offence against all propriety, in trifling with what his dearest relatives regarded as most sacred, this thoughtless trifling with the humble messengers of the Gospel, was the darkest feature in his character. To him it was the most natural course which the circumstances of his position could suggest, and, undoubtedly, appeared to be the least violation of former convictions and educational proprieties which would [30] allow him to stand as he did, in the favor and confidence of his unbelieving associates. He had not then become acquainted with the source of strength, by which he might have been sustained before the enemies of the Christian faith; he was unprepared to take the Christian position, and he became what the influences around him naturally determined. To give the true state of the case, the darker shades must appear with the lighter. He took the position of an unbeliever. But that he was not a deist of the rank type, will appear more fully from his own statements, especially in his letters while in the army, which will be presented in the next chapter.

We have thus stated Mr. Miller's social and public position; his worldly prospects, and his religious state. The long-suffering of God was still to be exercised towards him. He was to become satisfied with the insufficiency of the world. Then the light which had become darkness was to be revived within him; the breath of life from God would disclose the all-sufficient portion, and he would go forth to build again the faith he had destroyed.

Many were the prayers that ascended in his behalf; and some of those who were the most deeply interested for him would pass away before their prayers would be answered. But the great lessons of long-suffering, of faithfulness, and of power to deliver out of the most artful snare of the adversary, would be the more magnified, on the part of God; the praying, who were yet alive, would hail the answer with greater joy, and the delivered one would be the better prepared to take others, in the same fearful condition, by the hand, and lead them to Him who came to seek and save the lost! [31]

CHAPTER 3

His Military Life

The motives which led Mr. Miller to resign his public position as a civil officer, and enter upon the arduous and perilous theatre of military life, have been stated in the preceding chapter. Among the honors conferred on him in the military department, at the time of his advancement in the civil, was his election to the office of lieutenant, by superseding a commissioned officer, who expected it by promotion. His lieutenant's commission is dated July 21st, 1810. It is signed, "Jonas Galusha, Governor of Vermont."

To some of the readers of this work, the form of the oath taken on entering upon the duties of such an office may be of interest. A copy of that oath, found on the back of Mr. Miller's commission, is as follows:

> "I, William Miller, solemnly swear, that I will be true and faithful to the State of Vermont; that I will not, directly nor indirectly, do any act or thing injurious to the Constitution or Government thereof, as established by Convention. So help me God.
> "I also swear, that I will support the Constitution of the United States.
> W. M. MILLER.
>
> "*August 13th, 1810.* The foregoing oaths were taken and subscribed to before me.
> "CALEB HENDY, Jr., *Brig. Gen.*"

The reader will see that this commission is dated about two years prior to the declaration of war with England by the United States. The premonitions of that war, however, were already seen. On the 18th of June, 1812, the declaration was made in due form; and the first note of preparation found Mr. Miller, with hundreds of his hardy and patriotic Green Mountain neighbors, ready to take the field. A very short time after it was [32] announced that he would take his place at the head of a company of state volunteers, the ranks were filled. And on the day after the date of the act of the state government of Vermont which authorized the raising of such a body, his captain's commission is dated.

It is presumed that very few of Mr. Miller's particular friends will feel any special interest in these details of warlike affairs. He is nothing more nor less to them, on account of his connection with these matters. But it is not so with all who may read this work. The fact that he honored these public and responsible offices, which men are accustomed to regard with so much respect, would weigh more, on the question of competency, in the estimation of many very worthy people, than the purest Christian deportment in ordinary life. His true military station has also been misstated; and it is the work of the biographer and historian to give facts as they are. The question of Mr. Miller's rank and soldierly character can be presented in its true light, by the use of authentic documents, in fewer words than can do the question justice in any other form. And these documents must be decisive. No other reasons need to be stated for employing them. His captain's commission, in the Vermont volunteers, is in these words:

"L. S. By His Excellency, JONAS GALUSHA, Esquire, Captain-General, Governor, and Commander in Chief in and over the State of Vermont:

"To WILLIAM MILLER, Esq., greeting:

"You being elected a Captain of a Company of Infantry in the first Brigade of Volunteers of this State; and reposing special trust and confidence in your Patriotism, Valor, and good Conduct, I do, by virtue of these Presents, in the name and by the authority of the Freemen of the State of Vermont, fully authorize and empower you, the said William Miller, to take charge of the said Company as their Captain, pursuant to an act for raising a Corps of Volunteers, passed November 6th, 1812.

"You will, therefore, carefully and diligently discharge the said duty, by doing and performing every matter and thing thereunto relating. You will observe and follow such orders and directions as you shall, from time to [33] time, receive from the Governor of the State for the time being, or any other your superior officers, according to military discipline and the laws of this State: and all officers and soldiers under your command are to take notice hereof, and yield due obedience to your orders, as their Captain, in pursuance of the trust in you reposed.

"In testimony whereof, I have caused the Seal of this State to be hereunto affixed.

"Given under my hand, in Council Chamber, at Montpelier, this seventh day of November, in the year of our Lord one thousand eight hundred and twelve, and of the Independence of the United States the thirty-seventh.   JONAS GALUSHA.

"By his Excellency's command.

"R. C. MALLARY, *Secretary*."

This company being filled up, organized, and authorized to take the field, pursuant to orders, next came the scene of trial to a soldier – only inferior to the hour of battle – that of bidding adieu to home, and all that is dear to the heart of man associated with home. This was an exciting and deeply affecting scene. Skepticism was silenced before the working of nature, of reason, and the proprieties of such a moment, as decided by all nations, Pagan, Jewish, and Christian. How could these noble-hearted men – husbands, sons, brothers – part with those who were dearer to them than life itself, under circumstances they might properly regard as not very unlike to those of a dying hour, without asking the benediction of the Almighty? It was impossible. But it was not generally expected, by those who knew Captain Miller as a deist and a railer at the devout, that the devotions of this solemn leave-taking would be anything more than a ceremony, in which he would act the part of a constrained or indifferent spectator. Judge, then, of the effect, when he was seen to take his former friend, who was present with the multitude, by the hand; and, with a grace and tenderness which all felt to be in full tone with the occasion, and under deep emotion, present him to the company as the man of God, with whom they would join in prayer. The chaplain, on this occasion, was Elder Kendrick, who had felt and maintained a [34] special interest in Mr. Miller, in spite of his deism, from the first of his acquaintance with him. In his prayer, all the interest he felt in the members of the company, many of whom were his neighbors; in Captain Miller, as a promising family relative of his most intimate Christian friends; and in the great public occasion, as a patriot, was poured out with the most becoming solemnity, affection, and fervency. The effect was almost overpowering. It is fresh in the memory of those present, to this day.

Captain Miller's company, with the great body of volunteers raised in that region, was ordered to Burlington, which was expected to be the theatre of war for that campaign. The fatigue of the march, and an accident which proved almost fatal to Mr. Miller, are described in the following letter to his wife.

"Camp at Burlington, June 13th, 1813.

"DEAR LUCY: – I am now at this place, after a fatiguing march. My feet are worn all out, and my body is very sore. On our march from Bennington to this place, I met with an accident, which almost deprived me of life. The last day of our march, my feet and ankles being very lame, I hired a passage in a wagon, with four or five of my brother officers. Capt. Clark and myself got into the hind part of the wagon, and, while fixing the seat, the horses started, and threw me out. I fell on the back part of my head, and they have since informed me that I lay as if dead for fifteen or twenty minutes. They put me into the wagon, and carried me five or six miles, before I came to my senses. My head is still very sore. Ensign Dake was in the wagon, and paid the strictest attention to me.

"I have not much news of consequence to write. We expected the British in at Burlington every hour. There were about a thousand men came in yesterday and today from Bennington and Windsor, and we are ready to meet them with any force they can bring against us. I have nothing more to write, but to subscribe myself your ever-loving husband, "WM. MILLER."

On his arrival at Burlington, Mr. Miller was transferred from the volunteers of the State of Vermont to [35] the regular army of the United States. He first took the rank of lieutenant, and was immediately ordered back to Rutland County, to attend to the recruiting service, as the following "General Order" will show.

"Encampment, Burlington, June 13th, 1813.

"SIR, – You are hereby commanded to repair to the County of Rutland, and there attend to the recruiting service for the 30th Regt. Infantry in U. S. Army. You will govern yourself by the laws of the United States, and return to this post when commanded.

"MASON ORMSBIE, *Maj. Inf'ry.*

"To Lieut. W. MILLER, U. S. Army."

Such a transfer is considered honorable in the military sense; and the change of service, which allowed Mr. Miller to enjoy the comforts of home and the attention of friends, while suffering from his late accident, must have been very acceptable. But there were reasons for the arrangement which bear most favorably on his reputation. The army was in great want of men who could be relied upon, under the dangers which threatened from the enemy in the direction of Canada; and there were few men who could accomplish so much, in bringing them into the service, as Mr. Miller. He was very generally known, and highly respected, in the region assigned him; he was warmly devoted to the service, so that his example had a powerful effect; and the returns, which official documents fully exhibit, demonstrate the wisdom of directing his efficiency to this department of the service.

He was employed in raising recruits till 1814; but this period of comparative repose was of short duration. He was thus remanded to head-quarters:

"Cantonment, Burlington, July 7th, 1813.

"Lieut. W. MILLER, at Poultney. – You are hereby commanded to join your regt. at Burlington immediately, and report yourself to the commanding officer.

"ELIAS FASSET, *Col. 30th Inf'ry.*"

Soon after his return to Burlington, in July of 1813, Mr. Miller was called to suffer another of the dangers [36] of army life, which, on many accounts, is quite as serious as those of the battle-field. The army fever, which broke out among the troops at Burlington, has already been referred to. So alarming were its ravages, that the great body of the army, quartered in or near the town, was removed several miles into the more elevated country, east of the lake. A change from the humid atmosphere and bad water of one locality, which aggravated, if they did not cause the distemper, to the salubrious air and pure water of the other locality, could not fail of producing a happy effect. But those who were too feeble to be removed, and those who could obtain suitable accommodations in the town, remained. Mr. Miller was among these.

One of the very common, most lamentable and mortifying evils of war, is the absolute dependence of the poor soldier on those whose avarice or profligacy rob him of all the comforts, and often of the necessaries, which his country may provide for him. The medical department of the army too often furnishes this form of the horrors of war. When a mere reckless pretender to the title of his profession, who has become disqualified for any station in civil society, obtains a place in this department, the life of a soldier is thought as little of as the life of a dog. It would be far more desirable to face the cannon of the enemy, than to fall into such hands. How many of the brave soldiers at Burlington, who found so undesirable an end, were indebted to official aid for that result, is unknown. Happy were those who could provide for themselves. Mr. Miller was thus favored. His fever bore a greater resemblance to the common bilious fever than to the prevailing epidemic. But the same potations, dealt out so profanely by the bloated official to the dying around him, were prescribed for the young officer from Poultney. He knew the danger, and sternly refused to take the stuff. He immediately put himself under the care of one of the resident physicians of the village, Dr. Littlefield, whose name is still remembered in the family of Mr. Miller with sentiments of affectionate gratitude.

At the time now referred to, Burlington appeared [37] much more like a camp than like a place devoted to the peaceful pursuits of commerce and learning. As it was the most important United States settlement on the shores of Lake Champlain, it was generally expected that the English forces would be concentrated here, for its conquest or destruction. The regular routine of college exercises was suspended, and the halls of learning were appropriated to the sick and dying officers of the army. To enjoy such accommodations was esteemed a great favor. But these rooms were so much crowded, and such was the want of proper aid, that the air within every part of the building, occupied was like a pestilential solvent for everything that passed into it. In one of these rooms, Mr. Miller was confined for several days after he was taken sick. As soon, however, as the tidings of his sickness reached Poultney, his wife resolved to place herself at his bed-side with as little delay as possible. An anxious and hurried ride, in an open wagon, brought her to witness such a scene of suffering and death as she had not before known. She found her husband quite as comfortable as she expected; but on entering his apartment, she saw that the prospect of help for him, and of escape for herself, was about equally dark. But what could she do? He could not be taken home; she was among strangers, and all that the generosity of the inhabitants could furnish, which was nobly brought forward, was needed to meet the common demand. Most providentially, there was another of her own sex on the premises, who, although she had devoted her ample stock of bedding, and other conveniences for the sick room, to the common benefit of those who occupied the college, could still sympathize with a wife and mother in such affliction, and cheerfully make the sacrifice that was needed to meet the case. This noble-hearted woman was Mrs. Cushman, whose husband had charge of the college boarding-house. She invited Mrs. Miller into her spacious and airy parlor; she brought forward her unsoiled bed-linen, and other things on which the comfort of the sick so much depends, and generously devoted them, the parlor, and its ample appendages, to the use of her afflicted visitor. But little time was needed to put all in order for the [38] removal of the patient to this most inviting apartment. All the circumstances of the change combined to make its effects the most desirable. The fear of burdening Mrs. Cushman was the greatest difficulty in the way of feeling themselves at home. In the comparative quiet of this apartment, with the skillful attention of Dr. Littlefield, and the constant attention of his wife, Mr. Miller exhibited the most gratifying indications of recovery. But as hope became strong in reference to him, there were reasons for alarm about Mrs. Miller.

The fatigue of the journey to Burlington, the anxiety she felt for her husband, the constant care and labor required to make him comfortable, had prostrated her so far, that she became peculiarly exposed to the infection of the pestilence. She was permitted only to rejoice in her husband's improvement before the usual premonitions of the dreaded malady appeared in her own system. As it was no longer indispensable that she should continue at Burlington, she resolved to fly from the infected region, and run the risk of a failure in reaching home. Although her husband was afflicted by the thought of her leaving him, he was much more afflicted by the fear that she might be prostrated, and fall into unkind hands, on the journey; or even become helpless on the highway, and die, as his grandfather Phelps had, by the same disease, only a few months before. However, she ordered the lad who accompanied her to get the carriage ready, and bidding Mr. Miller farewell, she took the road towards Poultney, which leads through the hilly country above the almost level slope which borders the lake; and after a moderate ride of two days, she arrived home, in much better health than when she left Burlington. Although the sun was very hot – for this was in August – the pure, invigorating air of the mountains had restored the tone of her naturally vigorous constitution, and the alarming symptoms disappeared without medical aid. Mr. Miller was immediately informed of the beneficial effects of her journey, which had as good an effect on him as the best medicine could have; and his health soon became so much improved, that he could resume the post of duty.

As the enemy did not make their appearance in the [39] vicinity of Burlington, or on the east of Lake Champlain, arrangements were made to locate the American troops on the west side of the lake, and to advance into Canada. Plattsburgh became the head-quarters of one division of the troops; Burlington continued the headquarters for another. In the autumn of 1813, Mr. Miller had so far recovered as to cross over the lake; but the effects of his fever appeared in the form of a bad sore on his left arm. This became so painful, and was so much of annoyance, that a surgical operation was advised, which was to remove the affected parts of the flesh, so as to cleanse the bone by scraping it. If this was not done, possibly amputation would be necessary. He was somewhat displeased by the rudeness of the thoughtless medical students, or surgeon's mates, who too often seem to think that a disabled soldier is good for nothing but to cut up for experiments. And, as they handled the diseased limb one day somewhat roughly, and spoke very lightly of its amputation, as a matter of course, he reminded them that his sword arm was still sound; and, putting his hand on the hilt of his sword, then before him, gave them to understand that, whatever might be advised in the case, he should not submit to any unnecessary pain for their amusement. They understood him, and it ended their rudeness.

This danger, however, was shortly over, and he was able to join his regiment in actual service, while they were out in search of the enemy on the Canadian frontier. The particulars of this expedition are given in a letter to his wife, dated

"Chatuagay Four Corners, Oct. 31, 1813

"LUCY: – I once more have the pleasure of writing to you, and am very sorry that I cannot tell you of hairbreadth escapes and dismal sights, hideous yells and war-whoops; but so it is. I have seen nothing like an enemy, although I have been into Canada. I started from this place last Thursday, to join my regiment; but, meeting some officers, we were ordered to return to this place. The army is expected here in a few hours. They stayed only three or four miles back; they have had a number of skirmishes with Indians, and, last Tuesday, [40] they had a general engagement with the whole British force, consisting of regulars, militia and Indians, and it is said, would have taken the whole, was it not for the folly of some of our guides, who led that part of our army astray which should have fallen on their rear: and they being thus led astray and bewildered in the woods, the Indians fell upon them in the night, and made considerable havoc among them. Night before last, they had another encounter with our piquet guard, and there were some killed and wounded on both sides. You will undoubtedly hear many stories, but the truth you will hardly get, for there are as many different stories here as there are men. I expect we shall be posted at this place, that is, the 30th regt.; but wherever we may be, you will hear from me as often as you wish to. I have not heard from you since I came from home. Do write immediately, and direct your letter to "Lieut. Wm. Miller, of 30th Infantry, Northern Army.

"WM. MILLER.

"P. S. *Nov. 1st.* 1813. I have joined my regt., and find all our soldiers alive and well from Poultney. We lost none from our regt.; and only one wounded. It is said we lost 30 killed in said battle. We some expect an attack by the Indians soon.   "WM. MILLER."

These "skirmishes" closed the campaign of 1813 in this quarter; and, while the great body of the troops, under General Macomb, were preparing, at Burlington and Plattsburgh; for more efficient operations the following year, Mr. Miller was engaged in the recruiting service, in the vicinity of his residence, and through the State of Vermont generally. He was at home on a furlough, when he received the following orders from the colonel of his regiment:-

"Burlington, Jan. 10th, 1814.

"To Lieut. WILLIAM MILLER.

"You will immediately repair to Poultney, and such other places as you think proper, and there attend to the recruiting service, agreeable to your last instructions.

"ELIAS FASSET, *Col. 30th Inf'y.*" [41]

The year 1814 was to decide the contest between Great Britain and the United States. The former was able to bring her best troops into the field, and the latter must put forth all her resources to meet them. It seems almost impossible that human skill or strength could have brought about the result. There probably was no particular point of the general scene of the war where the circumstances of the American arms were of a more critical nature than at the point where Mr. Miller, with his brave countrymen, were to stand. Early in the year, and while he was searching out and sending into the field the recruits from the Green Mountains, he was promoted to the office of Captain in the regular army. As this is the point, in Mr. Miller's history, which has been misapprehended by some who have referred to him publicly, although the fact involved is, to his friends, of but little interest, the document which makes all clear is given:

"*The President of the United States of America to all who shall see these presents, greeting*:

"KNOW YE, That, reposing special trust and confidence in the patriotism, valor, fidelity, and abilities, of William Miller, I have nominated, and by and with the advice and consent of the Senate, do appoint him a Captain in the Thirtieth Regiment of Infantry, in the service of the United States: to rank as such from the thirty-first day of January, eighteen hundred and fourteen. He is, therefore, carefully and diligently to discharge the duty of Captain, by doing and performing all manner of things thereunto belonging. And I do strictly charge and require all officers and soldiers under his command to be obedient to his orders as Captain. And he is to observe and follow such orders and directions, from time to time, as he shall receive from me, or the future President of the United States of America, or the General or other superior Officers set over him, according to the rules and discipline of War. This Commission to continue in force during the pleasure of the President of the United States for the time being.

"Given under my hand, at the City of Washington, this first day of February, in the year of our Lord one [42] thousand eight hundred and fifteen, and in the thirty-ninth year of the Independence of the United States.

("L.S.)   JAMES MADISON.

"By the President,

"JAS. MONROE, *Secretary of War.*"

The summons which brought him to the post of danger is of the following form and date:

"Burlington, August 12th, 1814.

"To WM. MILLER, Capt. in the 30th Inf'y.

"SIR: – You are ordered to report yourself to the commanding officer of said regt., without delay, at Plattsburgh. I am, Sir, with respect, etc. etc.,

"ELIAS FASSET,

Col. 30th and Comd. recruiting."

His promotion to a more responsible position subjected him to some very painful duties; and if we may credit the uniform testimony of his companions in arms, few men ever met the difficulties before him with greater ability or success.

All the circumstances which led to the vacation of the office to which Mr. Miller was promoted need not be stated. But the said company of infantry passed under his command in a state of serious disorder. Such a state of things became the more threatening, as the approach of the enemy rendered it of the utmost importance that each company should be in a state of the greatest efficiency possible.

The nature of the difficulties to be met, the course he pursued, and the result, are stated in the following letter to his wife.

"Camp near Fort Moreau, in Plattsburgh, Sept. 4th, 1814.

Sunday, 9 o'clock evening.

"DEAR LUCY: – I received your letter of the 30th, and perceived, by the contents, that you received only eighty dollars. I enclosed 100, and think you must have been mistaken; for, if any person had robbed the letter, they would have taken the whole. My soldiers were paid their money to-day, and I have had to go out twice, since I have begun this letter, to still the noise. I have found [43] the company in a very wayward situation, but believe, by dint of application, I shall be able to bring them to good subordination. I have had to punish four or five of them very severely, and have reason to believe that they both love and fear me. One look is now sufficient to quell any disorder. This we call a pay-day, and, once in four days, we have a whiskey-day; on which days, I have six or seven soldiers who will take a little too much, and then, of all the devils in hell, I think they must exceed in deviltry. But, while in this situation, I do not punish. After they become sober, I then punish them as I told them I would, and I find it has a good effect. One punishment which I inflict on soldiers is *picketing*. First, a gallows is raised, about ten feet high; then their arms are extended and fastened above by ropes; then a picket drove into the earth, on which they are to stand until they receive sufficient punishment; and we seldom have to punish them the second time. I had one on the picket to-day, for threatening to shoot one of my sergeants, and swearing that he would not obey any officer except the captain. This, in an army, is a great crime; therefore, I could do no less than to make a public example. When he was first put up, he was very turbulent, and hoped he might die if he repented of what he said; but, after standing one hour, he became as penitent as a lamb, and prayed and begged to be released. 'Oh dear, Captain,' said he, 'do take me down – I shall die! I will never commit another crime. For Heaven's sake, release me!' I took him down, as you may well believe; and it wrung tears from my eyes to see how thankful the poor fellow was; .. but this is only the bad picture. In my next letter, I will show you the good side. The British are within ten miles of this place, and we expect a battle to-morrow; and I think they must be d–d fools if they do not attack us, as they are ten or eleven thousand strong, and we are only fifteen hundred; but every man is determined to do his duty. It may be my lot to fall; if I do, I will fall bravely. Remember, you will never hear from me, if I am a coward. I must close, as it is almost 11 o'clock.

"Remember your   WM. MILLER." [44]

This letter contains the only instance of the use of language approaching to the dialect of profanity, which has passed under the writer's notice, in a large amount of Mr. Miller's manuscripts. Considering that he was a deist and a soldier at the time, instances of a more objectionable form might have been expected. And this was evidently owing to the peculiar vexations of the time.

This letter is dated less than a week anterior to the most remarkable and bloody battle of Plattsburgh. It was daily expected when he wrote. It seems almost surprising, in view of the known strength of the two armies, that he should have spoken as he did: "This is only the bad picture; in my next letter, I will show you the good side!"

It is impossible to give a correct view of the perilous position of Mr. Miller and his fellow-soldiers, during this battle, without stating, to some extent, the details of its history. The reader will not consider it out of place, if quotations from works on such matters are here made, such as will place the danger and the courage of the subject of this memoir with other brave defenders of our country, and also the interposition of Providence, as it was regarded at the time, in their true light:-

> "It had become an object of solicitude with the belligerent parties on the northern frontier to obtain the superiority on the lakes. Indeed, the success of the land operations was considered to be entirely dependent on that of the marine. Commodore Perry had already established our dominion on Lake Erie: and that of Lake Ontario had been successfully disputed by Commodore Chauncey with Sir James Yeo. Vermont and New York were threatened from Lake Champlain. To counteract hostile attempts from this quarter, the command of the American squadron on this lake was intrusted to Commodore Macdonough, while the defense of Plattsburgh depended on the exertions of General Macomb, and his gallant little army. In September, 1814, an attack was anticipated on these youthful commanders; accordingly, on the 11th of that month, the expected event took place.

> "Early in the summer of 1814, the Canadian frontier [45] was reinforced by a large body of troops, which rendered the position of General Brown very critical. The British government, relieved from its long and severe struggle against Bonaparte, could dispose of many picked troops, disciplined under Wellington, and they were sent to Canada.

> "For several days, the enemy had been on his way to Plattsburgh, by land and water, and it was well understood that an attack would be made at the same time by his land and naval forces. Commodore Macdonough determined to await at anchor the approach of the latter.

> "General Macomb was frequently advised to retreat, to spare the blood and lives of his apology for an army, and save Plattsburgh from the fate of a conquered country. But the decision which he took, and to which

he unwaveringly adhered, in his apparently forlorn situation, proved the strength of his moral courage, and the wisdom of his measures.

"At eight o'clock in the morning, the look-out boat announced the approach of the enemy. At nine, he anchored in a line ahead, at about three hundred yards distance from the American line: his flag-ship, the Confiance, under Commodore Downie, was opposed to Commodore Macdonough's ship, the Saratoga; the brig Linnet was opposed to the Eagle, Captain Robert Henley; the enemy's galleys, thirteen in number, to the schooner, sloop, and a division of galleys; one of his sloops assisting his ship and brig, the others assisting his galleys; the remaining American galleys being with the Saratoga and Eagle.

"In this situation, the whole force on both sides became engaged; the Saratoga suffered much from the heavy fire of the Confiance, though the fire of the former was very destructive to her antagonist. The Ticonderoga, Lieutenant-commander Cassin, gallantly sustained her full share of the action. At half past ten o'clock, the Eagle, not being able to bring her guns to bear, cut her cable, and anchored in a more eligible position, between the Saratoga and the Ticonderoga, where she very much annoyed the enemy, but unfortunately left her commodore exposed to a galling fire from the enemy's [46] brig. The guns of the Saratoga on the starboard side being nearly all dismounted or not manageable, a stern anchor was let go, the bower cable cut, and the ship winded with a fresh broadside on the Confiance, which soon after surrendered. The broadside of the Saratoga was then sprung to bear on the brig, which surrendered within about fifteen minutes.

"The sloop that was opposed to the Eagle had struck some time before, and drifted down the line; the sloop which was with the enemy's galleys having also struck. Three of them were sunk, and the others pulled off. While Macdonough's galleys were in the act of obeying the signal to follow them, all the vessels were reported to him to be in a sinking state; it then became necessary to countermand the signal to the galleys, and order their men to the pumps.

"At this time, not a mast was standing, in either squadron, in a condition to hold up a sail; the lower rigging, being nearly all shot away, hung down along the mast.

"The action lasted, without intermission, two hours and twenty minutes.

"An attack made by the British army, under the Governor-general of the Canadas, Sir George Provost, on General Macomb, commanding at Plattsburgh, owed its defeat to the bravery of Commodore Macdonough on the lake, and the undaunted valor of Macomb, commanding on shore.

"Sir George, having collected all the disposable force in Lower Canada, with a view of conquering the country as far as Crown Point and Ticonderoga, entered the territories of the United States, on the first of September, with fourteen thousand men, and occupied the village of Champlain. As was before intimated, the cooperation of the naval force constituted an essential part of the arrangement. The consequence was, that, instantly on the discomfiture of the fleet, the army retired with great precipitation, having lost two thousand five hundred men, in killed, wounded, and missing.

"This victory was announced to the department of war, by Commodore Macdonough, on the day it was obtained, in the following brief and modest communication: [47] 'The Almighty has been pleased to grant us a signal victory on Lake Champlain, in the capture of one frigate, one brig, and two sloops of war of the enemy.' [7]

It was in the midst of this scene of terror and carnage that Mr. Miller's courage was tried. Its effect on him is described, so far as words can describe it, in two letters, one of which was written even before the battle ended, and is addressed to Judge Stanley, of Poultney; the other is addressed to Mrs. Miller. As both of these letters will be read with interest, they are inserted. The first is dated and reads as follows:

"Fort Scott, September 11, 1814.

20 minutes past 2 o'clock, P.M.

"Sir: – It is over! it is done! the British fleet has struck to the American flag! Great slaughter on both sides. They are in plain view, where I am now writing. My God! the sight was majestic, it was noble, it was grand. This morning, at ten o'clock, the British opened a very heavy and destructive fire upon us, both by water and land; their congreve rockets flew like hailstones about us, and round shot and grape from every quarter. You have no idea of the battle. Our force was small, but how bravely they fought! Sir Lord George Provost feels bad. His land force may expect to meet their fate, if our militia do their duty; but in time of action, they were not to be seen. The action on water lasted only two hours and ten minutes; the firing from their batteries has but just ceased – ours is still continuing; the small arms now are just coming to action. I have no time to write any more; you must conceive what we feel, for I cannot describe it. I am satisfied that I can fight; I know I am no coward; therefore, call on Mr. Loomis and drink my health, and I will pay the shot. Three of my men are

---

[7] "Glory of America."

wounded – by a shell which burst within two feet of me. The boat from the fleet, which has just landed under our fort, says the British commodore is killed. Out of 300 on board their ship, 25 remain alive. Some of our officers, who have been on board, [48] say the blood is knee deep. Their force we have taken consists of one ship, 36 guns; one brig of 18 guns, and two sloops.

"Huzza! huzza! Twenty or thirty British prisoners, taken by our militia, have just arrived in fort. I can write no more, for the time grows dubious.

"Yours forever,

"Wm. Miller.

"Give my compliments to all, and send this to my wife."

If it should be necessary, the forbearance of the reader is again appealed to, for noticing an incident, which, if it is of no other value, gave the greatest possible interest to the letter of Mrs. Miller, in the estimation of herself and family, at the time of its reception. It is one of those mysterious phenomena, the occurrence of which it is hard to deny, while the principle or agency from which they spring it is not easy fully to explain. The battle of Plattsburgh was fought on Sunday. The state of Mrs. Miller's health was such as to make her interest in the issue of the battle of the most affecting and absorbing character. She was near giving birth to a son, who is now living, and bears the strongest resemblance to his father of any one of the children. If there are any circumstances which would make it proper that an almost supernatural intercourse might be permitted between two souls which Heaven has united, it must be at such a time. While the battle was raging, nearly a hundred miles distant, Mrs. Miller became strangely affected. A hitherto unexperienced and unaccountable presentation was made to her mind, which to her was a demonstration of what was going on where she felt that so much was at stake. She was nearly frantic with agony, so that the friends who were with her became seriously alarmed on her account. Argument, ridicule, all the modes they could think of, to restore her usual cheerfulness and self-command, were alike unavailing. She could think and speak of nothing but the "trouble at the north!"

The form of this presentiment was very simple, but certainly it was highly emblematic. As she expressed it, – "A dark, furious, smothering tornado rushed down [49] on a poor, unsheltered flock of little birds!" There was ground enough for such a comparison in the antagonist forces, though there was anything but an apprehended sweep of a destructive tornado in the last letter of her husband. But the coincidence of time was the mystery.

The day passed; her agony subsided, but not her fears. The friends with her thought she had had a nervous time, or was slightly insane. Nothing was heard from the scene of conflict at the north till near the close of Monday. The first intimation of the tidings, to that family, was the strong peal of the village bell. A member of the family was sent out to inquire its meaning, and the glad shout of victory was heard on every hand. A fleet horse and rider had brought the news, and passed on south!

The sound of victory was most welcome. That was all that patriotism might ask. But family affection could not rest till it had learned the price of victory. An old, iron-hearted soldier has remarked, that "the next calamity to a defeat, in war, is a triumph!" Some must have fallen at Plattsburgh. And how many anxious hearts awaited the arrival of the next mail from the seat of war! That mail brought to Mrs. Miller the letter before referred to. It reads as follows:

"Fort Scott, September 12, 1814.
7 o'clock, morning.

"DEAR WIFE: – Yesterday was a day of great joy. We have conquered! we have drove them! About nine o'clock A. M., yesterday, the British fleet fired a salute as they passed Cumberland-head; it was a token for a general engagement. About twenty minutes after, they hove in sight. How majestic, how noble, our fleet lay in Plattsburgh Bay; and, like a saucy Yankee, paid no attention to their royal salute! The British fleet still bearing down upon us, bold as a lion, in a moment we were all prepared for action. The British had thrown up a number of batteries on all sides of us. The next minute the cannon began playing – spitting their fire in every quarter. What a scene! All was dreadful! – nothing but roaring and groaning, for about [50] six or eight hours. I cannot describe to you our situation. The fort I was in was exposed to every shot. Bombs, rockets, and shrapnel shells, fell thick as hailstones. Three of my men were wounded, and one killed; but none that were from Poultney, or that quarter. In one hour and forty-five minutes, the enemy's fleet was conquered. My God! what a slaughter on all sides! – out of 300 on board of one ship, 24 only remained unhurt! I cannot describe to you the general joy. At sundown, our forts fired a national salute, accompanied by a tune called 'Yankee Doodle,' and each gun was loaded with an eighteen pound shot. This soon frightened our foe to that degree, that, this morning, at daybreak, not a soul was to be seen; and they went off in so great a hurry that not one article of their baggage could they carry away. Some they burnt, and some they left behind. Their loss, in killed and wounded, is immense, besides one hundred taken prisoners, and three or four hundred deserters. Our loss was not so great, but considerable. Every officer and soldier is now singing for joy, and there is nothing now heard but the 11th day of September, and Lord George Provost retreating for Canada. You may well conceive, by my unconnected mode of writing, that I am as joyful as any of them. A naval and land engagement, within the compass of a mile or two, and fifteen or twenty thousand engaged at one and the same time, is superior to anything my eyes ever beheld before. How grand, how noble, and yet how awful! The roaring of cannon, the bursting of bombs, the whizzing of balls, the popping of small arms, the cracking of timbers, the shrieks of the dying, the groans of the wounded, the commands of the officers, the swearing of soldiers, the smoke, the fire, everything conspires to make the scene of a battle both awful and grand!

"The fort I was in was on the bank of the lake, and in plain view of everything which passed.

"Remember me to all my friends; and, in the mean time, accept of me, as I am, faithfully yours,

"WM. MILLER."

The triumph of the American arms at Plattsburgh was truly "a signal" one. And if ever it was proper to [51] ascribe such an event to "the Almighty," it was proper on this occasion. It is not very often the case, however, that an acknowledgment of this kind marks the official account of a battle, as it does that of Commodore Macdonough. It was perfectly in harmony with his well-known deportment at the time, and with the common feeling which pervaded, in an unusual degree, the whole United States force engaged. Napoleon had beaten the mightiest armies that Europe had ever raised, in an almost uninterrupted succession of battles, during more than ten years. The troops of England, with their allies, had now the reputation of having at last beaten Napoleon. And these English troops, with overwhelming numbers in their favor, entered the field against those of the

United States, at Plattsburgh. What, then, in all human estimation, had this "apology for an army" to expect?

One of the most sublime and appalling scenes, in which it falls to the lot of man to enact a part, is presented by the deadly encounter of fleets and armies. The attainment of a position; the skill and courage required, in each division of the body to be brought into action, in order to work out the plan on which the success of the day is presumed to depend; the ability and promptness needed to comprehend and execute any manoeuvre, the necessity of which may not be foreseen; the success of a stratagem or a surprise, are so many points, where the strength of the hostile forces is equal, in which the chances usually hang so much in doubt, that each man of the thousands in arms must feel his danger, in the same proportion that he feels his insufficiency to direct all to the desired result; and this sense of insufficiency must naturally dispose each one to look for aid to a power above that of man. Such a feeling is the usual accompaniment of a battle where the chances are equally balanced.

But when the strength of the forces is known to be very unequal, that party in the contest where the external weakness is felt, after all is done that devoted patriotism, union, intelligence and skill can accomplish, must faint, unless they are sustained by the hope of aid from on high; while the party which feel confident in [52] their own resources often become profanely arrogant, and fatally presumptuous. It is seldom that such an impressive exhibition of devout hope in God on one side, and such a painful exhibition of self-confidence on the other side, demands our attention, as were manifested in the battle of Plattsburgh.

When the hour of deadly strife had come, every preparation having been made for action on the American side, and the attention of all on board the Saratoga was called to the commodore, it is said that, in the stillness, which was soon to give place to scenes of tumult so unsuitable to the day, the voice of Macdonough was raised in fervent prayer to God, for the fleet, the army, and the success of the American cause. But this was only an expression of the deep feeling of every heart. In such circumstances, the stoutest, and even the profane, felt the propriety of prayer; for all were humbled before God. This sense of its propriety, if nothing else, gave them a new feeling of strength for the conflict. And when the day closed with an assurance of victory – for it was thought to be hardly possible, even when the English fleet had struck their colors – the hand of God seemed to be so manifest to all, that the hardest specimens of human nature in the fleet and army were seen in tears, while all were constrained to acknowledge their sense of providential favor.

The result of this battle deeply impressed the mind of Mr. Miller. He refers to it, in one of his published works, in these words:

> "Many occurrences served to weaken my confidence in the correctness of deistical principles. I was led frequently to compare this country to that of the children of Israel, before whom God drove out the inhabitants of their land. It seemed to me that the Supreme Being must have watched over the interests of this country in an especial manner, and delivered us from the hands of our enemies. I was particularly impressed with this view when I was in the battle of Plattsburgh, when, with 1500 regulars, and about 4000 volunteers, we defeated the British, who were 15,000 strong; we being also successful, at the same time, in an engagement with the [53] British fleet on the lake. At the commencement of the battle, we looked upon our own defeat as almost certain; and yet we were victorious. So surprising a result, against such odds, did seem to me like the work of a mightier power than man."

In another place it will be seen that arrangements for celebrating the anniversary of this battle gave rise to the Christian effort which arrested the attention of Mr. Miller, at the time of his conversion.

What passed on board the English fleet, or in their camp, as a contrast to what took place on the part of the Americans, has not been stated. Its statement is not necessary. But as it was assigned to Captain Miller, with other officers, to prepare the body of the English commodore for its interment, it may be remarked, in passing, that the sentiment, said to have been rashly expressed by that personage, when he took his accustomed drink at the close of his last meal, [8] imprecated such a termination of his career as he actually experienced. The first broadside from the American

---

[8] The sentiment, as uniformly stated, was to this import:- "If he did not eat his next meal in Plattsburgh, he hoped he might eat it in hell!"

fleet split off a massive splinter from a spar or timber of the Confiance, and dashed it with such force against Commodore Downie's person, in the region of the vitals, that he never breathed after he fell. It literally knocked the breath out of him.

The generous sympathy shown to the wounded of their enemies, and the honor paid to the dead, by the Americans, was as worthy of remembrance as the bravery with which they fought. Officers of the same rank received the same honors, without regard to the nation in whose service they fell. Mrs. Downie, who tarried in Canada, expressed her high sense of the honors paid to her husband, by an affecting and appropriate acknowledgment.

The battle of Plattsburgh was decisive as to any further hostilities in that quarter. A short armistice, arranged by the generals of the opposite forces, was followed by the ratification of peace. But the troops were still kept [54] at their post; and scenes as painful, if not so destructive of human life, as those just noticed, passed in the American camp. One of Mr. Miller's letters speaks in becoming terms of the scenes referred to. Other things are mentioned in the same letter, that might be omitted; but as the persons whose names are mentioned have passed away, and as a prominent trait in the character of the one who wrote the letter is here exhibited in its natural tenderness, the whole letter is inserted.

"Plattsburgh, Oct. 28, 1814.

7 o'clock, evening.

"Dear Lucy: – Again have I resumed my pen, in hopes to beguile those lonesome hours, (which, although in camp, I assure you are not a few.) In my last letter, sent by David Wyman, of Westhaven, I informed you of the intended execution of a few criminals. There were six of them launched into the other world in a hurry, to-day, and I think I had rather see one hundred fall in action.

"You, perhaps, remember Spencer; he was a sergeant, and gained the esteem of all his fellows. He is no more. He died yesterday of a fever – as is supposed – but I believe that a hopeless passion which he had formed for Charlotte Hyde hastened his end. I went to see him a few hours before his death; he was rational, and appeared to be warned of his approaching fate; he mentioned his friends in Poultney; he mentioned your name; regretted that he could not see you once more; but when he was a going to mention the name of Charlotte, his speech failed him. He could only squeeze my hand, and weep. I pitied him, from my soul. 'Young man,' said I, 'I know what you would say – endeavor to recover your health. You shall have a furlough, and go and see -'… 'Ah! no,' said he, 'it is all over with me. A few hours, and I shall be no more.' He hung to my hand; begged of me not to leave him; but my duty forced me, and, with difficulty, I tore myself from his grasp. I had him decently interred; and if any person was a mourner, I was one.

"Perhaps it would not be proper to mention this to Charlotte. You can do as you think best, as I believe [55] you are capable of judging as correctly as I can. The remainder of the soldiers from Poultney and that quarter are all well.

"I shall send this letter by Elnathan Phelps, Jr. I have sent to the post-office for a letter this evening, and the mail had not arrived; therefore, no letter from my Lucy. How unpropitious are these strong winds! – or is my Lucy unkind?

"But a short time, and, like Spencer, I shall be no more. It is a solemn thought. Yet, could I be sure of one other life, there would be nothing terrific; but to go out like an extinguished taper, is insupportable – the thought is doleful. No! rather let me cling to that hope which warrants a never-ending existence; a future spring, where troubles shall cease, and tears find no conveyance; where never-ending spring shall flourish, and love, pure as the driven snow, rest in every breast.

"Dear Lucy, do write to me, and let me know how you pass your time.

"Good-evening. I am troubled.   WM. MILLER."

As Mr. Miller has expressed his horror of the infidel doctrine of annihilation in the above letter, it may be proper here to show that it was this repulsive feature of deism which constituted the greatest difficulty connected with it in his mind. This fact is thus stated, in one of his published works:

"Before the close of this period, however," [the period of his deistical life] "I began to suspect that deism tended to a belief of annihilation, which was always very abhorrent to my feelings. In the fall of 1812, as I was returning to Poultney from the court at Rutland, in company with Judge Stanley, I asked him his opinion respecting our condition in another state. He replied by comparing it to that of a tree, which flourishes for a time, and turns again to earth; and to that of a candle, which burns to nothing. I was then satisfied that deism was inseparably connected with, and did tend to, the denial of a future existence. And I thought to myself, that rather than embrace such a view, I should prefer the heaven and hell of the Scriptures, and take my chance [56] respecting them. Still, I could not regard the Bible as inspired."

Another of his letters from the army is presented to the reader, rather to exhibit the ingenuity of its writer in administering a rebuke for what he supposed to be an omission, on the part of his wife, to forward the usual epistle to Camp Plattsburgh. It will be seen, that an arrangement had been made for a weekly correspondence. The large bundle of letters written by him, in fulfillment of this arrangement, is still preserved; each letter is numbered, and the whole furnishes an interesting illustration of the punctuality and order he carried into all the departments of life. This letter expresses the tender interest he felt in those at home. It shows that his pleasantry could adapt itself to the most serious subjects. And it undoubtedly presents a correct statement of his religious views at the time.

It should be stated, that the letter which he mourns the absence of, and which led him to suppose his wife must be "no more," was sent by a lad who expected to leave Whitehall and go to Plattsburgh by water, so as to get there about the time of the arrival of the mail. A storm detained the vessel some days, so that the letter was not received as intended. This afflicting letter – it is afflicting, full of irony as it is – reads as follows:

"Camp Plattsburgh, Nov 11th, 1814.

"DEAR LUCY: – Have you departed this life? Are you gone to the world of spirits? (I almost fancy that, while I am writing, your unembodied spirit is hovering around me.) Or, are you so engaged that you could not devote one hour in a week to your humble servant?

"The following are the words you wrote me not long since, to wit, – 'If I am alive, I shall write to you weekly, and put a letter into the post-office every Monday morning;' and, ever since Wednesday noon, I have been dressed in mourning. Shall I ever see my Lucy again? I have often exclaimed, Ah! no; she could not tell me a falsehood. She must be dead! What can I write, if she is gone? I cannot write anything; she cannot hear me. I can only write to my children, into whose hands [57] I hope this letter will fall, – 'Dear children, you have lost your mother, and but a little while, and your father must follow; perhaps, before you receive this, he will be no more; prepare, then, my children, to meet the frowns of fortune, and learn, in your youth, to repel the shafts of adversity. Your present time ought to be devoted to your studies. Remember the lives of your parents were short, and you know not the hour you will be called for. Life is uncertain, and you ought so to live as, when you come to die, that not one reflection will pass your mind but that you have so lived as to merit the good will of all good men. Your first study ought to lead you to look up to the Supreme Being as the Author of all things. When you learn his attributes, or as much as man is to know, you will ever keep in mind that he sees every action of your life, knows every thought, and hears every word. If you follow this rule, you cannot go far astray. You may be led, for a moment, into vices that human nature is subject to; but you cannot materially err, for, in your cooler moments, conscience will point to you the road you ought to follow. You must never give way to adversity, nor be raised up in prosperity; for pride is equally as dangerous as cowardice; for to give way to the first shows a weak and cowardly mind, and the latter indicates a vain and haughty spirit. Begin the world as you would wish you had when you come to die; endeavor to get the good will of all people; for it is better to have the good than the ill will of even a dog. Search not too far for vain and empty baubles; it is a more solid pleasure "to do as you would be done by." Yet, in this, you will find the ingratitude of man. Put not too much dependence on human favor; for there are but few who walk the narrow path. Remember, my children, that your father has vainly sought the friendship of man, and never could he discover any friendship only where there was a dependence. In the small circle in which I now move, this rule is manifest. Here are a hundred persons that depend upon me for every comfort, and each one professes a real love for me. Yet, if I was a citizen, or one of their own rank, I could never expect more than common friendship. Indeed, they seem to me like children, and, together with you, [58] claim my highest support. If my Lucy is no more, and I am doomed to lead a solitary life, you must calculate to live for yourselves. What pecuniary help I can afford you, I will; and I expect it will be but small. What little worldly store I have left at home may be divided equally among you when you arrive to years of discretion. In the mean time, I hope, William, that you will set so good an example to your brothers and sisters, as that, if they follow it, shall insure them peace, love, and friendship here, and happiness in the world to come. May you remember the virtues of your parents, and forget their vices: this is the constant prayer of your loving father,   Wm. Miller.'

"If Lucy is no more, or if she has forgotten Wm. Miller, then this letter is directed to Wm. S. Miller, his oldest son."

Mr. Miller remained at Plattsburgh as late as February of 1815; and, although the English had removed their forces into Canada, so that there was no fighting with them, there were some bad Yankees, whose cases called for occasional punishment. In the "Register of men tried and punished or pardoned," kept by our then military friend, we find nothing more severe inflicted, by any court martial of which "Capt. Miller" was "President," than this: "S- P-, Private. Jan. 20, 1815. Regt. C. Martial. Crime: disobedience of orders, neglect of duty, and stealing. Sentence: to be ducked in the lake, picketed two hours, and have his whiskey rations stopped sixty days." Rather a hard sentence for January!

In prosecuting the business designated in the following "Order" of General Macomb, he probably had an opportunity to make a flying visit to Poultney:

"Head-quarters, Plattsburgh, 3rd February, 1815.

"ORDERS. – Capt. Miller, of the 30th Regt., will proceed immediately to Whitehall, and procure clothing for the requisition of the commanding officer of his regt.

"ALEX. MACOMB."

Mr. Miller's connection with the scenes of military life [59] were drawing to a close. Peace had already been ratified; and, shortly after the news of that event arrived, he received permission to take a last farewell of the actual service of a calling which was as uncongenial with the aspirations of his soul as any of the scenes of his former life had been. The permit – perhaps it should be called a discharge – is in this form:

"Burlington, June 18, 1815.

"Capt. W. Miller has permission to depart till further orders, he having complied with the General Orders, as respects the five year men. By command,

"JNO. H. BURTON,

"*Lt. & Adj't 30th Inf'y.*"

A few reflections on this period of Mr. Miller's life, and the mention of an incident or two of some interest, must close this chapter. Everybody is familiar with the fact, that the army is a bad school of morality. Intemperance, licentiousness, gambling, fighting, stealing, profanity, and Sabbath-breaking, are the common vices of army life. It was the constant practice of these vices by those around him, which sickened Mr. Miller of their society. And that he should escape entirely from the contamination, would be too much to expect. However, it is both a matter of surprise, and highly creditable to him, that his moral integrity and habits were not affected to a hopeless extent. There were, however, some redeeming traits to the too generally dark moral picture of army life. There were a few men in the 30th regiment of infantry who were known as men of prayer, and undoubted piety. And an incident in their history, which Mr. Miller has often spoken of with great interest, should be mentioned. One of these praying men, if memory has not failed in the case, was Sergeant Willey. His tent was occasionally used for the purpose of holding a prayer-meeting. On one of these occasions, when Mr. Miller was "the officer for the day," he saw a light in this tent, and, wishing to know what was going on, as his duty required, he drew near, and heard the voice of prayer. He said nothing at the time; but, the next day, on recollecting it, he thought it was a good opportunity [60] to try the sergeant's piety, and indulge his own relish for a joke, by calling Sergeant Willey to account for having his tent occupied by a gambling party the night before. When the sergeant appeared, Captain Miller affected great seriousness, and spoke in a tone bordering on severity, as follows:- "You know, Sergeant Willey, that it is contrary to the army regulations to have any gambling in the tents at night. And I was very sorry to see your tent lit up, for that purpose, last night. We cannot have any gambling at such times. You must put a stop to it at once. I hope I shall not have to speak to you again about it!"

The poor sergeant stood thunderstruck, for a moment, to hear such an imputation cast on himself and his associates. And then, hardly daring to look up, he replied, with the most touching simplicity, and in a manner which showed that he was alike unwilling to suffer the scandal of entertaining gamblers, or to make a parade of his devotions, "We were not gambling, sir!"

Capt. Miller was touched with his appearance. But, still affecting greater severity than at first, being determined to press him to a confession, he said to the sergeant, "Yes, you were gambling! And it won't do! What else could have your tent lighted up for, all the evening, if you were not gambling?"

Sergeant Willey now felt himself under the necessity of being a little more explicit, and answered, in a manner deeply expressive of his grief and innocence, "We were praying, sir!"

Capt. Miller, by this time, was almost in tears; and indicating, by a motion of his hand, that he was satisfied, and that the praying sergeant might withdraw, he continued alone for some time, sensibly affected by the courage manifested by these Christians in that ungodly camp, by the becoming deportment of their representative under such a serious scandal, and by the doubtful course he had taken in reference to them.

There are but two particulars on which the writer has ever heard a hint that the subject of this memoir became in the least corrupted in his habits, during his connection with the army. On one of these particulars, he has written as follows: [61]

> "One day in May, 1816, I detected myself in the act of taking the name of God in vain – a habit I had acquired in the service; and I was instantly convicted of its sinfulness."

The other vice of his army life was that of gambling, particularly, if not exclusively, in the use of cards. To what extent he indulged the habit, cannot be stated; but, on returning home, at the close of the war, he abandoned the practice totally and forever. Facts might be presented to show that Mr. Miller's stern regard for the principles of personal virtue, and especially his abhorrence of the slightest violation of the laws of chastity, exposed him to the raillery of his less scrupulous, and even shameless, brother officers. It is sufficient to say, what all who have any knowledge of the question will confirm, that his personal integrity and official honor were such, throughout his connection with the army, as to command, in an almost unexampled degree, the respect and affection of all who were under him as an officer, and the hearty confidence and esteem of his official associates. For years after the war closed, it was a common thing for his brethren in arms to turn aside from the great route of travel, five or six miles, only to enjoy a short interview with one to whom they were so strongly attached; and some of the less provident, feeling sure that he would receive them with a sort of fatherly sympathy, which a poor, unfortunate soldier seldom finds in the world, were accustomed to tarry with him some days or weeks at a time.

One fact must be mentioned, which will speak more than volumes in behalf of his commanding integrity, as it shows the place he occupied in the respect and confidence of the soldiers. After the war, two members of his company, who lived as neighbors in the extreme northern part of Vermont, had some business difficulties, which grew to be so serious that they could hardly live together as neighbors on speaking terms, to say the least. This was a great affliction to themselves, as brother soldiers, to their families, and to the whole neighborhood. These men had often thought of their former captain, though they were much older than he was, and wished [62] the difficulties could be submitted to his examination and decision. But it was a long way to his residence, and the time and cost of the journey seemed too much to admit of such an arrangement. However, the matter became a source of so much trouble, that the proposition was made by one, and gladly accepted by the other, to visit Captain Miller; to submit the case to him, by telling each his own story, and to abide by his decision. The long journey was performed by these old soldiers separately, as duelists go to the place of single combat. They arrived at Captain Miller's nearly at the same time. Arrangements were made for a hearing. Each told his story. The decision was made known, after all the facts of the case had been duly considered. It was received in good faith by the parties. They took each other cordially by the hand, spent a little time with their captain, and returned to their homes in company, as friends and brothers. These men, now far advanced in life, it is believed are still living. Their names could be given, if it were necessary.

Paradoxical as it may appear, some of the most distinguished and honorable soldiers have been the most successful bloodless peace-makers, while, on the other hand, some of the most contemptible cowards, with peaceable pretensions always on their lips, have distinguished themselves by very little besides their successful contrivances to keep all engaged in war with whom they have had to do. Without claiming any special distinction for Mr. Miller on the score of what are styled brilliant achievements in the field of danger, the character of a great lover of peace belonged to him as a distinguishing personal trait. He delighted in peace, naturally; it is not known that he ever intentionally provoked a quarrel; and a considerable number of cases could be cited, in which he has been called to perform the office of a peace-maker, and in the duties of which he has been remarkably successful. But enough. More must be left unwritten than it would be practicable or necessary to write.

The watchful Providence which guarded him in the hour of deadly peril; the long-suffering which spared him while neglecting the talents bestowed, or misusing [63] them in rebellion against the Giver; and that wisdom and grace which overruled all the dangers experienced, and the derelictions practiced, as in many other persons of distinguished usefulness, demand our hearty adoration.

The close of Mr. Miller's military life was to be the commencement of a new era in his history. The circumstances which preceded that change, the means and instrumentalities employed in its accomplishment, and the practical results which immediately followed in the circle of his acquaintance, must be left to another chapter.

CHAPTER 4

Removal To Low Hampton – His Conversion – Study
Of The Bible – Rules Of Interpretation, Etc.

On the retirement of Mr. Miller from the army, he removed his family from Poultney, Vt., to Low Hampton, N. Y., to begin there the occupation of farming. His father had died there, in the year 1812, leaving the homestead encumbered with a mortgage. That was cancelled by Mr. Miller, who permitted his mother to live there, with his brother Solomon, while he purchased for himself another farm, in the neighborhood, about half a mile to the west. This lay mostly above the general level of the valley of the Poultney river, and comprised about two hundred acres of land, with a surface somewhat uneven, and with soil similar to that usually found in sections geologically marked by black slate and limestone. Two miles to the east was the village of Fairhaven, Vt., near the Poultney river; and eight miles to the west, on the southern extremity of Lake Champlain, at the foot of bold, precipitous hills, was the village of Whitehall, N. Y.

On this spot, in 1815, Mr. Miller erected a convenient farm-house, similar to those built throughout the interior of New England at that epoch. It was of wood, two stories high, with an ell projecting in the rear. The front and ends were painted white, with green blinds, and the back side was [64] red. It fronts to the north. A small yard, enclosed by a picket fence, and ornamented by lilacs, raspberry and rosebushes, separates it from the public road leading to Fairhaven, which is one of the interesting objects in the foreground of the extended view to the east, as seen from the window of the "east room," so full of tender and holy recollections to all visitors. [9]

To the west of the house, a few rods distant, is a beautiful grove, where, in later times, he often prayed and wept. This spot was selected by the political party to which Mr. Miller belonged, for the place of a public celebration of the national independence, on its anniversary, July 4th, 1816. Mr. Miller was selected as the marshal of the day; but, not fancying a party celebration, he used his influence so that all persons, irrespective

---

[9] See page 11.

of party, were invited to partake of its festivities. In those days of party excitement this was considered a wonderful stretch of charity.

Mr. Miller's grandfather Phelps was in the practice of preaching at the house of Mr. M.'s father, when he made his occasional visits. There was no church at the time in that section of the town. Through his labors Mr. Miller's mother was converted; and a little church was there organized, as a branch of the Baptist church in Orwell, Vt.

In 1812, Elisha Miller, an uncle of the subject of this memoir, was settled over the church in Low Hampton, and a small meeting-house was afterwards erected. On Mr. Miller's removal to Low Hampton, he became a constant attendant, except in the absence of the preacher, at that place of worship, and contributed liberally to its support. His relation to the pastor, and the proximity of his house, caused it to become the head-quarters of the denomination on extra as well as on ordinary occasions. There the preachers from a distance found food and shelter; and, though fond of bantering them on their faith, and making their opinions a subject of mirth with his infidel friends, they always found a home beneath his roof.

In the absence of the pastor, public worship was conducted by the deacons, who, as a substitute for the sermon, read a printed discourse, usually from "Proudfoot's Practical Sermons." Mr. Miller's mother noticed that, on such occasions, he was not in his seat, and she remonstrated with [65] him. He excused his absence on the ground that he was not edified by the manner in which the deacons read; and intimated that if *he* could do the reading, he should always be present. This being suggested to those grave officials, they were pleased with the idea; and, after that, they selected the sermon as before, but Mr. Miller did the reading, although still entertaining deistical sentiments.

The time had now come when God, by his providence and grace, was about to interpose to enlist the patriotic soldier in another kind of warfare; when to his mind, so fond of those departments of truth which appealed only to reason and sense, was to be opened a more inspiring field; when the persevering and delighted student of history was to see and appreciate the connection between the most stirring scenes and mightiest revolutions in this world's affairs and God's great plan of redemption, to which all the events of time are made subordinate.

Detecting himself in an irreverent use of the name of God, as before related, he was convicted of its sinfulness, and retired to his beautiful grove, and there, in meditation on the works of nature and Providence, he endeavored to penetrate the mystery of the connection between the present and a future state of existence.

As a farmer, he had had more leisure for reading; and he was at an age when the future of man's existence *will* demand a portion of his thoughts. He found that his former views gave him no assurance of happiness beyond the present life. Beyond the grave, all was dark and gloomy. To use his own words:

> "Annihilation was a cold and chilling thought, and accountability was sure destruction to all. The heavens were as brass over my head, and the earth as iron under my feet. *Eternity! – what was it? And death – why was it?* The more I reasoned, the further I was from demonstration. The more I thought, the more scattered were my conclusions. I tried to stop thinking, but my thoughts would not be controlled. I was truly wretched, but did not understand *the cause*. I murmured and complained, but knew not of whom. I knew that there was a wrong, but knew not how or where to find the right. I mourned, but without hope."

He continued in this state of mind for some months, [66] feeling that eternal consequences *might* hang on the nature and object of his belief.

The anniversary of the battle of Plattsburg – September 11 – was celebrated in all that region, for some years, with much enthusiasm. In 1816, arrangements had been made for its observance, by a ball, at Fairhaven. The stirring scenes of the late campaign being thus recalled, Captain Miller entered into the preparations for the expected festivities with all the ardor of the soldier. In the midst of these, it was announced that Dr. B. would preach on the evening previous to the ball. In the general gathering to that meeting, Captain Miller and his help attended, more from curiosity than from other actuating cause.

They left Captain Miller's house in high glee. The discourse was from Zechariah 2:4 – "Run! speak to this young man"! It was a word in season. On their return, Mrs. M., who had remained at home, observed a wonderful change in their deportment. Their glee was gone, and all were deeply thoughtful, and not disposed to converse, in reply to her questions respecting the meeting, the ball, etc. They were entirely incapacitated for any part in the festive arrangements. Other managers of the ball were equally unfitted for it: and the result was that it was indefinitely postponed. The seriousness extended from family to family, and in the several neighborhoods in that vicinity meetings for prayer and praise took the place of mirth and the dance.

On the Lord's day following, it devolved on Captain Miller, as usual in the minister's absence, to read a discourse of the deacons' selection. They had chosen one on the "importance of Parental Duties." Soon after commencing, he was overpowered by the inward struggle of emotion, with which the entire congregation deeply sympathized, and took his seat. His deistical principles seemed an almost insurmountable difficulty with him. Soon after, "Suddenly," he says,

> "the character of a Saviour was vividly impressed upon my mind. It seemed that there might be a Being so good and compassionate as to himself atone for our transgressions, and thereby save us from suffering the penalty of sin. I immediately felt how lovely such a Being must be; and imagined that I could cast myself into the arms of, and trust in the mercy of, such an One. But the question [67] arose, How can it be proved that such a Being does exist? Aside from the Bible, I found that I could get no evidence of the existence of such a Saviour, or even of a future state. I felt that to believe in such a Saviour without evidence would be visionary in the extreme. I saw that the Bible did bring to view just such a Saviour as I needed; and I was perplexed to find how an uninspired book should develop principles so perfectly adapted to the wants of a fallen world. I was constrained to admit that the Scriptures must be a revelation from God. They became my delight; and in Jesus I found a friend. The Saviour became to me the chiefest among ten thousand; and the Scriptures, which before were dark and contradictory, now became the lamp to my feet and light to my path. My mind became settled and satisfied. I found the Lord God to be a Rock in the midst of the ocean of life. The Bible now

became my chief study, and I can truly say, I searched it with great delight. I found the half was never told me. I wondered why I had not seen its beauty and glory before, and marveled that I could have ever rejected it. I found everything revealed that my heart could desire, and a remedy for every disease of the soul. I lost all taste for other reading, and applied my heart to get wisdom from God."

Mr. Miller immediately erected the family altar; publicly professed his faith in that religion which had been food for his mirth, by connecting himself with the little church that he had despised; opened his house for meetings of prayer; and became an ornament and pillar in the church, and an aid to both pastor and people. The die was cast, and he had taken his stand for life as a soldier of the cross, as all who knew him felt assured; and henceforth the badge of discipleship, in the church or world, in his family or closet, indicated whose he was and whom he served.

His pious relations had witnessed with pain his former irreligious opinions: how great were their rejoicings now! The church, favored with his liberality, and edified by his reading, but pained by his attacks on their faith, could now rejoice with the rejoicing. His infidel friends regarded his departure from them as the loss of a standard-bearer. And the new convert felt that henceforth, wherever he was, he must deport himself as a Christian, and perform his whole [68] duty. His subsequent history must show how well this was done.

To the church, his devotion of himself to his Master's service was as welcome as his labors were efficient. The opposite party, especially the more gifted of them, regarded him as a powerful, and, therefore, a desirable, antagonist. He knew the strength of both parties. That of the former he had often tested, when, in his attacks, though they might have been silenced, he had felt that he had a bad cause; and the weakness of the latter had been forcibly impressed on him in his fruitless efforts to assure himself that they were right. He knew all their weak points, and where their weapons could be turned against them. They were not disposed to yield the ground without a struggle, and began their attack on him by using the weapons and assailing the points which characterized his own former attacks on Christianity; and to this fact, under God, is probably owing his subsequent world-wide notoriety.

He had taunted his friends with entertaining "a blind faith" in the Bible, containing, as it did, many things which they confessed their inability to explain. He had enjoyed putting perplexing questions to clergymen and others, – triumphing in their unsatisfactory replies. These questions had not been forgotten; and his Christian friends, also, turned his former taunts upon himself.

Soon after his renunciation of Deism, in conversing with a friend respecting the hope of a glorious eternity through the merits and intercessions of Christ, he was asked how he knew there was such a Saviour. He replied, "It is revealed in the Bible." – "How do you know the Bible is true?" was the response, with a reiteration of his former arguments on the contradictions and mysticisms in which he had claimed it was shrouded.

Mr. Miller felt such taunts in their full force. He was at first perplexed; but, on reflection, he considered that if the Bible is a revelation of God, it must be consistent with itself; all its parts must harmonize, must have been given for man's instruction, and, consequently, must be adapted to his understanding. He, therefore, said, "Give me time, and I will harmonize all those apparent contradictions to my own satisfaction, or I will be a Deist still." [69]

He then devoted himself to the prayerful reading of the Word. He laid aside all commentaries, and used the marginal references and his Concordance as his only helps. He saw that he must distinguish between the Bible and all the peculiar and partisan interpretations of it. The Bible was older than them all, must be above them all; and he placed it there. He saw that it must correct all interpretations; and, in correcting them, its own pure light would shine without the mists which traditionary belief had involved it in. He resolved to lay aside all preconceived opinions, and to receive, with child-like simplicity, the natural and obvious meaning of Scripture. He pursued the study of the Bible with the most intense interest, – whole nights, as well as days, being devoted to that object. At times delighted with truth, which shone forth from the sacred volume, making clear to his understanding the great plan of God for the redemption of fallen man; and at times puzzled and almost distracted by seemingly inexplicable or contradictory passages, he persevered, until the application of his great principle of interpretation was triumphant. He became puzzled only to be delighted, and delighted only to persevere the more in penetrating its beauties and mysteries.

His manner of studying the Bible is thus described by himself:

> "I determined to lay aside all my prepossessions, to thoroughly compare Scripture with Scripture, and to pursue its study in a regular and methodical manner. I commenced with Genesis, and read verse by verse, proceeding no faster than the meaning of the several passages should be so unfolded as to leave me free from embarrassment respecting any mysticisms or contradictions. Whenever I found anything obscure, my practice was to compare it with all collateral passages; and, by the help of Cruden, I examined all the texts of Scripture in which were found any of the prominent words contained in any obscure portion. Then, by letting every word have its proper bearing on the subject of the text, if my view of it harmonized with every collateral passage in the Bible, it ceased to be a difficulty. In this way I pursued the study of the Bible, in my first perusal of it, for about two years, and was fully satisfied that it is its own interpreter. I found that, by a comparison of Scripture [70] with history, all the prophecies, as far as they have been fulfilled, had been fulfilled literally; that all the various figures, metaphors, parables, similitudes, etc., of the Bible, were either explained in their immediate connection, or the terms in which they were expressed were defined in other portions of the word; and, when thus explained, are to be literally understood in accordance with such explanation. I was thus satisfied that the Bible is a system of revealed truths, so clearly and simply given that the 'wayfaring man, though a fool, need not err therein.'"

In thus continuing the study, he adopted the following

RULES OF INTERPRETATION

I. Every word must have its proper bearing on the subject presented in the Bible. *Proof,* Matthew 5:18.

II. All Scripture is necessary, and may be understood by a diligent application and study. *Proof,* 2 Timothy 3:15-17.

III. Nothing revealed in Scriptures can or will be hid from those who ask in faith, not wavering. *Proof,* Deuteronomy 29:29. Matthew 10:26,

27. 1 Corinthians 2:10. Philippians 3:15; Isaiah 45:11. Matthew 21:22. John 14:13, 14; 5:7; James 1:5, 6. 1 John 5:13-15.

IV. To understand doctrine, bring all the Scriptures together on the subject you wish to know; then let every word have its proper influence; and if you can form your theory without a contradiction, you cannot be in error. *Proof*, Isaiah 28:7-29; 35:8. Proverbs 19:27. Luke 24:27, 44, 45. Romans 16:26. James 5:19. 2 Peter 1:19, 20.

V. Scripture must be its own expositor, since it is a rule of itself. If I depend on a teacher to expound to me, and he should guess at its meaning, or desire to have it so on account of his sectarian creed, or to be thought wise, then his guessing, desire, creed or wisdom, is my rule, and not the Bible. *Proof*, Psalm 19:7-11; 119:97-105. Matthew 23:8-10. 1 Corinthians 2:12-16. Ezekiel 34:18, 19. Luke 11:52. Matthew 2:7, 8.

VI. God has revealed things to come, by visions, in figures and parables; and in this way the same things are oftentime revealed again and again, by different visions, or in different figures and parables. If you wish to understand [71] them, you must combine them all in one. *Proof*, Psalm 89:19. Hosea 12:10. Habakkuk 2:2. Acts 2:17. 1 Corinthians 10:6. Hebrews 9:9, 24. Psalm 78:2. Matthew 13:13, 34. Genesis 41:1-32. Daniel 2nd, 7th & 8th. Acts 10:9-16.

VII. Visions are always mentioned as such. 2 Corinthians 12:1.

VIII. Figures always have a figurative meaning, and are used much in prophecy to represent future things, times and events, – such as mountains, meaning governments, Daniel 2:35, 44; beasts, meaning kingdoms, Daniel 7:8, 17; waters, meaning people, Revelation 17:1, 15; day, meaning year, etc. Ezekiel 4:6.

IX. Parables are used as comparisons to illustrate subjects, and must be explained in the same way as figures, by the subject and Bible. Mark 4:13.

X. Figures sometimes have two or more different significations, as day is used in a figurative sense to represent three different periods of time, namely, first, indefinite, Ecclesiastes 7:14; second, definite, a day for a year, Ezekiel 4:6; and third, a day for a thousand years, 2 Peter 3:8.

The right construction will harmonize with the Bible, and make good sense; other constructions will not.

XI. If a word makes good sense as it stands, and does no violence to the simple laws of nature, it is to be understood literally; if not, figuratively. Revelation 12:1, 2; 17:3-7.

XII. To learn the meaning of a figure, trace the word through your Bible, and when you find it explained, substitute the explanation for the word used; and, if it make good sense, you need not look further; if not, look again.

XIII. To know whether we have the true historical event for the fulfillment of a prophecy: If you find every word of the prophecy (after the figures are understood) is literally fulfilled, then you may know that your history is the true event; but if one word lacks a fulfillment, then you must look for another event, or wait its future development; for God takes care that history and prophecy shall agree, so that the true believing children of God may never be ashamed. Psalm 22:5. Isaiah 45:17-19. 1 Peter 2:6. Revelation 17:17. Acts 3:18.

XIV. The most important rule of all is, that you must have *faith*. It must be a faith that requires a sacrifice, and, if tried, would give up the dearest object on earth, the world [72] and all its desires, – character, living, occupation, friends, home, comforts and worldly honors. If any of these should hinder our believing any part of God's word, it would show our faith to be vain. Nor can we ever believe so long as one of these motives lies lurking in our hearts. We must believe that God will never forfeit his word; and we can have confidence that He who takes notice of the sparrow's fall, and numbers the hairs of our head, will guard the translation of his own word, and throw a barrier around it, and prevent those who sincerely trust in God, and put implicit confidence in his word, from erring far from the truth."

"While thus studying the Scriptures," – continuing the words of his own narrative, –

"I became satisfied, if the prophecies which have been fulfilled in the past are any criterion by which to judge of the manner of the fulfillment of those which are future, that the popular views of the spiritual reign of Christ – a temporal millennium before the end of the world, and the Jews' return – are not sustained by the word of God; for I found that all the Scriptures on which those favorite theories are based are as clearly expressed as are those that were *literally* fulfilled at the first advent, or at any other period in the past. I found it plainly taught in the Scriptures that Jesus Christ will again descend to this earth, coming in the clouds of heaven, in all the glory of his Father:[10] that, at his coming, the kingdom and dominion under the whole

---

[10] See John 14:3; Acts 1:11; 1 Thessalonians 4:16; Revelation 1:7; Matthew 16:27; 24:30; Mark 8:38; 13:26; Daniel 7:13.

heaven will be given to Him and the saints of the Most High, who will possess it forever, even for ever and ever:[11] that, as the old world perished by the deluge, so the earth, that now is, is reserved unto fire, to be melted with fervent heat at Christ's coming; after which, according to the promise, it is to become the new earth, wherein the righteous will forever dwell:[12] that, at his coming, the bodies of all the righteous dead will be raised, and all the righteous living be changed from a corruptible to an incorruptible, from a mortal to an immortal state; that they will all be caught up together to meet the Lord in the air, – [73] and will reign with him forever in the regenerated earth:[13] that the controversy with Zion will then be finished, her children be delivered from bondage, and from the power of the tempter, and the saints be all presented to God blameless, without spot or wrinkle in love;[14] that the bodies of the wicked will then all be destroyed, and their spirits be reserved in prison until their resurrection and damnation;[15] and that, when the earth is thus regenerated, the righteous raised, and the wicked destroyed, the kingdom of God will have come, when his will will be done on earth as it is done in heaven; that the meek will inherit it, and the kingdom become the saints.[16] I found that the only millennium taught in the word of God is the thousand years which are to intervene between the first resurrection and that of the rest of the dead, as inculcated in the twentieth of Revelation; and that it must necessarily follow the personal coming of Christ and the regeneration of the earth:[17] that, till Christ's coming, and the end of the world, the righteous and wicked are to continue together on the earth, and that the horn of the Papacy is to war against the saints until his appearing and kingdom, when it will be destroyed by the brightness of Christ's coming; so that there can be no conversion

[11] Daniel 7:14, 18, 22, 27; Matthew 25:34; Luke 12:32; 19:12, 15; 22:29; 1 Corinthians 9:25; 2 Timothy 4:1, 8; James 1:12; 1 Peter 5:4.

[12] 2 Peter 3:7-10; Isaiah 65:17-19; Revelation 21:22.

[13] 1 Corinthians 15:20, 23, 49, 51-53; Philippians 3:20, 21; 1 Thessalonians 4:14-17; 1 John 3:2.

[14] Isaiah 34:8; 40:2, 5; 41:10-12; Romans 8:21-23; 1 Corinthians 1:7, 8; 4:14; 15:54, 56; Ephesians 5:27; Colossians 1:22; 1 Thessalonians 3:13; Hebrews 2:13-15; Jude 24; Revelation 20:1-6.

[15] Psalm 1:3; 97:3; Isaiah 60:15, 16; 24:21, 22; Daniel 7:10; Malachi 4:1; Matthew 3:12; John 25:29; Acts 24:15; 1 Corinthians 3:13; 1 Thessalonians 5:2, 3; 2 Thessalonians 1:7-9; 1 Peter 1:7; 2 Peter 3:7, 10; Jude 6, 7, 14, 15; Revelation 20:3, 13-15.

[16] Psalm 37:9-11, 22, 28, 29, 34; Proverbs 2:21, 22; 10:30; Isaiah 40:21; Matthew 5:5; 6:10.

[17] Revelation 20-2-7.

of the world before the advent;[18] and that as the new earth, wherein dwelleth righteousness, is located by Peter after the conflagration, and is declared by him to be the same for which we look, according to the promise of Isaiah 65:17, and is the same that John saw in vision after the passing away of the former heavens and earth; it must necessarily follow that the various portions of Scripture that refer to the millennial state must have their fulfillment after the resurrection of all [74] the saints that sleep in Jesus.[19] I also found that the promises respecting Israel's restoration are applied by the apostle to all who are Christ's, – the putting on of Christ constituting them Abraham's seed, and heirs according to the promise.[20]

"I was then satisfied, as I saw conclusive evidence to prove the advent personal and pre-millennial, that all the events for which the church look to be fulfilled [in the millennium] before the advent, must be subsequent to it; and that, unless there were other unfulfilled prophecies, the advent of the Lord, instead of being looked for only in the distant future, might be a continually-expected event. In examining the prophecies on that point, I found that only four universal monarchies are anywhere predicted, in the Bible, to precede the setting up of God's everlasting kingdom; that three of those had passed away, – Babylon, Medo-Persia, and Grecia, – and that the fourth – Rome – had already passed into its last state, the state in which it is to be when the stone cut out of the mountain without hands shall smite the image on the feet, and break to pieces all the kingdoms of this world. I was unable to find any prediction of events which presented any clear evidence of their fulfillment before the scenes that usher in the advent. And finding all the signs of the times, and the present condition of the world, to compare harmoniously with the prophetic descriptions of the last days, I was compelled to believe that this world had about reached the limits of the period allotted for its continuance. As I regarded the evidence, I could arrive at no other conclusion.

"Another kind of evidence that vitally affected my mind was the chronology of the Scriptures. I found, on pursuing the study of the Bible, various chronological periods extending, according to my understanding of them, to the coming of the Saviour. I found that predicted events, which had been fulfilled in the past, often occurred within a *given time*. The one hundred and twenty years to the flood, Genesis 6:3; the seven days that were to precede it, with forty days of

---

18 Matthew 13:37-43; 24:14; Daniel 7:21, 22; 2 Thessalonians 2:8.

19 2 Peter 3; Isaiah 65:17; Revelation 21; 22.

20 Romans 2:14, 15; 4:13; 9:6; 10:12; 11:17; Galatians 3:29; Ephesians 2:14, 15.

predicted rain, Genesis 7:4; the four hundred years of the [75] sojourn of Abraham's seed, Genesis 15:13; the three days of the butler's and baker's dreams, Genesis 40:12-20; the seven years of Pharaoh's, Genesis 41:28-54; the forty years in the wilderness, Numbers 14:34; the three and a half years of famine, 1 Kings 17:1; the sixty-five years to the breaking of Ephraim, Isaiah 7:8; the seventy years' captivity, Jeremiah 25:11; Nebuchadnezzar's seven times, Daniel 4:13-16; and the seven weeks, threescore and two weeks, and the one week, making seventy weeks, determined upon the Jews, Daniel 9:24-27; the events limited by these times were all once only a matter of prophecy, and were fulfilled in accordance with the predictions.

"When, therefore, I found the 2300 prophetic days, which were to mark the length of the vision from the Persian to the end of the fourth kingdom, the seven times' continuance of the dispersion of God's people, and the 1335 prophetic days to the standing of Daniel in his lot, all evidently extending to the advent, with other prophetical periods, I could but regard them as 'the times before appointed,' which God had revealed 'unto his servants the prophets.' As I was fully convinced that 'all Scripture given by inspiration of God is profitable,' – that it came not at any time by the will of man, but was written as holy men were moved by the Holy Ghost, and was written for our learning, that we, through patience and comfort of the Scriptures, might have hope, – I could but regard the chronological portions of the Bible as being as much a portion of the word of God, and as much entitled to our serious consideration, as any other portion of the Scriptures.

"I, therefore, felt that, in endeavoring to comprehend what God had in his mercy seen fit to reveal to us, I had no right to pass over the prophetic periods. I saw that, as the events predicted to be fulfilled in prophetic days had been extended over about as many literal years; as God, in Numbers 14:34, and Ezekiel 4:4-6, had appointed each day for a year; as the seventy weeks to the Messiah were fulfilled in 490 years, and the 1260 prophetic days of the Papal supremacy in 1260 years; and as these prophetical days extending to the advent were given in connection with symbolic prophecy, I could only regard the time as symbolical, and as standing each day for a year, in accordance with the [76] opinions of all the standard Protestant commentators. If, then, we could obtain any clue to the time of their commencement, I conceived we should be guided to the probable time of their termination; and, as God would not bestow upon us an useless revelation, I regarded them as conducting us to the time when we might confidently look for the coming of the Chiefest of ten thousand, One altogether lovely.

"From a further study of the Scriptures, I concluded that the seven times of Gentile supremacy must commence when the Jews ceased to be an independent nation, at the captivity of Manasseh, which the best chronologers assigned to B. C. 677; that the 2300 days commenced with the seventy weeks, which the best chronologers dated from B. C. 457; and that the 1335 days, commencing with the taking away of the daily, and the setting up of the abomination that maketh desolate, Daniel 12:11, were to be dated from the setting up of the Papal supremacy, after the taking away of Pagan abominations, and which, according to the best historians I could consult, should be dated from about A. D. 508. Reckoning all these prophetic periods from the several dates assigned by the best chronologers for the events from which they should evidently be reckoned, they would all terminate together, about A. D. 1843. I was thus brought, in 1818, at the close of my two years' study of the Scriptures, to the solemn conclusion, that in about twenty-five years from that time all the affairs of our present state would be wound up; that all its pride and power, pomp and vanity, wickedness and oppression, would come to an end; and that, in the place of the kingdoms of this world, the peaceful and long-desired kingdom of the Messiah would be established under the whole heaven; that, in about twenty-five years, the glory of the Lord would be revealed, and all flesh see it together, – the desert bud and blossom as the rose, the fir-tree come up instead of the thorn, and instead of the briar the myrtle-tree, – the curse be removed from off the earth, death be destroyed, reward be given to the servants of God, the prophets and saints, and them who fear his name, and those be destroyed that destroy the earth.

"I need not speak of the joy that filled my heart in view of the delightful prospect, nor of the ardent longings of my soul for a participation in the joys of the redeemed. The [77] Bible was now to me a new book. It was indeed a feast of reason; all that was dark, mystical or obscure, to me, in its teachings, had been dissipated from my mind before the clear light that now dawned from its sacred pages; and O, how bright and glorious the truth appeared! All the contradictions and inconsistencies I had before found in the Word were gone; and, although there were many portions of which I was not satisfied I had a full understanding, yet so much light had emanated from it to the illumination of my before darkened mind, that I felt a delight in studying the Scriptures which I had not before supposed could be derived from its teachings. I commenced their study with no expectation of finding the time of the Savior's coming, and I could at first hardly believe the result to which I had arrived; but the evidence struck me with such force that I could not resist my convictions. I became nearly settled in my conclusions, and began to wait, and watch, and pray for my Saviour's coming."

The above are the conclusions to which he arrived on the general subject of prophecy; but his views on other scriptural topics may not be uninteresting in this connection. His general theological opinions may be inferred from his connecting himself with a Calvinistic Baptist church, as the one most congenial to his faith. But he has left, among his papers, an unfinished compendium of his belief, which bears date, and is appended to the annexed certificate, as follows:

"*Low Hampton, Sept. 5, 1822.*

"I hereby acknowledge that I have long believed it my duty ... to leave, for the inspection of my brethren, friends and children, a brief statement of my faith (and which ought to be my practice); and I pray God to forgive me where I go astray. I made it a subject of prayer and meditation, and, therefore, leave the following as my faith, – reserving the privilege of correction.

(Signed,) WM. MILLER.

"**ART. I.** I believe the Bible is given by God to man, as a rule for our practice, and a guide to our faith, – that it is a revelation of God to man."

"**ART. II.** I believe in one living and true God, and that [78] there are three persons in the Godhead, – as there is in man, the body, soul and spirit. And if any one will tell me how these exist, I will tell him how the three persons of the Triune God are connected."

"**ART. III.** I believe that God, by his Son, created man in the image of the Triune God, with a body, soul and spirit; and that he was created a moral agent, capable of living, of obeying, or transgressing the laws of his Maker."

"**ART. IV.** I believe that man, being tempted by the enemy of all good, did transgress and became polluted; from which act, sin entered into the world, and all mankind became naturally sinners, thrust out from the presence of God, and exposed to his just wrath forever."

"**ART. V.** I believe that God, knowing from eternity the use that man would make of his [free] agency, did, in his council of eternity, ordain that his Son should die; and that through his death salvation should be given to fallen man, through such means as God should appoint."

"**ART. VI.** I believe that, through the agency of the Holy Spirit, sinners are made the recipients of mercy, in conformity to the Divine plan, founded on the wisdom and knowledge of God; the fruits of which are manifested in the recipient by works of repentance and faith; and without which no man, coming to years of discretion and able to choose between good and evil, can have an interest in the blood and righteousness of Christ."

"**ART. VII.** I believe that Jesus Christ is an offering of God to sinners for their redemption from sin, and that those who believe in his name may take him by faith, go to God, and find mercy; and that such will in no wise be rejected."

"**ART. VIII.** I believe that Jesus Christ was the sacrifice for sin which justice demanded; and that all those who confess their sins on the head of this victim, may expect forgiveness of sin through the blood of the atonement, which is in Jesus Christ, the great High Priest in the Holy of Holies."

"**ART. IX.** I believe the atonement to be made by the intercession of Jesus Christ, and the sprinkling of his blood in the Holy of Holies, and upon the mercy-seat and people; by which means the offended is reconciled to the offender, the offender is brought into subjection to the will of God; [79] and the effect is, forgiveness of sin, union to the Divine person, and to the household of faith."

"**ART. X.** I believe all those for whom Christ intercedes, who are united to God by a living faith, and have received the forgiveness of sin through the sprinkling of the blood of Christ, can never perish; but are kept by the mighty power of God through faith unto salvation."

"**ART. XI.** I believe that all the promises of God are and will be accomplished in Christ Jesus; and that none of the human family are or can be entitled to the promises of grace, but those who are born of the Spirit in Christ Jesus, any more than the antediluvians could have been saved from the deluge without entering the ark."

"**ART. XII.** I believe that Jesus Christ will eventually take away the sin of the world, and cleanse the earth from all pollution, so that this earth will become the abode of the saints forever, by means which he has appointed; all believers being regenerated, sanctified, justified and glorified."

"**ART. XIII.** I believe that all final impenitents will be destroyed from the earth, and sent away into a place prepared for the Devil and his angels."

"**ART. XIV.** I believe Jesus Christ will come again in his glory and person to our earth, where he will accomplish his Divine purposes in the saving of his people, destroying the wicked from the earth, and taking away the sin of the world."

"**ART. XV.** I believe that the second coming of Jesus Christ is near, even at the door, even within twenty-one years, – on or before 1843."

"**ART. XVI.** I believe that before Christ comes in his glory, all sectarian principles will be shaken, and the votaries of the several sects scattered to the four winds; and that none will be able to stand but those who are built on the word of God."

"**ART. XVII.** I believe in the resurrection, both of the just and of the unjust, – the just, or believers, at Christ's second coming, and the unjust one thousand years afterwards, – when the judgment of each will take place in their order, at their several resurrections; when the just will receive everlasting life, and the unjust eternal condemnation." [80]

"**ART. XVIII.** I believe in the doctrine of election, founded on the will, purpose and fore-knowledge of God; and that all the elect will be saved in the kingdom of God, through the sanctification of the Spirit and the belief of the truth."

"**ART. XIX.** I believe in the ordinance of baptism by immersion, as a representation of Christ's burial and resurrection, – also of our death to sin and life to holiness."

"**ART. XX.** I believe in the ordinance of the Lord's supper, to be" -

The last article was left thus incomplete, and the series of articles was not extended, as it was evidently designed to have been, so as to give an expression of his faith on subjects not included in the foregoing. It is not known that his views, as above expressed, ever underwent any change, – excepting as his belief in the date of the second advent was afterwards shown, by the passing of the time, to be incorrect.

CHAPTER 5

Interval Between His Conversion And Public Labors – Letters – His Dream
– Acrostic – Letter From Elder Hendryx – Dialogue With A Physician, Etc.

From the time that Mr. Miller became established in his religious faith, till he commenced his public labors, – a period of twelve or fourteen years, – there were few prominent incidents in his life to distinguish him from other men. He was a good citizen, a kind neighbor, an affectionate husband and parent, and a devoted Christian; good to the poor, and benevolent, as objects of charity were presented; in the Sunday-school was teacher and superintendent; in the church he performed important service as a reader and exhorter, and, in the support of religious worship, no other member, perhaps, did as much as he. He was very exemplary in his life and conversation, endeavored at all times to perform the duties, whether public or private, which devolved on him, and whatever he did was done cheerfully, as for the glory of God. His leisure hours were devoted to reading and meditation; he kept himself well informed respecting [81] the current events of the time; occasionally communicated his thoughts through the press, and often, for his own private amusement, or for the entertainment of friends, indulged in various poetical effusions, which, for unstudied productions, are possessed of some merit; but his principal enjoyment was derived from the study of the Bible. His state of mind at this time can be better given in his own language.

"With the solemn conviction," writes Mr. Miller,

> "that such momentous events were predicted in the Scriptures, to be fulfilled in so short a space of time, the question came home to me with mighty power regarding my duty to the world, in view of the evidence that had affected my own mind. If the end was so near, it was important that the world should know it. I supposed that it would call forth the opposition of the ungodly; but it never came into my mind that any Christian would oppose it. I supposed that all such would be so rejoiced, in view of the glorious prospect, that it would only be necessary to present it, for them to receive it. My great fear was, that, in their joy at the hope of a glorious inheritance so soon to be revealed, they would receive the doctrine without sufficiently

examining the Scriptures in demonstration of its truth. I therefore feared to present it, lest, by some possibility, I should be in error, and be the means of misleading any.

"Various difficulties and objections would arise in my mind, from time to time; certain texts would occur to me, which seemed to weigh against my conclusions; and I would not present a view to others, while any difficulty appeared to militate against it. I therefore continued the study of the Bible, to see if I could sustain any of these objections. My object was not merely to remove them, but I wished to see if they were valid.

"Sometimes, when at work, a text would arise like this: 'Of that day and hour knoweth no man,' etc.; and how, then, could the Bible reveal the time of the advent? I would then immediately examine the context in which it was found, and I saw at once that, in the same connection, we are informed how we may know when it is nigh, even at the doors; consequently, that text could not teach that we could know nothing of the time of that event. Other texts, which are advanced in support of the doctrine of a temporal millennium, [82] would arise; but, on examining their context, I invariably found that they were applicable only to the eternal state, or were so illustrative of the spread of the gospel here, as to be entirely irrelevant to the position they were adduced to support.

"Thus all those passages that speak of the will of God being done on earth as in heaven, of the earth being full of the knowledge of the glory of God, etc., could not be applicable to a time when the Man of Sin was prevailing against the saints, or when the righteous and wicked were dwelling together, which is to be the case until the end of the world. Those which speak of the gospel being preached in all the world, teach that, as soon as it should be thus preached, the end was to come; so that it could not be delayed a thousand years from that time, nor long enough for the world's conversion after the preaching of the gospel as a witness.

"The question of the resurrection and judgment was, for a time, an obstacle in the way. Being instructed that all the dead would be raised at the same time, I supposed it must be so taught in the Bible; but I soon saw it was one of the traditions of the elders.

"So, also, with the return of the Jews. That question I saw could only be sustained by denying the positive declarations of the New Testament, which assert: 'There is no difference between the Jew and the Greek;' that 'The promise that he shall be the heir of the world was not to Abraham and his seed through the law, but through the righteousness of faith;' that 'There is neither Jew nor Greek, bond nor free, male nor female;' but that 'If ye are Christ's, then are ye Abraham's seed, and heirs according to the promise.' I was, therefore, obliged to discard an objection which asserts there *is* a difference between the Jew and Greek; that the children of the flesh *are* accounted for the seed, etc.

"In this way I was occupied for five years, – from 1818 to 1823, – in weighing the various objections which were being presented to my mind. During that time, more objections arose in my mind than have been advanced by my opponents since; and I know of no objection that has been since advanced which did not then occur to me. But, however strong they at first appeared, after examining them in [83] the light of the Divine Word, I could only compare them to straws, laid down singly as obstacles, on a well-beaten road: the car of truth rolled over them, unimpeded in its progress.

"I was then fully settled in the conclusions which seven years previously had begun to bear with such impressive force upon my mind; and the duty of presenting the evidence of the nearness of the advent to others, – which I had managed to evade while I could find the shadow of an objection remaining against its truth, – again came home to me with great force. I had, previously, only thrown out occasional hints of my views. I then began to speak more clearly my opinions to my neighbors, to ministers, and others. To my astonishment, I found very few who listened with any interest. Occasionally, one would see the force of the evidence; but the great majority passed it by as an idle tale. I was, therefore, disappointed in finding any who would declare this doctrine, as I felt it should be, for the comfort of saints, and as a warning to sinners."

His correspondence during this period shows ardent longings for the salvation of his relatives and friends.

In a letter to a sister, dated June 25, 1825, after writing on various subjects of family interest, he says:-

"DEAR BROTHER AND SISTER: – All the news that we had to tell having been told above, I will now add a few lines; and O! may they be directed by Infinite Wisdom! What are your prospects for eternity? Is there a land of eternal rest, beyond the confines of this world, in prospect? Do you believe that the blood of the everlasting covenant can and will cleanse you from all sin? Are you satisfied with your present evidence of an interest in that blood? That we shall die is certain; and due preparation for a better world is wisdom; and we ought, as rational beings, to make ourselves familiar with the road and acquainted with the inhabitants of said country. O, my soul! go thou to the mansions of the dead, and learn there the end of all living. That we ought to be cleansed from all sin, in order to be happy, is certain; for sin constitutes all misery; and a person living in the enjoyment (falsely so called) of sin cannot enter into rest. How necessary, then, is the work [84] of regeneration and sanctification! And may we obtain that evidence which will enable us, with Thomas, to say, 'My Lord and my God!' Redemption is the work of God. How proper, then, that Jesus should be called the Redeemer, the Holy One of Israel! Redemption is from sin. How improper, then, that we should live any longer therein! We ought as much to strive to attain to perfection as if it was attainable here below.

> 'Lord, I believe thy heavenly word;
> Fain would I have my soul renewed.
> I mourn for sin, and trust the Lord
> To have it pardoned and subdued.
>
> My King, my Saviour, and my God,
> Let grace my sinful soul renew;
> Wash my offences with thy blood,
> And make my heart sincere and true.
>
> O may thy grace its power display!
> Let guilt and death no longer reign;
> Save me in thine appointed way,
> Nor let my humble faith be vain.
>
> Ye favored lands, who have his word,
> Ye saints, who feel its saving power,
> Unite your tongues to praise the Lord,
> And his distinguished grace adore.'

"P.S. *June 30th.* – I have this day been to Whitehall, to see the celebrated Marquis de Lafayette, that made such a conspicuous figure, half a century ago, in our Revolution. He is a pleasant-looking old man, a friend to freemen, a terror to tyrants, and one that has spent his treasures, his blood, and the best part of his life in the cause of freedom and the rights of man. He has suffered much; yet he retains a good constitution. He goes a little lame, occasioned by wounds he received in the Revolution. He deserves the thanks of Americans, and he has received a general burst of gratitude from Maine to the

Mississippi. He has visited every State in the Union and almost every important town. I had the pleasure of dining with him; and after dinner he took a passage for New York.

"Yours, etc.,   WM. MILLER."

That Mr. M. was one of the men prominent in his section of the country is shown by his mingling with them, as above, on the various public occasions. [85]

He derived such pleasure from the study of the Bible, that it was almost his constant companion; and a portion of each day was devoted to its private perusal. He loved to meditate on its teachings and to talk about its promises.

Being naturally of a poetical temperament, it would not be strange if, occasionally, his dreams took shape from his waking thoughts. It is, however, due to Mr. Miller to say, that he had no peculiar faith in dreams; and the following is given more for its singularity, the simplicity with which it is related, and its devotional spirit, than for any other reason.

On the evening of the 4th of November, 1826, he sat up to a late hour, conversing with some friends on a religious subject, and retired to rest about twelve o'clock. Soon after he fell asleep. His sleeping thoughts assumed so distinct and vivid a form, and made so deep an impression on his mind, that, two years subsequently (January 17, 1828), he committed to writing

HIS DREAM.

"I thought I was in a barren, uninhabited country, apparently between sundown and dark – neither night nor day. The air appeared rather chilly; but not so cold as mid-winter, but like its beginning. I thought it stormed, but not severely: it appeared to me like a mixture of snow and rain. There appeared to be some wind, yet not a gale; and everything wore a gloomy aspect, yet I could not tell why. I seemed to be in danger, yet I knew of no danger. I thought I had two companions: one a Baptist minister, the other a Universalist. They had hold one of each arm, and were compelling me to come along, as though we were in great danger, and were fleeing for life. After travelling a northern course for some time, I inquired where we were. They said, 'Near home.' I thought they then took an eastward course, and came to a little spot of woods, consisting of small evergreen trees, about fifteen feet high. They then let go their hold of me, and lay down under these trees. I told them that I would not stay there. I then started, and they followed. Our course was then circuitous, from west to south and east, through a barren, level country, with nothing to be seen but now and then a bush. After travelling [86] for some time, we came in sight of a row of lights in the south-east, like a village light in the night. We steered our course for the lights, and soon came to a highway, running north and south. While we were consulting which road to take, there came down two women from the north, until they came against us. I then inquired of them where we were. They made no answer, but turned about, and went back. I here left my companions, and followed these women. We had not gone far before we came to an old log-house that stood by the wayside, into which they entered, and I followed, where I found a small fire, and attempted to warm myself; but, while I was thus warming myself, seeing some suspicious looks in the countenances of those present, I cast my eye around to see the cause, and beheld a great beast, like a bear, gnashing his teeth and growling at me. I started back to the other side of the house at the sight. I looked, and saw a chain fastened to the logs of the house and around his neck. I next saw a small dog, set on by one present, running around the bear, and barking at him. He soon caught the dog in his mouth, when a person present, in endeavoring to release the dog, got his hand caught between the teeth of the bear. I then looked for a weapon to relieve the person thus situated, and found a club about three feet long, with which I struck the bear on the head, and delivered the man. The bear then came at me, in a rage: The club now became a man's arm, with a hand having ten fingers, and those very long. With this I kept the bear off, and soon got out of the house and ran with all my might towards the north. After climbing a steep hill until I was weary, I sat down, when a person came to me, and informed me if I would follow him he would lead me out of danger. I followed him, and, after travelling up hill some time, we came to a small house, where we went in, and found a number of women spinning and making garments. After some conversation, my guide told me I must go on. We then went out, and followed the same northern course until we descended the hill, and came to a large, low, old house, where we went in, and saw a large number of people, of all ages and sexes. There appeared to be a man present, who went to each one of these, and whispered in their ears. All appeared solemn and silent. He came to me, and whispered [87] in my ears, 'Love God and your neighbor,' and told me to remember it. I thought I told him to write it on my heart. He said he would repeat it, and that I should not forget it. He did so, and left me. Here I had peculiar feelings. I found I had broken these two great commands all my life. It seemed as though I had never loved God or my neighbor. My whole life looked like a catalogue of crime; and if ever I had any repentance, I had it there. (O, my God! why not grant me such repentance when awake?) It was unmixed with any pride or thoughts of carnal things. I remembered all my sins, as I thought, and they looked exceeding sinful. If David felt as I then did, I do not wonder that he cried out, 'Against Thee, and Thee only have I sinned.' I thought that then my guide gave me a staff, and told me I must travel.

"I went out of the house, and, looking every way, to see which way I should go, I saw to the northward many roads branching off in different ways. While I was considering, I saw many people, young and old, come out of the house, and run in these roads. I then saw that the roads were wide, and well trod. I then thought of the broad way mentioned in the Scriptures, and turned away, determining within myself not to go therein. I then looked to the south, and saw a few people come out of the house, and one by one take a south-east course, and follow each other in a direct line, until I lost sight of them. While I stood thinking of them, I heard a voice, as from above, saying, 'This is the way; walk ye in it.' Although I saw no path, I followed the same course, and soon came to a strait way, cast up with two gulfs on either side. The path was marked with footsteps indented into the earth as deep as a shoe, and only wide enough for these tracks, one before the other, in a straight line. I soon overtook some travelling the same road, and one old man, apparently ninety or one hundred years of age, bowed down to the earth, and withered up. He appeared to be praising God that he had mercy on such an old, dry stick, while thousands younger were left to go in the broad way. I thought my road became more rugged, although the steps continued. When I came to any of these places, by setting my staff down it became long or short, as occasion might require, and I could step up or down with ease. My way was [88] principally in the ascent until I came to a precipice. I could look down and see the steps below; but how to get down I could not tell. While standing here the voice again spake: 'Pride must be humbled.' I then had a view of my proud heart, and all my ways seemed as though they were full of that sin. Even my devotions were nothing but pride; and in the bitterness of my soul I cried out: 'True, I am a proud, haughty wretch!' I then put my staff down the precipice, and it became a guide-pole, so that I, by clasping both my hands round it, slipped down, and then went on until I came to a low piece of wet ground. Here I lost my tracks, and while I was looking to find my way, the voice I had heard before again spoke: 'The way is marked with blood.' I then felt surprised that I had not remembered it. I then looked around to find the blood, and, looking a little way before me, I saw a rail-fence, and, stepping up to it, found a streak of blood from the top to the bottom, about two inches wide. I clasped it in my hands, and cried, 'This is the blood of my Saviour!' While in this situation I heard a voice as of a rushing wind. I looked up, and there was a small cloud over my head; and it began to sprinkle like great drops of rain. I looked on my hands and clothes, and saw great drops of blood. I heard the voice again saying: 'This is the blood of sprinkling, that speaketh better things than the blood of Abel.' I now had a view of the blood of Christ, its effects, and the great love wherewith he loved us. My mind, which all along had been more or less troubled, by fears and doubts, now became calm and serene, and, like Job, I could say, 'I know my Redeemer liveth.' My hard heart melted within me, and ran out with pure love to Christ. While in this ecstasy of mind, I looked up and saw a beam of wood, extending from east to west. I thought the voice said: 'Behold the cross!' I again looked down, and was wondering within myself what these things could mean, when the voice said: 'Garments rolled in blood.' I again looked up, and saw as it had been a cloak dipped in blood, hanging over the beam, fourteen or fifteen feet high.

"My feelings while viewing these things I cannot describe; but it now became light, and I saw the sun as if about three hours' high in the morning. I then travelled on the same strait way to the south-east, as before, with this difference – [89] only the streak of blood now marked my path. After travelling some time I came to a large house. It now appeared to be night. I went in, and saw many people there. The house extended from west to east, through the centre of which was a long hall, lighted up with lamps on each side; and on each side of this hall doors opened into small apartments like bed-rooms. I here found my former guide, who informed me that I must travel through this hall. He also gave me a little book, [21] and said that that would direct me. He then cautioned me to 'beware of the buttery.' [22] I put the book into my pocket, and walked through. As I passed along, the doors on each side of the hall would open, and spirits, as it then

---

[21] Mr. Miller never regarded this dream as at all ominous; and yet, through life, it often recurred to his mind. On the occasion of his first visit to Boston, he was presented with a small Polyglot Bible, which strongly reminded him of the book given him in his dream, and like that he made it his pocket companion.

[22] This is a very obscure phrase in the connection, unless it is to guard against the pleasures of the world.

appeared to me, would brush by me, and try to force me into these rooms. I kept right straight forward till I came to the east end of the room. Here I found two closed doors, and while I stood considering which door to enter, one of them opened and discovered to me a room filled with all the dainties man could wish to eat or drink; and some persons in the room invited me to enter. I was at a loss what to do; but, remembering the caution I had, I put my hand in my pocket to find my little book. I pulled out one, and found it was not the same, and so I threw it down, and pulled out two more, one after the other, and threw them down also. [23] I then pulled out the one that had been given me, and, on opening it, I read Isaiah 48:17, – 'Thus saith the Lord, thy Redeemer, the Holy One of Israel; I am the Lord thy God which teacheth thee to profit, which leadeth thee by the way that thou shouldest go.' The other door then opened, and I saw a dark, winding stairway. On the bottom lay a young child. I took it up, and reached it back to some that stood behind me. They refused to take it. I then laid it down again, and stepped in. All was [90] dark and gloomy as the door of death. I remembered no more until I arrived at the top of the stairs, where I found myself, as I then thought, in an upper room, filled with the purest light that my eyes had ever beheld. [24] I looked for the cause – there was none. The light was brighter than the brightest rays of the sun; yet it did not dazzle – it was as soft and easy to behold as the morning tints. The room appeared to be arched, yet I could not discover its height. The floor appeared like crystal glass, very thick, yet it did not restrain the sight, for I could see all below. The room extended from east to west. On each hand was a walk, on which I saw many walking. I was directed to walk with them, when I found that they were singing. The only words I could recollect were, 'Hallelujah to the Lamb!' The music was soft, and sweet; it fell on the ear without any jar or pain. I beheld many persons that I knew, – the old man that I had seen before. I congratulated him on his safe arrival at last. I heard him sing. No silent one was there. I thought

---

[23] When he first saw Dr. Dowling's work – *Miller Used up for a Shilling* – and other similar works, he was forcibly reminded of those spurious books which he threw away in his dream. He considered the little guide-book of more consequence than all these.

[24] The finding himself at the top of the stairs was a source of great consolation to him; and he often referred to it, in connection with the impression that he had, that, if called to the world of spirits, when absent from the body he should be present with the Lord. He had a desire to live till the Lord's coming, but would refer to this "upper room," as a very desirable place to spend the time before the resurrection, if he should not live till that event; and this, he thought, was designed to teach him that he should not, and to comfort him, in view of the prospect of death.

of the love they had one for another. I thought I felt its flame – its pure, un-adulterated love. No mixture of self beyond another. I saw persons of all denominations of Christians, yet all distinctions were taken away. Here was a communion indeed – here was no ennui – no hatred – no selfish principles to build up – no evil thoughts – nothing to hurt or annoy. (O! ye selfish votaries, could you but see this happy throng, you would cover your faces with shame; you would hide your-selves, if possible, from the face of the Lamb, and Him that sitteth on the throne.) I felt myself free from every clog, and all my soul was swallowed up in this celestial throng. I then thought it was a dream – a slight and disagreeable feeling passed over my mind, to think I must return and experience again the woes of life. I shuddered at the thought, and then awoke." [91]

By the following lines, written by Mr. Miller at the place of his birth, it appears that he visited the old homestead in Pittsfield, Mass., in 1827, – the lines being dated Oct. 16th of that year. They are an Acrostic on his own name, and are given, more as a memento of the past, than for any poetic merit. He must have been at this time forty-five years old.

> "Why was I here the light brought to behold?
> Inconstant life here first her pulses told;
> Life's blood here through my veins began to flow;
> Lo! here began my pilgrimage below;
> I here first lisped with infant's prattling tongue,
> And here heard mother's 'hush-a-baby' song.
> Murmuring, this pebbly brook taught me to play.
> Meandering stream, by thee I used to stray;
> In thee first saw the playful silvery fish;
> Learnt here t' express the infant's simple wish,
> Love, hope, and joy. I here my days began;
> Even here the broomstick rode, the circle ran;
> Rejoiced and prattled here to mimic man."

In the winter of 1828, the church in Low Hampton, of which Mr. Miller was a member, was refreshed by an out-pouring of the Holy Spirit. In a letter, dated March 12, written to Elder Hendryx, to whom reference has before been made, Mr. Miller says:

"One young man came to my house last night, after nine o'clock, to request prayers. He said he had been eight years under conviction, and appeared to be almost in despair. I thought I could say to him, as did John the Baptist to his disciples: 'Behold the Lamb of God, that taketh away the sin of the world!' Twelve or fourteen requested prayers last Sunday evening. It is really the work of the Lord. I never lived in a reformation so general, so solemn, and with so little noise. Surely, we have reason to rejoice and be glad. The Lord has remembered the low state of his people, and hath come down to deliver. Two of my children, William and Bellona, as I have a good degree of hope, are subjects of grace. Pray for us."

In the same letter he makes mention of trials, as well as blessings. He says:

"On Saturday, the first day of March, our meeting-house was consumed by fire. We should have almost despaired of ever building again, had not the Lord visited us by his grace, and likewise opened the hearts of our Christian friends from abroad. $400 have been subscribed from the adjoining towns. There is now some prospect that [92] we shall build. You know we are weak in numbers. We are really so in resources. I must bend my whole force to gain the above-mentioned object."

Mr. Miller succeeded in the accomplishment of his wishes, assisting according to his ability and known liberality.

He continued to make the Bible his daily study, and became more and more convinced that he had a personal duty to perform respecting what he conceived the Bible to teach of the nearness of the Advent. These impressions he thus describes:

"When I was about my business, it was continually ringing in my ears, 'Go and tell the world of their danger.' This text was constantly occurring to me: 'When I say unto the wicked, O wicked man, thou shalt surely die; if thou dost not speak to warn the wicked from his way, that wicked man shall die in his iniquity; but his blood will I require at thy hand. Nevertheless, if thou warn the wicked of his way to turn from it; if he do not turn from his way, he shall die in his iniquity; but thou hast delivered thy soul.' – Ezekiel 33:8, 9. I felt that, if the wicked could be effectually warned, multitudes of them would repent; and that, if they were not warned, their blood might be required at my hand. I did all I could to avoid the conviction that anything was required of me; and I thought that by freely speaking of it to all, I should perform my duty, and that God would raise up the necessary instrumentality for the accomplishment of the work. I prayed that some minister might see the truth, and devote himself to its promulgation; but still it was impressed upon me, 'Go and tell it to the world: their blood will I require at thy hand.' The more I presented it in conversation, the more dissatisfied I felt with myself for withholding it from the public. I tried to excuse myself to the Lord for not going out and proclaiming it to the world. I told the Lord that I was not used to public speaking; that I had not the necessary qualifications to gain the attention of an audience; that I was very diffident, and feared to go before the world; that they would 'not believe me nor hearken to my voice;' that I was 'slow of speech, and of a slow tongue.' But I could get no relief."

In this way he struggled on for nine years longer, pursuing the study of the Bible, doing all he could to present the [93] nearness of Christ's coming to those whom circumstances threw in his way; but resisting his impressions of duty to go out as a public teacher. He was then fifty years old, and it seemed impossible for him to surmount the obstacles which lay in his path, to successfully present it in a public manner.

His freedom to converse on the subject, and the ability with which he was able to defend his own views, and oppose those differing from him, had given him no little celebrity in his denomination in all that region; and some were rather shy in approaching him. Elder T. Hendryx, a Baptist clergyman now in the State of Pennsylvania, who has kindly furnished the biographer with many original letters from Mr. Miller, thus speaks of his first acquaintance with him:

"My first acquaintance with Brother Miller was in the summer of 1831. I had been requested to visit the Baptist church in Hampton, and concluded to go. When about to start, I was informed by a brother in the church of which I was a member, in Salem, N. Y., that there was a brother in the Hampton church, possessing considerable influence, who had many curious notions on doctrinal points, and on the prophecies, – particularly on the latter; and also (to use the brother's language) that he was 'hard on ministers who differed with him.' Having recently commenced preaching, without much confidence in my own ability, and not having made any engagement to the church, I at first almost concluded not to go. On further reflection I decided to go, and put my trust in Him, who had said, 'Lo, I am with you always.' On my way, I endeavored, by prayer and meditation, to divest myself of all prejudice against his peculiar notions, whatever they might be (for as yet I was ignorant of them), and at the same time to fortify myself against being led into error by him. I arrived at Bro. Miller's on the 6th of July, 1831. You may well suppose that my situation was not very enviable. I moved tremblingly and with the utmost caution. In spite of me, I could not act like myself; and it was not till I had been there nearly a week, and preached several discourses, that I could feel at home, or enjoy my wonted freedom in preaching the word. Several other ministering brethren visited at Bro. M.'s during my stay there, and I found that I was not altogether alone in [94] those feelings. But how perfectly groundless those fears! Instead of pouncing upon my errors like the tiger, no brother ever dealt with me more tenderly, or exhibited a better spirit in presenting his views.

"After being with Bro. M. some time, he asked me my views on the millennium. Having thrown off all reserve, I readily gave them. I had embraced the old view – the world's conversion a thousand years before the advent; and answered him accordingly. His reply was: 'Well, Bro. H., prove it! You know I want Bible for all that I receive.' 'Well,' said I; and, taking my Bible, I turned to the 20th of Rev., and was about to read, when I thought I would examine it again, and with very close attention. I was in a deep study. Bro. M. was waiting and watching me closely. He began to smile. 'Why don't you read, Bro. H.?' said he. I was astonished; for I could not make it out. At last I said: 'I go home next Monday. I will draw the passages off, and hand them to you when I return.' I took some four days for it, and gave him a long list of passages. He read them, and said: 'Bro. H., what has become of your old theory? This is mine.' 'Well,' said I, 'it is mine, too.' In my examination, *my* 'theory' had been overturned, and I came out where I now stand.

"One thing I observed in Bro. M.'s character: If he ever dealt harshly with a brother for holding an error, it was because he saw, or thought he saw, a spirit of self-importance in him."

The labors of Elder Hendryx were attended with a blessing as appears from a letter of Mr. Miller's to him, dated August 9, 1831. In it he says: "The Lord is pouring out his Spirit among us, but not in so powerful a manner as I could wish. Baptism has been administered every Sabbath but one since you were here. Two or three have obtained hope every week."

As Mr. Miller's opinions respecting the nearness and nature of the millennium became known, they naturally elicited a good deal of comment among his friends and neighbors, and also among those at a distance. Some of their remarks, not the most complimentary to his sanity, would occasionally be repeated to him.

Having heard that a physician in his neighborhood had [95] said, "Esquire Miller," as he was familiarly called, "was a fine man and a good neighbor, but was a monomaniac on the subject of the advent," Mr. M. was humorously inclined to let him prescribe for his case.

One of his children being sick one day, he sent for the doctor, who, after prescribing for the child, noticed that Mr. Miller was very mute in one corner, and asked what ailed him.

"Well, I hardly know, doctor. I want you to see what does, and prescribe for me."

The doctor felt of his pulse, etc., and could not decide respecting his malady; and inquired what he supposed was his complaint.

"Well," says Mr. Miller, "I don't know but I am a monomaniac; and I want you to examine me, and see if I am; and, if so, cure me. Can you tell when a man is a monomaniac?"

The doctor blushed, and said he thought he could.

Mr. Miller wished to know how.

"Why," said the doctor, "a monomaniac is rational on all subjects but one; and, when you touch that particular subject, he will become raving."

"Well," says Mr. Miller, "I insist upon it that you see whether I am in reality a monomaniac; and if I am, you shall prescribe for and cure me. You shall, therefore, sit down with me two hours, while I present the subject of the advent to you, and, if I am a monomaniac, by that time you will discover it."

The doctor was somewhat disconcerted; but Mr. Miller insisted, and told him, as it was to present the state of his mind, he might charge for his time as in regular practice.

The doctor finally consented; and, at Mr. Miller's request, opened the Bible and read from the 8th of Daniel. As he read along, Mr. Miller inquired what the ram denoted, with the other symbols presented. The doctor had read Newton, and applied them to Persia, Greece, and Rome, as Mr. Miller did.

Mr. Miller then inquired how long the vision of those empires was to be.

"2,300 days." [96]

"What!" said Mr. Miller, "could those great empires cover only 2300 literal days?"

"Why," said the doctor, "those days are years, according to all commentators; and those kingdoms are to continue 2300 years."

Mr. M. then asked him to turn to the 2nd of Daniel, and to the 7th; all of which he explained the same as Mr. Miller. He was then asked if he knew when the 2300 days would end. He did not know, as he could not tell when they commenced.

Mr. Miller told him to read the 9th of Daniel. He read down till he came to the 21st verse, when Daniel saw "the man Gabriel," whom he had "seen in the vision."

"In what vision?" Mr. Miller inquired.

"Why," said the doctor, "in the vision of the 8th of Daniel."

"'Wherefore, understand the matter and consider the vision.' He had now come, then, to make him understand that vision, had he?"

"Yes," said the doctor.

"Well, seventy weeks are determined; what are these seventy weeks a part of?"

"Of the 2300 days."

"Then do they begin with the 2300 days?"

"Yes," said the doctor.

"When did they end?"

"In A. D. 33."

"Then how far would the 2300 extend after 33?"

The doctor subtracted 490 from 2300, and replied, 1810. "Why," said he, "that is past."

"But," said Mr. Miller, "there were 1810 from 33; in what year would that come?"

The doctor saw at once that the 33 should be added, and set down 33 and 1810, and, adding them, replied, 1843.

At this unexpected result the doctor settled back in his chair and colored; but immediately took his hat and left the house in a rage.

The next day he again called on Mr. Miller, and looked as though he had been in the greatest mental agony.

"Why, Mr. Miller," said he, "I am going to hell. I have not slept a wink since I was here yesterday. I have [97] looked at the question in every light, and the vision must terminate about A. D. 1843; and I am unprepared, and must go to hell."

Mr. Miller calmed him, and pointed him to the ark of safety; and in about a week, calling each day on Mr. M., he found peace to his soul, and went on his way rejoicing, as *great a monomaniac* as Mr. Miller. He afterwards acknowledged that, till he made the figures 1843, he had no idea of the result to which he was coming.

CHAPTER 6

*Commencement Of Public Labors – Publishes His Views
In Pamphlet – Interview On The Hudson River Boat –
His Regard For The Bible – Correspondence, Etc.*

The public labors of Mr. Miller, according to the best evidence to be obtained, date from the autumn of 1831. He had continued to be much distressed respecting his duty to "go and tell it to the world," which was constantly impressed on his mind. One Saturday, after breakfast, he sat down at his desk to examine some point, and, as he arose to go out to work, it came home to him with more force than ever, "Go and tell it to the world." He thus writes:-

"The impression was so sudden, and came with such force, that I settled down into my chair, saying, 'I can't go, Lord.' 'Why not?' seemed to be the response; and then all my excuses came up – my want of ability, etc.; but my distress became so great, I entered into a solemn covenant with God, that, if he would open the way, I would go and perform my duty to the world. 'What do you mean by opening the way?' seemed to come to me. 'Why,' said I, 'if I should have an invitation to speak publicly in any place, I will go and tell them what I find in the Bible about the Lord's coming.' Instantly all my burden was gone, and I rejoiced that I should not probably be thus called upon; for I had never had such an invitation. My trials were not known, and I had but little expectation of being invited to any field of labor. [98]

"In about half an hour from this time, before I had left the room, a son of Mr. Guilford, of Dresden, about sixteen miles from my residence, came in, and said that his father had sent for me, and wished me to go home with him. Supposing that he wished to see me on some business, I asked him what he wanted. He replied, that there was to be no preaching in their church the next day, and his father wished to have me come and talk to the people on the subject of the Lord's coming. I was immediately angry with myself for having made the covenant I had; I rebelled at once against the Lord, and determined not to go. I left the boy, without giving him any answer, and retired in great distress to a grove near by. There I struggled with the Lord for about an hour, endeavoring to release myself from the covenant I had made with him; but I could get no relief. It was impressed upon my conscience, 'Will you make a covenant with God, and break it so soon?' and the exceeding sinfulness of thus doing overwhelmed me. I finally submitted, and promised the Lord that, if he would sustain me, I would go, trusting in him to give me grace and ability to perform all he should require of me. I returned to the house, and found the boy still waiting. He remained till after dinner, and I returned with him to Dresden.

"The next day, which, as nearly as I can remember, was about the first Sabbath in August, 1833,[25] I delivered my first public lecture on the Second Advent. The house was well filled with an attentive audience. As soon as I commenced speaking, all my diffidence and embarrassment were gone, and I felt impressed only with the greatness of the subject, which, by the providence of God, I was enabled to present. At the close of the services on the Sabbath, I was requested to remain and lecture during the week, with which I complied. They flocked in from the neighboring towns; a revival commenced, and it was said that in thirteen families all but two persons were hopefully converted. [99]

"On the Monday following I returned home, and found a letter from Elder Fuller, of Poultney, Vt., requesting me to go and lecture there on the same subject. They had not heard of my going to Dresden. I went to Poultney, and lectured there with similar effect.

"From thence I went, by invitation, to Pawlet, and other towns in that vicinity. The churches of Congregationalists, Baptists and Methodists, were thrown open. In almost every place I visited my labors resulted in the reclaiming of backsliders, and the conversion of sinners. I was usually invited to fields of labor by the ministers of the several congregations whom I visited, who gave me their countenance; and I have never labored in any place to which I was not previously invited. The most pressing invitations from the ministry, and the leading members of the churches, poured in continually from that time, during the whole period of my public labors, and with more than one half of which I was unable to comply. Churches were thrown open everywhere, and I lectured, to crowded houses, through the western part of Vermont, the northern part of New York, and in Canada East; and powerful reformations were the results of my labors."

---

[25] The printed article from which this is copied was written in 1845. By an examination of his correspondence, it appears that he must have begun to lecture in August, 1831. So that this date is a mistake of the printer or an error in Mr. Miller's memory. As no mention is made of this in the letter to Elder Hendryx, from which the previous extract is made, he could not have gone to Dresden before the second Sabbath in August, 1831.

Soon after he began to lecture on the subject, Mr. Miller began to be importuned to write out and publish his views. In a letter to Elder Hendryx, dated January 25, 1832, he says:

> "I have written a few Numbers on the coming of Christ and the final destruction of the Beast, when his body shall be given to the burning flame. They may appear in the Vermont Telegraph; if not, in pamphlet form. They are written in letters to Elder Smith, of Poultney, and he has liberty to publish."

On the same occasion, he adds: "I am more and more astonished at the harmony and strength of the word of God; and the more I read, the more I see the folly of the infidel in rejecting this word."

The articles referred to were sent as anonymous to the editor of the Telegraph, who declined their publication unless informed of the name of the writer. This being communicated to him, they appeared, in a series of sixteen articles, over the initials of W. M. The first article was published [100] in the paper of May 15, 1832, and they caused much conversation and discussion.

Soon after this, he addressed another letter to Elder Hendryx, which is so quaintly written, contains so much of general interest, and is so illustrative of his habits of thought and modes of expression, that it is here given:

> "*Hampton, March* 26th, 1832.
>
> "Dear Bro. Hendryx: – I received your favor of the 19th inst. day before yesterday, and should have begun to answer it then, but, on coming home, I found Bro. D. at my house, a licentiate from Hamilton, who came on purpose to learn these strange notions of 'crazy Miller's,' or at least to save Bro. Miller, if possible, from going down to the grave with such an error. He was a stranger to me; but, after he introduced himself, we went to work, night and day, and he has just left me, – Monday, 3 o'clock, P.M. He has got his load, and, as he says, he never was so loaded before.
>
> "You may say this is boasting. No, no, Bro. Hendryx, you know better. I only made him read Bible, and I held the Concordance. No praise to me; give God the glory. At any rate, he will find it hard to resist the truth. He wants me to let him come and board with me, two or three months, to study the Bible. He is a young man, of brilliant talents; he preached two sermons here yesterday, and they were very well

done. I have somebody to labor with almost daily. I have been into Poultney, and some other places, to lecture on the coming of Christ; and, in every instance, I have had large assemblies. There is increasing anxiety on the subject in this quarter; but they will see greater signs of these times soon, so that Christians will believe in his coming and kingdom. The harvest is about closing up, and the wrath of God is about to be poured upon our world. Pestilence, sword, and famine, will succeed each other in swift succession, and the kingdoms of this world will soon be destroyed by the 'stone cut out of the mountain without hands.' Yes, brother, – it will soon be over when sinners can be converted. I would, therefore, advise you to lead your hearers by slow and sure steps to Jesus Christ.

"I say *slow*, because I expect all are not strong enough to run yet; and *sure*, because the bible is a sure word; – [101] and where your hearers are not well indoctrinated, you must preach *Bible*; you must prove all things by *Bible*; you must talk *Bible*; you must exhort *Bible*; you must pray *Bible*, and love *Bible*; and do all in your power to make others love *Bible*, too. One great means to do good is to make your parishioners sensible that you are in earnest, and fully and solemnly believe what you preach. If you wish your people to feel, feel yourself. If you wish them to believe as you do, show them, by your constant assiduity in teaching, that you sincerely wish it. You can do more good by the fire-side, and in your conference circles, than in the pulpit. Pulpit preaching is, and has long been, considered as no more than a trade. 'Why, he is hired to preach! – he must, of course, tell a good story,' etc., etc. And the very reason why there is more good done in conference meetings, and protracted meetings, is simply this: the god of this world is shut out. They will say, He expects nothing for this; surely our salvation is his anxious desire. Reflections of this sort make strong impressions of conviction on the mind. If this man of God will make so much sacrifice, surely I ought to think, at least, how much my brother has my benefit in view in his preaching.

"*May 20th*, 1832. It is now almost two months since I began this letter, and I ought to make some apology for my long neglect. But I hate apologies; for we never tell the whole truth. You have, undoubtedly, seen, or will see, two numbers in the Telegraph before you receive this letter. A number more will soon follow. I expect it will start some queries, if nothing more. There is much opposition expressed by some who ought to have taught the same things. But people will think and reflect; and truth will in the end prevail. Do come, on the 13th and 14th of June, to our Association. I expect Bro. Sawyer will be ordained then. *Do come.* I have much to say to you; but I cannot write as I wish…

"I have just come from a prayer-meeting this morning, at our school-house, at sunrise. We are praying for the second coming of our dear Redeemer, when the 'sanctuary will be cleansed.' Pray with us, my brother. I am more and more satisfied that the end of the world is at hand. The evidence flows in from every quarter. 'The earth is reeling [102] to and fro, like a drunkard.' One short year ago, and Zion was rejoicing with her multiplied converts; now she is down 'by the cold streams of Babylon.' One year since, and we were enjoying a plentiful harvest; now, we are sleeping in the cold, and the staff of life is neglected. Is the harvest over and past? If so, soon, very soon, God will arise in his anger, and the vine of the earth will be reaped. See, see! – the angel with his sharp sickle is about to take the field! See yonder trembling victim fall before his pestilential breath! High and low, rich and poor, trembling and falling before the appalling grave, the dreadful cholera. Hark! – hear those dreadful bellowings of the angry nations! It is the presage of horrid and terrific war. Look! – look again! See crowns, and kings, and kingdoms tumbling to the dust! See lords and nobles, captains and mighty men, all arming for the bloody, demon fight! See the carnivorous fowls fly screaming through the air! See, – see these signs! Behold, the heavens grow black with clouds; the sun has veiled himself; the moon, pale and forsaken, hangs in middle air; the hail descends; the seven thunders utter loud their voices; the lightnings send their vivid gleams of sulphurous flame abroad; and the great city of the nations falls to rise no more forever and forever! At this dread moment, look! look! – O, look and see! What means that ray of light? The clouds have burst asunder; the heavens appear; the great white throne is in sight! Amazement fills the universe with awe! He comes! – he comes! Behold, the Saviour comes! Lift up your heads, ye saints, – he comes! he comes! – he comes!

"WM. MILLER."

A letter, written about the same time with the above, to a sister of Mr. Miller's, whose husband was a Universalist, is particularly severe on those sentiments. Beginning with subjects of mere family interest, he proceeds to those of a religious; and, in speaking of the nearness of the advent, he says:

"I now tell you that I am more and more convinced of its truth. I have lectured on it, in a number of places, this winter, and many people believe that the calculation is right. Some are afraid of it, and others will not believe; but [103] among them all it makes a great deal of talk.

Some say Esq. Miller is crazy; others, that he is a fool; – and neither of them are wide from the truth. But Bro. J. and sister A. will say, 'We wish Bro. William would let that subject alone. We do not want to hear so much about Christ's second coming, the end of the world, the judgment-day, and the destruction of the wicked. He knows no more about it than the man in the moon.' So say I. But the Bible tells us; and that will never fail. You will see, within a few weeks, some numbers in the Vermont Telegraph, signed W. M. Read, and then judge. If it is not printed in the paper, I will send it to you in pamphlet form. I think it will be printed, at any rate.

"I want to know if J– is a Universalist yet; and, if so, whether he can tell me who are the partakers of the second death, and what the second death is? You will find the description of them in Revelation 20th chap., and 21:8. Be sure you are not deceived, Bro. J.; for the time is shortly coming that will try every man's work, whether it be good or evil; and if you love the Lord Jesus, show your love by believing his word, and being reconciled to his word and will. How little love to Christ do we show when we are unreconciled to his justice, his word, or the righteous judgment of God on the finally impenitent! Yes, brother; it is not contrary to the carnal mind of man to be happy, *if* we can be happy in our own way. Neither should we be very angry with God, if he made all others so, if we thought that was the *only* hope for us. But, if the Universalists could contrive any plan, that would be plausible, to save themselves, and condemn the Calvinists, or those who preach endless misery, their actions show that they would do it quickly; or why do they rail at those who preach as Christ did? 'Except a man is born again he cannot see the kingdom of God.' 'And these shall go away into everlasting punishment.' Why do they oppose those meet-ings where souls are brought to cry out, as in the days of the apostles, 'Men and brethren, what shall we do to be saved?' Did you ever hear such a cry in a Universalist meeting, – where brethren and sisters were all together in prayer, with one accord praying and agonizing for the souls of their brethren according to the flesh? No! [104]

"'Do you think they are fools, Brother William? You know they do not believe in damnation. They preach *all men* will be saved.'

"Ah, ha! What fools the apostles were! If they had preached thus they would have saved many a bitter cry; and Father Paul might have saved himself many a bitter groan in endeavoring to save his kinsmen according to the flesh, and not have wished himself accursed from Christ for their sakes. I really wish – if it is true that all men will be saved – that Paul had known it before he made that expression, that he might save '*some*,' when he might have said that he had the promise of God that '*all*' would be saved. Paul must have been as crazy as Bro. William. O, how many long arguments it would have saved, – how many twistings of texts, and windings and turnings, – if Paul, Peter, John, Matthew, Mark, Luke, Jude, and even Christ, had not said anything about two classes of mankind in a future state, and nothing about punishment being everlasting! But the Universalist is wiser than all these, now-a-days; for they do not preach so now, do they, J-?

"WM. MILLER.

"*March* 27, 1832."

During the summer of 1832, Mr. Miller appears to have been much engaged in attending protracted meetings, which were at that time very common in many parts of the country. Under date of "Hampton, Oct. 1, 1832," he wrote to Elder Hendryx:

"... When your letter arrived I was attending a protracted meeting, in Westport; and the next day after I got home I went to Poultney, to attend one there. I went to Keesville, to attend one, as soon as we left Poultney, and only arrived home last Saturday ... I have spent a great share of my time in attending protracted meetings this summer and fall."

In the same letter he thus exhibits his fondness for the Bible, and points out the great doctrines which he believed it inculcated:

"I want to see you more than ever, and when we have less company, so that we can sit down and have a good dish of Bible together. The light is continually breaking in; [105] and I am more and more confirmed in those things of which I told you, namely, redemption by grace; the efficacy of Christ's blood; justification by his righteousness imputed to us: sanctification through the operation of the Divine Spirit; and glorification by our gathering together unto him at his appearing. I also believe those things to be founded upon election, particular, personal, and certain; governed by the mind, will, and plan of God, which was, is, and will be eternal; and which is revealed to us so far as to give us confidence, hope, and full assurance that nothing in the Divine plan, either of the means or end, can or will fail of their accomplishment."

The church in Low Hampton being destitute of a pastor, in a letter to the same, dated Nov. 17, 1832, Mr. Miller describes the kind of minister they wished for.

"We do not want one who thinks much of his own gifts, and is lifted up with pride; neither do we want a novice – I mean, a fool; one who knows nothing about the Gospel of Christ. We want one who will stir up our minds, will visit, is good to learn, apt to teach, modest, unassuming, pious, devotional, and faithful to his calling. If his natural talents are brilliant, with those qualifications, they would not hurt him. If they are only moderate, they may do well enough for us. Some of our people want 'a quick gab.' But I should prefer a quick understanding ... I set out for Salem to-morrow morning."

In a letter to the same, dated Hampton, Feb. 8, 1833, he writes:

"The Lord is scattering the seed. I can now reckon eight ministers[26] who preach this doctrine, more or less, besides yourself. I know of more than one hundred private brethren who say that they have adopted my views. Be that as it may, 'truth is mighty and will prevail.' If I should get my views printed, how many can you dispose of, in pamphlet form? ... Our people are about giving me a license to lecture. I hardly know what to do. I am too old, too wicked, and too proud. I want your advice. Be plain, and tell me the whole truth." [106]

Shortly after, he published his views, in a pamphlet of sixty-four pages, entitled:

"Evidences from Scripture and History of the Second Coming of Christ, about the year 1843; and of his Personal Reign of One Thousand Years. By William Miller. 'Prove all things: hold fast that which is good.' 1 Thessalonians 5:21. Brandon, Vermont, Telegraph Office, 1833."

Soon after the publication of this pamphlet, he had occasion to visit the city of New York. As he was passing down the Hudson, in a steamboat, a company of men standing near him were conversing respecting the wonderful improvements of the day. One of them remarked, that it was impossible for things to progress, for thirty years to come, in the same ratio as they had done; "for," said he, "man will attain to something more than human." Mr. Miller replied to him, that it reminded him of Daniel 12:4, – "Many shall run to and fro, and knowledge shall be increased." A pause ensuing, Mr. M. continued, and observed, that the improvements of

---

[26] The first minister who publicly adopted his views, was Elder Fuller, of Poultney, Vt.

the present day were just what we should expect at this time, in the fulfillment of Daniel's prophecy. He then commenced with the 11th chapter of
Daniel, and, comparing the prophecy with the history, showed its fulfillment – all listening with close attention.

He then remarked, that he had not intended trespassing so long on
their patience, and, leaving them, walked to the other end of the boat. The
entire company followed, and wished to hear more on the subject. He
then took up the 2nd, 7th, 8th and 9th chapters of Daniel. His hearers
wished to know if he had ever written on the subject. He told them that
he had published the above pamphlet, and distributed among them what
copies he had with him.

This was one of his first audiences, and some gentlemen of high
standing listened to his remarks.

He scattered the most of his pamphlets gratuitously, sending them
as a response to letters of inquiry respecting his views, and to places which
he could not visit.

Under date of April 10, 1833, in writing to Elder Hendryx, and
speaking of the evil of resorting to excommunication from the church for
slight causes, in view of a particular case, he says:

> "Is the remedy better than the disease? Should we cut off a man's leg
> because he has a thorn in his [107] toe? I think not. Should we set a
> wheat field on fire and burn the whole crop, because of a few tares
> in the field? No: let both grow until the harvest. O, how much injury
> is done in church discipline! The hypocrite uses it as a tool to make
> others think he is very pious. The envious use it as a weapon to bring
> down those they imagine are getting above them. The bigot uses it to
> bring others to his faith; and the sectarian, to bring others to his creed,
> etc. But, my dear brother, how many difficulties do you think we have
> in our churches where the spirit of Christ is manifested through the
> whole trial, or where it began with 'Father, forgive them, for they
> know not what they do'? Therefore, I can frankly and honestly say, the
> remedy which has been applied to cure this moral disease, is worse, a
> thousand times worse, than the original cause."

In the same letter, he says:

> "We have no preacher, as yet, except the old man [Mr. M.] with his
> Concordance. And he is so shunned, with his cold, dull and lifeless

performance, that I have strong doubts whether he will attempt again. But – hush – not a word of what I tell you! I had a letter from brother S-, a few days since. He wants me to go down and spend a few days in lecturing on the prophecies with his folks [in Jay, N. Y.] But the *cross!* … Last Sunday, in the P.M., I tried to hold forth the truth from Isaiah 65:25; the Sabbath before, from the same chapter, 17-19 verses. I wish I had the tongue of an Apollos, and the mental powers of a Paul: what a field might I not explore: and what powerful arguments might be brought to prove the authenticity of the Scriptures! But I want one thing more than either – the spirit of Christ and of God; for he is able to take worms and thresh mountains. O my brother, let us pray for each other, especially on the Sabbath, each that the Lord would bestow this gift of the Holy Spirit upon the other. Peradventure the Lord will answer."

In the same letter he thus expresses his regard for the word of God:

"O may the Bible be to us a rock, a pillar, a compass, a chart, a statute, a directory, a polar star, a traveller's guide, a pilgrim's companion, a shield of faith, a ground of hope, a history, a chronology, an armory, a store-house, a mirror, a [108] toilet, a closet, a prayer-book, an epistle, a love letter, a friend, a foe, a revenue, a treasury, a bank, a fountain, a cistern, a garden, a lodge, a field, a haven, a sun, a moon, a star, a door, a window, a light, a lamp, a luminary, a morning, a noon, an evening, an hour-glass, a daysman, a servant, an handmaid.

"It is meat, food, drink, raiment, shelter, warmth, heat, a feast, fruit, apples, pictures, wine, milk, honey, bread, butter, oil, refreshment, rest, strength, stability, wisdom, life, eyes, ears, hands, feet, breath; it is a help to hearing, seeing, feeling, tasting, smelling, understanding, forgiving, loving, hoping, enjoying, adoring, and saving; it teaches salvation, justification, sanctification, redemption, and glorification; it declares condemnation, destruction, and desolation; it tells us what we were, are, and shall be; begins with the beginning, carries us through the intermediate, and ends only with the end; it is past, present, and to come; it discovers the first great cause, the cause of all effects, and the effects of all causes; it speaks of life, death, and judgment, body, soul, and spirit, heaven, earth, and hell; it makes use of all nature as figures, to sum up the value of the gospel; and declares itself to be the Word of God. And your friend and brother believes it.

"WILLIAM MILLER.

"*Hampton, April* 10th, 1833."

CHAPTER 7

*Becomes A Licensed Preacher – Visits Different Places – Letter
On Universalism – Poetical Letter To Elder Hendryx –
Record Of His Labors – Sketch Of A Discourse, Etc.*

In the autumn of this year, Mr. Miller received a license to preach, from the church of which he was a member, as follows:

> "Let brotherly love continue: the Baptist Church of Christ, in Hampton and Whitehall, do certify that Brother William Miller is a member in regular standing in this Church. Brother Miller has been improving his gifts with us in expounding the words of Divine Truth, in public, for some [109] time past, to the approbation and edification of the church. We are satisfied that Brother Miller has a gift to improve in public; and are willing he should improve the same, wherever his lot may be cast among the Zion of God, – that the name of the Lord may be glorified, and his followers edified. Done in Church Meeting, Saturday, Sept. 14, 1833. By order of the Church.
>
> "(Signed,)   BYRON S. HARLOW, *Clerk pro tem.*"

In a letter to his sister, before referred to, written two days subsequent to the date of the above, and dated "Low Hampton, Sept. 16, 1833," he speaks of the above license, and of his labors, as follows:

> "I have just returned from Dresden, where I have been to spend a Sabbath, and to preach to them the word of life. My texts, yesterday, were Hosea 13:1; Isaiah 61:7; and Psalm 102:16… I do feel anxious to come and see you; and, if the Lord will, and your people should not object, to try to speak to them of the things of the kingdom. My brethren have given me a license – unworthy and old and disobedient as I am. Oh, to grace how great a debtor!"

He then proceeds with matters of mere family interests; and closes with the following exhortation to his brother-in-law, respecting the doctrine of Universalism:

> "Just as sure as the word of God is *true*, depend upon it, universal salvation is *not* true. Was this what David saw, when he saw the end of the wicked? Enter into the sanctuary of your own conscience, my brother, and you will find 'No,' or declarations as plain. 'Strive to enter

in at the strait gate; for *many* shall strive to enter in, and shall *not* be able.' Look at Daniel 12:9, 10; – here we have the *end* described. What does conscience say? Be careful, my brother; remember that eternal consequences hang on your decision; and what is the answer? 'Many (not all) shall be purified, and made white, and tried; but the wicked shall do wickedly; and *none* of the wicked shall understand.' See Malachi 4:1-3. Where are the wicked, the proud, and all that do wickedly? Do they enjoy the healing beams of the Sun of righteousness? [110] 'No.' Again, in Matthew 13:49, 50. Are the wicked permitted to dwell with the just? Is heaven and happiness their abode? Enter into the sanctuary, and what do you hear? *No*! No! Again, in Matthew 25:12, 30, and 46. Do the foolish virgins enter in to the marriage supper? or are they ever married to the Lamb? *No*! Is the unprofitable servant 'in light and glory?' *No*! No! And are the goats enjoying the same communion with the sheep? or are they going 'into life eternal?' *No*! No! No! Read, again, Romans 1:18, to the fifth verse of the second chapter. Would it be unjust for God to condemn the characters there described? Your judgment tells you *No*. Your conscience responds the same answer, *No*! Your tongue must *one day* answer No! For every tongue must and will confess to the glory of God. Oh! my brother, enter into the sanctuary, and knock while the door may be opened; seek while you may find; look while you may live; and you will most assuredly learn '*their end*.' All the plausible reasoning of all the Universalists under the whole canopy of heaven, cannot save *one soul*. 'Except a man is born of the Spirit he cannot enter the kingdom of God.'"

During the fall of 1833, and the ensuing winter, Mr. Miller seems to have been constantly occupied in lecturing in Dresden and other towns in New York and Vermont. The very modest estimate which he had of his own abilities and qualifications as a preacher, is apparent in all his correspondence where any reference is made to his public labors. In writing to Eld. Hendryx, under date of Low Hampton, Feb. 25th, 1834, he says;

"… You have undoubtedly heard that I have been trying *to preach* (as some call it) about in this vicinity. I have been laboring, it is true, in my weak manner, in Dresden, two or three months; and the Lord has seen fit to bless us with a little reformation. I have likewise preached in Putnam, Wrentham, Poultney, and in this place. You laugh, Bro. Hendryx, to think old Bro. Miller is preaching! But laugh on: you are not the only one that laughs; and it is all right – I deserve it. If I could preach the truth, it is all I could ask."

Being now recognized as a regularly licensed preacher, his Bro. Hendryx naturally addressed him as the "Rev. [111] William Miller." To a letter thus directed, Mr. Miller, under date of "Hampton, March 22, 1834," thus replied:

"DEAR BRO. HENDRYX: – I wish you would look into your Bible, and see if you can find the word Rev. applied to a sinful mortal like myself; and govern yourself accordingly... Let us be determined to live and die on the Bible. God is about to rise and punish the inhabitants of the world. The proud, the high, the lofty must be brought low; and the humble, the meek, and the contrite will be exalted. Then, what care I for what the world calls great or honorable? Give me Jesus, and a knowledge of his word, faith in his name, hope in his grace, interest in his love, and let me be clothed in his righteousness, and the world may enjoy all the high-sounding titles, the riches it can boast, the vanities it is heir to, and all the pleasures of sin; and they will be no more than a drop in the ocean. Yes, let me have Jesus Christ, and then vanish all earthly toys. What glory has God revealed in the face of Jesus Christ! In him all power centres. In him all power dwells. He is the evidence of all truth, the fountain of all mercy, the giver of all grace, the object of all adoration, and the source of all light; and I hope to enjoy him to all eternity. What! such a sinful wretch as I enjoy Christ? How can this be? Yes, yes; through the electing love of God, the sprinkling of the blood of the covenant, and the work of regeneration, such a sinner as I may be cleansed from sin, purified, and made white, and glorified in the New Jerusalem, together with him, and with all who love our Lord and Saviour Jesus Christ, and who love his appearing. Bro. H., shall you and I appear together in that general assembly and church of the first born? If God will, I hope we shall there meet, to part no more. How can I realize the glory that will there be manifested? And how could I bear the thought to be banished from the face of Jesus, and from the glory of his power? Forbid it, O my Redeemer! Forbid! and let grace reign through righteousness unto eternal life, by Jesus Christ our Lord."

The same devotional feelings are manifest in all his epistles, and also evince that he experienced nearness of access to God, and great religious enjoyment. [112]

Many of his unstudied letters contain sentiments poetically expressed. Some of these have been given in the preceding pages. The following one contains so full a synopsis of his views, that it is here inserted entire:

"North Hampton, August 17, 1834.

"DEAR BROTHER HENDRYX: – Your favor of last month was duly received. I have delayed writing, for fear my letter would arrive at Locke before you. Since I saw you, I have been on a tour north. I was gone from home twenty-eight days, and delivered thirty-two lectures on the second coming of our dear Redeemer and his personal reign, as follows:- two at Keene, nine at Jay, (there a reformation broke out while I was lecturing, and Brother Sawyer writes me that it is still progressing, and that about eighty have been the fruits thus far), seven at a place called the Forks (here three were converted before I left, and eight or ten were under conviction, not heard from since), nine at Keesville (a great concourse of people, spent two Sabbaths and one week, some Universalists shaken), five at Peru Village (large audience, and some conversions – one strong Universalist). I have spent a few Sabbaths in this vicinity; but shall take another tour next week.

"How thankful, Brother Hendryx, we ought to be, that God can and does make use of feeble, frail, broken instruments, for the salvation of immortal souls! Yes, thanks be to God! Let all glory belong to him. I have had invitations from twelve other places to visit them and lecture on the same subject. After haying and harvesting are over, I shall go again. If I am correct, how important is time! Nine years will pass soon; and then, my dear brother, you and I must render our account before the solemn bar of our omnipotent Judge.

"Come, come, dear Saviour, nor let time delay! ....Revelation 22:17, 20.
Break, sacred morning! usher in the day, ...Isaiah 58:8.
When all the happy throng, the heavenly band, ...Daniel 7:10.
Shall descend from above, 'the spirit land;' ....1 Thessalonians 4:14.
When the seventh trump its solemn blast shall sound,...........1 Thessalonians 4:16.
And Gabriel's voice shall shake the solid ground; ....Isaiah 2:19, 21.
When sleeping myriads from their graves shall rise,..............1 Thessalonians 4:16.
And meet thee, Jesus, in these nether skies; ....1 Thessalonians 4:17.
When those who yet remain, by sin oppressed,...................1 Thessalonians 4:17.
Will feel a sudden change and join the blessed........1 Corinthians 15:51, 52. [113]
There all the Spirit's fruits unite to praise ....Galatians 6:8.
The Father, Son, and Spirit – 'Ancient of days.' ....Daniel 7:9, 22.

"Yes, my brother, if we are found looking, longing and believing, happy will that meeting be. 'Blessed and holy is he that hath part in the first resurrection,' etc. But if, on the contrary, we are hypocrites, what a sad scene, what a dismal morning to us!

"When from the East we see the cloud arise, ...Acts 1:9, 11.

And bring to view a Saviour long despised, ...Revelation 1:7.

When we shall hear the trump's portentous roll, ...Isaiah 27:13.

That shakes the earth from centre to the pole; ....Psalm 18:7.

When, from the great white throne, indignant ire ....Revelation 20:11.

Shoots forth its blaze, and sets the world on fire: ....Malachi 4:1.

Then all the wicked, all that pride can boast, ...Malachi 4:1.

'Shall be as stubble,' saith the Lord of hosts; ....Malachi 4:1.

When kings, and captains, tyrants, mighty men, ...Revelation 19:18.

Are the great supper for the fowls of heaven; ....Revelation 19:17.

And kingdoms, thrones, and powers, dominions riven, ...Daniel 2:44.

Like chaff before the angry whirlwind driven. ....Daniel 2:35.

The dragon, papal beast, the great arch-foe, ...Revelation 19:20.

Shall sink in endless night, – eternal woe; ....Revelation 20:10.

The orb of day, his face be hid in gloom, ...Isaiah 24:23.

And the old reeling earth in Nature's tomb. ....Isaiah 24:20.

"But we, my brother, if we are what we profess to be, look for a new heavens and a new earth, wherein dwelleth righteousness.

"When this dark orb shall from its ashes rise, ...Isaiah 65:17.

And the new heavens, descending from the skies, ...Revelation 21:10.

The bride, adorned in robes of righteousness, ...Revelation 21:2.

Shall with the Bridegroom enter into rest. ....Hebrews 4:9.

Then, O my soul, shall you, permitted, view ....Psalm 130:5-8.

The word fulfilled: 'created all things new;' ....Revelation 21:5.

And all be banished – trials, sins and fears, ...Revelation 21:4.

To live and reign with Christ a thousand years. ....Revelation 20:6.

The beloved city, filled with boys and men, ...Zechariah 8:4, 5.

Will constitute the New Jerusalem, ...Zechariah 8:3, 8.

And there, as priests of God, with Christ to dwell, ...Revelation 20:6.

While Satan and his hosts are chained in hell. ....Revelation 20:1-3.

But, lo! a thousand years are past and gone, ...Revelation 20:7.

Since the new world was from the old one born; ....Isaiah 42:5-9.

When death gives up the particles of dust, ...Revelation 20:13.

And hell lets loose the spirits of the curs'd. ....Revelation 20:13.

Then on the surface of the earth they stand,.............................Revelation 20:9.

A company unnumbered as the sand;.....................................Revelation 20:8.

For in the flesh they sinned in time that's pass'd...........................Romans 7:5.

So in the flesh must they be judg'd at last;.....................................1 Peter 4:6.

Deceived and gathered, round the city come,..........................Revelation 20:8.

To hear their sentence and receive their doom.................Revelation 20:13. [114]

But can they scale those walls, so great and high?...................Revelation 21:22.

No; nothing enters that doth make a lie................................Revelation 21:27.

Now from the golden gates, from tower to tower,...............Revelation 21:12-18.

The saints look forth for the decisive hour! ....1 Corinthians 6:2.Revelation 14:7.

Then justice, from on high, in fiery breath,..................Daniel 9:3.Hebrews 12:29.

Destroys the rebels – this 'the second death!'................Revelation 20:9, 14; 21:8.

"But stop; what am I about? Writing poetry, when I ought to have been writing sober prose! for I am almost certain I shall never see you again, until the morning of that day comes, 'and the Sun of righteousness arises.' – Malachi 4:2.

"With healing wings shall grace on grace distil,...........................Zechariah 4:7.

And cleanse the church on Zion's holy hill;.................................Daniel 8:14.

Where sin no more controls, nor death by sin,.........................Romans 5:12-21.

But justified and glorified with him:.....................................Romans 8:30-39.

No need of sun or moon, for He's our light;...........................Revelation 21:23.

No changing seasons there, nor gloomy night;.........................Revelation 22:5.

No parting there of friends, nor farewells given,.......................Romans 8:35-39.

But gathered all in one from earth and heaven..........................Ephesians 1:10.

On this my faith is fixed, my hope is rais'd;...........................1 Corinthians 13:13.

To him the glory, and his name be prais'd.....................................Psalm 148.

Then, while I stay in this unfriendly state,...........................1 Corinthians 15:9.

Lord, give me grace, and patiently I'll wait...............................Romans 5:4, 5.

"Poetry again! Indeed, Brother Hendryx, you must forgive me, for my pen refuses to write anything except it hobbles along in verse; and this may be wholly uninteresting to you.

"For poets say, and surely they can tell, ...Song of Solomon 1:7.

To read a poet right, 'drink from his well;'...........Song of Solomon 5:1. Acts 8:29.

To catch the spirit, touch the spirit's flame,...................1 John 4:1. Romans 8:9.

And kindred spirits kindle back again.....................................1 Timothy 4:12.

Then read my quotings, brother, and believe,.................2 Corinthians 1:12-14.

If I'm not right, I'm happy being deceived;..............................Galatians 6:3, 4.

For hope's an anchor, – all in this agree, – ....Hebrews 6:19.

And faith a helmsman – so at least with me; ....2 Corinthians 5:7.

The word of God my compass, love the pole, ...Revelation 15:2. Isaiah 60:9.

Experience my sails, and Christ the whole. ....Ezekiel 27:7.

Grace is my ballast, for it keeps me low; ....Romans 7:7-25.

The Spirit is the wind, that bears me through; ......Song of Solomon 4:16. Acts 2:2.

Perfection is the haven for which I run, ...Ephesians 4:13.

Consigned to him who gave for me his Son; ....1 Corinthians 15:24. John 3:16.

Life is the voyage, and I am 'homeward bound,' ....Jeremiah 45:5.

Time is my log-book, death my anchor-ground; .....Revelation 2:10. Psalm 116:15.

The resurrection is my ship o'erhauled, ...Revelation 20:6. Psalm 17:15.

Eternity unites us all in all. ....1 Corinthians 15:28. [115]

"And now, surely, brother, your patience will be relieved; for my paper is filled up, and I can only say, my respects to all you and yours. Mrs. Miller sends hers also.

"I remain your brother in the Gospel,

"WILLIAM MILLER.

Mr. Miller kept no journal, nor any record of the places he visited, till October, 1834. Beginning at a place called "The Forks," supposed to be "Moore's Forks" in Clinton county, N. Y., the names of places where, the dates when, and the texts from which, he preached, are given in two small memorandum-books, as follows:

PLACE.	TIME.	TEXT.	TEXT.
Forks, N. Y.	Oct. 1, 1834.	Luke 15:18.	Revelation 8:13.
Keesville, N. Y.	Oct. 5, 1843.	Revelation 1:20.	Job 23:24.
Beekmantown,	Oct. 6, 1843.	Daniel 8:13, 14.	Job 10:14.
Plattsburgh,	Oct. 8, 1843.	Daniel 8:13, 14.	Revelation 20:6.
Keesville,	Oct. 11, 1843.	1 Corinthians 3:11.	
Keesville,	Oct. 12, 1843.	Romans 8:6, 7.	Luke 15:18.
Westport,	Oct. 14, 1843.	Daniel 8:13, 14.	Luke 10:14.
Westport,	Oct. 15, 1843.	Revelation 20:6.	

After visiting the above places, he returned home to Low Hampton, and soon after wrote to Elder Hendryx, as follows:

"North Hampton,[27] Oct. 23, 1834.

"MY DEAR BROTHER HENDRYX:- Your favor of Sept. 17 came to hand while I was absent on a tour into Clinton county, of about six weeks, I gave thirty-six lectures on the Second Coming of Christ, was at two covenant meetings, attended two protracted meetings in said time, saw a number of new-born babes in Christ, and now, being at home, I shall write to Brother H. and rest myself a little. ...

"You ask me to give you a skeleton of some discourse. My last was from Romans 8:6. And,

"**I.** I show the exercise of the carnal mind.

"**II.** I show the exercise of the spiritual mind.

"**III.** Explain Death, Life and Peace.

"How I treated my first and second heads you well know. [116]

"**III.** Death is a separation.

"**1st.** Natural death is a separation of soul and body. All mankind are its subjects. It is not the penalty of the law; for Christ became the end of the law for us, etc.

"**2nd.** *Death moral* is a separation from *holiness* and *happiness*. All men were under this *death* by reason of sin. This is the penalty – and Christ bore this in his own body on the tree, when he cried, 'My God, my God,' etc. This death is *eternal*, unless we are delivered by some power that can give life. And we must be born of the Spirit, or be morally dead forever.

"**3rd.** *Death spiritual* is a separation from piety, or from spiritual life; and none but those who have been born of the Spirit can become subjects of this *death*, and those only while in the body, 'absent from the Lord.' 2 Corinthians 1:9.

"Life is the opposite of *Death*; and is *natural, moral* and *spiritual*. *Natural life* is animal, and may and doth exist in transgressors of the holy law of God. This all men have and will possess, both before and after the resurrection. *Moral life* is that life enjoyed by all perfectly holy beings, as the holy angels, man in his original state, and the church of the First-born made perfect. It is God with us, saints glorified, etc. *Spiritual life* is the life enjoyed by spiritual men; those who live not after the flesh, but after the Spirit; those who are born of the spiritual man, the Lord from heaven. This is more or less enjoyed by the Christian in this imperfect state, is the fruit of the Spirit, and is

---

27 The north part of Hampton is called Low or North Hampton, to distinguish it from the main part of the town.

manifested by *love, faith* and hope, and all the graces of the Spirit. These are the spiritual seed, children of the promise; which have the promise not only of this (spiritual) life, but of that (moral life) which is to come, which is eternal, out of the reach of sin or temptation.

"*Peace* is that holy exercise of love to God and man, which constitutes the happiness of all souls reconciled to the government of God; makes them at peace with God, with man, and their own conscience, and gives a taste of heaven, happiness, and the world to come.

"I am every day more convinced that the whole word of God is given for our instruction, reproof and correction; and that the prophecies contain the strongest evidences of the divinity and truth of the Bible; and present to saint and [117] sinner the strongest motives for a holy life, and repentance and faith towards God, that can be produced. When John preached repentance, he prophesied that the kingdom of heaven was at hand, as a principal motive. The apostles prophesied that God had appointed a day, in which he would judge the world in righteousness, by that man, Jesus Christ; and your unworthy brother in Christ proclaims that the day is at hand, when 'he that is filthy will be filthy still, and he that is holy will be holy still'; and that Christ is now standing at the door and knocking for the last time. And, my dear brother, I can truly say 'that the testimony of Jesus is the spirit of prophecy.' And yet how many professed ministers of Christ, at the present day, treat that part of the word with total neglect, and even laugh and jeer at those who would warn the people of their approaching danger. But God has supported me beyond my most sanguine expectation. And although they say much before they hear, yet when they do hear they seem confounded.

"The evidence is so clear, the testimony is so strong, that we live on the eve of the present dispensation, towards the dawn of the *Glorious Day*, that I wonder why ministers and people do not wake up and trim their lamps. Yes, my brother, almost two years since you heard the news, '*Behold, the bridegroom cometh!*' – and yet you cry, A little more sleep, a little more slumber. Blame not your people if they go to sleep under your preaching. You have done the same. Bear with me, my brother. In every letter you have written me, you have promised to study this all-important subject, and in every letter you confess your negligence. The day draws near. More than one sixth of the time is gone since my Brother Hendryx promised, and yet asleep! Oh! God, forgive him! Are you waiting for all the world to wake up before you dare get up? 'Where has your courage fled?' Awake! awake! O sluggard! Defend your own castle, or take sides with the word of God; *destroy*, or *build*. You must not, you cannot, you shall not be neutral.

Awake! awake! Tell Deacon Smith to help wake you. Tell him, for me, to shake you, and not give out shaking, until Bro. H. will put on the whole armor of light.

"In every church where I have lectured on this important subject, many, very many, seem to awake, rub open their [118] eyes, and then fall back to sleep again. But the enemy is waking up. In one town (North Beekmantown) I received a letter, the day after my first lecture, from some bullies and blackguards, 'that if I did not clear out of the state, they would put me where the dogs could never find me.' The letter was signed by ten of them. I staid, and, blessed be God! he poured out his Spirit, and began a work which gain-sayers could not resist.

"Some ministers try to persuade their people not to hear me; but the people will go, and every additional lecture will bring an additional multitude, until their meeting-houses cannot hold them. Depend upon it, my brother, God is in this thing; and he will be glorified; and blessed be his holy name! Do pray for me, my brother, that I may have grace equal to my need, and that I may always see my need, feel my weakness, and be kept humble, and that I may always declare the truth. *Do pray!*

"I think, if the Lord will, I shall be in your section of country next spring or summer. Do give me a list of some brethren between here and your place, if you can.

"I remain yours in Christ,

Rev. T. HENDRYX.   "WILLIAM MILLER."

Two days subsequent to the date of the above, Mr. M. was again in the field; and, according to his memorandum-book, gave lectures as follows: Oct. 25 and 26, at Paulet, Vt.; Nov. 6, 8 and 9, at Orwell, Vt.; 10 and 12, in Cornwall, Vt.; and Nov. 16, in Hampton, N. Y. His success in the above places is indicated in the following extract from a letter which he wrote Elder Hendryx from Low Hampton, on the 28th of Nov., 1834:

"I have had good success since I wrote you before. The Lord has been with me. I have been into a number of towns in Vermont. Some old, hardened rebels have been brought to plead for mercy, even before my course of lectures was finished. Blessed be the holy name of God! He has given me more than I should have dared to ask. How good, my brother, it is to preach, having God for paymaster! He pays down. He pays in souls. He paid the Shepherd thus, and he was satisfied: will he not pay his servants too? Yes, yes. Bless his name, O my soul, for all his benefits! [119]

"I find that studious Christians are the best hearers; and the reason is obvious. The more we know of mankind, the less room there is for bigotry, superstition, and prejudice. Those are evils always attending ignorance."

With the exception of a single Sabbath in Orwell, Vt., Mr. Miller remained at home during the remainder of the year.

CHAPTER 8

New Doors Open – His Labors Countenanced By Ministers Of
His Denomination – His First Donation Of Two Half-Dollars –
Death Of His Mother – Incident At Shaftsbury – Results Of His
Labors – Testimony Of A Convert From Infidelity – Letter Of
Rev. C. Fitch – Urgent Appeals To Visit Various Towns, Etc.

After the commencement of the new year (1835) he lectured, during the first week of January, in Addison, Vt., and the second in Cornwall, Vt. He then returned home, where he remained till the 12th of February, writing on the 11th to Elder Hendryx as follows:

> "The Lord opens doors faster than I can fill them. Tomorrow I have
> an appointment in Whiting, which will occupy a week. The next week
> I shall be in Shoreham; the last week in this month, at Bridgport;
> the first week in March, in Middletown; the second, in Hoosac. I
> have calls from Schroon, Ticonderoga, Moriah, Essex, Chazy, Champlain, Plattsburgh, Peru, Mooretown, Canton, Pottsdam, Hopkinton,
> Stockholm, Parishville, and other places too numerous to mention.
> The Lord has blessed me thus far; in almost every place where I have
> lectured, the Spirit has given fruit. Where I went forth expecting trials
> and persecution, I have found God a present help. Pray for me, that
> my faith fail not, and that I may ever feel my weakness, and that my
> dependence may be on Israel's God. Pray that I may do my duty in
> the fear of God, and in the [120] love of the truth; and then, whatever
> may become of me, God will be glorified and souls saved."

After filling the two former of those appointments, he returned home till the 8th of March, when he lectured in Bridgport, Vt., three days, and gave six lectures. He lectured in Granville on the following Sabbath, March 15th, and again returned home.

It seems to have been his intention, when he left home on the 7th of March, to have returned to Whiting – he having received an invitation to that effect. A powerful work of grace had followed his lectures there, and several infidels had acknowledged the authenticity of the Scriptures as demonstrated by the fulfillment of prophecy, and were under deep conviction, and wished to see him. Whether he went there or not, does not appear. But, on the 21st of March, he writes, "I have been very sick with a cold, for a day or two past, and I am only able to sit up for a short time."

On the 19th of April he again visited Granville, where he also lectured on the 20th and 21st. On the 26th, he lectured at Middletown, N. Y. On the 28th, he again wrote from Low Hampton.

> "I have been laid up with a severe cold, and have been only to two or three places since I wrote last (March 21st). But I have now recovered my health again, so that I have been the last two weeks at Granville and Middletown. Next Sunday (May 3) I am to be at Fort Ann Village, N. Y., if the Lord will; and when I shall get through lecturing in this region, I cannot tell. Doors open faster than I can fill them. I have calls from Wells, Bishop's Corner, and Tinmouth."

These lectures and sermons of Mr. Miller met the approval of a large number of the ministers of his denomination, with whose approbation, from this time, he went forth as a public laborer, endorsed and sanctioned by the following certificate:

> "March 19, 1835.
>
> "This may certify, to whom it may concern, that we, whose names are hereunto affixed, – being ministers in the denomination of regular Baptists, – are personally acquainted with Bro. William Miller, the bearer of this certificate; that he is a member, and a licentiate in good regular standing, in [121] the particular Baptist church, in Hampton, N. Y.; that we have heard his lectures on the subject of the *Second Coming and Reign of our Lord Jesus Christ*; and that we believe his views on that particular subject, as well as others pertaining to the gospel, are worthy to be known and read of all men. As such an one, we commend him to God, and the affectionate acceptance of our brethren in the precious Saviour.
>
> J. Sawyer, Jr., South Reading.
> E. Halping, Hampton.
> Amos Stearns, Fort Ann.
> Emerson Andrews, Lansingburgh.

"June 28, 1836.

"Having heard the above-mentioned lectures, I see no way to avoid the conclusion that the coming of Christ will be as soon as 1843.

 R. S. Palmer, Stockholm, N. Y.

 Joel H. Green, Parishville.

 Silas Pratt, Nicholsville.

 Wareham Walker, Shaftsbury, Vt.

 Edw. B. Crandell, Lansingburgh, N. Y.

 James Ten Brooke, Panton, Vt.

 Edward Mitchell, Canada.

 Samuel B. Ryder, Jr., Canada.

 S. C. Dillaway, West Granville, N. Y.

 Wakeman G. Johnson, Whiting, Vt.

 B. Carpenter, Addison.

 J. Fuller, Poultney.

 Holland Turner, Plattsburg.

 A. Jones, Jr., Middlebury.

 Anthony Case, Cornwall.

 Albert Stone, Johnston.

 Prosper Powell, Troy, Vt.

 Samuel Marshall, Fort Ann, N. Y.

 Isaac Wescott, Stillwater.

 William W. Moor, Bristol.

 Edward S. Soullard, Middletown. [122]

"I do cordially recommend the above, and its bearer, Brother Miller.

 George Norris, Granville.

 Jehial K. Wright, Weybridge.

 M. D. Miller, Monkton.

 Simon Fletcher, Bridgeport, Vt.

 John A Dodge, Ferrisburg.

 Elias Hurlbut, Andover, Vt.

 Samuel Pollard, Weston, "

 Edmund Goodnough, Agent B.G.T.S.

 Arurah Allen, West Haven.

 Hiram Safford, Keeseville.

 Friend Blood, Brookfield.

> Benjamin Willard, East Williamstown.
> Lyman Culver, Barre.
> Isaiah Huntley, Jericho.
> John Lord, East Randolph, Mass.
> James M. Beeman, Westford, Vt.
> Oliver Ayer, Littleton, Mass."

"The above I certify to be a true copy of an original Ministerial Recommendation, signed by the above-named persons. The sentiments I believe correct, and according to the word of God. I think it will be fulfilled in 1843, or thereabouts.

JUSTUS DA LEE, Cambridge."

After visiting Fort Ann, N. Y., on the 3rd of May, he lectured in Whitehall, N. Y., on the 10th and 17th of the same month; in West Haven, on the 7th of June, and in Middlebury, Vt., on the 14th. From that place he went into the province of Lower Canada, and lectured, on the 21st and 23rd, at Bolton; the 25th, at Hutting; the 28th, 29th, and July 1st, at Derby; July 2nd, at Georgeville; the 5th and 6th, at Bolton, again; the 7th, at Outlet; and the 8th and 9th at Stanstead Plain. On the 12th, he lectured at Derby, Vt.; the 13th, at Troy, Vt.; the 14th, at Lowell, Vt.; the 15th, at Eden, Vt.; the 16th, at Cambridge, Vt.; the 17th, at Jericho, Vt.; and the 19th, at Orwell, Vt.

During this tour, while in Canada, a woman placed two half-dollars in his hand, which was all the assistance he received [123] previous to 1836. His expenses for travel, etc., were paid from his own funds.

On his way home from Canada, he was much depressed in his spirits. To use his own words, he was overwhelmed with a dark cloud, for which he could not account. He felt impelled to hasten home, with a presentiment that there was trouble there. Leaving Jericho, Vt., instead of filling several appointments, he took the nearest route, and hastened home with all speed. Calling at Orwell, by the urgent request of his Uncle Phelps, he stopped to speak to the church on the Sabbath, leaving immediately after service for home, where he arrived late at night. His family were astonished to see him return so soon, and he was delighted to find them all well.

At an early hour on Monday he went to visit his mother, to take to her a present from her daughter in Canada. His mother lived about half a mile from Mr. Miller's, with her son, Solomon. He found her in the enjoyment of good health, and he spent the day with her, returning home unusually interested with his visit. His mother did not receive his views, but always told him to preach the whole truth, as he believed it, and do his duty. Soon after Mr. Miller had left his mother she was seized with the palsy. Mr. M. was sent for. She was unable to converse any; but, by the pressure of the hand, signified that she knew him, and before the close of the week expired. Had not Mr. Miller been impressed with a sense of "trouble at home," he would have taken a more circuitous route, and filled several appointments, according to previous arrangements. By thus changing his original purpose he enjoyed the opportunity of a day's conversation with his mother, which he would otherwise have been deprived of. He often recurred to this as a signal instance of God's favor.

On the 2nd of August, he lectured at South Bay, N. Y.; on the 9th, at Dresden, N. Y.; and, on the 23rd, at South Bay, again. On the 28th, he again writes from Low Hampton, to Elder Hendryx, as follows:

> "I am yet engaged in warning the inhabitants to be prepared for the great day of God Almighty, and am endeavoring to prove by the Scriptures that it is near, even at the [124] doors ... I always present this as an inducement for men to repent. I call on them in the name of my dear Master to turn, repent, believe, and obey him. I beseech them, for the value of their souls, to believe in Christ. I implore them to lay up treasures in heaven. I importune with them, again and again, to read, reflect, examine, and see if the word of God is not true. I show them its complete fulfillment thus far, and then I pray God to direct the arrow to the heart. I ask God, through Jesus Christ, to nerve the arm that pulls the bow, and to sharpen the arrow that twangs from it. I then put all my confidence in God, and in his promise, 'Lo, I am with you even to the end of the world.' ...
>
> "I have this moment received a letter from Bro. Wescott [the Baptist clergyman], to be in Stillwater next Sabbath [August 30th]; and I shall be under the necessity of leaving in a few minutes. I shall be absent until about the 1st of October.

"My good old mother Miller is dead. She died about four weeks since. The rest of us are all in good health.

"Yours in gospel bonds,   WM. MILLER."

He visited Stillwater, N. Y., according to invitation, and continued there one week, lecturing each day. On the 13th he was at Bristol. On the 1st of November he visited Middletown, N. Y., and gave a course of eight lectures. He then lectured again, five days, at Bristol, commencing on the 15th of November; and, beginning on the 29th, he labored five days longer at Middletown, – usually giving two lectures each day. On the 6th of December he was at Whitehall, N. Y.; on the 20th, at Poultney, Vt.; and on the 27th, at Westhaven. This terminated his labors for the year 1835.

On the 3rd of January, 1836, he lectured at a "Brother Aborn's;" on the 24th, at Dresden, N. Y.; on the 7th of February, at Fort Ann Village, N. Y.; on the 13th of March, at Orwell, Vt.; and on the 14th, at Shoreham, Vt. His public lectures during these winter months were interrupted by the preparation of his course of sixteen lectures for the press, which were published in Troy, N. Y., in the spring of this year, by Elder Wescott. All the copies of [125] that edition supplied to Mr. Miller he purchased at the regular prices.

On the 24th of April he again visited Stillwater, N. Y.; and, on the 15th of May, New Haven, Vt. On the 16th, he commenced a course of lectures at Weybridge, Vt., which closed on the 20th. On the day following, he began his labors at Monkton, N. Y., which continued eight days.

On the 19th of June he visited Lansingburgh, N. Y., and continued till the 26th. To pay his stage-fare he received, on this occasion, four dollars, which, with the two half-dollars received in Canada, was all the remuneration he had thus far received for his expenses. Subsequent to that time, as he says in his "Apology and Defence," he never received enough to meet his expenses of travel to the places where he was invited; so that his public labors were never of any pecuniary advantage to him, as has been currently reported and believed; but, on the contrary, they were a heavy tax on his property, which gradually decreased during that period of his life.

On the 21st of July, he writes, from Low Hampton, to Elder Hendryx:–

> "I have been confined at home, for three weeks past by a bilious complaint. I was taken unwell while lecturing at Lansingburgh, N. Y.; but I finished my course of lectures, and returned home, and have not been well since. My lectures were well received in that place, and excited attention. The house was filled to overflowing for eight days in succession. I feel that God was there, and believe that in his glorified kingdom I shall see the fruits. ... Infidels, Deists, Universalists and sectarians, were all chained to their seats, in perfect silence, for hours, – yes, days, – to hear the old stammering man talk about the second coming of Christ, and show the manner, object, time, and signs of his coming. O, my brother! it makes me feel like a worm, – a poor, feeble creature; for it is God only who could produce such an effect on such audiences. Yet it gives me confidence; for I solemnly believe it is truth; and God will support his word, and will be present where it is preached, however feeble the instrument; for 'Lo, I am with you even to the end of the world.' Therefore, if I were preaching before all the kings of the earth, why should I fear? for the King of kings is with me. If all the [126] lords were there, yet He is Lord of lords, and of the great men of the earth."

Mr. Miller again lectured in Dresden, N. Y., on the 7th of August; in Orwell, Vt., on the 11th of September; and in Keesville, N. Y. on the 18th. He then gave courses of lectures, beginning at Lawrence, N. Y., on the 22nd; Stockholm, on the 29th; Parishville, on the 7th of October; Massena, N. Y., on the 14th. He gave ten lectures at Fort Covington, N. Y., beginning on the 20th, and was at Chatauguay, N. Y., on the 27th. This terminated his labors for the year 1836. In allusion to these last visits, he wrote on the 23rd of December:

> "I have not visited a place where the Lord has not given me one or two souls for my hire. I have spent eight weeks in St. Lawrence county, and delivered eighty-two lectures this fall. Next week I am going to Shaftsbury and vicinity."

He visited Shaftsbury, Vt., the 23rd of January, 1837, and gave his full course of sixteen lectures. At the close of one lecture, a Baptist clergyman arose, and stated that he had come there for the purpose of exposing the folly of Mr. M., but had to confess that he was confounded, convicted and converted. He acknowledged that he had applied various unhandsome appellations to Mr. Miller, calling him "the end of the world man," "the old visionary," "dreamer," "fanatic," and for which he felt covered with shame and confusion. That confession, evidently so honest, was like a thunderbolt on the audience.

Very few particulars of interest have been gathered respecting his labors during the year 1837. According to his memorandum-book, he lectured in Wells, Vt., on the 3rd of February; in Shrewsbury, Vt., on the 3rd of March; in Andover, Vt., from the 5th to the 12th of March; in Weston, Vt., four days, beginning with the 13th; in Mt. Holly, Vt., on the 17th; in Orwell, Vt., on the 23rd of April and 7th of May; in Danby, Vt., on the 14th of May; in Poultney, Vt., eight days, beginning with the 21st of May; in Orwell, again, on the 4th of June; in North Springfield, Vt., from the 11th to the 17th; in Ludlow, Vt., from the 19th to the 21st; in Mt. Holly, Vt., from the 25th of June to [127] the 2nd of July;[28] in Orwell, Vt., on the 9th of July; at Fairhaven, Vt., from the 11th to the 20th; in Whiting, Vt., on the 23rd; in Fairhaven, Vt., on the 13th of Aug.; in Moriah, Vt., from the 14th to the 22nd of October; in Ludlow, Vt., from the 29th to the 6th of November, and at Stillwater, N. Y., on the 31st of December.

With the 1st of January, 1838, he commenced a second course of lectures at Lansingburgh, N. Y., in compliance with the urgent request of the Baptist church in that place, and of E. B. Crandall, their pastor. The lectures continued nine days, and were listened to by crowded and attentive audiences. The result also was most heart-cheering. Infidelity had several strongholds in that neighborhood, and many of that class attended his lectures, and were greatly affected by them. In a letter dated on the 25th of that month, two weeks after the close of the lectures, a gentleman of that place writes to Mr. Miller:

> "I have never witnessed so powerful an effect in any place, as in this, on all who heard. I am of the opinion that not less than one hundred

---

[28] At this place they raised, and placed in his hands, quite a sum of money for his services. He took $1.50 to pay his stage fare to the next place, and directed them to give the balance to some benevolent object.

persons, who held infidel sentiments, are brought to believe the Bible. Infidelity is dumb in this place, as if frightened, and converts are many."

The following testimony of one who was converted from infidelity during these lectures, is copied from the Boston Investigator (an infidel paper) of January, 1845.

"Mr. Editor: – I was a warm supporter of the views of Abner Kneeland, attended his lectures and *protracted dances*, disbelieved in Divine Revelation and a future existence, and fully accorded with Mr. Kneeland's views of religion. Having read every work of note that I could obtain, and having heard many lectures opposed to God and the Bible, I considered myself prepared to overthrow the Christian faith, and feared no argument that could be brought from the Bible. With these feelings, I attended a full course of Mr. Miller's lectures. He gave his rules of interpretation, and pledged himself to prove his position. I approved of his rules, – to which I refer you, – and the result [128] was, he established the fact that the Bible is what it purports to be – the Word of God – to my mind, beyond a doubt; and I have taken it as the man of my counsel. I notice your doubts of the truth of the statement in relation to hundreds of infidels being converted under the preaching of Mr. Miller. This may possibly be owing to your never having given Mr. Miller a candid and thorough hearing. He is a man mighty in the Scriptures, and has done terrible execution in the ranks of the 'King's enemies,' with the sword of the Spirit, which is the Word of God. I am personally acquainted with nearly one hundred, who held to similar views with Abner Kneeland, who were converted under the preaching of Mr. Miller; and we did not yield the point without a struggle, nor without due consideration. Each and every prop and refuge of infidelity and unbelief were taken away from us, and our sandy foundation was swept by the truth of the Almighty as chaff is driven by the wind. Yet we parted with them much as a man parts with a *diseased tooth*. We tried to cure and keep it there, and when made to know that the *root* and foundation was rotten, it was painful to part with; but we rejoiced and felt better after the separation; for there is balm in Gilead – there is a Physician there.

"*Lansingburgh, N. Y.*, January, 1845."

On the 14th of January, Mr. Miller lectured at Westhaven, N. Y., and two weeks from that day at Low Hampton, N. Y. On the 4th of February he commenced a course of lectures at Panton, Vt., which he continued eight days. He then returned to Westhaven, N. Y., and lectured seven days, beginning February 18th.

On returning to Low Hampton, he found the following letter from Rev. Charles Fitch, pastor at the Marlboro' Chapel, Boston. It was the beginning of an acquaintance between those dear brethren in Christ, and as such will be read with interest by all.

"Boston, March 5, 1838.

"MY DEAR BROTHER: – I am a stranger to you, but I trust that, through the free sovereign grace of God, I am not altogether a stranger to Jesus Christ, whom you serve. I am the pastor of an Orthodox Congregational church in this city. A few weeks since your lectures on the Second Coming of Christ were put into my hands. I sat down to read the [129] work, knowing nothing of the views which it contained. I have *studied* it with an overwhelming interest, such as I never felt in any other book except the Bible. I have compared it with Scripture and history, and I find nothing on which to rest a single doubt respecting the correctness of your views. Though a miserable, guilty sinner, I trust that, through the Lord's abounding grace, I shall be among those that 'love his appearing.' I preached to my people two discourses yesterday on the coming of our Lord, and I believe a deep and permanent interest will be awakened thereby in God's testimonies. My object in writing you, my dear sir, is twofold.

"1st. Will you have the kindness to inform me, by letter, in what history you find the fact stated that the last of the ten kings was baptized A. D. 508, and also that the decree of Justinian, giving the Bishop of Rome power to suppress the reading of the Scriptures, was issued in 538? All the other data which you have given I have found correct, and I know of no reason to doubt your correctness in these. But, as I have not yet been able to find a statement of those facts, you will do me a great favor by just informing me where I may find them; and I shall then feel prepared to defend the truth, and to point others to the right source of information.

"There is a meeting of our Ministerial Association to-morrow, and, as I am appointed to read an essay, I design to bring up this whole subject for discussion, and trust that I may thereby do something to spread the truth.

"2nd. My second object in writing was to ask if you would put me in the way to obtain a dozen copies of your lectures. I know of none to be obtained here. I know of several individuals who are very desirous to obtain the work, and if you can tell me of any place where it can be obtained in this city, or in New York, you will greatly oblige me. If you can give me any information of importance on the subject, not contained in your book, I should greatly rejoice, because, as I stand a watchman on the walls, I wish to '*give the trumpet a certain sound*,' and to make that sound as full, and explicit, and convincing as possible.

"Yours in the faith of Jesus Christ,

"CHARLES FITCH." [130]

On the 12th of March, Mr. M. commenced a course of lectures, and continued eight days, at Benson, Vt. Previous to this he had received urgent requests from the Rev. Mr. Hill, of the First Church in Troy, N. Y., and Rev. Mr. Parke, of the church in West Troy, uniting with their respective churches, for a course of lectures in each place; and they were expected, in West Troy, to have been commenced previous to those in Benson, Vt. Their disappointment, and the great anxiety of ministers and people, at that period, to secure his services, may be judged of by the following letter from the pastor of the church in that place:

"West Troy, March 12th, 1838.

"WILLIAM S. MILLER, ESQ.:[29] Dear Sir, – I received a line from you, dated March 1st, and was glad to hear that Father Miller had concluded to visit West Troy on Saturday last. With much anxiety all looked forward to that day, expecting the privilege of hearing something upon the subject of Christ's Second Coming. But, alas! we are *disappointed*. Dear sir, I write these few lines, letting you know something of the state of feeling in this place upon the subject of Mr. Miller's lectures. In the street, in the house, in short, wherever (almost) you meet an individual, the first thing is, Has Mr. Miller come yet? When is Mr. Miller going to be here? What is the reason he does not come? etc. If the old gentleman can possibly come down to West Troy, I wish him to come as soon as possible. I hope he will not delay. I think we have a little claim upon him, if our wishes may be brought into account. Dear sir, upon the reception of this, please write me the reason of the *disappointment*; also, when he will come, if at all, that I may give an answer to them that ask.

"Yours in haste,

"FREDERICK S. PARKE."

---

[29] A son of Mr. M., who was at that time Postmaster in Low Hampton.

At the same date, Mr. Miller's son received a letter from Troy, N. Y., stating that

> "Rev. Mr. Hill is at present very anxious, and most of his church, for your father to come to East Troy first, and he has undertaken a negotiation with [131] Elder Parke for your father to visit them half of the time."

In compliance with these urgent requests, he commenced a course of lectures at West Troy, N. Y., on the 8th of March, and continued till the 15th, when he began in East Troy, where he continued till the 25th. These were attended with happy results. In March of the next year, the Rev. Mr. Parke wrote Mr. Miller as follows:

> "It is my privilege to say that God in mercy is doing a great work in West Troy. Old and young and middle-aged are alike made the happy recipients of grace. The Dutch Reformed church are enjoying an interesting state of things. The Methodists are full of the Spirit, and the Baptists are pressing on in the good cause. Praise the Lord! A number date their awakening to your lectures on the Second Coming of Christ. ... You have great reason to rejoice that God is pleased to make you the honored instrument of awakening poor sinners."

Previous to these lectures, he had received the following urgent request from Rev. Emerson Andrews, of the Baptist church in Rome, N. Y.:

> "Rome, N. Y., March 20, 1838.
>
> "DEAR BROTHER MILLER: – ... We have heard something of you and yours, and want to see you here in person, and hear your whole course of lectures. I feel as if the time had arrived for you 'to preach the Gospel at Rome also.' There is more attention to religion now than formerly, and some anxiety. The desire to hear from you is very great. We want you to come immediately, the first Sunday if possible. Don't, I beg of you, make *any delay, or excuse,* but come right off. ... I want you to be here before the time if possible."

Engagements at Troy made it necessary to defer compliance with the above till they were attended to. After a few days' rest, he visited Rome, N. Y., began his lectures there on the 6th of May, and continued till the 16th. In the absence of any journal, or of any reference to these lectures in any of the letters preserved by him, their results cannot be here recorded. [132]

In June following, he again visited his friends in Canada East, and lectured at Outlet on the 10th and 11th, and at Bolton from the 12th to the 14th, – returning home before the end of the month. After this he gave courses of lectures, commencing on the 26th of August, at Braintree, Vt.; on the 16th of September, at White Creek, Vt.; on the 3rd of October, at Pittsfield, Vt.; on the 7th, at Randolph, Vt., and on the 16th at Brookfield, Vt.

This last course was given at the urgent request of Rev. Jehiel Claflin and the Baptist church in that place. As early as the 26th of June, Mr. C. wrote him: "There are a great many people in this and the adjoining towns who are very anxious to hear you lecture on the subject of the Millennium." And, on the 16th of July, he wrote: "I received your favor of the 30th ult., and read the same with much delight, to find that you could gratify the wish of so many friends in this and the adjacent towns. I read your letter in meeting, yesterday, to my congregation; and, some being present from abroad, I consulted them according to your request, and found an increasing anxiety in their minds that you should come and lecture in this vicinity, or near by."

On the 7th of November he commenced a course of lectures at Montpelier, Vt., which he continued there and in the neighborhood till the 23rd. On the 17th, he writes from that place to his son:

> "There is a great excitement on the subject in this place. Last night we had a solemn and interesting meeting. There was a great breaking down, and much weeping. Some souls have been born again. I can hardly get away from this people. They want me to stay another week; but I shall go to the next village on Monday. Mr. Kellogg, the Congregational minister here, is a good man, and his church are living Christians. Montpelier is quite a considerable village, and contains some very intelligent people, who appear to listen with much interest. This afternoon I meet the citizens, and am to give them an opportunity to ask questions and state objections. ... May God help me to give his truth! I know my own weakness, and I know that I have neither power of body nor of mind to do what the Lord is doing by me. It is the Lord's doings and marvelous in our [133] eyes. The world do not know how weak I am. They think much more of the old man than I think of him."

A gentleman in this place, on the 20th of February following, wrote to Mr. M. as follows:

> "I am happy to inform you that your labors with us have been blessed, and twenty have united with our church [the Baptist] since you left Montpelier, and twenty or thirty more will soon join, all of whom date their awakening at the time you lectured here. Brother Kellogg (the Congregationalist minister) is strong in the faith, and his views are with Brother Miller on the second coming of Christ."

On the 24th of November, he commenced a series of lectures in Jericho, Vt., which continued till the 2nd of December. On the 28th of this month, he went to Stockbridge, Vt., and on the 30th to Rochester, where he continued till the 6th of January, 1839.

On the 7th of January, 1839, he wrote to his son from Bethel, Vt., that he had lectured in those places to large audiences, and was on his way to Woodstock. He arrived at that place on the 7th, and commenced a second course of lectures, which continued to the 14th. From that date to the 20th, he lectured at Pomfret, Vt.; from the 21st to the 27th, at Bethel, Vt.; and from the 28th to the 31st, at Gaysville, Vt.; – from which place he returned home. On the 28th, he wrote from Gaysville to his son:

> "There has been a reformation in every place that I have lectured in since I left home, and the work is progressing in every place rapidly. The meeting-houses are crowded to overflowing. Much excitement prevails among the people. Many say they believe; some scoff; others are sober and thinking. Give my love to all – mother and the children. I remain yours, etc.   WM. MILLER."

On the 10th of March, he commenced in Essex, Vt., and lectured till the 17th. From the 18th to the 24th, he was at Williston, Vt.; and on the 26th he commenced another course of lectures at Waterbury, Vt., which closed on the 1st of April. Having projected a tour into Massachusetts about this time, he was obliged to disappoint a large number who had solicited visits from him. As evidence of the [134] great desire to hear him, he then had on file urgent requests from Frederic Daley, "preacher in charge," Northfield, Vt., – with fifteen signatures from Strafford, Vt., – expressing "a great anxiety on the part of the public to hear a course of lectures;" from Joseph Chase, Middlesex, announcing that the meeting-house had been opened for him without a dissenting vote, and urging him to come, by all means; Wm. D. Leavett, Grantham, N. H. – urging his presence there "at as early a day as possible;" Z. Delano, Hartford, Vt., wishing him to come as early "as practicable;" Jonathan Woods, Dover, Vt. – "many people being desirous to hear;" Hiram Freeman, pastor of the Congregationalist church in Middlesex, Vt. – stating that "the church would gladly see him, and were generally anxious for him to come," etc., etc.; – none of which appear to have been complied with.

CHAPTER 9

*Visits Massachusetts – Invitation To Lowell – Extract From The
Lynn Record – Is Invited To Boston – Conversation With Elder
Himes – Publication Of His Lectures By Mr. Mussey – Labors
In Portsmouth – Interview With Elder Robinson, Etc.*

In compliance with an invitation from Mr. Seth Mann, of Randolph,
Mass., dated January 15th, 1839, informing him that "I, myself, and many
of our Baptist and Pedo-Baptist friends here, wish you to come and preach
to us," Mr. Miller visited Massachusetts, and arrived, for the first time, in
Boston, on the evening of April 18th. The next day he wrote as follows:

> "Boston, April 19th, 10 o'clock A. M., 1839.
>
> "Dear Son: – I am now in this place, hearty and well. Start at half-past
> twelve for Randolph, where I expect to be next week. Roads were
> very bad. Snow-storm night before last in Keene, N. H. – pleasant
> yesterday and to-day. I have been running about this morning – visited
> India wharf, the new Market, Faneuil Hall, etc., etc. Busy time [135] in
> Boston. I have no news as yet. Will write as often as you will wish to
> hear. I stopped at the Pemberton House, No. 9 Howard Street.
>
> "Yours, etc.   WM. MILLER."

He reached Randolph, and commenced his first course of lectures
in Massachusetts on the 21st of April of that year. He closed his lectures
there on the 28th; commenced in Stoughton, Mass., on the 29th, and
continued to the 6th of May; lectured at Braintree, Mass., on the 7th and
8th, and from the 9th to the 13th in East Randolph, Mass. His lectures in
these places were attended by powerful revivals. On the 27th of May, Mr.
Mann wrote to him from Randolph, saying:

> "The Lord, we trust, is doing a gracious work in this place. There have
> been twelve or fourteen already converted, and at the close of the last
> meeting about twenty arose for prayers. Our last conference meeting
> was so crowded that we had to adjourn to the meeting-house. …
> There appears to be a great solemnity on the minds of nearly all in Mr.
> M'Leish's society. A powerful work is going on in East Randolph."

In July following, Rev. Charles Peabody transmitted to Mr. M. the unanimous vote of the church for him to repeat his lectures in Randolph; but he does not appear to have done so.

Previous to Mr. Miller's visit to Massachusetts, Elder T. Cole, of Lowell, had heard of the results attending his labors in Vermont, and had written for him to visit that city. The dress of Mr. Miller was very plain and ordinary, much more befitting his profession of a farmer than of a preacher. Elder Cole, from the reports of his great success, expected him to appear like some distinguished doctor of divinity. When Mr. M. came to Randolph, Elder C. obtained a promise of his services in Lowell, to commence on the 14th of May, and was requested to meet him at the cars. He had heard that Mr. Miller wore a camlet cloak and white hat, but expected to see a fashionably-dressed gentleman. On the arrival of the cars, he went to the depot to meet him. He watched closely the appearance of all the passengers as they left the cars, but saw no one who corresponded with his expectations of Mr. M. Soon he saw an [136] old man, shaking with the palsy, with a white hat and camlet cloak, alight from the cars. Fearing that this one might prove to be the man, and, if so, regretting that he had invited him to lecture in *his* church, he stepped up to him, and whispered in his ear, -

"Is your name Miller?"

Mr. M. nodded assent.

"Well," said he, "follow me."

He led the way, walking on ahead, and Mr. M. keeping as near as he could, till he reached his house. He was much chagrined that he had written for a man of Mr. M.'s appearance, who, he concluded, could know nothing respecting the Bible, but would confine his discourse to visions and fancies of his own.

After tea, he told Mr. M. he supposed it was about time to attend church; and again led the way, Mr. M. bringing up the rear. He showed Mr. M. into the desk, but took a seat himself among the congregation. Mr. M. read a hymn; after it was sung he prayed, and read another hymn, which was also sung. He felt unpleasant at being left in the pulpit alone, but took for his text: "Looking for that blessed hope, and the glorious appearing of Christ. Elder C. listened for about fifteen minutes, when, seeing that he presented nothing but the word of God, and that he opened the Scriptures in a manner that did honor to the occasion, like a workman who needeth not to be ashamed, he walked up into the pulpit, and took his seat. Mr. M. lectured there from the 14th to the 22nd of May, and again from the 29th to the 4th of June. A glorious revival followed, and Elder C. embraced his views in full, continuing for six years a devoted advocate of them. On the 25th of July, Elder C. wrote Mr. M. that, since the lectures, he "had baptized about forty, sixty in all having joined the church; and there are yet some who are seeking the Lord." Mr. Miller says of his visit: "At Lowell I also became acquainted with my Bro. J. Litch, who had previously embraced my views, and who has since so aided their extension by his faithful lectures and writings, and energetic and consistent course." [137]

From the 24th to the 28th of May, Mr. M. lectured in Groton, Mass., and from the 3rd to the 9th of June, in Lynn, Mass. In connection with his visit to this place, he made the following entry in his memorandum-book: "Thus ends my tour into Massachusetts, making eight hundred lectures from October 1, 1834, to June 9, 1839 – four years, six months, nine days." The editor of the "Lynn Record" gave the following notice of Mr. Miller, and his visit to that place: -

"MILLER AND THE PROPHECIES.

"We took a prejudice against this good man, when he first came among us, on account of what we supposed a glaring error in interpreting the Scripture prophecies so that the world would come to an end in 1843. We are still inclined to believe this an error or miscalculation. At the same time we have overcome our prejudices against him by attending his lectures, and learning more of the excellent character of the man, and of the great good he has done and is doing. Mr. Miller is a plain farmer, and pretends to nothing except that he has made the Scripture prophecies an intense study for many years, understands some of them differently from most other people, and wishes, for the good of others, to spread his views before the public. No one can hear him five minutes without being convinced of his sincerity, and instructed by his reasoning and information. All acknowledge his lectures to be replete with useful and interesting matter. His knowledge of Scripture is very extensive and minute; that of the prophecies, especially, surprisingly familiar. His application of the prophecies to the great events which have taken place in the natural and moral world is such, generally, as to produce conviction of their truth, and gain the ready assent of his hearers. We have reason to believe that the preaching or lecturing of Mr. Miller has been productive of great and extensive good. Revivals have followed in his train. He has been heard with attention wherever he has been ...

"There is nothing very peculiar in the manner or appearance of Mr. Miller. Both are at least equal to the style and appearance of ministers in general. His gestures are easy and expressive, and his personal appearance every way [138] decorous. His Scripture explanations and illustrations are strikingly simple, natural, and forcible; and the great eagerness of the people to hear him has been manifested wherever he has preached."

On his way home he lectured at the following places: – Commencing on the 16th of June at Westford, Vt.; the 23rd, at Cambridge, Vt., and on the 30th at Colchester, Vt. As a result of his labors in Colchester, twenty-three were added to the Baptist church between that time and the 2nd of December following.

The letters addressed to him and his son at this period show that a report was in circulation that he was dead; and, as soon as that was successfully contradicted, another was current that, on reexamining his calculations, he had discovered a mistake of one hundred years. Both of these rumors were several times subsequently revived, and had to be as often contradicted.

On the 15th of September, in compliance with "the wish of many in Rutland, Vt.," who were "very anxious to hear" his "course of lectures," he visited that place, and lectured each day, to the 22nd, when he returned to his family, and made arrangements for a second visit to Massachusetts.

He commenced his labors at Groton, Mass., on the 13th of October, and lectured ten days. In reference to these lectures and others in neighboring towns, Rev. Silas Hawley, Congregational minister, wrote from Groton, on the 10th of April, 1840, as follows:-

"Mr. Miller has lectured in this and adjoining towns with marked success. His lectures have been succeeded by precious revivals of religion in all those places. A class of minds are reached by him not within the influence of other men. His lectures are well adapted, so far as I have learned, for shaking the supremacy of the various forms of error that are rife in the community."

Closing his lectures in Groton, Mr. M. gave a third course of lectures in Lowell, continuing from the 23rd of October to the 1st of November. These, like the previous lectures in that place, were attended with precious fruits.

From the 2nd to the 10th of November, he lectured in [139] Haverhill, Mass., where he made the acquaintance of Elder Henry Plummer, pastor of the Christian church, who embraced his views, and was a steadfast friend till Mr. Miller's decease.

On the 11th of November Mr. M. commenced a course of lectures in Exeter, N. H., which continued till the 19th. On the 12th a conference of the Christian Connection was in session there, and they called on Mr. Miller in a body. He was a stranger to nearly all of them; and few of them regarded his views with anything more than mere curiosity. Several of them questioned him respecting his faith; but they were speedily silenced by the quotation of appropriate texts of Scripture.

It was on this occasion that he became acquainted with Elder Joshua V. Himes, then pastor of the Chardon-street church, Boston. Elder H. had written to Mr. M., on the 19th of October, inviting him to give a course of lectures in his chapel. He now renewed his invitation, and got the promise of a course of lectures in December. Before commencing there, Mr. Miller gave a second course of lectures in Stoughton, Mass., from the 24th to the 29th of November, and one in Canton, Mass., from the 1st to the 6th of December. In this last place, he writes to his son, he "lectured three times on the last day, to a house jammed full." Pressing invitations for further labors in the surrounding region had to be disregarded, in order to fulfill his engagement in the metropolis of New England.

He arrived in Boston on the 7th of December, and from the 8th to the 16th lectured in the Chardon-street chapel, – his first course of lectures in that city.

On the 12th of December Mr. Miller writes from Boston to his son: –

> "I am now in this place lecturing, twice a day, to large audiences. Many, very many, go away unable to gain admittance. Many, I am informed, are under serious convictions. I hope God will work in this city."

At this time he stopped at the house of Elder Himes, who had much conversation with him respecting his views, his plans for the future, and his responsibilities. Elder H. became impressed with the correctness of Mr. M.'s views respecting the nearness and nature of Christ's coming; but was not fully satisfied respecting the time. He was, however, [140] sufficiently convinced that Mr. Miller was communicating important truths, to feel a great interest in their promulgation.

> "When Mr. Miller had closed his lectures," says Elder H., "I found myself in a new position. I could not believe or preach as I had done. Light on this subject was blazing on my conscience day and night. A long conversation with Mr. Miller then took place, on our duties and responsibilities. I said to Bro. Miller, 'Do you really believe this doctrine?'
>
> "He replied, 'Certainly I do, or I would not preach it.'
>
> "'What are you doing to spread or diffuse it through the world?'
>
> "'I have done, and am still doing, all I can.'
>
> "'Well, the whole thing is kept in a corner yet. There is but little knowledge on the subject, after all you have done. If Christ is to come in a few years, as you believe, no time should be lost in giving the church and world warning, in thunder-tones, to arouse them to prepare.'
>
> "'I know it, I know it, Bro. Himes,' said he; 'but what can an old farmer do? I was never used to public speaking: I stand quite alone; and, though I have labored much, and seen many converted to God and the truth, yet *no one*, as yet, seems to enter into the *object* and *spirit of my mission*, so as to render me much aid. They like to have me preach, and build up their churches; and there it ends, with most of the ministers, as yet. I have been looking for help, – I want help.'
>
> "It was at this time that I laid myself, family, society, reputation, all, upon the altar of God, to help him, to the extent of my power, to the end. I then inquired of him what parts of the country he had visited, and whether he had visited any of our principal cities.
>
> "He informed me of his labors," [as given in the foregoing pages].
>
> "'But why,' I said, 'have you not been into the large cities?'

"He replied that his rule was to visit those places where invited, and that he had not been invited into any of the large cities.

"'Well,' said I, 'will you go with me where doors are opened?' [141]

"'Yes, I am ready to go anywhere, and labor to the extent of my ability to the end.'

"I then told him he might prepare for the campaign; for doors should be opened in every city in the Union, and the warning should go to the ends of the earth! Here I began to 'help' Father Miller."

With this epoch commenced an entire new era in the spread of the doctrine of the Advent. B. B. Mussey, Esq., a distinguished Boston publisher, undertook the publication of a revised edition, of five thousand copies, of Mr. Miller's Lectures, on condition that Mr. Miller would secure the copyright. Mr. M. did so, which subjected himself to some blame, where the reason for the act was not known. Mr. M. gave to Mr. Mussey the entire profits of the edition for two hundred copies of the work, which Mr. Mussey gave him.

On the 17th of December Mr. M. lectured in Westford, where he was refused the use of the Congregational church, – the first place of worship that was ever closed against him. From the 19th to the 26th of December, he lectured in Littleton, Mass. The result of these lectures is indicated by a letter of Rev. Oliver Ayer (Baptist), who writes, in January: – "I baptized twelve at our last communion. I shall, probably, baptize from fifteen to twenty next time. There have been from thirty-five to forty hopeful conversions. There is also quite a work in Westford, – ten or twelve conversions, and twenty or thirty inquirers. The work is still going on."

On the 28th he returned to Boston, and repeated his course of lectures in Mr. Himes' chapel, closing on the 5th of January, 1840. The day following, by request of the Baptist church under the care of the Rev. Mr. Parker, he visited Cambridgeport, and lectured there each day till the 13th of January. From the 14th to the 20th, he gave a second course of lectures to Elder Plummer's society, in Haverhill, Mass.

On the 21st of January, 1840, he visited Portsmouth, N. H., and commenced his first course of lectures in that city. The following article, in reference to them, from the pen of Elder David Millard, pastor of the

Christian Society there, appeared in the columns of the Christian Herald, a few weeks subsequently: [142]

"On the 21st of January Bro. William Miller came into town, and commenced, in our chapel, his course of lectures on the Second Coming of Christ. During the nine days that he remained crowds flocked to hear him. Before he concluded his lectures a large number of anxious souls came forward for prayers. Our meetings continued, every day and evening, for a length of time after he left. Such an intense state of feeling as now pervaded our congregation we never witnessed before in any place. Not unfrequently from sixty to eighty would come forward for prayers on an evening. Such an awful spirit of solemnity seemed to settle down on the place that hard must be that sinner's heart that could withstand it. Yet, during the whole, not an appearance of confusion occurred; all was order and solemnity. Generally, as soon as souls found deliverance, they were ready to proclaim it, and exhort their friends, in the most moving language, to come to the fountain of life. Our meetings thus continued, on evenings, for six weeks; indeed, they have thus continued, with very little intermission, up to the present.

"Probably about one hundred and fifty souls have been converted in our meetings; but a part of these were from other congregations, and have returned to their former meetings. Among the converts are a considerable number from the Universalist congregation; these still remain with us. From our meetings this blessed work soon spread into every congregation in town favorable to revivals. In several of them it is at present spreading with power. For weeks together, the ringing of bells, for daily meetings, rendered our town like a continual Sabbath. Indeed, such a season of revival was never witnessed before in Portsmouth by the oldest inhabitant. It would be difficult, at present, to ascertain the exact number of conversions in town; it is variously estimated at from five hundred to seven hundred. We have received into fellowship eighty-one; nine of these were received on previous profession. We have baptized sixty-seven, and the others stand as candidates for baptism. Never, while we linger on the shores of mortality, do we expect to enjoy more of heaven than we have in some of our late meetings, and on baptizing occasions. At the water-side thousands would gather to witness this solemn institution [143] in Zion, and many would return from the place weeping. Our brethren at the old chapel have had some additions, – we believe some over twenty."

The Rev. Mr. Peabody, of Portsmouth, in a sermon, published soon after, spoke of the revival which commenced there in connection with Mr. Miller's labors, as follows:

> "If I am rightly informed, the present season of religious excitement has been, to a great degree, free from what, I confess, has always made me dread such times, – I mean those excesses and extravagances which wound religion in the house of its friends, and cause its enemies to blaspheme. I most cheerfully express my opinion that there will be, in the fruits of the present excitement, far less to regret, and much more for the friends of God to rejoice in, – much more to be recorded in the book of eternal life, – than in any similar series of religious exercises which I have ever had the opportunity of watching."

At the time of these lectures, Elder D. I. Robinson was stationed in Portsmouth, as the pastor of the Methodist church, and attended a part of the course. He writes: -

> "I heard him all I could the first week, and thought I could stop his wheels and confound him; but, as the revival had commenced in the vast congregation assembled to hear, I would not do it publicly, lest evil should follow. I, therefore, visited him at his room, with a formidable list of objections. To my surprise, scarcely any of them were new to him, and he could answer as fast as I could present them. And then he presented objections and questions which confounded *me*, and the commentaries on which I had relied. I went home used up, convicted, humbled, and resolved to examine the question."

The result was that Elder R. became convinced of the nearness of the Advent, and has since been a faithful preacher of the kingdom at hand. Elder Thomas F. Barry, also, at this time embraced Mr. Miller's views, and continued an able and consistent advocate of the same till his death, at Oswego, N. Y., July 17th, 1846.

On the 30th and 31st of January, Mr. M. again lectured in Exeter, N. H., and from the 2nd to the 6th of February in Deerfield, N. H., after which he returned to Boston. [144]

CHAPTER 10

Publication Of The "Signs Of The Times" – Visit To Watertown, Portland, New York City, And Other Places – Letters Of Elders Medbury, Fleming, And Green – His Sickness, Resignation, Etc.

From the 8th to the 29th of February, Mr. M. gave his third course of lectures in Boston, in the Marlboro' Chapel and other places, as the doors opened. It was during this series of meetings that the publication of a journal, devoted to the doctrine of the Advent, was effected. Mr. Miller (in 1845) thus narrates its origin: -

> "For a long time previous to this, the papers had been filled with abusive stories respecting my labors, and they had refused to publish anything from me in reply. I had greatly felt the need of some medium of communication to the public. Efforts had been frequently made to commence the publication of a paper which should be devoted to the advocacy of the doctrine, and the communication of information on the fulfillment of prophecy. We had, however, never been able to find a man who was willing to run the risk of his reputation and the pecuniary expense, in such a publication.

> "On my visit to Boston in the winter of 1840, I mentioned to Brother Himes my wishes respecting a paper, and the difficulties I had experienced in the establishment of one. He promptly offered to commence a paper which should be devoted to this question, if I thought the cause of truth would be thereby advanced. The next week, without a subscriber or any promise of assistance, he issued the first No. of the Signs of the Times, on the 20th of March, [28th of February,] 1840 – a publication [now Advent Herald] which has been continued to the present time.

> "With this commenced an entire new era in the spread of information on the peculiar points of my belief. Mr. Mussey gave up to him the publication of my lectures, and he published them in connection with other works on the prophecies, which, aided by devoted friends, he scattered [145] broadcast everywhere to the extent of his means. I cannot here withhold my testimony to the efficiency and integrity of my Bro. Himes. He has stood by me at all times, periled his reputation, and, by the position in which he has been placed, has been more instrumental in the spread of these views than any other ten men who have embarked in the cause. His course, both in laboring as a lecturer

and in the manner that he has managed his publications, meets my full approval." – *Apology and Defence*, p. 21.

After the issue of the first No., its printers, Messrs. Dow & Jackson, proposed to Elder Himes to issue the paper semi-monthly for one year, he to furnish the editorial matter gratuitously, and they to have all the proceeds of it. These terms being accepted, they reissued the first No. on the 20th of March, and continued it, as per agreement, for one year, when it reverted to Elder Himes, its projector, by whom it has been continued to the present time [1853].

On the 1st of March, 1840, Mr. M. visited Watertown, Mass., and commenced his first course of lectures in that place. These continued nine days, and were attended by a crowded audience. Mr. M. was much pleased with his reception there, and, after leaving, wrote to his son:-

"I have never seen so great an effect in any one place as there. I preached last from Genesis 19:17. There were from a thousand to fifteen hundred present, and more than one hundred under conviction. One half of the congregation wept like children when I parted from them. Mr. Medbury, the Baptist minister, a good man, wept as though his heart would break when he took me by the hand, and, for himself and people, bade me farewell. He and many others fell upon my neck, and wept and kissed me, and sorrowed most of all that they should see my face no more. We could not get away for more than an hour, and finally we had to break away. About twenty were converted while I was there."

Rev. R. B. Medbury afterwards gave the following account of the result of Mr. Miller's lectures there, through the "Signs of the Times":-

"For several months past we have enjoyed, and are still enjoying, a pleasing work of grace among us. This revival, as stated in the account published in the Christian Watchman of the 8th instant, was in progress when Mr. Miller [146] commenced lecturing here. In speaking of the results of his labors, however, it is but just to say that his influence here preceded him. It will be recollected that, some time in January, he lectured at Cambridgeport, about four miles from us. Many, both of our church and congregation, attended one or more of those lectures. The first two subjects of the present work among us, as well as some others, who have since been hopefully converted, regarded those lectures as instrumental of fastening permanent conviction upon their minds. Several Christians, too, were awakened to a new sense of their duty.

"There had, however, been rather more feeling than usual in several of our meetings previous to that time. And in the interval which elapsed between this time and the commencement of Mr. Miller's lectures here, the blessing of God had accompanied the means of grace at home to the hopeful conversion of about twenty. The work evidently received a new impulse while Mr. Miller was here. His lectures were attended by crowds, who listened with profound attention, and, we have reason to believe, in not a few cases with profit. Many persons from neighboring villages shared the benefit of his labors in common with us, and, in several cases, returned to their homes rejoicing. Other means of grace were, however, mingled with his labors, which were, no doubt, in a great degree owned and blessed of God.

"Among those who have since united with our church, many have mentioned Mr. Miller's lectures as the means, under God, of bringing them to repentance. They have generally stated that, for months or years, they had thought more or less on the subject; but that, on hearing him, they felt it was time to take a stand. The things of eternity assumed to them an unwonted reality. Heaven was brought near, and they felt themselves guilty before God. It was not so much the belief that Christ might come in 1843 as it was the *certainty* of that event, with the conviction that they were not prepared to hail his coming with joy. Many, however, who listened to his whole course of lectures with a heart unmoved, have since been melted into contrition, and become the hopeful subjects of renewing grace.

"Many Christians who attended Mr. Miller's lectures here have regarded them as the means of quickening them [147] to new spiritual life. I know not that any one has embraced all his peculiar views; but many have been made to feel that time is short, that the coming of Christ is at hand, and that what they do for their fellow-men must be done quickly. They have felt that hitherto the doctrine of the second coming of Christ has had little or no practical effect upon them, and that, while they could suppose at least one thousand years between that event and the present time, its influence must be less than if it were a matter of constant expectation. They think that the contemplation of this subject has awakened feelings which the anticipation of death never kindled in their breasts. Earth has receded, and their attachment to all sublunary objects has been loosened. Eternity has seemed to open near before them, and its scenes have become more distinct objects of vision; while the soul, with all that pertains to its immortal weal or woe, has been felt to eclipse every other object of earth. In a word, they profess to have consecrated themselves unto the service of God, and to labor to be found watching whenever the Master of the house shall come, 'whether at even, or at midnight, or at the cock-crowing, or in the morning, lest, coming suddenly, he should find them sleeping.'

"*Watertown, May* 21, 1840."

In compliance with the wishes of Elder L. D. Fleming, pastor of the Christian church in Portland, Me., Mr. Miller visited and gave his first course of lectures in that city, from the 11th to the 23rd of March. The result of these was thus stated by Elder Fleming, in April following:

"There has probably never been so much religious interest among the inhabitants of this place, generally, as at present; and Mr. Miller must be regarded, directly or indirectly, as the instrument, although many, no doubt, will deny it, as some are very unwilling to admit that a good work of God can follow his labors; and yet we have the most indubitable evidence that this is the work of the Lord. It is worthy of note that in the present interest there has been, comparatively, nothing like mechanical effort. There has been nothing like passionate excitement. If there has been excitement, it has been out of doors, among such as did not attend Brother Miller's lectures. [148]

"At some of our meetings, since Brother M. left, as many as two hundred and fifty, it has been estimated, have expressed a desire for religion, by coming forward for prayers; and probably between *one* and *two hundred* have professed conversion at our meetings; and now the fire is being kindled through this whole city and all the adjacent country. A number of rum-sellers have turned their shops into meeting-rooms, and those places that were once devoted to intemperance and revelry are now devoted to prayer and praise. Others have abandoned the traffic entirely, and are become converted to God. One or two gambling establishments, I am informed, are entirely broken up. Infidels, Deists, Universalists, and the most abandoned profligates, have been converted, – some who had not been to the house of worship for years. Prayer-meetings have been established in every part of the city, by the different denominations, or by individuals, and at almost every hour. Being down in the business part of our city, on the 4th inst., I was conducted into a room over one of the banks, where I found about thirty or forty men, of different denominations, engaged, with one accord, in prayer, at about eleven o'clock in the daytime! In short, it would be almost impossible to give an adequate idea of the interest now felt in the city. There is nothing like extravagant excitement, but an almost universal solemnity on the minds of all the people. One of the principal booksellers informed me that he had sold more Bibles in *one month*, since Mr. Miller came here, than he had in any four months previous."

An article in the Maine "Wesleyan Journal" gave the following account of his person, and style of preaching:

"Mr. Miller has been in Portland, lecturing to crowded congregations in Casco-street Church, on his favorite theme, the end of the world, or literal reign of Christ for one thousand years. As faithful chroniclers of passing events, it will be expected of us that we should say something of the man and his peculiar views. Mr. Miller is about sixty years of age; a plain farmer, from Hampton, in the State of New York. He is a member of the Baptist church in that place, from which he brings satisfactory testimonials of good standing, and a license to improve publicly. He has, we understand, numerous testimonials, also, from clergymen of different [149] denominations, favorable to his general character. We should think him a man but of common-school education; evidently possessing strong powers of mind, which, for about fourteen years, have been almost exclusively bent to the investigation of Scripture prophecies. The last eight years of his life have been devoted to lecturing on this favorite subject.

"In his public discourse, he is self-possessed and ready; distinct in his utterance, and frequently quaint in his expressions. He succeeds in chaining the attention of his auditory from an hour and a half to two hours; and in the management of his subject discovers much tact, holding frequent colloquies with the objector and inquirer, supplying the questions and answers himself in a very natural manner, and, although grave himself, sometimes producing a smile from a portion of his auditors.

.　.　.　.　.　.　.　.　.

"Mr. Miller is a great stickler for literal interpretations; never admitting the figurative, unless absolutely required to make correct sense, or meet the event which is intended to be pointed out. He doubtless believes, most unwaveringly, all he teaches to others. His lectures are interspersed with powerful admonitions to the wicked, and he handles Universalism with gloves of steel."

In connection with the foregoing was appended a statement of Mr. M.'s opinions, which elicited from him the following comment:

> "In all the cities which I have visited, the editors of religious news-papers have almost invariably misstated and ridiculed my views, doctrines, and motives; but in Portland I found, as I honestly believe, an honest editor. He gave a candid, honest, and impartial account."

Mr. Miller was strongly urged by "the wardens of the First Baptist Society, worshipping in Pleasant-street," where he lectured a portion of the time, to give them "another course of lectures," but he was obliged to decline the invitation; and, on the last Tuesday in March, left Portland, and by stage and railroad reached his home in Low Hampton on Friday night following, – "being absent from home nearly six months, and having delivered three hundred and twenty-seven lectures." [150]

On his way home, a young man, dressed in black, who, Mr. M. after-wards learned, was a clergyman in a neighboring town, became his companion for a short distance in the stage. The young man was very talkative respecting the ministers of his acquaintance, – remarking what a smooth preacher A was, how learned B was, and how popular C was, etc. When the stage stopped for the passengers to dine, the young man proved to be an acquaintance of the landlord's, and they commenced conversation respecting "the prophet Miller." The landlord inquired of the gentleman in black if he had read Mr. Miller's lectures, which the former had loaned him a few days previous. "No," the clergyman said, "he read the introduc-tion, and found that Mr. M. was not a *learned* man, and therefore he had no confidence in the work." This reply struck Mr. M. with much force, as evidence of the manner in which many let those reputed to be learned do their thinking for them.

From the 5th to the 29th of April, he lectured in Hampton, N. Y., to full houses, and a good work followed. On the 2nd of May he commenced a course of lectures in the Baptist church in Benson, Vt., and lectured there and in the church of the Rev. Mr. Francis (Orthodox) nine days. On leaving this place, Mr. Miller wrote to his son:

"The several clergymen in the town met with us. The Lord came down in his power, and by his Spirit; a gracious influence was felt, and many a stout heart yielded to the gospel of Christ. About thirty had obtained a hope, and about one hundred more were anxious, when I left."

Mr. Miller next visited New York city, and commenced his first course of lectures there, from the 16th to the 29th of May, at the corner of Norfolk and Broome streets, to good assemblies. On the 19th, he wrote: "Last night we had a solemn time. An anxious and deep attention was given by the whole congregation." Considerable interest was excited by this course, and the ground was prepared for subsequent labors. At the close of these lectures, Mr. Miller returned home, where he remained a few days, and then made another visit to Canada East. He lectured at Hatly on the 21st of June, and at Bolton on the 24th. On the 28th he commenced a course of lectures in Georgeville, which closed on [151] the 5th of July. Writing from this place, on the 29th of June, he speaks of "large congregations," "serious attention," and of the prospect "that much good would be done there." He then returned to Low Hampton, where he lectured on the 12th of July.

He remained at home about four weeks, when he visited Dresden, N. Y., and lectured from the 9th to the 12th of August. Of that place he writes, under date of August 13th: "We had a good time; the Lord was there." He then adds: "I do not know what to say about coming to Massachusetts again. Day after to-morrow I begin a course of lectures at Fort Ann. The next week I go north, where I have three places, which will take three weeks at least. I have more business on hand than any two men like me should perform. I must lecture twice every day. I must converse with many – answer a host of questions – write answers to letters from all parts of the compass, from Canada to Florida, from Maine to Missouri. I must read all the candid arguments (which I confess are not many) which are urged against me. I must read all the slang of the drunken and sober. ... The polar star must be kept in view; the chart consulted, the compass watched; the reckoning kept; the sails set; the rudder managed; the ship cleared; the sailors fed; the voyage prosecuted; the port of rest, to which we are destined, understood; and to the watchman call, 'Watchman, what of the night?'"

On the 15th of August, 1840, he commenced his anticipated lectures at South Bay, in the town of Fort Ann, N. Y., and continued to the 20th.

On the 2nd, in compliance with a previous invitation, he commenced a second course of lectures in Colchester, Vt., which terminated on the 29th. Of these meetings Elder Columbus Green thus writes:

> "The audiences were very large, notwithstanding it was a time of great excitement, and our place of worship was as still as death. His lectures were delivered in the most kind and affectionate manner, convincing every mind that he believed the sentiments he uttered. He made the most powerful exhortations that I ever heard fall from the lips of any one. A deep solemnity pervaded the minds of the [152] community. Young men and maidens, amid the pleasures of early years; men in the meridian of life, hurrying on with locomotive speed in pursuit of the treasures of earth; gray-haired sires, and matrons whose hoary locks gave evidence that many winters had passed over them, all paused and pondered on the things they heard, inquiring, 'Am I ready?' Many came to the conclusion that they were unprepared to meet their Saviour, repented of their sins, and, through the merits of Jesus, obtained pardon full and free. For two years after this, there was a constant state of revival in that place; and many were the souls that dated their convictions of sin at that time, when the faithful old man warned them of the world's approaching doom. No man was more highly esteemed than he was; and it was not uncommon for impenitent men to vindicate his character when his motives were impeached.
>
> "Many there regarded him as 'a chosen vessel of the Lord,' who had been instrumental in building them up 'in the most holy faith;' who had taken them, as it were, to Pisgah's top, and shown them the promised land, that better country for which patriarchs and prophets sighed. Among the public servants of the Most High, to them most dear, our departed brother held a conspicuous place. Years have passed since I enjoyed those happy seasons with them, and swift-rolling rivers and snow-capped hill-tops now lie between us. But, in whatever light they may now regard the efforts of him who sleeps in death, they then appreciated them. For one, I have never since seen the time when I was not thankful to God that I was counted worthy to see the light, and rejoice in it. And my prayer is that the torch of truth may illume our path through time, and that we may at last have an abundant entrance into the everlasting kingdom of our Lord Jesus Christ.
>
> "*Montgomery, Vt., March 14, 1850.*"

Mr. Miller next lectured in Burlington, Vt., from the 30th of August to the 5th of September; in Salisbury, Vt., from the 12th to the 20th of September; and from the 26th of the same month to the 1st of October, in Sudbury, Vt., after which he returned to Low Hampton.

In anticipation of attending the first General Conference [153] of believers in the second coming of Christ, which was to assemble on the 14th of October, 1840, in Boston, Mr. Miller left home on the 8th, and proceeded as far as Fairhaven, Vt., about two miles from home, where he was taken with a severe attack of typhoid fever. In the afternoon of the same day he was carried back to Low Hampton. He was thus deprived of the long-desired privilege of meeting fellow-laborers in the work in which he was engaged. On the 15th of October he was able to dictate a few lines to those assembled in conference, as follows:

> "... Why was I deprived of meeting those congenial minds in this good, this glorious cause of light and truth? Why am I to bear this last affliction, and not enjoy this one pleasure of meeting fellow-laborers in a cause so big with prospects, so glorious in its results, so honoring to God, and so safe to man? Why are the providences of God so mysterious? I have often inquired. Am I never to have *my will*? No, never, until my will shall harmonize with thine, O Father! Yes, God is right; his providence is right; his ways are just and true; and I am foolish to murmur or complain.
>
> "... O, I had vainly hoped to see you all, to breathe and feel that sacred flame of love, of heavenly fire; to hear and speak of that dear blessed Saviour's near approach! ... But here I am, a weak, a feeble, toilworn old man, upon a bed of sickness, with feeble nerves, and, worse than all, a heart, I fear, in part unreconciled to God. But bless the Lord, O my soul! I have great blessings yet, more than I can number. I was not taken sick far from home. I am in the bosom of my family. I have my reason; I can think, believe, and love. I have the Bible – O blessed book! If I cannot read, I have a daughter who loves that book, and she can read for me. How pleasant it is to hear these infant voices read that holy book! How soft the couch of sickness may be made by dutiful children and the book of God! I have a hope, – yes, yes, 'a blessed hope,' – founded on that Word that never fails. My hope is in Him who soon will come, and will not tarry. I love the thought; it makes my bed in sickness; I hope it will in death. I wait for him. My soul, wait thou on God. I have the Spirit; O blessed Holy Spirit! He

whispers in [154] my heart, 'Fear not, I am with thee; be not dismayed,' I will sustain thee. I have a promise from the great I Am: 'Though after my skin, worms destroy this body, yet in my flesh shall I see God.' I have many friends, and I am persuaded they will last forever. I am confident that I have daily prayers from many hearts." ...

When sufficiently restored, he returned to Fort Ann, and lectured from the 26th to the 30th of December, 1840, in compliance with the "unanimous invitation" of the Baptist church there, Rev. J. O. Mason pastor, who had dispatched a messenger for him. From the 2nd to the 8th of January, 1841, he lectured at Ballston Spa, N. Y.; and again, from the 9th to the 12th, at Fort Ann.

CHAPTER 11

Lectures In Boston (4th, 5th, And 6th Courses), In Andover, Providence,
Galway, N. Y., Claremont, N. H., Benson, Vt. – His Illness – Incident At
Sandy Hill, At Worcester – The Phrenologist – Meetings At Hartford

On the 31st of January, 1841, Mr. Miller again visited Boston, and commenced his fourth course of lectures in that city. He continued there till the 19th of February. The first eighteen lectures were given in the Chardon-street Chapel, "which was crowded almost to suffocation, and thousands were obliged to retire for want of room." Beginning on the 9th, a second course of eighteen lectures was delivered, by invitation of the Baptist church in South Boston, Thomas Driver pastor.

In compliance with an invitation from Rev. N. Hervey, pastor of the Baptist church in Andover, Mass., Mr. M. commenced a course of lectures in their house on Sunday, February 21, 1841. The students of the Orthodox institution there requested him to lecture only evenings, that they might attend his full course; but he could not consistently [155] comply with their wishes. His labors continued there till March 2nd, and were attended by a very large and attentive audience. Mr. Hervey, in whose church they were delivered, has given the following sketch of them.

> "His exposition of the prophecies, together with his earnest and impressive appeals to Christians and sinners to prepare for the coming of the Lord, were the means of arousing Christians to action, and of the conversion of a number of persons, who before were without hope and without God in the world. In the course of the lectures, an incident occurred, which shows his familiar acquaintance with the scriptures and promptness to meet objectors to his views. About the fourth day of his labors he received a letter, signed 'Anonymous,' containing a long list of passages from the Old and New Testaments, which were evidently quoted by 'Anonymous' from *memory*, without naming their chapter and verse. These passages were thought by the author of the letter to be directly opposed to Mr. Miller's view of the near approach and personal reign of Christ on earth. To these texts was affixed a single question. The letter, on being taken from the office, was presented to Mr. Miller, who read it through, and immediately said: '"Anonymous" has not quoted a single text right.' In the

evening, previous to his lecture, he took the letter from his pocket, and inquired if there was a person in the audience by the name of *Anonymous*. If so, he would like to have him stand up. The house was filled on that evening by a large congregation. Mr. Miller waited some time for the appearance of 'Anonymous;' the congregation remained in breathless silence to see the stranger. But no one answered to the call. Mr. Miller then read the letter, and, as he read each passage, also read the same from the Bible. The audience were satisfied that not one text was correctly quoted. Mr. Miller again repeated the call for 'Anonymous' to stand up, if he was present. No one arose. Mr. Miller then read the question which closed the letter, namely – 'Mr. Miller, how dare you assert your theory with so much confidence without a knowledge of the Hebrew and Greek languages?' To this Mr. Miller promptly replied, 'If I am not acquainted *with the HEBREW and GREEK*, I know enough to quote the *English* texts of the Scriptures rightly.' – 'Anonymous' never made [156] himself known, and it was the impression of many of the audience that the author of the letter, if he *was* skilled in the Hebrew and Greek, was *exceedingly deficient* in his knowledge of the *English* Scriptures.

"During Mr. Miller's stay in Andover several persons called to converse with him on the topics of his lectures, and he was very ready to devote his time to conversation with persons desirous of receiving information. He entered into the conversation with all his heart, and hundreds will remember with delight and devout gratitude to God the interviews they have enjoyed with him, and the instructions they have received from his lips. He was ever ready to answer all reasonable questions, and could generally distinguish between the caviler and the sincere inquirer after truth. Two young men, who were in the course of study at the Theological Seminary at Andover, called to see Mr. Miller while at the house of the writer, and spent some time in conversation with him upon the Advent of Christ. After the conversation, as they were about leaving, one of the young men asked Mr. Miller the following question:

"'Well, if the Lord is coming so soon, Mr. Miller, what shall *we do* who are *studying* for the ministry? We have some time yet to prepare for the pastoral office.'

"To this the good man promptly replied: 'Young men, if God has called you to study, keep on in your course, and I will aid you all in my power; but if he has called you to preach, study your Bibles, and commence preaching immediately.'

"The young men bade their adviser good day. N. H."

From the 3rd to the 13th of March, he lectured to crowded audiences at the Marlboro' Chapel, his fifth course of lectures in Boston. From the 13th to the 19th of the same month, he lectured in Fairhaven, Mass.; from the 20th to the 26th, in New Bedford, Mass.; and from the 27th of March to the 5th of April, to large audiences in Providence, R. I. The Town Hall, a commodious building, was granted by the City Council for that purpose. On Sunday, the 4th, by the invitation of Rev. Mr. Jameson, of the 3rd Baptist Church, he lectured there all day to full and solemn congregations. His keeping no journal, makes it impossible to give [157] the particular results of these lectures; but in each of the last three places a large number of intelligent members, in the several churches, embraced his views.

From the 8th to the 15th of April, 1841, he labored in Lowell, Mass., when, after an absence of three months, he returned home, to enjoy a season of rest. At this time he estimated that, since the 1st of October, 1839, he had "travelled four thousand five hundred and sixty miles, and preached six hundred and twenty-seven lectures, averaging one and a half hours each, resulting in about five thousand hopeful conversions."

On the 23rd of May, in compliance with a very urgent request from Addison, Vt., he commenced a course of lectures there, which continued till the 30th, when he was taken sick with a painful inflammation in his left limb. He immediately returned home, when the other limb was similarly affected. This terminated in painful swellings and copious discharges, which began to heal about the 10th of June, but confined him to his room till the last of August; so that he rested from labor during the summer.

From the 12th to the 20th of September he lectured in Hartford, N. Y., to crowded houses. On the 26th of September, and onward to October 6th, he lectured at Ballston, N. Y.; and, on the 10th of October, he commenced a course of lectures at Galway, N. Y., which closed on the 17th. With these lectures a revival commenced, which, according to a letter from Rev. Wm. B. Curtis, pastor of the Baptist church, extended into the neighboring towns. Under date of March 12th, 1842, he wrote to Mr. Miller as follows:

> "The glorious work soon became general and powerful, and we continued our meetings (including the week you were with us) eight

weeks, with only a day or two intermission. I find I have over one hundred names who profess to have obtained hope in the pardoning mercy of God. Including those converted in other meetings originating from this revival, it is probable that from one hundred and fifty to two hundred have been converted to God in this vicinity since your labors here. In justice to yourself and the truth, I must say that the extent and power of this glorious revival was greatly promoted by your lectures. Many converts date their first impressions from hearing you. The work [158] has prevailed principally in the Baptist, Methodist, and Christian societies, while there have been but few conversions among the Presbyterians, who stood aloof from you when here."

On the 18th of October he returned to Low Hampton, and presided at a conference of Second Advent believers, which assembled in the Baptist church there, from the 2nd to the 5th of November, 1841.

On the 10th of November, in compliance with an invitation numerously signed, he commenced a course of lectures in the townhouse at Claremont, N. H., and continued to the 18th. A letter, signed "J. Andrews," written soon after, states that, "Now all the town is aroused to the subject of religion. The Baptist, Methodist, and Congregational societies are all united in this work. Some are converted, and from sixty to seventy-five are anxiously seeking the Lord."

On the 14th of November, the First Baptist Church, Mr. Parker pastor, in Cambridgeport, Mass., voted unanimously to renew an invitation, which they had some time before extended to Mr. Miller, and with which he had been unable to comply, to give a course of lectures there. In compliance with that request, he made arrangements to commence there on Sunday, the 21st of November; but, in consequence of the breaking down of the stage on Saturday, he was detained in Nashua over the Sabbath, and gave three lectures to the citizens of that place. He reached Cambridgeport on the 23rd, and continued till the 28th. On the day following, he commenced his sixth course of lectures in Boston, at Boylston Hall, where he addressed large audiences each day and evening till the 9th of December.

These repeated series of discourses in Boston had a powerful effect on the community. As usual, large numbers went away, unable to gain admittance, and many were hopefully converted from sin to holiness. This last was a common feature in all his labors, and was one great reason why calls from those who did not entertain his views were so frequent and urgent. This reason is given in an invitation extended to him by the Baptist church in New Ipswich, N. H., November 29th, 1841. Their pastor, J. M. Willmarth, thus writes: "The majority desire you to come, principally because they have understood that your addresses to sinners [159] are plain and pungent, and frequently attended with the divine blessing in the conversion of souls."

A course of lectures in Dover, N. H., continuing from the 11th to the 19th of December, terminated his labors for the year 1841.

From the 8th to the 16th of January, 1842, he lectured at Fonday's Bush, N. Y.; from the 17th to the 26th of January, in Jamesville, N. Y.; and, from the 27th of January to the 3rd of February, in the Presbyterian church at Sandy Hill, N. Y. A conference of Advent believers was held in this church, commencing on the 1st of February and closing on the 4th. The services were held the last evening at the court-house. On that occasion about one hundred persons arose for prayer, and a revival commenced which continued for weeks. On this evening an incident occurred which did much to deepen the impressions made by the lecture. H. B. Northop, Esq., a prominent lawyer of that county, arose, at the close of the meeting, and remarked that

> "he had stood at that bar many times and addressed a jury of twelve sensible men, presenting evidence and arguments which he knew were weak and fallacious, and he knew others might have seen it; but he had sat down with the confident expectation that those twelve men would give him their verdict. He had attended these lectures, and had done it with a mind strongly predisposed to reject the doctrine, and exceedingly skeptical. He had attended with a determination, if possible, to overthrow the theory, and to exult with a feeling of triumph if he succeeded. He had watched every word and sentence, and made an effort at every point where he thought there was a possibility of making a breach; but had been unable to do it. And now, after making himself acquainted with history, sacred and profane, with prophecies and prophetic periods, so far as his circumstances would permit him to do, he would frankly confess that he had never found any theory that would compare with this for strength

of evidence. He would not say he believed the event would come in 1843, or within ten years of that; but he could see no reason why it would *not* take place then! At any rate, he was satisfied, if there was any truth in the Bible, the event was near; and this is [160] the nearest calculation we can possibly come to respecting the time."

The effect of such a declaration, from such a source, can be better imagined than described. Rev. Seth Ewer, in a letter of the 2nd of March following, wrote:

"For about four weeks we continued meetings, day and evening. … We find new cases of conviction daily, and frequent hopeful conversions. Our house of worship is thronged every evening. Last Sabbath evening the question was put, whether they wished to continue the services; and hundreds arose in the affirmative. … Between fifty and sixty profess to have obtained a hope."

From the 12th of February, 1842, to the 17th, he lectured in Benson, Vt. At the close of this meeting he took a violent cold, which prevented him from speaking for a few days. He commenced a course of lectures at Nashua, N. H., on the 24th of February; but, after speaking a few times to crowded houses, the state of his lungs, and the want of a suitable place to speak in, compelled him to relinquish his labors there on the third day.

From the 6th to the 9th of March, Mr. Miller lectured in Medford, Mass. While here a friend took him to a phrenologist in Boston, with whom he was himself acquainted, but who had no suspicion whose head he was about to examine. The phrenologist commenced by saying that the person under examination had a large, well-developed, and well-balanced head. While examining the moral and intellectual organs, he said to Mr. Miller's friend:

"I tell you what it is, Mr. Miller could not easily make a convert of *this man* to his hair-brained theory. He has too much good sense."

Thus he proceeded, making comparisons between the head he was examining and the head of Mr. Miller, as he fancied it would be.

"O, how I should like to examine Mr. Miller's head!" said he; "I would give it one squeezing."

The phrenologist, knowing that the gentleman was a particular friend of Mr. Miller, spared no pains in going out of the way to make remarks upon him. Putting his hand on the organ of marvelousness, he said: "There! I'll bet you anything that old Miller has got a bump on his head [161] there as big as my fist;" at the same time doubling up his fist as an illustration.

The others present laughed at the perfection of the joke, and he heartily joined them, supposing they were laughing at his witticisms on Mr. Miller.

> "He laughed; 't was well. The tale applied Soon
> made him laugh on t' other side."

He pronounced the head of the gentleman under examination the reverse, in every particular, of what he declared Mr. Miller's must be. When through, he made out his chart, and politely asked Mr. Miller his name.

Mr. Miller said it was of no consequence about putting his name upon the chart; but the phrenologist insisted.

"Very well," said Mr. M.; "you may call it Miller, if you choose."

"*Miller, Miller,*" said he; "what is your first name?"

"They call me William Miller."

"What! the gentleman who is lecturing on the prophecies?"

"Yes, sir, the same."

At this the phrenologist settled back in his chair, the personation of astonishment and dismay, and spoke not a word while the company remained. His feelings may be more easily imagined than described.

The following description of Mr. Miller's phrenological developments were furnished by a phrenological friend in 1842, and may be of some interest to those acquainted with that science:

ORGANS VERY LARGE. – Amativeness, Adhesiveness, Combativeness, Firmness, Conscientiousness, Benevolence, Constructiveness, Ideality, Calculation, Comparison.

LARGE. – Philoprogenitiveness, Alimentiveness, Acquisitiveness, Self-esteem, Imitation, Mirthfulness, Form, Size, Order, Locality, Eventuality, Time, Language, Causality.

FULL. – Inhabitiveness, Concentrativeness, Caution, Approbation, Wonder, Veneration, Weight, Color, Tune.

MODERATE. – Marvelousness, Secretiveness, Hope, Individuality.

From the 12th to the 20th of March he lectured in the Town Hall in Worcester, Mass. The meetings were well [162] attended, – the hall being crowded during most of the time; two thousand people were judged to have been present. While explaining the 7th chapter of Daniel, Mr. M. very significantly inquired how there could be a millennium, according to the common understanding of it, while the Little Horn warred with the saints, which he was to do till the coming of the Ancient of Days? A Baptist clergyman arose, and offered to answer that question the following morning. The next morning he came in and requested additional time, and his answer was postponed another day. When that time arrived he came in and presented the common view respecting the millennium, and inquired if there was no way to harmonize that text with it. Mr. M. said, that was what they were waiting for him to do! But he left it there. This caused Mr. M. to be listened to with more than usual interest. A revival attended his labors, and considerable effect was produced on the public mind.

From the 22nd to the 28th, he lectured in the City Hall in Hartford, Ct. From two hundred to three hundred persons in that city became favorable to his views as the result of those lectures. Mr. M. was prevented from giving his whole course of lectures, on this occasion, by a severe attack of catarrh and influenza, which made him unable to proceed. The Hartford "Christian Secretary," a Baptist periodical, said of these meetings:

> "One fact connected with this conference struck us somewhat forcibly; and that was, the immense crowd which attended the whole course of lectures. We are unable to speak of the attendance during the day, but in the evening the large hall was filled to overflowing with attentive listeners. Probably not less than from fifteen hundred to two thousand persons were in attendance every evening. This large mass of hearers was made up from nearly or quite every congregation in the city. How many of them have become converts to this new doctrine we have no means of judging, but presume the number is not very small. Of one thing we are satisfied, and that is this: unless the clergy, generally, present a better theory than the one offered by Mr. Miller, the doctrine will prevail to a very general extent."

It was on this occasion that the writer of this became convinced that the Second Advent is to be pre-millennial; and [163] the first resurrection, a "resurrection out from among the dead." At the close of these labors Mr. M. returned to Low Hampton, for that rest which his over-tasked frame now greatly needed.

CHAPTER 12

*Lectures In New York – Newark – Saratoga – Newburyport
– Palmer – The East Kingston Camp-Meeting – Brandon
– Benson – Chickopee – New Haven, Etc.*

On the 24th of April he commenced a course of lectures in the large hall of the Apollo, 410 Broadway, in the city of New York, as usual to large audiences, closing on the 10th of May.

On the 7th of May, he visited Newark, N. J., and gave two discourses in the Universalist chapel in that city. In compliance with three very urgent requests from Rev. Joshua Fletcher, pastor, and the unanimous vote of the Baptist church, in Saratoga, N. Y., Mr. M. again visited that place, and lectured from the 14th to the 22nd of May. From the 24th to the 28th of May, he gave his seventh course of lectures in Boston; and from the 29th of May to the 3rd of June, 1842, he lectured in Newburyport, Mass. At the commencement of his lecture, in the evening of the first day, an egg was thrown into the hall, at him, but fell upon the side of the desk. At the close, stones were thrown through the windows, by a mob outside, who indulged in some characteristic hootings and kindred noises. The congregation dispersed without damage, save the glass of lamps and windows. Under those circumstances, the town authorities closed the hall, and the lectures were adjourned to the chapel in Hale's Court. They continued till Friday, June 3rd – a goodly number having received Christ to the joy of their souls.

From the 4th to the 12th of June, he gave a second course of lectures in the Casco-street church, Portland, Me. They were attended by crowds of anxious hearers, and many Christians were refreshed, while some sinners were converted to God. From the 16th to the 26th of June, he lectured at [164] Three Rivers (in Palmer, Mass.) A member of the Baptist church there afterwards wrote, through the "Christian Reflector," the organ of that denomination, as follows:

> "DEAR BROTHER GRAVES:- It is with gratitude to God that I am able to turn aside from the joyful scenes around me, to inform the friends in Zion what God hath wrought for us. Rev. William Miller,

on the 16th of June last, commenced a course of lectures on the Second Advent of Christ to this world in 1843. The lectures were delivered in our meeting-house, which, however, would hold but a small part of the audience, it being estimated at five thousand; and notwithstanding prepossessions, prejudices, and the slanderous reports circulated about this man of God, the people gave heed to the word spoken, and seemed determined to examine the Scriptures, to see if these things were so; and deep solemnity pervaded the vast assembly. The children of God were soon aroused to a sense of their duty; sinners were seen weeping, and heard to say, 'Pray for me!' The number increased, until one hundred, in an evening prayer-meeting, were seen to arise to be remembered in the prayers of the saints. Soon converts began to tell us what the Lord had done for them. Some Deists, some Universalists, and many of the thoughtless, of both the middle-aged and the youthful part of the community, have been brought to submit their hearts to God, and are now waiting for and hasting to the coming of the day of God. As to the character of the work, let me say, I have never seen a more thorough conviction of the total depravity of the heart, and the utter helplessness of the sinner, and that, if saved, it must be by the sovereign grace of God, than has been manifest in all that have given a relation of their experience."

On the 29th of June, 1842, Mr. M. commenced a course of lectures on the camp ground at East Kingston, N. H. This was the first camp-meeting held by believers in the Advent near, and was noticed by a writer in the Boston Post as follows:

"The Second Advent camp-meeting, which commenced at East Kingston, N. H., on Tuesday, June 29th, and continued from day to day until Tuesday noon, July 5th, was [165] attended by an immense concourse of people, variously estimated at from seven to ten thousand. ...

"The meeting was conducted with great regularity and good order from beginning to end. The ladies were seated on one side, and the gentlemen on the other, of the speaker; meals were served uniformly and punctually at the times appointed, and the same punctuality was observed as to the hours appointed for the services.

"The preachers were twelve or fifteen. Mr. Miller gave the only regular course of lectures – the others speaking occasionally. Many of the people, without doubt, assembled from motives of curiosity merely; but the great body of them, from their solemn looks and close attention to the subject, were evidently actuated by higher and more important motives. Each tent was under the supervision of a tent-master, who was responsible for the good order within the same, where religious exercises were kept up at the intermissions between the public exercises and meals, and where lights were kept burning through the night. ...

"Some fault was found, or dissatisfaction felt, with that part of the regulations which precluded all controversy – *i.e.*, which prevented people of opposite theological sentiments from occupying the time or distracting the attention of the audience, which would otherwise have introduced confusion and defeated the object of the meeting. Nothing could be more reasonable than this regulation, and no peace-loving person would make any objection. ... The meeting broke up with harmony and good feeling."

A few years later, a distinguished American writer and poet, J. G. Whittier, who was present at this meeting, made the following reference to it:

"Three or four years ago, on my way eastward, I spent an hour or two at a camp ground of the Second Advent in East Kingston. The spot was well chosen. A tall growth of pine and hemlock threw its melancholy shadow over the multitude, who were arranged upon rough seats of boards and logs. Several hundred – perhaps a thousand – people were present, and more were rapidly coming. Drawn about in a circle, forming a background of snowy whiteness to the dark masses of men and foliage, were the white tents, and [166] back of them the provision stalls and cook shops. When I reached the ground, a hymn, the words of which I could not distinguish, was pealing through the dim aisles of the forest. I know nothing of music, having neither ear nor taste for it – but I could readily see that it had its effect upon the multitude before me, kindling to higher intensity their already excited enthusiasm. The preachers were placed in a rude pulpit of rough boards, carpeted only by the dead forest leaves and flowers, and tasseled, not with silk and velvet, but with the green boughs of the sombre hemlocks around it. One of them followed the music in an earnest exhortation on the duty of preparing for the great event. Occasionally he was really eloquent, and his description of the last day had all the terrible distinctness of Anelli's painting of the 'End of the World.'

"Suspended from the front of the rude pulpit were two broad sheets of canvass, upon one of which was the figure of a man, – the head of gold, the breast and arms of silver, the belly of brass, the legs of iron, and feet of clay, – the dream of Nebuchadnezzar! On the other were depicted the wonders of the Apocalyptic vision – the beasts – the dragons – the scarlet woman seen by the seer of Patmos – oriental types and figures and mystic symbols translated into staring Yankee realities and exhibited like the beasts of a travelling menagerie. One horrible image, with its hideous heads and scaly caudal extremity, reminded me of the tremendous line of Milton, who, in speaking of the same evil dragon, describes him as

'Swingeing the scaly horrors of his folded tail.'

"To an imaginative mind the scene was full of novel interest. The white circle of tents – the dim wood arches – the upturned, earnest faces – the loud voices of the speakers, burdened with the awful symbolic language of the Bible – the smoke from the fires rising like incense from forest altars – carrying one back to the days of primitive worship, when

'The groves were God's first temples, ere men learned
To hew the shaft, and lay the architrave,
And stretch the roof above it.'"

There were near thirty tents on the ground, and the interest of the meeting continued to the last. Mr. Miller left [167] the ground on the 4th of July, for Northampton, Mass., where he lectured from the 5th to the 7th, and then proceeded to Low Hampton.

He remained at home till past the middle of August. On the 20th of that month he commenced a course of lectures at Brandon, Vt., which continued till the 28th. On the 25th, a large tent had been pitched at Chicopee, Mass., where Mr. Miller was anxiously expected; but he did not arrive so as to commence his lectures till the 1st of September. He then lectured each day till the 4th, when the meeting closed. That was a very large gathering, and, as was estimated, some four hundred or more found peace in believing.

From the 7th to the 11th of September, he lectured at Castine, Maine. On returning to Boston, on the 12th, at the request of the passengers, he gave a lecture on the boat. He went to Albany on the 13th, lectured there in the evening, and on the next day took the canal-boat, on which he also lectured, on his way to Granville, N. Y., where he lectured from the 18th to the 23rd of September. From the 8th to the 16th of October, he lectured in Whitehall, N. Y., and from the 20th to the 30th, at Benson, Vt., where Mr. Himes held a tent-meeting in connection with his lectures.

On the 3rd of November, Mr. Himes erected the Big Tent in Newark, N. J. Mr. Miller was not able to be present till the 7th, from which time to the 14th he gave fifteen discourses. Five days before the close of that meeting the weather became so inclement that the meetings could not be continued in the tent, and they were adjourned to the Presbyterian church in Clinton-street, which was kindly opened during the week. On Sunday, the 13th, the meeting was held in the morning in Mechanic's Hall, which was crowded to suffocation, and found to be altogether too strait for them. At 2 P.M., Mr. Miller spoke from the steps of the court-house to near five thousand people. Notwithstanding the inclemency of the weather, and their being thus driven from pillar to post, the meetings were very interesting, and were productive of much good.

At the close of the meeting in Newark, he commenced a course of lectures in New York city, which continued till the 18th of November. On the 19th of November, [168] he commenced a course of lectures in New Haven, Ct., in the M. E. Church, Rev. Mr. Law pastor. On Sunday, the 20th, although the house was large, it was crowded; and in the evening many were unable to gain admittance. He continued there till the 26th, the interest continuing during the entire course. "The Fountain," a temperance paper published in that city, gave the following account of the meeting:

> "Mr. William Miller, the celebrated writer and lecturer on the Second Advent of our Saviour, and the speedy destruction of the world, has recently visited our city, and delivered a course of lectures to an immense concourse of eager listeners in the First Methodist Church. It is estimated that not less than three thousand persons were in attendance at the church, on each evening, for a week; and if the almost breathless silence which reigned throughout the immense throng for two or three hours at a time is any evidence of interest in the subject of the lectures, it cannot be said that our community are devoid of feeling on this momentous question.

> "Mr. Miller was accompanied and assisted by Rev. J. V. Himes, who is by no means an inefficient coadjutor in this great and important work. We did not attend the whole course, the last three lectures being all we had an opportunity of hearing. We were utterly disappointed. So

many extravagant things had been said of the 'fanatics' in the public prints, and such distorted statements published in reference to their articles of faith, that we were prepared to witness disgusting and perhaps blasphemous exhibitions of 'Millerism,' as the doctrine of the Second Advent is called.

"In justice to Mr. Miller we are constrained to say, that he is one of the most interesting lecturers we have any recollection of ever having heard. We have not the least doubt that he is fully convinced of the truth of the doctrine he labors so diligently to inculcate, and he certainly evinces great candor and fairness in his manner of proving his points. And he proves them, too, to the satisfaction of every hearer; – that is, allowing his premises to be correct, there is no getting away from his conclusions.

"There was quite a number of believers in attendance from other places, and a happier company we have never seen. [169] We have no means of ascertaining the precise effect of these meetings on this community, but we know that many minds have been induced to contemplate the Scripture prophecies in a new light, and not a few are studying the Bible with unwonted interest. For our own part, this new view of the world's destiny is so completely at variance with previous habits of thought and anticipation, that we are not prepared to give it entire credence, though we should not dare hazard an attempt to disprove it.

"The best part of the story is, that a powerful revival has followed the labors of Messrs. Miller and company. We learn that over fifty persons presented themselves for prayers at the altar of the Methodist church on Sunday evening. On Monday evening the number was about eighty."

In the month of May following, Rev. A. A. Stevens (Orthodox Cong.), then a member of Yale College, in a letter to the "Midnight Cry," stated that "the powerful and glorious revival which then commenced continued for some two months, with almost unabated interest."

At the close of these lectures, Mr. M. returned to New York city, where he gave six discourses, from the 27th to the 29th of November, and then returned to Low Hampton. Arriving home, he wrote as follows:

Low Hampton, December 7th, 1842.

"Dear Brother Himes. ... I did not get home till 10 o'clock on Saturday night. On Wednesday, at 6 o'clock, P. M., same day we left

New York, we were brought up all standing in a snow-bank, which we kept bunting, with two or three locomotives, until the next evening at 6 o'clock. On Thursday, by the mighty power of three locomotives, we gained twelve miles from Great Barrington, where we were brought up the night before, to the state line, where they left us and we waited for the Boston cars, which had been due thirty hours. That night we slept in the cars, as the night before, and Friday we got as far as Lansingburg. Saturday I came home, cold and weary, worn out and exhausted. On my arrival, I found a messenger after me and my wife, to visit her mother, who was supposed to be dying; my wife went, and soon returned with the news of her death. After attending the funeral, we [170] came home on Monday night, and yesterday I got some rest. This morning I feel some refreshed. But the fatigue of body and mind has almost unnerved this old frame, and unfitted me to endure the burdens which Providence calls upon me to bear. I find that, as I grow old, I grow more peevish, and cannot bear so much contradiction. Therefore I am called uncharitable and severe. No matter; this frail life will soon be over. My Master will soon call me home, and soon the scoffer and I shall be in another world, to render our account before a righteous tribunal. I will therefore appeal to the Supreme Court of the Universe for the redress of grievances, and the rendering of judgment in my favor, by a revocation of the judgment in the court below. The World and Clergy vs. Miller. ...

"I remain, looking for the blessed hope,

"WILLIAM MILLER."

CHAPTER 13

M R. MILLER had not been sufficiently definite respecting the time of the Advent, in the estimation of some who embraced his views. The expression "about the year 1843" they regarded as too general. As he was about to enter on the long looked-for year, he prepared and published the following

SYNOPSIS OF HIS VIEWS

"**I**. I believe Jesus Christ will come again to this earth. – Proof. John 14:3; Acts 1:11; 1 Thessalonians 4:16; Revelation 1:7.

"**II**. I believe he will come in all the glory of his Father. – Matthew 16:27; Mark 8:38.

"**III**. I believe he will come in the clouds of heaven. – Matthew 24:30; Mark 13:26; Daniel 7:13. [171]

"**IV**. I believe he will then receive his kingdom, which will be eternal. – Daniel 7:14; Luke 19:12, 15; 2 Timothy 4:1.

"**V**. I believe the saints will then possess the kingdom forever. – Daniel 7:18, 22, 27: Matthew 24:34; Luke 12:22, 29; 1 Corinthians 9:25; 2 Timothy 4:8; James 1:12; 1 Peter 5:4.

"**VI**. I believe at Christ's second coming the body of every departed saint will be raised, like Christ's glorious body. – 1 Corinthians 15:20-29; 1 Corinthians 3:2.

"**VII**. I believe that the righteous who are living on the earth when he comes will be changed from mortal to immortal bodies, and, with them who are raised from the dead, will be caught up to meet the Lord in the air, and so be forever with the Lord. – 1 Corinthians 15:51-53; Philippians 3:20, 21; 1 Thessalonians 4:14-17.

"**VIII**. I believe the saints will then be presented to God blameless, without spot or wrinkle, in love. – 1 Corinthians 4:14; Ephesians 5:27; Colossians 1:22; Jude 24; 1 Thessalonians 3:13; 1 Corinthians 1:7, 8.

"**IX**. I believe, when Christ comes the second time, he will come to finish the controversy of Zion, to deliver his children from all bondage, to conquer their last enemy, and to deliver them from the power of the tempter, which is the devil. – Deuteronomy 24:1; Isaiah 34:8; 40:2, 5; 41:10-12: Romans 8:21-23; Hebrews 2:13-15; 1 Corinthians 15:54, 56; Revelation 20:1-6.

"**X.** I believe that when Christ comes he will destroy the bodies of the living wicked by fire, as those of the old world were destroyed by water, and shut up their souls in the pit of woe, until their resurrection unto damnation. – Psalm 50:3; Psalm 97:3; Isaiah 66:15, 16; Daniel 7:10; Malachi 4:1; Matthew 3:12; 1 Corinthians 3:13; 1 Thessalonians 5:2, 3; 2 Thessalonians 1:7-9; 1 Peter 1:7; 2 Peter 3:7, 10; Isaiah 24:21, 22; Jude 6-15; Revelation 20:3-15; John 5:29; Acts 24:15.

"**XI.** I believe, when the earth is cleansed by fire, that Christ and his saints will then take possession of the earth, and dwell therein forever. Then the kingdom will be given to the saints. – Psalm 37:9-11, 22-34; Proverbs 2:21, 22; 10:30; Isaiah 60:21; Matthew 5:5; Revelation 5:10.

"**XII.** I believe the time is appointed of God when these things shall be accomplished. – Acts 17:31; Job 7:1; 14:14; [172] Psalm 81:3; Isaiah 40:2; Daniel 8:19; 10:1; 11:35; Habakkuk 2:3; Acts 17:26.

"**XIII.** I believe God has revealed the time. – Isaiah 44:7, 8; 45:20, 21; Daniel 12:10; Amos 3:7; 1 Thessalonians 5:4.

"**XIV.** I believe many who are professors and preachers will never believe or know the time until it comes upon them. – Jeremiah 8:7: Matthew 24:50; Jeremiah 25:34-37.

"**XV.** I believe the wise, they who are to shine as the brightness of the firmament, Daniel 12:3, will understand the time. – Ecclesiastes 8:5; Daniel 12:10; Matthew 24:43-45; 25:6-10; 1 Thessalonians 5:4; 1 Peter 1:9-13.

"**XVI.** I believe the time can be known by all who desire to understand and to be ready for his coming. And I am fully convinced that some time between March 21st, 1843, and March 21st, 1844, according to the Jewish mode of computation of time, Christ will come, and bring all his saints with him; and that then he will reward every man as his works shall be. – Matthew 16:27; Revelation 22:12."

With the commencement of the new year, he issued the following

Address To Believers In The Near Advent

"**Dear Brethren:** – This year, according to our faith, is the last year that Satan will reign in our earth. Jesus Christ will come, and bruise his head. The kingdom of the earth will be dashed to pieces, which is the same thing. And he, whose right it is to reign, will take the kingdom, and possess it for ever and ever.

"And the God of peace shall tread Satan under your feet shortly. Therefore, we have but a little time more to do as our good brother, Paul, was commanded, Acts 26:18, – 'to open their eyes, and to turn them from darkness to light, and from the power of Satan unto God, that they may receive forgiveness of sins, and inheritance among them which are sanctified by faith that is in me.' Let us then put forth our best energies in this cause; let every one of us try, by persuasion, by the help and grace of God, to get one, at least, of our friends to come to Christ, in this last year of redemption; and, if we succeed, what an army of regenerated souls may we not hail in the new heavens and new [173] earth! I pray God, my brethren, that nothing may deter you from this work. Let scoffers scoff, and liars tell lies; we must not suffer ourselves to be drawn from our work. Yes, the glorious work of salvation, within a few short months, will be finished forever. Then I need not exhort you more on this point; you yourselves know the value of this great salvation.

"And another thing it is well for us to remember. The world will watch for our halting. They cannot think we believe what we speak, for they count our faith a strange faith; and now beware, and not give them any vantage-ground over us. They will, perhaps, look for the halting and falling away of many. But I hope none who are looking for the glorious appearing will let their faith waver. Keep cool; let patience have its perfect work; that, after ye have done the will of God, ye may receive the promise. This year will try our faith; we must be tried, purified and made white; and if there should be any among us who do not in heart believe, they will go out from us: but I am persuaded that there cannot be many such; for it is a doctrine so repugnant to the carnal heart, so opposite to the worldly-minded, so far from the cold professor, the bigot and hypocrite, that none of them will, or can, believe in a doctrine so searching as the immediate appearing of Jesus Christ to judge the world. I am, therefore, persuaded better things of you, brethren, although I thus speak. I beseech you, my dear brethren, be careful that Satan get no advantage over you by scattering coals of wild-fire among you; for, if he cannot drive you into unbelief and doubt, he will try his wild-fire of fanaticism and speculation to get us from the word of God. Be watchful and sober, and hope to the end, for the grace that shall be brought unto you at the revelation of Jesus Christ.

"Think not, my brethren, that I stand in doubt of your perseverance. I know your faith, your love, and hope, to be rooted and grounded on the word of the Almighty; you are not dependent on the wisdom or commandments of men; many, if not all of you, have examined for yourselves; you have studied, and found true, what at first was only reported unto you; you have found the Bible much more precious than you had before conceived; its doctrines to be congenial [174] with the holy and just character of God; its precepts to be wise, benevolent, and kind; and its prophecies to be clear and lucid, carrying conviction of the truth and inspiration of the Scriptures, by a harmony of manner and matter from Genesis to Revelation. In one word, you have found a new bible, and I hope and believe you have read it with new delight. I fear not that you can ever be satisfied with the views of our opponents; their manner of explaining Scripture is too carnal to satisfy the devoted child of God.

"Then let me advise to a continual searching for truth, both for faith and practice; and, wherever we have wandered from the word of God, let us come back to the primitive simplicity of the gospel once delivered to the saints. Thus we shall be found ready at his coming to give an account of our stewardship, and hear our blessed Master say, 'Well done, thou good and faithful servant; enter thou into the joy of thy Lord.' Every truth we get from the blessed book prepares us better for his coming and kingdom. Every error prevents us, in part, from being ready. Let us, then, stand strong in the faith, with our loins girt about with truth, and our lamps trimmed and burning, and waiting for our Lord, ready to enter the promised land, the true inheritance of the saints. This year the fullness of time will come, the shout of victory will be heard in heaven, the triumphant return of our great Captain may be expected, the new song will commence before the throne, eternity begin its revolution, and time shall be no more.

"This year – O blessed year! – the captive will be released, the prison doors will be opened, death will have no more dominion over us, and life, eternal life, be our everlasting reward. This year – O glorious year! – the trump of jubilee will be blown, the exiled children will return, the pilgrims reach their home, from earth and heaven the scattered remnant come and meet in middle air, – the fathers before the flood, Noah and his sons, Abraham and his, the Jew and Gentile, all who have died in faith, of every nation, kindred, tongue, and people, will meet to part no more. This year! the long looked-for year of years! the best! it is come! I shall hope to meet you all, through faith in God and the blood of the Lamb. Until then, farewell. May God bless you, and sustain you in the faith. [175]

"May you be patient in all tribulation, and endure unto the end. May you this year be crowned with immortality and glory. And finally, my brethren, 'I pray God, your whole body, soul, and spirit, be preserved blameless unto the coming of the Lord Jesus Christ.'

"WILLIAM MILLER.

"*Low Hampton, January* 1, 1843."

In compliance with the wishes of Elder Marvin Eastwood and his congregation, in Waterford, N. Y., Mr. Miller lectured there from the last day of December, 1842, to the 8th of January, 1843. On the morning of the third day, the Congregational minister called on him, with a deacon of his church, and wished to ask him a few questions.

Five other gentlemen soon came in, and took seats in the room.

Mr. Miller told the clergyman that he might ask any question he pleased, and he would answer the best he could.

The minister accordingly asked him some twenty questions, each one of which Mr. M. answered by quoting a text of Scripture. He then thanked Mr. M. for his politeness, and acknowledged that he had answered him fairly. "But," said he, "I do not believe your doctrine."

"What doctrine?" said Mr. M.

"I don't believe God has revealed the time."

Mr. M. asked him if he would answer three questions.[30]

The minister replied that he did not come there to *answer* questions.

One of the gentlemen present then inquired of the minister why he would not answer.

He said he did not come for the purpose of answering questions, and did not choose to.

The gentleman then said to him: "I have disbelieved the Bible, but have been one of your principal supporters many years; and, when Mr. Miller has answered so many of your [176] questions, if you will not let him

---

[30] Mr. M. was in the habit of replying to those who denied that God has revealed the time by asking them: "What 'wonders' are referred to in Daniel 12:6?" "Who gave the answer to the inquiry there asked?" and "If those 'wonders' include the resurrection, – and the Lord has sworn with an oath that it shall be for a time, times, and a half, – is not the time revealed?" adding, "Whether we understand it correctly or not, is another question." – *See* p. 265.

ask you three, I can pay you no more of my money." He added, "I have seen more evidence in proof of the truth of the Bible in the few lectures I have heard from Mr. M. than in all the sermons you have ever preached."

"Why," said the minister, "how does Mr. Miller prove the truth of the Bible?"

"By the fulfillment of prophecy."

"And do not I prove it in the same way? Do not I show how all the prophecies in reference to Christ were fulfilled in him?"

"Why, yes, you do that; but you have never shown that those prophecies were written before Christ; and it is very easy to write a history. But Mr. M. has shown us how the prophecies are being fulfilled in our own day; he has shown us how the history of Napoleon is a perfect fulfillment of prophecy; and I *know* that that prophecy was written before the time of Napoleon."

The minister and deacon retired. The gentleman then turned to Mr. Miller, and said that he and his four companions were infidels; that they had attended his lectures; had become quite interested; but had very curious feelings, and wished to know what ailed them.

Mr. M. inquired whether they would attend any more of his lectures.

They replied that they should lose none of them.

"Well," said Mr. M., "I think I will not tell you what ails you; but, if you will give close attention during the week, I think you will find out."

They attended his lectures, and, before the end of the week, with a number of others who had been infidels, were rejoicing in the goodness and forgiveness of God. At the close of his last lecture, one hundred and twenty persons voluntarily arose for prayers; a goodly number were soon rejoicing in the Saviour, and a glorious result followed.

On the 10th of January, 1843, Mr. M. began a course of lectures in the Presbyterian church in Utica, N. Y., where an interest was elicited which extended to surrounding places. Invitations were received from many of the neighboring towns, which could not be complied with. The meetings closed on the 17th, when forty or fifty were [177] inquiring what they should do to be saved. A good work had been commenced, which continued for several weeks. The "Methodist Reformer," published in that city, announced that "many thoughtless sinners and cold professors were stirred up to duty by them;" and the "Baptist Register" said, "Mr. Miller's appeals were often very pungent, and made a deep impression on the audience, and many came forward for prayer."

HOAX IN WASHINGTON

The great rush there was at this time, to hear Mr. Miller lecture on the prophecies, is well illustrated by the following, from the Washington correspondence of the Boston "Mercantile Journal":

"Washington, January 22nd, 1843.

"MR. SLEEPER: – I wrote you yesterday, among other news, that Mr. Miller, the end-of-the-world man, was here. It was announced yesterday, by hand-bills, stuck up all over the city, that he would preach to-day [Sunday] at 3 o'clock, P.M., from the steps of the Patent Office; and, immediately after dinner, crowds were observed wending their way in that direction. The commissioner of the public buildings, or some other officer, had had erected a barricade about halfway up the steps, for the purpose of keeping off the crowd; and when I went to the place of meeting, the space between Seventh and Ninth streets, in front of the Patent Office, was nearly filled with people, their numbers variously estimated from five to ten thousand, of all sexes, ages, and colors. I should think there were over five thousand.

"The space above the barricades was guarded by police officers, who had permitted some few persons, principally members of Congress, to pass over, which filled some of the unfavored ones with no little indignation, and the democratic spirit of the people began to work.

"A number of abortive attempts were made to pass the barrier, but, except to the privileged few, unsuccessfully. One person, however, more determined than the rest, showed fight, and was rather roughly handled by the officers, when the crowd, taking his part, and presuming he was abused, made a rush to the barrier, to break it down, but for the [178] moment unsuccessfully. The crowd became, however, more calm, until a gentleman, whom I understood to be a clergyman, stepped forward, and said that he had been requested to inform the people before him *that there was no certain information that Mr. Miller was in the city;* upon which a shout arose, unlike anything I have heard since the shouts on Bunker Hill, in September, 1840, intermingled with cries of 'Hoax!' Humbug!' etc. The crowd, however, became still enough in a few minutes for the clergyman to continue his remarks, which were as follows: 'As I said before, Mr. Miller is, probably, not in the city; but, as it is a pity that such a concourse should be entirely disappointed of receiving benefit on such a day, I think it would be well for you to call on a distinguished gentleman, Mr. Briggs, a member of Congress from Massachusetts, to give you a temperance address. He is now on the platform.' Cries of 'Briggs!' 'Briggs!' ensued; but Mr. Briggs had no notion of being called out in this unceremonious manner, and, though urgently solicited by his friends, declined. The crowd, perceiving that there was to be no 'fun' made for them, determined to make some for themselves; and again rushing against the barricade, this time success-fully, succeeded in obtaining a footing on the platform, and drove the privileged ones, *ladies and all*, through the Patent Office, – the door of which was kicked open, – into the basement, and from thence into the street; and then, as far as I know, quietly dispersed.

"The hoax was undoubtedly got up by some printer's *devil*, or other mischievous *boys*, who had the handbills printed and distributed. A great many people from the neighboring parts of the district were arriving during the day, and a number of vehicles and horsemen were on the ground. In fine, it was not a bad hoax – pretty well got up; but if it had been on any other day than Sunday, it would have been better."

From the 21st to the 29th of January, 1843, Mr. Miller lectured in Bennington, Vt. He then went to Philadelphia, Pa., and lectured in the large hall of the Chinese Museum, which was crowded to excess, from the 3rd to the 10th of February. On the evening of the 7th, a gentleman arose [179] and confessed that he had been an infidel, but could now praise God for what he had done for his soul. Many others followed, bearing testimony to God's pardoning mercy.

The interest attending the lectures continued to increase from the first till the evening before their close. On that evening the house was filled to overflowing at an early hour.

When the lecture commenced, the crowd and confusion were so great as to render it almost impossible to hear the speaker; and it was thought best, after notifying the people what was to be done, and giving an opportunity for all who wished so to do to go out, to close the doors, and thus secure silence. This was done, and the speaker proceeded to his subject. For about half an hour there was profound silence, and deep interest was evinced by the immense audience, with the exception of a few unruly boys. This would have undoubtedly continued, had it not been for the circumstance of a lady's fainting, and it becoming necessary to open the doors for her to go out. When the door was opened, there was a rush of persons who stood outside for admittance. As soon as this was done, and a few had come into the room, an unruly boy raised the cry of "Fire," which threw the whole assembly into confusion, some crying one thing, and some another. There did not appear to be any disposition on the part of the multitude to disturb the meeting; but all came from the rush and cry. The disorder arose more from the excited fears of the people than from any other cause. Order was again restored, and the speaker proceeded for a few moments, when another rush was made, and the excitement became so great within as to render it expedient to dismiss the meeting.

The police of the city were willing to do what they could, but there was nothing for them to do; for they could not govern the excited nerves of the audience.

On Friday morning the multitude were again assembled at an early hour for service, and Mr. Miller proceeded to answer numerous questions which had been proposed. A most profound attention was manifested until the meeting was about half through, when a man arose and wished to propose some questions, which interrupted the order of the meeting.

The owners became alarmed for the safety of the hall, and [180] ordered the meetings to be closed after the afternoon service. Although this fact was unknown except by a few persons, yet the room was literally packed with a mass of living beings, who listened with breathless silence to Mr. Miller's last lecture.

There had been no intimation given throughout of what had transpired to close the meetings, until he came to bid them farewell. There were then bitter tears and strong sighs. The announcement of the fact came unexpectedly. The appeal was melting beyond expression. Probably more than a thousand persons arose to testify their faith in the truth of the Advent near, and three or four hundred of the unconverted arose to request an interest in his prayers. Mr. Miller closed the services by a most feeling and appropriate prayer and the benediction. No blame was attached to the owners of the Museum for their course.

About this time it was announced, by a correspondent of Bennett's N. Y. Herald, that Mr. Miller had fixed on the 3rd of April for the Advent. This being industriously circulated, led Prof. Moses Stuart to say of "the men of April 3rd, 1843," "I would respectfully suggest, that in some way or other they have, in all probability, made a *small mistake* as to the *exact day* of the month when the grand catastrophe takes place, – the *1st of April* being evidently much more appropriate to their arrangements than any other day in the year." – *Hints*, 2nd ed., p. 173. The New York Observer of February 11, 1843, in commenting on this suggestion of Prof. Stuart, thought it sufficient "to quiet every feeling of *alarm!*" As remarks like these, and other equally foolish stories which are referred to in the following letter, met the eye of Mr. Miller, he thus denied them through the columns of the "Signs of the Times":

> "DEAR BROTHER HIMES: – At the request of numerous friends, I herein transmit to them, through you, a brief statement of facts, relative to the many stories with which the public are humbugged, concerning the principles I advocate, and the management of my worldly concerns.
>
> "My principles, in brief, are, that Jesus Christ will come again to this earth, cleanse, purify, and take possession of the same, with all his saints, some time between March 21, [181] 1843, and March 21, 1844. I have never, for the space of more than twenty-three years, had *any other time preached or published by me*; I have never fixed on any month, day, or hour, during that period; I have never found any mistake in reckoning, summing up, or miscalculation; I have made no provision for any other time; I am perfectly satisfied that the *Bible* is *true*, and is the *Word of God*, and I am confident that I rely wholly on the blessed Book for my faith in this matter. I am not a prophet. I am not sent to prophesy, but to read, believe, and publish what God has inspired the ancient prophets to administer to us, in the prophecies of the Old and New Testament. These have been, and now are my principles, and I hope I shall never be ashamed of them.
>
> "As to worldly cares, I have had but very few for twelve years past. I have a wife and eight children; I have great reason to believe they all are the children of God, and believers in the same doctrine with myself. I own a small farm in Low Hampton, N. Y.; my family support themselves upon it, and I believe they are esteemed frugal, temperate

and industrious. They use hospitality without grudging, and never turn a pilgrim from the house, nor the needy from the door. I bless God my family are benevolent and kind to all men who need their sympathy or aid; I have no cares to manage, except my own individual wants; I have no funds or debts due me of any amount; 'I owe no man any thing;" and I have expended more than two thousand dollars of my property in twelve years, besides what God has given me through the dear friends, in this cause.

"Yours respectfully,   WILLIAM MILLER.

"Philadelphia, Feb. 4th, 1844."

The almost unparalleled abuse to which Mr. Miller was subject, through most of the secular and some of the religious papers, during this period, called forth the following manly rebuke from the "Sandy Hill Herald," a paper published in Mr. Miller's own county:

"FATHER MILLER.

"While we are not prepared to subscribe to the doctrine promulgated by this gentleman, we have been surprised at [182] the means made use of by its opponents to put it down. Certainly all who have ever heard him lecture, or have read his works, must acknowledge that he is a sound reasoner, and, as such, is entitled to fair arguments from those who differ with him. Yet his opponents do not see fit to exert their reasoning powers, but content themselves by denouncing the old gentleman as a 'fanatic,' a 'liar,' 'deluded old fool,' 'speculator,' etc., etc. Mr. Miller is now, and has been for many years, a resident of this county, and as a citizen, a man, and a Christian, stands high in the estimation of all who know him; and we have been pained to hear the gray-headed, trembling old man denounced as a 'speculating knave.'

"Speculating, forsooth! Why need he speculate? He has enough of the good things of this world to last him through the few days which at longest may be his on earth, without travelling from city to city, from town to village, laboring night and day like a galley-slave, to add to a store which is already abundant. Who, that has witnessed his earnestness in the pulpit, and listened to the uncultivated eloquence of nature, which falls in such rich profusion from his lips, dare say that he is an impostor? We answer, without fear of contradiction from any candid mind, None! We are not prepared to say how far the old man may be from correct, but one thing, *we doubt not that he is sincere*; and we do hope that some one of his many opponents will take the pains to investigate the subject, and, if it be in their power, drive the old man from his position. It is certainly a subject worthy of investigation, and one fraught with momentous consequences; and no matter who the individual is that promulgates the doctrine, if he offers good reasons and sound arguments, drawn from the word of God and from history, we say he is entitled to his position until, by the same means, he is driven from it. Mr. Miller certainly goes to the fountain of knowledge, revelation and history, for proof, and should not be answered with low, vulgar and blasphemous witticisms.

"We like the following remarks, copied from an exchange, in relation to this subject:

"'MILLERISM. – This is the term by which the opinions of those who oppose the idea of a millennium, and maintain [183] that the end of the world will take place in 1843, are distinguished; and they are thus denominated because Mr. Miller first propagated it.

"'We certainly are not a convert to the theory; but we feel bound in duty to lift our voice in reproof of, and enter our protest against, the *infidel scurrility and blasphemous witticisms* with which some of our exchanges abound, and from which religious periodicals are not wholly exempt.

"'If Mr. Miller is in error, it is possible to prove him so, but not by vulgar and blasphemous witticisms and ribaldry; these are not arguments. And to treat a subject of such overwhelming majesty, and fearful consequences.– a subject which has been made the theme of prophecy in both Testaments; the truth of which, occur when it will, God has sealed by his own unequivocal averments – we repeat it, to make puns and display vulgar wit upon this subject, is not merely to sport with the feelings of its propagators and advocates, but is to make a jest of the day of judgment, to scoff at the Deity himself, and contemn the terrors of his judgment bar.'"

The "Pittsburg (Pa.) Gazette" also said:

"We do not concur with Mr. Miller in his interpretations of the prophecies; but we can see neither reason nor Christianity in the unmerited reproach which is heaped upon him for propagating an honest opinion. And that he is honest we have no doubt. True, we think him in error, but believe he is honestly so. And suppose he does err in his views of prophecy, does that make him either a knave or a fool? Have not some of the greatest or best men who have lived since the days of the apostles erred in the same way? And who will say that all these, including Whitby, Bishop Newton, and others of equal celebrity, were monomaniacs, and driven by a pitiable or culpable frenzy to the adoption of their opinions? The truth is, as we apprehend, that many of those who are so indecorous and vituperative in their denunciations of Miller, are in fearful trepidation, lest the day being so near at hand, 'should overtake them unawares,' and hence, like cowardly boys in the dark, they make a great noise by way of keeping up their courage, and to frighten away the bugbears." [184]

The editor of the "Countryman," in giving the Synopsis of Mr. Miller's views, added:

"The abstract of Miller's views, which we give on our fourth page, so far as we give it in this paper, is and has been, according to what we have been able to ascertain, the professed belief of orthodox Christians, from the day of Christ's ascension into heaven until the present hour. Therefore they are not merely Mr. Miller's views, but the acknowledged views of the Christian church, the received Bible doctrine; and if Bible doctrine, then are they the truth.

"One of the apostles, who shared as largely in the confidence and personal instruction of his Master as any, concludes a reference to this subject in these words: 'Wherefore, beloved, seeing that ye look for such things, be diligent, that ye may be found of him in peace, without spot and blameless.' 2 Peter 3:14. If the things here referred to have not taken place, – and who will say they have? – they, of course, are yet to transpire. If so, is not the caution of the apostle as important in this our day, as it was when he uttered it? And if it was an event to be looked for and hoped for *then*, should it be an object of less solicitude *now*? Every intelligent, free moral agent upon earth, whether aware of it or not, has an interest in this issue. He may absorb his mind in other matters, he may drown reflection in the whirl of business or pleasure, he may wrap his soul in projects of wealth or ambition, and fill his aspiring eye with the anticipated glories of some dazzling height, but his interest still cleaves to the immortality of his nature, and, sooner or later, he must discover that it is the most important interest ever presented to his consideration, or that is attached to his being or his destiny. Is it not, then, the height of wisdom to give heed to these things, and examine them with all that diligence and dispassionate attention their importance merits?" [185]

CHAPTER 14

*Mr. Miller And His Reviewers – Doctors Dowling, Chase,
Jarvis, Etc. – The Fourth Kingdom – The Little Horn – Prophetic
Numbers – Seventy Weeks – Coming Of Christ, Etc.*

As it will be proper to take some notice of the controversy between Mr. Miller and those who entered the lists against him, it may as well be referred to in this connection. As his views gained adherents, various publications of sermons, reviews, etc., were issued from the press – the design of which was to counteract his expositions of prophecy. Some of these were direct attacks on him, and others only indirect, by opposing the long established principles of Protestant interpretation. The controversy had respect principally to the following points:

1. The Fourth Kingdom of Daniel 7th chapter.
2. The Little Horn of the same.
3. The Little Horn of the 8th.
4. The Length of the Prophetic Periods.
5. The Commencement of the Seventy Weeks of Daniel 9th.
6. Their Connection with the 2300 days of Daniel 8th.
7. The Rise of the Little Horn of the 7th.
8. The Nature of Christ's Second Advent.
9. The Return of the Jews.
10. The Epoch of the Resurrection.

Mr. Miller laid no claim to *originality* in his position respecting any of the above points; but maintained that they were established opinions of the church, and, being so, that his conclusions from such premises were well sustained by human as well as by divine teachings. While his opponents attacked the view he took of these points, no one of them assailed the whole; but each admitted his correctness on some of the points; and, among them, the whole were admitted.

1. *The Fourth Kingdom of Daniel.* This he claimed to be the *Roman.* In this, he had the support of the ablest and most judicious expositors of every age. William Cunninghame, Esq., [186] of England, an eminent

expositor, in speaking of the four parts of the great image of the dream of Nebuchadnezzar, says, that they are "respectively applied by Daniel himself to *four kingdoms, which have, by the unanimous voice of the Jewish and Christian churches, for more than eighteen centuries, been identified with* the empires of Babylon, Persia, Greece, and Rome." Should this be questioned, the witnesses are abundant. In the Jewish Church, we have the Targum of Jonathan Ben Uzziel, Josephus, and the whole modern synagogue, including the names of Abarbanal, Kimchi, David Levi, and others. In the Christian Church, such as Barnabas, Irenaeus, Chrysostom, Cyril of Jerusalem in his catechism, Jerome, and according to him, all ecclesiastical writers, Hyppolitus and Lactantius in the early ages; since the Reformation, Luther, Calvin, Mede, T. H. Horne,[31] Sir Isaac Newton, Bishop Newton, Dr. Hales, Scott, Clarke, Brown,[32] Watson,[33] Bishop Lloyd, Daubuz, Brightman, Faber, Noel, Dr. Hopkins, and almost every biblical expositor of any note in the Protestant church. Those who make this application of the four parts of the image have no difficulty in making a like application of the four beasts of Daniel seventh. The remarkable similarity of the two visions requires this.

This long established opinion was controverted by Prof. Stuart of Andover, in his "Hints," before referred to. He said:

> "The fourth beast in Daniel 7:6, etc., is, beyond all reasonable doubt, the divided Grecian dominion, which succeeded the reign of Alexander the Great." – *Hints*, p. 86.

Prof. Irah Chase, D.D., said:

> "The fourth empire was that of the successors of Alexander, among whom Seleucus was preeminent." – *Remarks on the Book of Daniel*, p. 20.

Others, of lesser note, copied from these, and took a similar position respecting the fourth kingdom.

---

[31] See Introduction, vol. 1, p. 333; vol. 4, pp. 189, 191

[32] See Harmony of Scripture.

[33] Theol. Dic., p. 228

Of those who opposed Mr. Miller on other points, John Dowling, D.D., of New York city, in his "Exposition of the Prophecies," did not assail this.

Rev. W. T. Hamilton, D.D., of Mobile, Ala., in his "Lecture on Millerism," said: "I freely admit, that in his [187] general outline of interpretation (excluding his dates), following, as he does much abler men who have gone before him, Mr. Miller is correct. The several dynasties prefigured in the great metallic image of Nebuchadnezzar – in the vision of the four beasts, and of the ram and he-goat – Daniel himself points out. Mistake there is not easy." – p. 18.

Dr. Jarvis, D.D., LL.D., of Middletown, Ct., in his "Two Discourses on Prophecy," also applies the fourth beast in the same manner. – p. 42.

J. T. Hinton, A.M., of St. Louis ("Prophecies Illustrated"), said:

> "The dream of the image, the vision of the four beasts, that of the ram and he-goat, and the 'scriptures of truth,' give us four detailed descriptions of the history of the world, from the time of Daniel to the 'time of the end;' and the Apocalyptic visions refer to the same period as the latter portion of the prophecies of Daniel." – p. 25.

> "The dream of the image is of the greatest importance; it leaves *without excuse* those who would reduce the remaining prophecies of Daniel to the narrow compass of the little acts of the reign of Antiochus Ephiphanes. Nothing can be clearer than that the gold, the silver, the brass, the iron, and the clay, are designed to cover the history of the world in all its successive ages." – p. 27.

Again he says:

> "We think our readers will concur with us, and with the great mass of writers on prophecy, that the 'ten horns,' or Daniel's 'fourth beast,' and 'the beast rising out of the sea, having seven heads,' of the Apocalyptic visions, refer to the ten kingdoms into which the Roman empire was divided. Of the identity of the ten-horned beasts of Daniel and John there can be no reasonable doubt." – p. 232.

2. *The Little Horn of the seventh chapter of Daniel.* This he held to be the Papacy. This was no novel view of that symbol, being, as it was, the view of the whole Protestant world. See Dr. Clarke's Notes on 2 Thessalonians 2., Croly on the Apoc., pp. 113-117, Horne's Int., vol. 4, p. 191, Watson's Theol. Dic., p. 62, G. T. Noel, Prospects of the Church of Christ, p. 100,

William Cunninghame, Esq., Political Dest. of the Earth, p. 28, Mede, Newton, Scott, Daubuz, Hurd, Jurieu, Vitringa, Fleming, [188] Lowman, and numerous others of the best standard expositors.

Prof. Stuart, Prof. Chase, and others who applied the "fourth beast" to the four divisions of Alexander's successors, applied the little horn of the same chapter to Antiochus Epiphanes.

Mr. Hinton took the same view that Mr. Miller did of this symbol. He said:

> "If any other events of history can be set forth and made to fill out *all the particulars* mentioned by Daniel and John, we should be happy to see them stated; till then, we shall believe the little horn rising up amidst the ten horns, and having three of them plucked up before it, to refer to the rise of the Papacy in the midst of the kingdoms into which the Roman empire was divided in the sixth century." – p. 237.

Dr. Dowling, Dr. Hamilton, and others, who admitted that the fourth beast symbolized the Roman empire, also applied its little horn to the Papacy.

3. *The Little Horn of the eighth chapter of Daniel, that became exceeding great.* This Mr. Miller believed to be a symbol of Rome. In this view he was sustained by Sir Isaac Newton, Bishop Newton, Dr. Hales, Martin Luther, Dr. Prideaux, Dr. Clarke, Dr. Hopkins, Wm. Cunninghame, and others.

Dr. Horne said of the first three above named:

> "Sir Isaac Newton, Bishop Newton, and Dr. Hales, have clearly shown that the Roman power, and no other, is intended; for, although some of the particulars may agree very well with that king (Antiochus), yet others can by no means be reconciled to him; *while all of them agree and correspond exactly with the Romans, and with no other power.*" – *Intro.*, vol. 4, p. 191.

In addition to these, almost all the old writers who applied it to Antiochus Epiphanes did so only as the type of Rome, where they looked for the Antichrist. St. Cyril, Bishop of Jerusalem, in the fourth century, said,

> "This, the predicted Antichrist, will come when the times of the (Pagan) Roman empire shall be fulfilled, and the consummation of the world approach. Ten kings of the Romans shall rise together, in

different places indeed, but they shall reign at the same time. Among these, the eleventh is [189] Antichrist, who, by magical and wicked artifices, shall seize the Roman power."

Prof. Stuart, Prof. Chase, and even Dr. Dowling, with others, applied this symbol to Antiochus Ephiphanes.

Rev. R. C. Shimeal, of New York ("Prophecy in Course of Fulfilment"), dissented from Mr. Miller, and also from the foregoing, and understood this horn to symbolize the Mahommedan power. Mr. Hinton took the same view.

Mr. Miller was sustained in his application of this point by Dr. Hamilton and Dr. Jarvis. The latter said:

> "Sir Isaac Newton, with that sagacity which was peculiar to him, was the first, I believe, who showed clearly that this little horn was the Roman power." – p. 43.

4. *The Length of the Prophetic Numbers*. In explaining these, Mr. Miller adopted the Protestant view, that they represent years. There is probably no point respecting which Protestant commentators have been more agreed than this. Faber, Prideaux, Mede, Clarke, Scott, the two Newtons, Wesley, and almost every expositor of note, have considered this a *settled question*. Indeed, so universal has been this interpretation of these periods, that Professor Stuart says:

> "It is a singular fact that the great mass of interpreters in the English and American world have, for many years, been wont to understand the *days* designated in Daniel and the Apocalypse as the *representatives or symbols of years*. I have found it difficult to trace the origin of this general, *I might say*, almost universal custom." – *Hints*, p. 77.

He also says:

> "For a long time these principles have been so current among the expositors of the English and American world, that scarcely a serious attempt to vindicate them has of late been made. They have been regarded as *so plain* and so well *fortified* against *all objections*, that *most expositors* have deemed it quite useless even to attempt to defend them. One might, indeed, almost compare the ready and unwavering assumption of these propositions, to the assumption of the first

self-evident axioms in the science of geometry, which not only may dispense with any process of ratiocination in their defense, but which do not even admit of any." – *Hints*, p. 8.

Prof. Stuart, however, dissented from this "almost universal [190] custom,' and claimed that the prophetic days – the 1260, 1290, 1335, and 2300 – indicated only days. Of the 1260 he said:

> "The very manner of the expression indicates, of course, that it was not the design of the speaker or writer to be *exact* to a day or an hour. A little more or a little less than three and a half years would, as every reasonable interpreter must acknowledge, accord perfectly well with the general designation here, where plainly the aim is not statistical exactness, but a mere generalizing of the period in question." – *Hints*, p. 73.

Again he says:

> "A statistical exactness cannot be aimed at in cases of this nature. Any near approximation to the measure of time in question would, of course, be regarded as a sufficient reason for setting it down under the general rubric."

"By the 1260 days," he said, "no more than three and a half years literally can possibly be meant" (p. 75); and of the 2300: "We must consider these 2300 evening-mornings as an expression of simple time, *i.e.*, of so many days, reckoned in the Hebrew manner." – p. 100.

Prof. C. E. Stowe, D.D., of Andover, Mass., in his "Millennial Arithmetic," claimed that "*day* does not mean *year* in the prophecies any more than elsewhere;" and that "a definite designation of time was not here intended, but only a general expression." – p. 13.

Prof. Chase agreed with Prof. Stuart respecting the 1260 days; but said of the 2300: "The period predicted is *not* two thousand and three hundred *days*, but only *half* that number – 1150." – *Remarks*, p. 60.

Dr. Dowling agreed with Prof. Chase, that the 2300 were half days; but differed both from him and Prof. Stuart respecting the 1260, of which he says:

"I believe, as Mr. Miller does, and indeed most Protestant commentators, that the 1260 years denote the duration of the dominion of the Papal Antichrist. After comparing these passages, and the entire prophecies to which they belong, with the history and character of Papacy, I cannot doubt that this is the mystical Babylon, whose name is written in Revelation 17:5; and that, when the 1260 years are accomplished, then shall that great city, Babylon, be thrown down, and shall be found no more at all." – *Reply to Miller*, p. 27. [191]

Prof. Pond, D.D. (of Bangor, Me.), in his "Review of Second Advent Publications," was in doubt whether the periods of Daniel could be proved to be years; but was willing to cut the matter short by conceding the point that it may be so." – p. 22.

Dr. Jarvis, Mr. Hinton, Mr. Shimeal, and Prof. Bush, sustained Mr. Miller respecting the significance of the prophetic days.

In speaking of the application of the 2300 days to the time of the persecution of Antiochus Epiphanes, Dr. Jarvis says:

"This interpretation would, of course, be fatal to all Mr. Miller's calculations. It is not *surprising*, therefore, that it should be eagerly embraced by many of his opponents. But, with all due deference, I think there are insuperable difficulties in the way of this scheme, which makes Antiochus Epiphanes the little horn."

"I make no difficulty, therefore, in admitting the evening-morning to mean a prophetic day." – *Sermons*, p. 46.

He further says that Daniel was told to shut up the vision, "because the fulfillment of it should be so far distant; a strong collateral argument, as I understand it, for the interpretation of 2300 prophetic days." – *Ib.*, p. 47. And "The vision is the whole vision of the ram and he-goat." – p. 45.

Prof. Bush, in writing to Mr. Miller, said:

"I do not conceive your errors on the subject of chronology to be at all of a serious nature, or in fact to be *very wide of the truth*. In taking a *day* as the prophetical time for a *year*, I believe you are *sustained* by the *soundest exegesis*, as well as *fortified* by the high names of Mede, Sir Isaac Newton, Bishop Newton, Faber, Scott, Keith, and a host of others, who have long since come to *substantially your conclusions* on this head. They *all agree* that the leading periods mentioned by

Daniel and John *do actually expire about this age of the world*; and it would be strange logic that would convict you of heresy for holding in effect the same views which stand forth so prominently in the notices of these eminent divines."

"Your results in this field of inquiry do not strike me as so *far out of the way* as to affect any of the great interests of truth or duty." – *Ad. Her.*, vol. 7, p. 38.

Writing to Prof. Stuart, Prof. Bush said:

"I am not [192] inclined precipitately to discard an opinion *long prevalent in the church*, which has commended itself to those whose judgments are entitled to profound respect. That such is the case in regard to the *year-day* calculations of prophecy I am *abundantly satisfied*; and I confess, too, at once to the pleasure that it affords me to find that that which is sustained by *age* is also sustained by *argument*."

Again he says:

"Mede is very far from being the first who adopted this solution of the symbolic term, day. It is the solution naturally arising from the construction put, in *all* ages, upon the oracle of Daniel respecting the seventy weeks, which, by Jews and Christians, have been interpreted weeks of years, on the principle of a day standing for a year. This fact is obvious from the Rabbinical writers *en masse*, where they touch upon the subject; and Eusebius tells us (Dem. Evangl. 8, p. 258 – Ed. Steph.), that this interpretation in his day was *generally*, if not *universally admitted*."

"I have, in my own collection, writers on the prophecies, previous to the time of Mede, who interpret the 1260 days as so many years, and who are so far from broaching this as a *new* interpretation, that they do not even pause to give the grounds of it, but proceed onwards, as if no risk were run in taking for granted the soundness of the principle which *came down to them accredited by the* immemorial *usage of their predecessors*." – *Hierophant*, vol. 1, p. 245.

If the old established principle of the year-day theory is wrong, then, said Prof. Bush,

"not only has the whole Christian world been led astray for ages by a mere *ignis fatuus* of false hermeneutics, but the church is at once cut loose from every chronological mooring, and set adrift in the open sea, without the vestige of a beacon, light-house, or star, by which to determine her bearings or distances from the desired millennial haven to which she had hoped she was tending."

5. *The Commencement of the Seventy Weeks.* – These were believed by Mr. Miller to be weeks of years, – four hundred and ninety years, – and commenced with the decree of Artaxerxes Longimanus to restore and build Jerusalem, according to Ezra seventh, B. C. 457. This has also long been considered by commentators to be a settled point; and [193] it probably would not have been disputed were it not for a desire to avoid the conclusion to which Mr. Miller came, on the supposition that it was the beginning of the 2300 days. On so settled a point as this it is only necessary to mention such names as Horne (see Int., vol. 1, p. 336, vol. 4, p. 191), Prideaux (see Connection, pp. 227-256), Clarke (see Notes on 9th of Daniel), Watson (Theol. Dic., p. 96), William Howel, LL.D. (Int. of Gen. His., vol. 1, p. 209), Scott, and Cunninghame.

This point was not much questioned by any. A Mr. Kindrick, in a "New Exposition of the Prophecies of Daniel," said: "They are seventy years only, and commenced with the birth of Christ and ended with the destruction of the Jewish nation." – p. 4. Rev. Calvin Newton affirmed, in the Christian Watchman, that they were fulfilled in seventy literal weeks. And Prof. Stuart said:

> "It would require a volume of considerable magnitude even to give a history of the ever-varying and contradictory opinions of critics respecting this *locus vexatissimus*; and perhaps a still larger, to establish an exegesis which would stand. I am fully of opinion that no interpretation as yet published will stand the test of thorough grammatico-historical criticism." – *Hints*, p. 104.

Mr. Shimeal, while he admitted that they are weeks of years, commenced them four years later than Mr. M.

Dr. Hamilton sustained Mr. Miller on this point. He said:

> "The interpretation which Mr. Miller gives of Daniel's seventy weeks, commencing with the decree of Artaxerxes Longimanus, in the seventh year of his reign (B. C. 457), for the rebuilding of Jerusalem, and terminating with the death of Christ, A. D. 33, is, in the main, correct, because here Mr. M. but gives a tolerably faithful

report of the result of the labors of the learned Prideaux and others in this field of research." – p. 18.

This interpretation was not denied by Dr. Jarvis, Mr. Hinton, and Mr. Morris. And Dr. Dowling said: "Mr. Miller says the four hundred and ninety years begin B. C. 457, which is correct. He says they end A. D. 33, which is also correct." – p. 49.

6. *The Connection between the 70 Weeks and 2300 Days.* – This was a *vital* point in the chronology of Mr. M. to bring the end in 1843. The Rev. William Hales, D.D., [194] the most learned modern chronologer, says:

> "This simple and ingenious adjustment of the chronology of the seventy weeks, considered as forming a branch of the 2300 days, was originally due to the sagacity of Hans Wood, Esq., of Rossmead, in the county of Westmeath, Ireland, and published by him in an anonymous commentary on the Revelation of St. John, Lon., 1787." – *New Anal. Chro.*, vol. 2, p. 564.

He elsewhere calls it "the most ingenious of its class."

The argument which Mr. Miller used in support of this point was based upon the literal meaning of the Hebrew word, which, in our version of Daniel 9:24, is rendered "determined" – *cut off,* or *cut out,* – and the circumstances in which Gabriel appeared to Daniel, as stated in the ninth chapter, with the instruction given.

In the 8th chapter of Daniel is recorded a vision which was to extend to the cleansing of the sanctuary, and to continue 2300 days. Daniel had "sought for the meaning" of that vision, and a voice said: "Gabriel, make this man to understand the vision." Gabriel said to Daniel: "I will make thee know what shall be in the last end of the indignation; for, at the time appointed, the end shall be;" and then proceeded to explain the symbols, but said nothing of their duration. At the close of the explanation Daniel fainted, and was sick certain days; and he says he "was astonished at the vision, but none understood it."

Three years subsequent to that vision, Daniel – understanding "by books the number of the years whereof the word of the Lord came to Jeremiah the prophet, that he would accomplish seventy years in the desolations of Jerusalem," – set his face unto the Lord to seek by prayer and supplications, with fasting, and sackcloth, and ashes. He proceeded to confess his own sins and the sins of his people, and to supplicate the Lord's favor on the sanctuary that was desolate. While he was thus speaking, Daniel says:- "Gabriel, whom I had seen in *the vision* at the beginning, being caused to fly swiftly, touched me about the time of the evening oblation; and he informed me, and talked with me, and said: 'O Daniel, I am now come forth to give thee skill and understanding. At the beginning of thy supplications the commandment came forth, and I am come to show [195] thee; for thou art greatly beloved; therefore understand the matter and consider *the vision*. Seventy weeks are *determined*,'" etc., "from the going forth of the decree to restore and to build Jerusalem unto Messiah the Prince:" – after which Jerusalem was to be made desolate "until the consummation." – Daniel 9:20-27.

Dr. Gill, a distinguished divine and scholar, rendered the word "determined" *cut off*, and is sustained by good scholars.

Hengstenberg, who enters into a critical examination of the original text, says:

> "But the very use of the word, which does not elsewhere occur, while others, much more frequently used, were at hand, if Daniel had wished to express the idea of determination, and of which he has elsewhere, and even in this portion, availed himself, seems to argue that the word stands from regard to its original meaning, and represents the seventy weeks, in contrast with a determination of time (*en platei*), as a period cut off from subsequent duration, and accurately limited." - *Christology of the Old Test.*, vol. 2, p. 301. Washington, 1839.

Gesenius, in his Hebrew Lexicon, gives cut off as the definition of the word, and many others of the first standing as to learning and research, and several versions have thus rendered the word. [34] [196]

---

[34] A Hebrew scholar, of high reputation, makes the following remarks upon the word: "The verb *chathak* (in the Niphal form, passive, nechtak) is found *only* in Daniel 9:24. Not another instance of its use can be traced in the entire Hebrew Testament. As Chaldaic and Rabbinical usage must give us the true sense of the word; if we are guided by these, it has the *single* signification of CUTTING, or CUTTING OFF. In the Chaldeo-Rabbinic dictionary of Stockius, the word '*chathak*' is thus defined: –

Such being the meaning of the word, and such the circumstances under which the prophecy of the seventy weeks was given, Mr. Miller claimed that *the vision* which Daniel was called on to consider, and respecting which Gabriel was to give him skill and understanding, was *the vision* of the 8th chapter; of which Daniel sought the meaning, which Gabriel was commanded to make him understand, but which, after Gabriel's explanation, none understood; and that the seventy weeks of years – *i.e.*, four hundred and ninety that were *cut off* – were cut off from the 2300 days of that vision; and, consequently, that those two periods must be dated from the same epoch, and the longer extend 1810 years after the termination of the shorter.

The same view was advocated by several English divines. Rev. M. Habershon says:

> "In this conclusion I am happy in agreeing with Mr. Cunninghame, who says, 'I am not aware of any more probable era which can be selected for the commencement of the 2300 years than that which has been chosen by some recent writers, who supposed this period to have begun at the same time with the seventy weeks of Daniel, or in the year B. C. 457, and consequently that it will terminate in the year 1843.'" – *Hist. Dis.*, p. 307.

"'Scidit, abscidit, conscidit, inscidit, excidit' – *To cut*, to cut away, to cut in pieces, to cut or engrave, *to cut off*.

"Mercerus, in his 'Thesaurus,' furnishes a specimen of Rabbinical usage in the phrase chathikah shelbasar – 'a piece of flesh,' or 'a cut of flesh.' He translates the word as it occurs in Daniel 9:24, by 'præcisa est' – WAS CUT OFF.

"In the literal version of Arias Montanus it is translated 'decisa est' – WAS CUT OFF; in the marginal reading, which is grammatically correct, it is rendered by the plural 'decisae sunt' – *were cut off*.

"In the Latin version of Junius and Tremellius, nechtak is rendered 'decisæ sunt' – *were cut off*.

"Again: in Theodotion's Greek version of Daniel (which is the version used in the Vatican copy of the Septuagint as being the most faithful), it is rendered by συνετμήθησαν – *were cut off*; and in the Venetian copy by τετμήνται – *have been cut*. The idea of *cutting off* is pursued in the Vulgate, where the phrase is 'abbreviatæ sunt,' have been shortened.

"Thus *Chaldaic and Rabbinical authority*, and *that of the earliest versions*, – *the Septuagint and Vulgate*, – *give the* SINGLE SIGNIFICATION OF CUTTING OFF TO THIS VERB."

The celebrated Joseph Wolf, though dating the seventy weeks and 2300 days from B. C. 453, commenced them at the same epoch. – *Missionary Labors*, p. 259. And Dr. Wilson, of Cincinnati, who is high authority in the Presbyterian church, in a discourse on "Cleansing the Sanctuary," says:

> "I undertake to show that Daniel's 'seventy weeks' is the beginning or first part of the 'two thousand three hundred days' allotted for the cleansing of the sanctuary; that Daniel's 'time, times, and a half' is the last or concluding part of the 2300 days."

Prof. Stuart, Dr. Dowling, Prof. Chase, and others, who denied the year-day calculation when applied to the 2300 days, of course dissented from Mr. Miller on this point. Dr. [197] Dowling went so far as to *deny* (!) that the Hebrew article *hai* (the) is in the phrase "the vision," in the original of Daniel 9:23.

Of those who admitted the year-day theory, Dr. Hamilton, Dr. Jarvis, Mr. Hinton, and Dr. Pond, denied any connection between the two periods. Dr. Hamilton commenced the 2300 days B. C. 784, and ended them with the era of the Reformation, A. D. 1516. The others did not hazard any opinion respecting the time of their commencement.

Mr. Miller was supposed to be sustained on this point by Prof. Bush, who did not consider him in any serious error respecting the time. And Mr. Shimeal said, "I trust it will not be deemed a violation of that modesty which becomes me, if, for the reasons here given, I withhold my assent from the conclusion of the Rev. Dr. Jarvis on this subject; which is that the seventy weeks form no part of the two thousand three hundred days." – p. 34.

7. *The Rise of the Papacy – the Little Horn of Daniel 7th.* – Mr. Miller claimed that the one thousand two hundred and sixty years of the Papacy were to be reckoned from A. D. 538, by virtue of the decree of Justinian. This decree, though issued A. D. 533, did not go into full effect until 538, when the enemies of the Catholics in Rome were subjugated by Belisarius, a general of Justinian. In this view, as to the rise of Papacy, he was sustained by Croly (see his work on Words of Encouragement to Self-supporting Workers, 113-117); G. T. Noel (see Prospects of Ch., p. 100); Wm. Cunninghame, Esq. (Pol. Destiny of the Earth, p. 28); Keith,

vol. 1, p. 93; Encyclopedia of Rel. Knowl., art. Antichrist; Edward King, Esq., and others.

Prof. Stuart and Prof. Chase, in applying this little horn to Antiochus, and the beast of the Apocalypse to Nero, explained these numbers in days, satisfactorily to themselves.

Dr. Jarvis, who admitted that they symbolize years, denied Mr. Miller's commencement, without assigning any other. He said:

> "I would rather imitate the caution of the learned Mr. Mede, with regard to the time of the great apostasy, 'and curiously inquire not, but leave it unto him who is the Lord of times and seasons.'"

And of the 1260, 1290, and 1335 days, Mr. Dowling said:

> "If I am asked the question, – As you reject the interpretation [198] Mr. Miller gives of these prophetic times, can you furnish a better? I reply, *I do not feel myself bound to furnish any*"! – *Reply to M.*, p. 25.

Dr. Hamilton rather agreed with Faber and Scott, in dating from the decree of Phocus, A. D. 606.

Mr. Shimeal sustained Mr. Miller in dating from the decree of Justinian, but reckoned from the *date* of its *issue*, instead of from its going into effect. – p. 45.

8. *The Coming of Christ.* – Mr. Miller contended that this was to be literal and personal. This was the view which had been entertained by the church in all ages, and is recognized in the formulas of faith adopted by all evangelical churches. Whether his coming is to be pre or post millennial, is another question; but that Christians, in all ages, have believed that Christ will come again in person to judge the world, will not be questioned.

That Christ will ever thus return was denied by Prof. Stuart and Prof. Bush. The former said that he had "a deeper conviction than ever of the difficulties which attend the supposition of a *personal, actual,* and *visible* descent of Christ and the glorified saints to the earth." – *Hints*, 2nd ed., p. 153. Again: "All the prophecies respecting the Messiah are invested with the costume of figurative language." – *Ib.*, p. 183. And again: "Christ himself assumed a visible appearance," at his first advent, "only that he might take on him our nature and die for sin. When he appears a second time, there is no necessity for assuming such a nature." – *Ib.*, p. 185.

Prof. Bush gave, as his opinion, that

> "the second advent of the Saviour is not affirmed to be *personal*, but *spiritual* and *providential*; and that the event so denominated is to be considered as having entered upon its incipient fulfillment at a very early period of the Christian dispensation." – *Anastasis*, p. 9.

Mr. Dowling and others, who admitted the personal coming of Christ at the *close* of the millennium, claimed that the predicted reign of Christ on earth during that period is to be *spiritual*.

But Mr. Shimeal sustained Mr. Miller in his belief that the advent will be personal and pre-millennial. And Bishop Hopkins, of Vermont (Two Discourses on the Advent), [199] while he claimed that the time was not revealed, said, nevertheless, "we would admonish you, with still greater earnestness, to keep your souls in constant readiness for your Lord's advent, and in a state of sacred desire to behold him in his glory." – p. 29.

9. *The Return of the Jews.* – Mr. Miller looked for no return of the Jews previous to the resurrection of the just; and the righteous of that nation, who have died in the faith of Abraham, with all Gentile believers of like precious faith, he regarded as the subjects of all unfulfilled promises to Israel, – the fulfillment of which will be in the new earth, and in the resurrection out from among the dead.

That the promise to Abraham has reference to the resurrection state, is no novel or unscriptural view.

Rabbi Eliezer the Great, supposed to have lived just after the second temple was built, applied Hosea 14:8 to the pious Jews, who seemed likely to die without seeing the glory of Israel, saying: "As I live, saith Jehovah, I will raise you up in the resurrection of the dead; and I will gather you with all Israel."

The Sadducees are reported to have asked Rabbi Gamaliel, the preceptor of Paul, whence he would prove that God would raise the dead; who quoted Deuteronomy 9:21: "Which land the Lord sware that he would give to your *fathers*." He argued, as Abraham, Isaac, and Jacob had it not, and as God cannot lie, that they must be raised from the dead to inherit it.

Rabbi Simai, though of later date, argues the same from Exodus 6:4, insisting that the law asserts in this place the resurrection from the dead, when it said, "And also I have established my covenant with them, to give them the Canaan;" for, he adds, "it is not said to *you*, but to them."

Mennasseh Ben Israel says:

> "It is plain that Abraham and the rest of the patriarchs did not possess that land; it follows, therefore, that they must be raised in order to enjoy the promised good, as, otherwise, the promises of God would be vain and false." – *De Resurrect. Mort.*, L. i., c. 1, sec. 4.

Rabbi Saahias Gaion, commenting on Daniel 12:2, says: "This is the resuscitation of the dead Israel, whose lot is eternal life, and those who shall not awake are the forsakers of Jehovah."[200]

"In the world to come," says the Sahar, fol. 81, "the blessed God will vivify the dead and raise them from their dust, so that they shall be no more an earthly structure."

Of the early Christian fathers, Irenaeus, Eusebius, Chrysostom, Ambrose, Augustine, Jerome, and others, looked for no return of the Jews previous to the resurrection, though some of them convey the idea that the risen saints are then to be trained for a higher glory.

Luther, Calvin, and many other divines of the era of the Reformation, apply the promises to Abraham in a like manner; as do many divines of the present time.

Of those who entered the lists against Mr. Miller, Dr. Dowling, Mr. Shimeal, and Dr. Hamilton, strenuously contended for the return of the Jews in the flesh to Palestine.

Prof. Stuart sustained Mr. Miller so far as the question has respect to the true Israel, applying the promises to all who are of the faith of Abraham.

10. *The Epoch of the Resurrection.* – Mr. Miller held that the resurrection of the just will be pre-millennial, and that that of the wicked will be at the close of the millennium. This hinges on the interpretation given to Revelation 20:4-6. It is worthy of note, that during the first two centuries

there was not an individual who believed in any resurrection of the dead, whose name or memory has come down to us, who denied that a literal resurrection is there taught.

Eusebius admits that Papias was a disciple of John the Evangelist, and that he taught that, "after the resurrection of the dead, the kingdom of Christ shall be established corporeally on this earth." – [Hist. Lib. 3, Sec. 39.] And Jerome quotes Papias [De Script. Eccles.] as saying, that "he had the apostles for his authors, and that he considered what Andrew, what Peter said, what Philip, what Thomas said, and other disciples of the Lord." Irenaeus taught that at the resurrection of the just the meek should inherit the earth; and that then would be fulfilled the promise which God made to Abraham.

Justyn Martyr, who was born A. D. 89, seven years before the Revelations were written, says that he and many others are of this mind, "that Christ shall reign personally on earth," and that "all who were accounted orthodox so believed." He also says, "A certain man *among us*, [201] whose name is John, being one of the twelve apostles of Christ, in that Revelation which was shown to him, prophesied that those who believe in our Christ shall fulfill a thousand years at Jerusalem."

Tertullian, who wrote about A. D. 180, says it was a custom of his times for Christians to pray that they might have part in the first resurrection: and Cyprian, who lived about A. D. 220, says that Christians "had a thirst for *martyrdom*, that they might obtain a better resurrection," – the martyrs being raised at the commencement of the thousand years.

The first of whom we have any account that opposed this doctrine was Origen, in the middle of the third century, who styled those who adhered to it "the simpler sort of Christians." Mosheim assures us that the opinion "that Christ was to come and reign a thousand years among men" had, before the time of Origen, "met with *no opposition*." – *Ch. Hist.*, vol. 1, p. 284.

At the era of the Reformation this doctrine was revived, and taught by Luther and Melancthon; it is in the confession of Augsburg (A. D. 1530); was the belief of Latimer, Cranmer, and Ridley; is in the Articles of the Church (Ed. vi., A. D. 1552); is not denied in the more prominent creeds and confessions of faith of the churches, and was believed by Mede, Sir Isaac Newton, Bishop Newton, Milton, Knox, Bunyan, Gill, Cowper, Heber, Pollok, Greswell, and many other distinguished names of modern times.

This point was vital to Mr. Miller's theory, for, however correct he might be in his *time*, without this *event* he must fail in his application of prophecy.

Prof. Bush, while he admitted that all "the leading periods mentioned by Daniel and John do actually expire *about* this age of the world" (*Letter to Mr. M.*, p. 6), claimed that "the great event before the world is not its *physical conflagration*, but its *moral regeneration.*" – p. 11.

Mr. Hinton said:

> "It is possible we may have reached the goal of the world's moral destiny. It is, indeed, our deliberate opinion that we are in the general period of termination of the 23rd century alluded to by the prophet … and that the events alluded to in the phrase 'then shall the [202] sanctuary be cleansed' are now actually passing before us." – p. 121. But he considered the *event* "a resurrection from death in trespasses and sins." – p. 336.

Dr. Dowling, Dr. Hamilton, and others, while they did not admit, with Prof. Bush, that the present age "is just opening upon the crowning consummation of all prophetic declarations," contended that the millennium

> "is to be ushered in, not by a literal resurrection of the bodies of the saints, but by the figurative resurrection of the holy men of all past ages, in the numerous instances of eminent piety that shall appear in every nation under heaven." – *Dr. H.*, p. 30.

Prof. Stuart, while he admitted that the resurrection here brought to view was a resurrection of the body, limited it to the martyrs, and denied that there is to be a descent of Christ to the earth, or a *visible* reign of the martyrs with him.

Dr. Jarvis did not deny the event for which Mr. Miller looked; and Mr. Shimeal taught, with Mr. Miller, the resurrection of the glorified saints, and their visible reign with Christ on the earth; but he held that they would reign over the converted nations, and denied the conflagration previous to the end of the thousand years.

And Bishop Hopkins gave as his opinion that the consummation "is drawing nigh; how nigh none can tell."

There were various other issues between Mr. Miller and his reviewers; but they were more collateral than vital to the question at issue, and are not, therefore, particularly noticed in this connection.

It is seen, from the foregoing, that Mr. Miller's points, taken separately, were not new or original with him; and that the peculiarity of his theory consisted in putting them *together*; and that, while none of his opposers condemned the whole, and each point separately was admitted by some of them, there was no more unanimity among them, than between him and them. They had not only to battle with Mr. Miller's theory, but each had to disprove those of the others.

It was, therefore, not surprising that the reviewers of Mr. Miller made no impression on those who held his opinions. It was seen that to oppose him they were ready [203] to abandon old established principles of Protestant interpretation. Even the "Boston Recorder" (Orthodox Cong.) said:

> "It must needs be acknowledged that our faith is greatly shaken in the interpretations on which, in common with most of our own brethren, we have heretofore relied, and which forms the foundation of the baseless theories of Miller!"

And the "Christian Advocate and Journal" (Meth. Epis.) said:

> "If his (Prof. Chase's) views in regard to the prophecies of Daniel be correct, the long-established opinion, that the Roman empire is the fourth kingdom of the prophet, must give way to the more successful researches of Dr. Chase. Some other opinions, which have been thought to be settled beyond a doubt, are terribly shaken."

Those who adhered to the established principles of interpretation did not fail to perceive that Prof. Stuart, Dr. Dowling, and Prof. Chase, etc., had not fairly met Mr. Miller, and that their expositions would not stand the test of sound criticism.

Of Professors Stuart and Bush the New York Evangelist said:

"The tendency of these views is to destroy the Scripture evidence of the doctrine of any real end of the world, any day of final judgment, or general resurrection of the body. The style of interpretation, we assert, tends fearfully to Universalism. This tendency we are prepared to prove."

The Hartford "Universalist" said of Professor Stuart:

"He puts an uncompromising veto upon the popular interpretations of Daniel and Revelation, and *unites with Universalists* in contending that most of their contents had special reference to, and their fulfillment in, scenes and events which transpired but a few years after those books were written." – *Oct.* 15, 1842.

Mr. Hinton said of the same:

"We regret that, in the midst of the great moral conflict with Antichrist, which is now carrying on, those into whose hands the saints were so long 'given' should find so able a coadjutor. We have, however, no fears that Christians of sound common sense, and capable of independent thought, will, after a candid consideration of the scheme which excludes Papacy from the page of prophecy, and that which traces in the prophetic [204] symbols a faithful portraiture of its abominations, make a wrong decision. Since we have read the work of the learned Stuart, we have rejoiced the more that our humble abilities have been directed to the defense of the old paths." – *Proph. Illus.*, p. 231.

Of Mr. Dowling, Dr. Breckenbridge said:

"As for this disquisition of Mr. Dowling, we may confidently say, that it is hardly to be conceived that anything could be printed by Mr. Miller, or Mr. Any-body-else, more shallow, absurd and worthless. There is hardly a point he touches on which he has not managed to adopt the very *idlest conjectures* of past writers on the prophecies; and this so entirely without regard to any coherent system, that the only clear conviction a man of sense or reflection could draw from his pamphlet, if such a man could be supposed capable of believing it, would be that *the prophecies themselves are a jumble of nonsense.* Such answers as his can have no effect, we would suppose, except to bring the whole subject into ridicule, or to *promote the cause he attacks.*" – *Spirit of the 19th Century, March No.*, 1843.

Again he says, in speaking of "the general ignorance which prevails on this subject," that of it "no greater evidence need be produced than the fact that this pamphlet of Mr. Dowling has been extensively relied on, yea, *preached*, as a sufficient answer" to Mr. Miller.

On surveying the whole field of controversy, Professor Bush, while he claimed that the Spiritualists were nearer the truth, said of them:

> "They have not answered the arguments of their opponents, nor can they do it on the ground which they themselves professedly occupy in respect to a millennium. Assuming that that period is yet future, and its commencement of no distant date, the Literalists, or Adventists, bear down with overwhelming weight of argument upon them, maintaining that the Second Coming precedes and ushers in that sublime era. The Spiritualists say nay, but refuse to commit themselves to a defined position. All that they know is, that there is to be a millennium of some kind, occurring at some time, introduced in some way, and brought to an end from some cause; and that immediately thereupon the Lord is to descend from heaven, burn up the earth, raise the dead, and administer the judgment; but as [205] to the what, the when, the how, the why – on these points they rest content in *knowing nothing*, because of the impression taken up that *nothing is to be known*." – *N. C. Repos.*, 1849, p. 248.

Dr. Jarvis, in his sermons, was particularly severe on Mr. Miller, but afterwards did him ample justice, as in the following. He said:

> "Mr. Miller, in his eagerness to make out his scheme, absolutely falsifies the language of the Bible. He makes Jehoram to have reigned five years, where the Scripture positively says he reigned eight; and between Amaziah and Azariah, or Uzziah, he introduces an interregnum of eleven years, for which he has not even the shadow of an authority in the Bible. He quotes, indeed, chapters 14th and 15th of the 2nd book of Kings; and this may be sufficient for those who are ready to take his opinions upon trust. But, if you examine the chapters to which he refers, you will be astonished to find that there is not in either of them one word upon the subject." – *Sermons*, p. 55.

In his preface to his sermons Dr. Jarvis makes the following correction of the above. He says:

"It will be seen that in speaking of the curtailment of the reign of Jehoram, the son of Jehoshaphat, from eight to five years, and the introduction of eleven years of interregnum between the reigns of Amaziah and Uzziah, he has censured Mr. Miller in too unmeasured terms. These particulars he is bound to explain.

"It would have been easier, and perhaps more advantageous to the author, to have made the alterations silently, and omitted the censure. But would it have been equally honest?

"In preparing the introductory volume of his 'Ecclesiastical History,' he had carefully avoided reading modern writers on chronology, for fear of being biased by their systems. For this reason he had never read the learned work of Dr. Hales; and though familiar with Petavius, Usher, and Marsham, a good while had elapsed since he had consulted them on the parts of history connected with the prophecies. But these great writers being entirely silent as to any interregnum in the kingdom of Judah, the existence of such an interregnum was entirely a new idea to him. Mr. Miller quoted 2 Kings 14, 15, without mentioning the [206] verses from which he drew the inference; and it was not till the author had read Dr. Hales' 'Analysis' that he saw the correctness of that inference. If this admission gives Mr. Miller an advantage, he is fairly entitled to it. We cannot, for one moment, suppose that he knew anything about Dr. Hales or his work. As a plain, unlettered man, his perspicuity in reading his Bible, and *his Bible only*, is much to his credit; and we ought to consider it as giving additional force to the reasons assigned by Dr. Hales, that an ignorant man, as Mr. Miller confessedly is, should, from the mere examination of the Bible, have arrived at the same conclusion. The censure, however, in the sermon, holds good with regard to the reign of Jehoram, the son of Jehoshaphat (2 Kings 8:17; 2 Chronicles 21:5); but, being equally applicable to Archbishop Usher, should not have been laid particularly at Mr. Miller's door."

CHAPTER 15

*His Treatment Of Opponents – Specimens Of His Preaching
– Colloquial, Expostulatory, Expository, Etc.*

Mr. Miller did not consider that his reviewers always treated him and his arguments with the utmost fairness; and, in speaking of them, he sometimes retorted in terms of great severity. Considering his treatment, by the religious and secular press, and the contumely which was incessantly heaped on him, that he should, at times, manifest a degree of impatience, was more an occasion of regret than of surprise. Few men have been called to endure so great an amount of reproach as fell to his lot; and few could have endured it as he did. He was human, and shared in all the weaknesses common to humanity; but, whenever he failed to endure the smart of undeserved wounds with all the sweetness of gospel charity, no one more sincerely regretted it than he did; and his liability to err in this respect was with him a subject of many prayers and tears.

His severity, however, was often richly merited; and he [207] knew how to be severe, without being uncourteous. Those who used their learning to fritter away the plain meaning of Scripture, and to make it teach something which the common reader would never have perceived in it, – merely for the purpose of opposing his conclusions, – he had little inclination to spare.

In speaking of the 8th chapter of Daniel, and the question, "How long shall be the vision?" he says,

> "The answer is, 'Unto 2300 days.'"
>
> "'But,' says the critic, 'it is "evenings-mornings."'"
>
> "No matter: all men seem to understand it *days*; for it is so translated in every language with which we are acquainted at the present day. Therefore, this can never be made plainer, if this compound Hebrew word should be criticized upon until the judgment shall set. I am sick of this continual harping upon words. Our learned critics are worse on the waters of truth than a school of sharks on the fishing-banks of the north, and they have made more infidels in our world than all the heathen mythology in existence. What word in revelation

has not been turned, twisted, racked, wrested, distorted, demolished, and annihilated by these voracious harpies in human shape, until the public have become so bewildered they know not what to believe? 'They have fouled the waters with their feet.' I have always noticed where they tread the religious spirit is at a low ebb; it becomes cold, formal, and doubtful, at least. It is the mind of the Spirit we want, and God's word then becomes spirit and life unto us.

"'The words "*evenings-mornings*" convey to our mind the idea of days; thus this vision is 2300 days long,' says the reader.

"'Yes. But how can all this be?' says the inquiring mind. 'Can three kingdoms rise up and become great; from a small people become a strong nation; conquer all the nations of the earth, and then, in its turn, be subdued and conquered by a kingdom still more fortunate; and so on through three successive kingdoms, and do this in little over six years? Impossible.'

"'But God has said it, and I must believe. Now the only difficulty is in time.'

"'How can this be?' [208]

"'Very well,' says the dear child of God; 'I remember me: God says I must "dig for the truth as for hid treasure." I will go to work, and, while I am digging, I will live by begging. Father in heaven, I believe it is thy word; but I do not understand it; show me thy truth.'

"I had rather have one humble prayer of this kind, with an English Bible in my hand, than all the Hebrew, Greek, and Latin Bro. S. ever knew.

"The child then takes the word *day*, and compares spiritual things with spiritual, to find what his heavenly Father means by days in a figurative sense. The first text he lights upon is in Numbers 14:34, '*each day for a year.*'

"'May this not be it?' says the child.

"He takes hold of it by faith, carries it home, lays it up in his cell of sweets, richer than a lord, and again goes forth in search of more. He now lights upon Ezekiel 4:6: '*I have appointed thee each day for a year.*' He is now rich in very deed – two jewels in one cell. He does not stop to criticize, like a Stuart, and query, and reason himself out of common sense and reason too; but, Abraham-like, he believes, and lays up his treasure at home.

"'I see,' says the child, 'this use of days was so ordained by my Father in two cases; and two witnesses are enough. But I am not certain that I have a right to use these jewels in this place. I will go and beg, and dig again.'

"In this excursion he lights on Daniel 9:23-27: 'Seventy weeks are determined upon thy people.'

"'Seventy weeks of what?' says the critic.

"'I do not care a fig,' says the believing child, 'whether you call it *days* or *years*: I know how long it was in fulfilling.'

"'How long?'

"'Exactly four hundred and ninety years: from the decree given in the seventh year of Artaxerxes, four hundred and fifty-seven years before Christ, unto his death, thirty-three years after the birth of Christ, making exactly four hundred and ninety years, or seventy sevens of years of the vision.'"

Prof. Stuart having applied the days in Daniel 12th to the times of Antiochus, when the context shows that the resurrection will follow their termination, Mr. Miller said:

"Suppose Prof. Stuart had been a believing Jew, and [209] lived in the time of Antiochus, and had been of the same mind he is now, or says he is, and one of his brother Jews had come along and prophesied or preached that the Jews were to be a scattered and a peeled people, *dashed* and scattered among all nations, more than two thousand years, then to come; and suppose the professor had been then an expounder of the law and the prophets, and was called upon to explain this text as being then fulfilled, what would he say to his brother Jew, the prophet? He would say, as any man must say by him:

"'Sir, you are a false prophet; for God has told us plainly, in this very text, that, when this three and a half years are fulfilled under which we are now groaning, then our scattering or dashing will be accomplished – yes, and finished, too. So says the word. Therefore do you keep away from my flock of Pharisees, for I do not want my people excited by your false, alarming doctrine. Do you not see that, at the end of 1335 days, Daniel will stand in his lot? And do you not see, sir, that his standing in his lot means the resurrection? Read the first three verses of this chapter.'

"'Ah,' says the prophet, 'that does not mean the resurrection, but –'

"'But what?' says the professor.

"'O! I do not know – difficult to understand,' says the prophet.

"'I see,' says the professor, 'you are a Sadducee. You do not understand either the Hebrew or the Chaldaic, or the exegesis of the Scriptures. How dare you prophesy evil of this nation, when God hath spoken peace after these days? I say you are a Sadducee. I will have no fellowship with you. You must not come into my synagogue.'

"Would not this be the natural result of such a case? I leave it for the reader to judge.

"Or, suppose that the professor was now in controversy with a Jew, – a Sadducee, – and was under the necessity of proving the doctrine of the resurrection by the Old Testament, would he not put into requisition this very text, and prove by the same a resurrection unto eternal life; and, if he did not believe such plain and positive proofs as these texts would be, would he not consider him a poor, blinded [210] Sadducee? Let us be careful that our own mouths do not condemn us.

"If, then, these days can only end with the resurrection, it is impossible that these Scriptures can apply to Antiochus. And, as the rules which he has given us in his Hints are the same, in substance, which I was forced to adopt more than twenty years ago, I cannot believe that Antiochus Epiphanes is even hinted at from Daniel 11:14 to the end of the 12th chapter. And, if the prophecy does not belong to Antiochus, then he must acknowledge that the little horn can apply only to the Papal power; and must agree with nearly all Protestant writers that 'time, times, and a half,' are, together with the other numbers in this chapter, to be understood in a symbolical sense."

In writing, he sometimes indulged in a colloquial style. In the following he hints at an objection often urged against him, that he, being a farmer, should not presume to teach. He says:

"*As it was in the days of Noah, so shall it be in the days of the Son of Man.* They were eating and drinking, marrying and giving in marriage, until Noah entered into the ark. Methinks I can almost see the scenes of that day. See you not that elegant building yonder, near that ark of gopher-wood? That building was reared at a great expense, by the host, for the purpose of entertaining strangers who might come to visit that ark, and to ridicule and laugh at that old, white-headed man you see yonder pitching the ark. The host, you see, has become rich by the great gain he has made, from the furnishing of the workmen, citizens and strangers, with food and drink of the most costly kind. Look into the dining-hall of that establishment. See the table loaded with all the delicate viands of the season. See those bottles filled with the sparkling juice of the grape. See the host at his door, beckoning to each passer-by to enter and regale himself. Hear the conversation between the host and the stranger guest who has just entered his mansion:

"*Guest.* What great building is that in yonder field, on that eminence?

"*Host.* That is called 'Noah's Ark.'

"*Guest.* But what use is he going to put it to? It [211] seems to be built for sailing. Surely the old man does not expect to sail on dry land.

"*Host.* Yes; you are right. The old man says the world is coming to an end (Genesis 6:13), and he has prepared an ark to save himself and family; for all flesh will be destroyed by water, as he says.

"*Guest.* But how does he know this?

"*Host.* He says God told him.

"*Guest.* What kind of a man is he? He must be a great fanatic, I am thinking.

"*Host.* Why, yes; we think he is crazy a little; but you cannot discover it in anything else but his building that great ark, and neglecting his farm and other worldly matters. But what he has lost I have gained.

"*Guest.* A farmer, say you? – a farmer! Why did not God tell some of our 'mighty men, which are men of renown'? (Genesis 6:4.) A farmer, too! There is no truth in it. But do any believe him?

"*Host.* Believe him! No. We have other things to attend to, and cannot spend time to hear the old farmer. But we were all very much startled, no longer ago than yesterday; for the old man has been telling some that he had prepared rooms for the beasts of the field, and for the fowls of the air, and every creeping thing; and yesterday they came, two and two of every sort, and entered the ark, apparently of their own accord. (Genesis 7:8, 9.) This, you may be sure, startled us some; but the banquets and feasts of last night have dissipated the fears of all, and to-day things are as they should be.

"*Guest.* It is rather strange; yet it cannot be true. God will not destroy the world in the midst of this hilarity and glee, and in the height of all these improvements at the present day. Much, much of the earth remains yet to be cultivated and inhabited. Our western wilderness is yet to be explored and settled. Then the world is yet in its infancy – not two thousand years old yet; and you know we have a tradition that the earth is to wax old like a garment. It cannot be true, what the old man tells you. I will warrant you the earth will stand many thousand years yet.

"*Host.* Look! look! there goes the old fool and his family now, I dare say, into the ark. I remember me now, [212] the old man told us, four days ago, that, in seven days (Genesis 7:4-10), God would cause it to rain sufficient to destroy every living thing from the face of the earth. I shall have a chance to laugh at the old man four days hence. I told him to his face that, after his seven days were ended, he would be ashamed to preach any more, and we should have some quiet then.

"*Guest*. But do your priests let him preach in their congregations and societies?

"*Host*. O no! by no means; that is, none that are called respectable, or of the higher class. Why, sir, they held a meeting last night at my banqueting house. After the cloth was removed, and while the wine was circulating freely, old Noah was the subject of the toast. And it would have done you good to have heard their sharp cuts and squibs; it caused a roar of laughter among the guests. See, yonder come some of them now. Let us go in, and enjoy another treat. *(They go in.)*

"Ah, said I, were these scenes acted before the flood, and will it be so in the end of the world? And will the generation of the righteous not pass off until they behold these things acted over again? So says our blessed Saviour, *and so I believe.*

"Then shall 'heaven and earth pass away.' The righteous will pass off to meet their Lord, and the wicked be consumed to cleanse the world. Then will the prophecy in this chapter be fulfilled, and 'the word of God will not pass away.'

"Prepare, ye servants of the Most High, to render up your steward-ship. Ye scoffers, take warning; cease your revilings, your newspaper squibs, your bombast, your revellings, and your banquetings. And you, my dear reader, prepare! prepare! for lo! -

'He comes, he comes, the Judge severe;
The seventh trumpet speaks him near.'"

The foregoing will also serve as a specimen of his mode, at times, of addressing an audience. At other times he was very earnest and solemn. In arguing that we must be beyond the end of the 1260 days of Daniel and John, from the fact that the church is not now in the wilderness, he said: [213]

"Can we be mistaken in the fulfillment of this prophecy? Is the church now in the wilderness? And if you should respond, She is, – I ask you, When, then, was she out? Not in the apostolic age; for she was not more free then than now. And then, let me inquire, where are your twelve hundred and sixty years? They can have no meaning. O, Christian! I beg of you, believe in the word of God; do not, I pray you, discard time, any more than manner. Is it not selfishness in us to discard the set times which God has fixed, and not man? Where is our faith? Why are we so slow of heart to believe? Three times we have witnessed, – yes, in the lifetime of some of us, – the fulfillment of the 'time, times, and an half,' in the accomplishment of the 'forty-two months,' in the completion of the 'twelve hundred and three-score days,' and yet, O God, we refuse to believe! Shame on that professor who will not open his eyes!

"They tell us we cannot understand prophecy until it is fulfilled.

"But here it is three times fulfilled in this day in which we live. What excuse have you now, O ye heralds of the cross? Ah! say you, that is *your* construction; we are not bound to follow your explanations. No, no! But for ages you and your fathers have been telling us that these prophecies were true; and you have told us that when they come to pass we should know what they meant; and, although ages on ages have rolled their rapid course, yet nothing has transpired, as you will own; and we, if we should search, and find, as we believe, the prophecies fulfilling, and tell our reasons, you then can taunt us with a skeptic argument, – 'this is *your* construction,' – and then not dare to tell us what it means! Awake, awake, ye shepherds of the flock! Come, tell us why these things are not fulfilled. Deceive us not. You stand upon the walls, both night and day; then tell us what it means. We have a right to ask, 'Watchman, what of the night? Watchman, what of the night?' An answer we must have; or you must leave your towers. It will not do to answer us, 'I am under no obligation to tell you.' [35] Has Zion no better watchmen on her walls than this? Alas! alas! then we may sleep, and [214] sleep, until the trumpet's dreadful blast shall shake our dusty beds, and the last angel raise his hand and swear 'that time shall be no longer.' Why are you thus negligent and remiss in duty? If I am not right in my construction of God's holy word, pray tell us what is truth, and make it look more plain, – and will we not believe? Thus you will cleanse your garments from our blood, and we must bear the shame. What time of night? Come, tell us plainly. There are portentous clouds hanging over our heads; we hear the murmurs of the fitful winds; we see sad omens of a dreadful storm; and where is our watchman's voice? Your silence gives us fears that we are betrayed. Awake! awake! Ye watchmen, to your post! It is no false alarm. There are judgments, heavy judgments, at the door. 'Our God shall come, and shall not keep silence; a fire shall devour before him, and it shall be very tempestuous round about him. He shall call to the heavens

---

[35] Dowling's Reply to Miller.

from above, and to the earth, that he may judge his people.' How shall the fearful stand in that great day, when heaven and earth shall hear his mighty voice, and they that hear must come to judgment? Where will the unbelieving scoffer then appear? When God makes inquisition for the blood of souls, and when the under-shepherds stand, with their flocks, around the 'great white throne,' to have each motive, thought, word, act, and deed, brought out to light, before a gazing world, and tried by that unerring rule, 'the word.' – I ask you, scorner, jester, scoffer, how will you appear? Stop, stop, and think, before you take a fatal leap, and jest away your soul!"

In closing a discourse on the text, "We shall reign on the earth," he thus proceeds:

"We shall reign on the earth, says our text. Not under its present dispensation, but after it is cleansed by fire; after the wicked are destroyed by fire, as the antediluvians were by water; after the resurrection of the saints, and when Christ's prayer, taught to his disciples, shall be answered, *Thy will be done on earth, even as in heaven.*' When the bride has made herself ready, and is married to the bridegroom, he will then move her into the New Jerusalem state, prepared as a bride adorned for her husband, where we shall reign with him for ever and ever, on the new earth and in the new heavens; [215] 'and God shall wipe away all tears from their eyes, and there shall be no more death, neither sorrow nor crying, neither shall there be any more pain; for the former things are passed away.' Then the whole earth 'shall be full of his glory;' and then, as says the prophet Isaiah 54:5, 'For thy Maker is thine husband; the Lord of Hosts is his name; and thy Redeemer, the Holy One of Israel; the God of the whole earth shall he be called.'

"And then, my dear hearer, if you have had your heart broken off from sin; if you have by faith been united in spirit to the Lamb of God; if you have patiently endured tribulation and persecution for his name, – then you will live and reign with him on the earth, and this earth will be regenerated by fire and the power of God; the curse destroyed; sin, pain, crying, sorrow, and death, banished from the world, and mortality clothed upon by immortality, death swallowed up in victory. You will rise up in that general assembly, and, clapping your hands with joy, cry, 'Holy, holy, holy is the Lord God Almighty, which was, and is, and is *now come.*' Then you will be in a situation to join the grand chorus, and sing the new song, saying, 'Thou art worthy, for thou wast slain, and hast redeemed us to God by thy blood, out of every kindred, and tongue, and people, and nation, and hast made us unto our God kings and priests, and we shall reign on the earth, saying, with a loud voice, Worthy is the Lamb that was slain to receive power, and riches, and wisdom, and strength, and honor, and glory, and blessing.' And all who meet in that grand assembly will be then heard to shout, 'Blessing, and honor, and glory, and power, be unto Him that sitteth upon the throne, and unto the Lamb for ever and ever.' And methinks I can now see every one who loves our Lord and Saviour Jesus Christ in this assembly rising upon their feet, and in one united prayer of faith, crying, 'Come, Lord Jesus, O come quickly!'

"But you, O impenitent man or woman! where will you be then? When heaven shall resound with the mighty song, and distant realms shall echo back the sound, where, tell me, where will you be then? *In hell!* O Think! *In hell!* – a dreadful word! Once more think! *In hell!* lifting up your eyes, being in torment. Stop, sinner; think! *In hell!* [216] where shall be weeping, wailing, and gnashing of teeth. Stop, sinner, stop; consider on your latter end. *In hell!* 'where the beast and false prophet are, and shall be tormented day and night for ever and ever.' I entreat of you to think – in hell! I know you hate to hear the word. It sounds too harsh. There is no music in it. You say it grates upon the ear. But think, when it grates upon the soul, the conscience, and the ear, and not by sound only, but a dread reality, when there can be no respite, no cessation, no deliverance, no hope! You will then think, – yes, of this warning, of a thousand others, perhaps of this hour, with many more that are lost, – yes, worse than lost, – that have been squandered in earthly, vain, and transitory mirth, have been abused; for there have been many hours the Spirit strove with you, and you prayed to be excused. There was an hour when conscience spake; but you stopped your ears and would not hear. There was a time when judgment and reason whispered; but you soon drowned their cry by calling in some aid against your own soul. To judgment and reason you have opposed *will* and *wit*, and said '*in hell*' was only *in the grave*. In this vain citadel, in this frail house of sand, you will build until the last seal is broken, the last trump will sound, the last woe be pronounced, and the last vial be poured upon the earth. Then, impenitent man or woman, you will awake in everlasting woe!

"Be warned; repent; fly, fly for succor to the ark of God, to Jesus Christ, the Lamb that once was slain, that you might live; for he is worthy to receive all honor, power, and glory. Believe, and you shall live. Obey his word, his Spirit, his calls, his invitations; there is no time for delay; put it not off, I beg of you, – no, not for a moment. Do you want to join that heavenly choir, and sing the *new song*? Then come in God's appointed way; repent. Do you want a house not made with hands, eternal in the heavens? Then join in heart and soul this happy people, whose God is the Lord. Do you want an interest in the New Jerusalem, the beloved city? Then set your face as a flint Zionward; become a pilgrim in the good old way. 'Seek first the kingdom of heaven,' says Christ, 'and then all these things shall be added unto you.'" [217]

At other times his discourse was of the most mild and gentle kind. Thus, in speaking of the Church of Christ under various circumstances, he says:

"In tracing her history from the patriarch Abraham to the present day, we find her variable as the wind, and changeable as the weather.

"To-day, she is coming up out of the wilderness leaning on the arm of her Beloved; to-morrow, 'like a young roe leaping upon the mountains, and skipping upon the hills.'

"Now she is seen among the trees of the woods; next in a palace of silver enclosed in boards of cedar.

"There we saw her in the clefts of the rock; here we behold her in the broad way, in the streets of the great city.

"Again we find her among the foxes of the desert; and anon we perceive her seeking Him whom her soul loveth.

"She is asleep on her bed by night; and the same night the watch finds her in the city.

"Behold her Lord knocking at the door for admittance, while she is too indolent to arise and let him in. The next moment she is opening to her Beloved, but he had withdrawn himself. At one time the voice of her Beloved, sounding over the hills and echoing among the mountains like the roar of distant thunder, has no impression; next, the soft whisper of love gains all her attention.

"Here blows the rough north wind and strong south wind upon her spices, yet they put forth no fragrancy. And there the lightest breeze makes her roses blossom, and all the air is perfume.

"See her countenance to-day black as the tents of Kedar; and to-morrow comely as the daughters of Jerusalem, and fair as the purple curtains of Solomon. To-day she is 'a garden barred, a spring shut up, a fountain sealed;' to-morrow, 'a garden open, a well of living waters, and streams from Lebanon.' Now she is weak as a babe; a single watchman can 'smite, wound, and take away her veil;' and then she is courageous and valiant, 'terrible as an army with banners.' To-day she is made to keep another's vineyard; to-morrow she is realizing a thousand pieces of silver from her own. She is truly a changeable being, carried about by the slightest circumstances." [218]

The following extract from a discourse, is another specimen of this mode of address:

"'Come, and let us return unto the Lord; for he hath torn, and he will heal us; he hath smitten, and he will bind us up. After two days will he revive us; in the third day he will raise us up, and we shall live in his sight. Then shall we know, if we follow on to know the Lord; his going forth is prepared as the morning; and he shall come unto us as the rain, as the latter and former rain unto the earth.' – Hosea 6:1-3.

"The text to which I have directed your attention, in the above paragraph, is one of the richest and most interesting prophecies that was ever delivered to mortals by any prophet since the world began. Every word speaks, and is full of meaning; every sentence is a volume of instruction. No wisdom of man could communicate as much in as few words. It is a pearl of great price, lying deep in the waters of prophecy; it is a diamond, which will cut the film that covers the visual organ of the readers of God's word; it is a gem in the mountain of God's house, shining in the darkness, and the darkness comprehendeth it not. It puzzled the Pharisee, confounded the Scribe, and perplexed the Sadducee. It has, and will continue to have, the same influence on similar characters until the end of time. The great men of the earth will not stoop to its light, because it lies too low. The small men of the earth will not pick it up, for fear of ridicule from those above them. And now, dear reader, I am afraid you will go and do likewise, – either treat it with contempt or ridicule. But you will find, if you will examine, that in it is contained, -

"I. OUR DUTY TO GOD.

"'Come, let us return unto the Lord;' and, 'If we follow on to know the Lord.' Here is the whole duty of man, as clearly described as any crystal could make it. Repent, believe, and obey, are clearly inculcated. What better words could an orator make use of, to excite the minds of men to noble deeds of daring, than are here used by the prophet? 'Come' – he invites – 'let us' – he will go with them – 'return.' Ah! what a word – return! Traveller, have you ever wandered far from home, in a cold, unfeeling world, among strangers, among robbers, enemies, thieves, and hard-hearted worldlings? Have you been sick and weak, wounded and torn, spoiled and robbed, smitten and cheated, hated and reviled, and this, too, for [219] days, months, or years? Have you at last 'returned' to your family, your friends, your native land? Do you remember those familiar objects, as you returned – the way, the mountain, the hill, the valley, and the plain; the grove, the turn, the house, and the brook? Do you remember the tree, the rock, the barberry-bush, the gate and the post, the doorway and latch? 'O, yes,' say you; 'I remember, too, my beating and palpitating heart, and the falling tear which I stopped to wipe away from my blanched cheek, while my hand was on the latch. I remember how I listened to hear the loved ones breathe, although it was then in the dark watches of the night.'

"Thus tells the wanderer the tale of his 'return;' and in like manner could all the wandering sons of Zion speak of their 'return.' You, then, who have experienced these things, can realize the value of the word 'return.' And from my soul I pity the wanderer that never has returned 'unto the Lord;' to him that loved us, to him who died for us; more, vastly more, than mortal friends could ever do – he died. And so, say you, can fathers die for children, and mothers for their sons; children can give their lives, though rare the gift, to save the life of parents; husbands, and wives, and friends have fallen, to save each other from death. All this is true. But here is love greater than these; 'for while we were enemies Christ died for us.' Yea, more: he left his Father's presence, his glory, and that heaven where angels dwell; where he, the brightest star in all the upper world, stood highest; where seraphim and cherubim in glory cast down their crowns, and worshipped at his feet. 'He became poor, that we through his poverty might be made rich.' Again: he bore our shame, and by his stripes we are healed. He was buffeted for our offences, and despised by mortals, for whom he suffered in the flesh. He rose from death for our justification, and ascended on high, to intercede for sinners, and has sent down his Spirit to bring us wanderers home.

"'For he hath torn.' True, he suffers our sins to tear us, and those earthly powers, in whom we trust, to break our proud hearts, and, therefore, tears away our vain supports. He tears our affections from earthly things, that he may place them on a more enduring substance. He tears our [220] hearts from idol gods, that he may place them on God supreme. He tears our soul from the body, that we may no longer live in the flesh to sin, but depart in the spirit, and be with Christ.

"'And he will heal us.' Yes, he will heal us from all our backslidings, and love us freely for his own name's sake. He will heal us from sin, by showing us its deadly nature. He will heal us from worldly affections, by placing our affections in heaven. He will heal our hearts of idolatry, by the taking possession of them himself. He will heal us from death, by the resurrection from the grave.

"'*He hath smitten.*' God has so ordered, in his providence, that his children cannot have intercourse and association with men of the world, and with the kingdoms of this earth, but that persecution, or loss of Christian character, is sure to follow. The prophet is showing the present state of the church, while the tares and wheat are growing together. The children of God shall be smitten – meaning they shall be chastised, persecuted, ruled over. See the Roman power, from the days of their connection with the Jews until the present time, ruling over, persecuting, and trampling under foot the church of God. Our text is not only showing us our duty to God, but it teaches us the sufferings of the church, the dealings of God with her, and her final redemption; the first and second coming of her Lord; her final deliverance from death and all enemies, and her glorified reign.

"'*And he will bind us up.*' which is a promise of God, that, although the church should be torn and smitten, yet he would heal them, and bind them up. In due time he would gather them into one fold; he would bind up all their wounds, and heal them of all their maladies. He would visit their transgressions with a rod, and their iniquities with stripes; but his loving kindness he would not take from them."

An extract from his lecture on the parable of the "ten virgins." will close these specimens. He thus gives his understanding of what is denoted by their "trimming" their lamps.

"The world, for a number of years, have been trimming their lamps, and the wise and foolish have been engaged in translating the word of God into almost every language [221] known to us upon the earth. Mr. Judson tells us that it has been translated into one hundred and fifty languages within thirty years; that is, three times the number of all the translations known to us before. Then fourfold light has been shed among the nations, within the short period of the time above specified; and we are informed that a part, if not all, of the word of God is now given to all nations in their own language. This, surely, is setting the word of life in a conspicuous situation, that it may give light to all in the world. This has not been done by the exertions of Christians or professors only, but by the aid of all classes and societies of men. Kings have opened their coffers and favored those engaged in the work; nobles have used their influence, and have cast into the treasury of the Lord of their abundance; rich men have bestowed of their riches; and, in many cases, the miser has forgotten his parsimony, the poor have replenished the funds of the Lord's house, and the widow has cast in her mite. How easy to work the work of the Lord when the hearts of men are made willing by his power! But shall we forget those who have forsaken the land of their fathers, the home of their nativity, and have spent lonesome years of toil among strangers, – yes, worse than strangers, – among heathen idolaters, and the savages of the wilderness, in the cold regions of the north, and under the scorching rays of a vertical sun, among the suffocating sands of the desert, or in the pestilential atmosphere of India; who have risked their lives to learn a language, and prepare themselves to trim a lamp for those who sit in darkness and the shadow of death? No, we will not forget them; the prayers of thousands have ascended before the golden altar, morning and evening, on their behalf, and Israel's God has been their protector. Surely we may hope that these have oil in their lamps, who have sacrificed so much to bestow a lamp upon others. But remember, my brethren, the Lord he is God, and let him have all the glory. This is the time, and the same time that Gabriel informed Daniel, 'Many should run to and fro, and knowledge should increase.' This, too, is the same time when the angel flying through the midst of heaven had the everlasting gospel to preach to them who dwelt upon the earth. Here are Christ's words, fulfilled, where he says, 'And this gospel of the kingdom [222] shall be preached in all the world for a witness unto all nations; and then shall the end come.'

"2nd. It is plain, to any diligent observer of the signs of the times, that all the societies for moral reform in our world at the present day are parts of the fulfillment of the parable, giving more light. What of our Bible societies? Are not these trimming the lamp for millions of human beings? Thirty years past, more than three-fourths of the families in what we call Christian lands were without the lamp of life, and now nearly all are supplied. Many of those who sat in heathenish darkness then are now rejoicing in the light of God's book. And much of this has been performed through the instrumentality of Bible societies; and not only through the agency of the church, but political men, men of the world, the great men, merchants of the earth, and those who trade in ships, all who live under the influence of the gospel, – the 'kingdom of heaven,' – have engaged in the work. Will not the most skeptical acknowledge that this society has succeeded beyond the most sanguine expectation of its most ardent advocates? And is not this strong circumstantial evidence that the Bridegroom is near, even at the door?

"3rd. The missionary societies, of all sects and denominations, which have been established within forty years, have as far exceeded all former exertions of this kind as the overflowing Nile does the waters of the brook Kidron. See the missionary spirit extending from east to west, and from north to south, warming the breast of the philanthropist, giving life and vigor to the cold-hearted moralist, and animating and enlivening the social circle of the pious devotee. Every nation, from India to Oregon, from Kamtschatka to New Zealand, has been visited by these wise servants (as we hope) of the cross, proclaiming 'the acceptable *year* of the Lord, and the *day* of vengeance of our God,' carrying the lamp, the word of God, in their hands, and oil, faith in God, in their hearts. All classes of men are engaged in this cause, from the gray hairs of old age down to the sprightly youth of ten years. Who, then, can doubt but that the virgins, in this sense, have and are trimming their lamps, and the bride is making herself ready? 'Go ye out to meet him.'

"4th. The Sabbath-schools and Bible-classes are but a part [223] of the fulfillment of the parable, yet clearly an evidence that the virgins are now trimming their lamps. This system of teaching the young and ignorant took its rise between forty and fifty years since, at the very time that the Christian world were praying, and ardently praying, for the coming of Christ, before that part of the Saviour's prayer was forgotten, 'Thy kingdom come.' From a little fountain this stream of water has become a great river, and encompassed the whole land. Every quarter of the globe is drinking at this fountain or stream of knowledge, and the youth are taught to trim their lamps. And when the Bridegroom shall come may we not reasonably hope that the thousands of the young men and young women, who have assisted in giving light to others, may be found having oil in their vessels, and their lamps trimmed and burning, and they looking and waiting for the coming of their Master, that when he comes they may rise to meet him in the air, with ten thousand of their pupils, who will sing the new song in the New Jerusalem for ever and ever? Search diligently, my young friends, and see to it that ye believe in this word, 'which is able to make you wise unto salvation.'

"5th. Tract societies are of much use, and are an efficient means to help to trim the lamps. Like snuffers that take away the preventives to the light, so are tracts. They take away from the mind the prejudice that thousands have against reading the word of God; they remove those rooted and groundless opinions, which many have, that they cannot understand the Bible; they serve to excite the mind to this kind of reading; they enlighten the understanding in some scriptural truths; they are pioneers, in many instances, to conversion; they can be sent where the word of God cannot at first be received; in one word, they are the harbingers of light, the forerunners of the Bible. And in this, too, all men in this probationary state seem to be more or less engaged, from the king on the throne, down to the poor peasant in the cottage, writing, printing, folding, transporting, paying, or reading, those silent little messengers of the virgins' lamp. 'Then all those virgins arose and trimmed their lamps.' Has not God's hand been seen in all this? And glory be to him who hath disposed the hearts of men to work the work that God bids them, and to fulfill the blessed [224] word which he hath given them. This institution took its rise about the same time with the Bible society.

"6th. Temperance societies. These serve one purpose in trimming the lamps and preparing the way for the virgins to go out and meet the Bridegroom. Our world, twenty years ago, might be called a world of fashionable drunkards; almost all men drank of the intoxicating bowl, and thought it no harm. But when the lamp began to dart its rays around our tabernacles, it was found by woful experience that those who drank of the poisonous cup were totally and wholly unprepared to receive the warning voice, or to hear the midnight cry, 'Behold, the Bridegroom cometh!' No, 'they that were drunken were drunken in the night,' says the apostle. 'Therefore let us watch and be sober.' And Peter tells us, 'But the end of all things is at hand; be ye therefore sober, and watch unto prayer.' How foolish would it have been for a drunken man to be set on a watch, or a praying man to be found drunk! Therefore, in order that men might be in a suitable frame of mind to receive instruction at the close of this dispensation, and be in a situation to listen to the midnight cry, God ordered the virgins, and they arose and trimmed their lamps; and in all human probability thousands, who would have met a drunkard's grave if this society had not arose, are now watching, with their lamps trimmed and burning, ready to meet the Bridegroom at his coming. perhaps this temperance society is the virgins' last resort. The Judge stands at the door; go ye out to meet him. This society, like the others before mentioned, is a general thing, and all sects, denominations, and classes of men, are engaged in it, and it has an important influence upon all men who are in this probationary state, and who may be termed, as in our text, 'virgins.' This society is of later origin than the others, and seems to be a rear-guard to wake up a few stragglers which the other societies could not reach. And now, drunkards, is your time; Wisdom stands at the door and knocks; let go the intoxicating bowl; be sober, and hear the midnight cry, 'Behold, the Bridegroom cometh!' For your souls' sake drink not another draught, lest he come and find you drunken, 'and that day come upon you unawares and find you sleeping.' O, be wise, ye intemperate men! for they only went into the marriage who were found ready, [225] 'and the door was shut.' 'Then came also the other virgins, saying, Lord, Lord, open to us. But he answered and said, Verily, I say unto you, I know you not. Watch, therefore, for ye neither know the day nor the hour when the Son of Man cometh.' 'But the wise shall understand,' says Daniel 12:10.

"And now, my Christian friends, let me inquire, Are your lamps trimmed and burning? And have you oil in your vessels? Are you prepared for the coming Bridegroom? And are you awake to this important subject? What say you? If this parable, to which I have directed your minds, has reference to the last day and the coming of Christ; if the 'virgins' have reference to all men in the probationary state, and dividing them into two classes, wise and foolish; if the 'lamp' is the word of God, and 'oil' means faith in his word, or grace in the heart, as some say, – then my conclusions are just, and the evidence is strong that we live at the end of the gospel kingdom, and upon the threshold of the glorified state of the righteous. Then examine your Bibles, and if you can more fairly prove any other exposition of this parable than I have this, then believe yours, and time must settle the issue; but if you can find nothing in the Scriptures to controvert plainly my explanation, then believe, and prepare to meet the Bridegroom; for, behold, he cometh! Awake, ye fathers and mothers in Zion! ye have long looked and prayed for this day. Behold the signs! He is near, even at the door. And, ye children of God, lift up your heads and rejoice, for your redemption draweth nigh. For these things have begun to come to pass. And, ye little lambs of the flock, remember, Jesus has promised to carry you in his arms, and that he will come and take you to himself, that where he is there ye may be also. But remember, all of you, the wise had oil in their lamps, and they were trimmed and burning. Search deep; examine yourselves closely; be not deceived; and may the Spirit, which searcheth all things, and knoweth what is in the mind of man, assist you.

"But, my impenitent friends, what shall I say to you? Shall I say, as the Master in the parable, 'Behold, the Bridegroom cometh: go ye out to meet him'? Prepare to meet your Judge. Now he has given you a time for repentance; [226] you have a probationary season, and possibly now the sceptre of mercy is held out to you. Repent, or it will soon be said to you, as Jeremiah said to the virgin, the daughter of Egypt, 'In vain shalt thou use many medicines; for thou shalt not be cured;' or, as in the parable, 'I know you not.' Have you no oil in your lamps?

Delay not a moment; believe the gospel, and you will live; believe the word of God; receive the love of the Bridegroom, and make no delay; for while they went to buy, the Bridegroom came; and they that were ready went in with him to the marriage, and the door was shut. O, think what must be the exercise of your minds when these things shall be real; when you will stand without and knock, saying, 'Lord, Lord, open to us!' Again I ask, will you repent, believe, and be saved? Are you determined to resist the truth until it is too late? Say, sinner, what think ye?

"'We will risk the consequence. We do not believe in your day you tell us of. The world is the same it always was, – no change, nor ever will be; but if it should come, it will not this ten thousand years, – not in our day, certainly. You do not believe yourself. If you did, we should call you a fool.'

"Are these your arguments, sinner?

"'Yes.'

"Well, if I had brought no more, no stronger arguments than these, I would not blame you for not believing, for not one of yours can you or have you supported with a particle of proof. They are mere assertions; your believing or not believing will not alter the designs of God. The antediluvians believed not. The citizens of the plain laughed at the folly of Lot. And where are they now? Suffering the vengeance of eternal fire." [227]

CHAPTER 16

His Sickness – Visit To Massachusetts – Fanaticism
– Mr. Miller Repudiates It

At the close of his lectures in Philadelphia, Mr. Miller went to Trenton, N. J., to spend the Sabbath (February 12, 1843). By invitation of the mayor of that city, he lectured there three days, and was listened to by crowded houses.

From Trenton he returned to New York city, but held no public meeting there. He improved the opportunity to visit a brother at Williamsburg, Long Island, where he had an interview with the editor of the "Gazette and Advertiser," who thus referred to it:

> "Our curiosity was recently gratified by an introduction to this gentleman, who has probably been an object of more abuse, ridicule and blackguardism, than any other man now living. A large number of the veracious editors of the political and religious newspapers have assured us that Mr. Miller was totally insane, and sundry preachers had confirmed this assurance. We were somewhat surprised to hear him converse on religious subjects with a coolness and soundness of judgment which made us whisper to ourselves,

> 'If this be madness, then there is method in 't.'

> "When our interview closed, we were left wondering at the cause of that malignant spirit of slander and falsehood with which a man has been assailed, who has spent his time and substance in a course of unceasing toils to persuade men 'to flee from the wrath to come.'"

From New York, Mr. M. went up the Hudson river as far as Lansingburg, N. Y., where he lectured from the 17th to the 21st of February. The day following, in compliance with the urgent request of the Baptist church in Half Moon, N. Y., he visited that place, and commenced a course of lectures, which continued till the 5th of March.

At the request of Mr. Davis, pastor of the Presbyterian church in Ballston Centre, Mr. M. next lectured in his house from the 6th to the

11th of March; and, on the 12th, [228] gave two discourses at the Spa. As usual, a large number were present, and God's blessing was manifested.

On the 15th of March, he delivered two discourses at Rock City, in the town of Milton, N. Y., about six miles from Saratoga Springs. He had attempted to go as far as Albany, to fulfill an engagement there; but, after getting within fourteen miles of that city, he was obliged to return to Rock City, where he was taken sick with his old complaint, erysipelas, in his right arm. He remained at the house of Dea. Dubois, where he received the kindest attention, till the 23rd of March. On that day he was removed to the house of Herman Thomas, in the same place. He was carefully provided for there till the 30th, when he was so far convalescent as to be removed by his son. By short and easy journeys he reached his home at Low Hampton on the 31st, as comfortably as could have been hoped for.

On the 6th of April he commenced a letter to Mr. Himes, in which he says: "I am now at home; was brought home six days since. I am very weak in body, but, blessed be God! my mind, faith, and hope, are yet strong in the Lord, – no wavering in my belief that I shall see Christ this year," etc. This letter not being completed on the 13th of April, his son forwarded it to Mr. Himes, adding, "father is quite low and feeble, and we fear he may be no better."

His complaint manifested itself in a multiplicity and succession of carbuncle boils, which were a great drain on his system, and wasted his strength rapidly. On the 3rd of May, when their violence had greatly abated, he wrote: "My health is on the gain, as my folks would say. I have now *only* twenty-two boils, from the bigness of a grape to a walnut, on my shoulder, side, back, and arms. I am truly afflicted, like Job, and have about as many comforters, only they do not come to see me, as Job's did." Two weeks later, he was again much more feeble, and his physicians prohibited visitors from seeing him.

On the 28th of May, his son wrote: "Father's health is no better, on the whole. He continues very weak and low, confined to his bed most of the time." In addition to his numerous boils, he had, by a fever, been brought near to death's door.

About the 1st of July he was so far recovered as to be [229] able to walk about his house, and his health continued to improve, so that, from the 6th to the 9th of September, he gave a course of lectures in N. Springfield, Vt. He lectured in Claremont, N. H., on the 11th; in Springfield, N. H., on the 12th; in Wilmot, N. H., on the 14th; in Andover, N. H., on the 17th; in Franklin, N. H., on the 18th; in Guilford, N. H., from the 21st to the 24th; in Gilmanton, N. H., on the 25th; and at Concord, N. H., on the 26th and 27th. On the 2nd of October he gave two addresses at the camp-meeting in Exeter, N. H., and arrived at Lowell, Mass., on the 3rd. He went to Boston on the 6th, gave three discourses, and then returned home to Low Hampton, where he remained till the 9th of November.

During this tour, Mr. Miller was much pained by witnessing a tendency to fanaticism on the part of some who held to his views. As he had no sympathy for anything of the kind, and has been unjustly identified with it in the minds of the public, it becomes necessary to show its origin, that its responsibility may rest where it rightly belongs.

The views of Mr. Miller being embraced by persons belonging to various religious denominations, it was impossible, from the nature of the case, for those of any particular faith to teach their own private opinions in connection with the Advent, without exciting the jealousy of those who held opposite sentiments. To avoid any such clashing of opinions, the following platform was adopted by the first conference held by believers in the Advent (October 14, 1840), in their Address unanimously presented to the public, namely:

> "Our object in assembling at this time, our object in addressing you, and our object in other efforts, separate and combined, on the subject of the kingdom of heaven at hand, is to revive and restore this ancient faith, to renew the ancient landmarks, to 'stand in the way, and see and ask for the old paths, where is the good way' in which our fathers walked, and the martyrs 'found rest to their souls.' We have no purpose to distract the churches with any new inventions, or to get ourselves a name by starting another sect among the followers of the Lamb. We neither condemn nor rudely assail others of a faith different from our own, nor dictate in matters of conscience for our brethren, [230] nor seek to demolish their organizations, nor build new ones of our own; but simply to express our convictions, like Christians, with the reasons

for entertaining them, which have persuaded us to understand the word and promises, the prophecies and the gospel of our Lord, as the first Christians, the primitive ages of the church, and the profoundly learned and intelligent reformers, have unanimously done, in the faith and hope that the Lord will come quickly in his glory, to fulfill all his promises in the resurrection of the dead.

"We are agreed and harmonize with the published creed of the Episcopal, Dutch Reformed, Presbyterian, and Methodist churches, together with the Cambridge Platform of the Congregational church, and the Lutheran and the Roman Catholic churches, in maintaining that Christ's second and only coming now will be to judge the world at the last day.

"We are not of those who sow discord among brethren, who withdraw from the fellowship of the churches, who rail at the office of the ministry, and triumph in the exposure of the errors of a secular and apostate church, and who count themselves holier than others, or wiser than their fellows. The gracious Lord has opened to us wondrous things in his word, whereof we are glad, and in view of which we rejoice with fear and trembling. We reverently bless his name, and we offer these things, with the right hand of our Christian fellowship and union, to all disciples of our common Lord, of every sect and denomination, praying them, by the love of the crucified Jesus, to regard the promise of his coming, and to cultivate the love of his appearing, and to sanctify themselves in view of his approaching with power and great glory; although they conscientiously differ from us in minor points of faith, or reject some of the peculiarities which exist in individuals of this Conference.

"We do not seek to excite the prejudices of our fellowmen, or to join with those who mock at sin, or who scoff at the word or promise of the great Jehovah, or who lightly esteem offices and ordinances of the church, or who empty of their power the threatenings of the holy law, or who count the blood of the atonement a useless thing, or who refuse to worship and honor the Son of God even as they [231] honor the Father; nor do we refuse any of these, or others of divers faith, whether Roman or Protestant, who receive and heartily embrace the doctrine of the Lord's coming in his kingdom; for experience and reason unite to teach, in the words of the apostle, that 'every man's work shall be made manifest, for the day shall declare it;' and the vivid apprehension of its approach tries and consumes the wood, and hay, and stubble, among our opinions, and we all become, by gentle necessity, the lambs of one flock, and are led into one fold, under the hand of the Chief Shepherd and Bishop of souls."

It was thus unanimously agreed, that the sectarian questions which divide Christians should be avoided in the presentation of the Advent doctrine, and that "minor points of faith," and the "peculiarities" in the belief of any, should not be made prominent, to impede their united labors.

In the autumn of 1842, Mr. Miller's views were embraced by John Starkweather, a graduate of the Andover Theological Seminary, and a minister of good standing in the Orthodox Congregational denomination. He had been a minister at the Marlboro' Chapel, in Boston, and at other places, and was regarded as a man of peculiar sanctity. He was, at that time, unemployed by any people, and Elder Himes being obliged to spend much of his time in preaching in other places than Boston, Mr. Starkweather was called as an assistant pastor of his church, at the chapel in Chardonstreet.

Mr. Starkweather commenced his labors there in October, 1842. He was tall, well formed, and had a voice of great power and not unpleasant tones. His personal appearance was thus prepossessing, which, with his reputation for superior sanctity, enabled him easily to secure the confidence of his hearers, who nightly thronged the chapel.

His principal theme was the necessity of a preparation for the Saviour's coming. At such a time no subject seemingly could be more appropriate. But Mr. Starkweather had embraced peculiar views respecting personal sanctification; and, contrary to the understanding which had been had on the subject of sectarian views, he made his own notions not only a test of readiness for the Lord's coming, but of Christian fellowship, – demanding the largest liberty [232] for himself, and granting none to others. He taught that conversion, however full and thorough, did not fit one for God's favor without a second work; and that this second work was usually indicated by some bodily sensation.

During the winter, the losing of strength and other cataleptic and epileptic phenomena became manifested, and were hailed by him as evidences of the great power of God in the sanctification of those who were already devoted Christians. He denominated such "the sealing power."

These manifestations were new to a majority of his hearers. Some looked on in wonder and awe, while others were suspicious of the new development, but feared to "offend against the Holy Ghost," as dissent from it was termed; and those who were favorably impressed were anxious to experience on themselves the "sealing power."

Those who were familiar with the history of fanaticism in past ages, who had read with pain the termination of the career of the eloquent Edward Irving in England, who knew the devastation caused by fanaticism in the time of the Reformation, of its effects in the early ages of Christianity, and of the results produced by it even in many portions of our own country during the infancy of some of the sects among us, were at no loss respecting its character.

It was at first supposed that Mr. Starkweather was an innocent cause of this, and that he was ignorant of his strong mesmeric powers, by which he had obtained a sympathetic influence over some of his hearers. He was reasoned with on the subject, but to no purpose. His mind was bent in a certain direction, and pursue his course he would. His actual spirit was not discovered until leading brethren publicly dissented from such exercises as any necessary part of Christianity. At this the uncaged lion was aroused, and it became evident what manner of spirit he was of.

Near the close of April, 1843, it was deemed necessary to take a decided stand on the subject. A meeting had been appointed for the afternoon, and Mr. Himes, who had been absent during these occurrences, with judicious brethren determined to endeavor to stem the current of fanaticism which had commenced. In a calm and faithful manner, he gave them the history of various movements which had been destroyed or greatly injured by fanaticism; and, without [233] intimating that evidences of such then existed, he exhorted them to learn from past experience, and see to it that they avoid the rocks on which others had been shipwrecked.

Mr. Starkweather arose in reply, and was so vehement that Mr. Himes felt justified in again addressing the audience, exposing the nature of the exercises that had appeared among them, and their pernicious tendency.

This so shocked the sensibilities of those who regarded them as the "great power of God," that they cried out and stopped their ears. Some jumped upon their feet, and some ran out of the house. "You will drive out the Holy Ghost!" cried one. "You are throwing on cold water!" said another.

"Throwing on cold water!" said Mr. Himes; "I would throw on the Atlantic Ocean before I would be identified with such abominations as these, or suffer them in this place unrebuked."

Starkweather immediately announced that "the saints" would thenceforth meet at another place than the Chardonstreet Chapel; and, retiring, his followers withdrew with him.

From this time he was the leader of a party, held separate meetings, and, by extending his visits to other places, he gained a number of adherents. He was not countenanced by the friends of Mr. Miller; but the public identified him and his movement with Mr. Miller and his.

This was most unjust to Mr. Miller; but to this day the Romanists identify, in the same manner the fanaticism consequent on the Reformation, with Luther and those who repudiated the doings of Munzer, Storch and others.

While Starkweather was thus repudiated, he persisted in forcing himself, wherever he could, upon the public, as a religious teacher and lecturer on the Advent.

On the 9th of August, 1843, a camp-meeting commenced at Plainfield, Ct., at which Starkweather was, and some manifestations were exhibited which were entirely new to those present, and for which they could not account. Another meeting was held at Stepney, near Bridgeport, on the 28th of the same month, where the developments were more marked. A few young men, professing to have the gift of discerning spirits, were hurried into great extravagances. [234] Elder J. Litch published a protest against such exhibitions, in which he said:

> "A more disgraceful scene, under the garb of piety, I have rarely witnessed. For the last ten years I have come in contact nearly every year, more or less, with the same spirit, and have marked its developments, its beginning, and its result; and am now prepared to say that it is evil, and only evil, and that continually. I have uniformly opposed it wherever it has made its appearance, and as uniformly have been denounced as being opposed to the power of God, and as resisting the operations of the Spirit. The origin of it, is the idea that the individuals thus exercised are entirely under the influence of the Spirit of God, are his children, and that he will not deceive them and

lead them astray; hence every impulse which comes upon them is yielded to as coming from God, and, following it, there is no length of fanaticism to which they will not go." – *Midnight Cry*, Sept. 14, 1843.

This fanaticism was the result of Starkweather's teaching that "gifts" were to be restored to the church. Even he seemed at first amazed at the results.

As a specimen of the hallucination, a young man by the name of M---- imagined that he had power to hold the cars from moving on the railroad, by the mere effort of his will. As they were about starting, he said: "Don't you go." The wheels of the locomotive made several revolutions before the heavy train started. "Now go," said he; and it moved. "There!" said he, "did I not stop the train?"

Returning home, "Father," said he, "do you believe I have the power of God?"

"Yes," said the father, who had been fascinated at the meeting.

"Well, then, drive the horse on to that rock by the roadside;" and he was obeyed, somewhat to their discomfort.

On the 13th of September, another meeting was held at Windsor, Ct. The same spirit appeared there, and is described by Elder L. C. Collins in the Signs of the Times, September 27, 1843. One female, believing that, as Peter walked on the sea by faith, so she by faith might walk across the Connecticut river, resolved to make the attempt, but [235] was prevented. They kept the meeting in confusion an hour or more, and would listen to no remonstrances.

During Mr. Miller's confinement by his sickness, he had not come in contact with any of these things; but, on his last tour into Massachusetts, he had seen something of it, and took the earliest opportunity to do his duty respecting it, by a prompt disclaimer. Before reaching home, he stopped a day at Castleton, Vt., and wrote the following letter, which was published in the Signs of the Times, November 8, 1843:

"DEAR BROTHER:- My heart was deeply pained, during my tour east, to see in some few of my former friends a proneness to wild and foolish extremes and vain delusions, such as working miracles, discerning of spirits, vague and loose views on sanctification, etc.

"As it respects the working of miracles, I have no faith in those who pretend beforehand that they can work miracles. See Revelation 13:13, 14: 'And he doeth great wonders, so that he maketh fire come down from heaven on the earth in the sight of men. And deceiveth them that dwell on the earth by the means of those miracles which he had power to do in the sight of the beast.' Whenever God has seen fit to work miracles, the instruments have seemingly been unconscious of having the power, until the work was done. They have, in no instance that I recollect, proclaimed as with a trumpet that they could or would work a miracle. Moses and the apostles were more *modest* than these modern pretenders to this power. You may depend upon it, whosoever claims the power has the spirit of Antichrist. Revelation 16:14: 'For they are the spirit of devils, working miracles, which go forth to the kings of the earth, and of the whole world, to gather them together to the battle of that great day of God Almighty.' I know they pretend to prove that men are to have this power unto the end of the world, by Mark 16:17. But take the whole passage together, and what does it prove? Not that all believers can do these miracles, but that these miracles would follow those who believe; that is, those who believed in the record that God had given would, in the apostolic age, have a confirmation of the truth of that word by those miracles, which would [236] follow them. The word would be thus confirmed by miracles, performed by prophets and apostles, who were inspired to write the Old and New Testament. I see no reason for the working of miracles in this age; 'for if they believe not Moses and the prophets, neither would they believe though one should arise from the dead.' Since the apostles' day, none have worked miracles but the anti-Christian beast.

"The discerning of spirits is, I fear, another fanatical movement to draw off Adventists from the truth, and to lead men to depend on the feeling, exercise, and conceit of their own mind, more than on the word of God. It builds up a spirit of pride and self-righteousness, and thus loses sight of the humbling doctrine, to account others better than ourselves. If all Christians were to possess this gift, how should we live by faith? Each would stand upon the spiritual gifts of his brother, and, if possessed of the true spirit of God, could never err. Surely the devil has great power over the minds of some at the present day. And how shall we know what manner of spirit they are of? The Bible answers: 'By their fruits ye shall know them.' Then it is not by the spirit. I think those who claim this power will soon manifest, by their fruits, that they have another rule than the Bible. I have observed that those persons, who think that they have been baptized by the Holy Ghost, as they term it, become more sensitive of themselves, and very jealous for their own glory; less patient, and full of the denunciatory spirit against others, who are not so fortunate as themselves. There are many spirits gone out into the world; and we are commanded to try the spirits. The spirit that does not cause us to live soberly, righteously, and godly, in this present world, is not the spirit of Christ. I am more and more convinced that Satan has much to do in these wild movements. He has come down, having great wrath, knowing he hath but a short time; and he will, if possible, deceive the very elect.

"On sanctification I have but little at present to say. Sanctification has two prominent meanings in Scripture: setting apart for holy purposes; and being cleansed from all sin and pollution. Every soul converted to God is sanctified in the first sense. He devotes himself to God, to love, serve, and obey him forever. Every one who obtains complete redemption, [237] body, soul, and spirit, is sanctified in the second sense. The first kind is, or ought to be, now enjoyed by every *true believer* in Christ. The other will never be accomplished till the resurrection of the just, when these vile bodies shall be changed. We are sanctified, in the first sense, through faith and a knowledge of the truth; and, in my opinion, are not perfect until we are perfect in faith and knowledge of the word of God. Yet many among us, who pretend to be wholly sanctified, are following the traditions of men, and apparently are as ignorant of truth as others who make no such pretensions, and are not half so modest. I must confess that they have to me an appearance of boasting. I would not judge harshly; but I cannot see any reason to believe them any more holy than many others, who make no such claims. I would say nothing to prevent any man or woman from living holy. This is what we are all seeking after, and what I expect to attain, when Christ shall come and blot out my sins, according to his promise. – Acts 3:19. I think those with whom I have conversed, who pretend to have obtained this grace, instead of enjoying more than others, labor, in their arguments, to lower down the standard of holiness to their present capacity. Instead of looking for a blessed hope at the appearing of Jesus Christ, who shall change our vile bodies, and raise our capacity to enjoy and adore him forever, in an infinitely higher state of perfection, they think they are actually enjoying all the promises *now*, and are not in need of any further work of grace to give them a right to the eternal inheritance of the saints. If this be so, and we are truly perfect, sanctified, and prepared for our possession in heaven, then every moment we are debarred our right of entering and taking possession of our inheritance would be an illegal withholding of us from our just rights of participating in the enjoyment of the will of our blessed Master. But it is not so. We are minors, and subjects of chastisements. Proverbs 3:11, 12: 'My son, despise not the chastening of the Lord, neither be weary of his correction; for whom the Lord loveth he correcteth; even as a father the son in whom he delighteth.' Hebrews 12:5-9: 'And ye have forgotten the exhortation which speaketh unto you as unto children, My son, despise not thou the chastening of the Lord, nor faint [238] when thou art rebuked of him; for whom the Lord loveth he chasteneth, and scourgeth every son whom he receiveth. If ye endure chastening, God dealeth with you as with sons; for what son is he whom the father chasteneth not? But if ye be without chastisement, whereof all are partakers, then are ye bastards, and not sons. Furthermore, we have had fathers of our flesh which corrected us, and we gave them reverence; shall we not much rather be subject to the Father of spirits, and live?' Therefore, let us all be modest, unassuming, and godlike, pressing on to the mark. Let us not, therefore, judge one another any more. Romans 14:13: 'But judge this rather, that no man put a stumbling-block or an occasion to fall in his brother's way.' 1 Corinthians 8:9-13: 'But take heed lest by any means this liberty of yours become a stumbling-block to them that are weak. For if any man see thee, which hast knowledge, sit at meat in the idols' temple, shall not the conscience of him that is weak be emboldened to eat those things which are offered to idols; and through thy knowledge shall the weak brother perish, for whom Christ died? But when ye sin so against the brethren, and wound their weak conscience, ye sin against Christ. Wherefore, if meat make my brother to offend, I will eat no flesh while the world standeth, lest I make my brother to offend.' If my brother is truly perfect in every good work, he will bear with me and my weakness. Romans 15:1: 'We, then, that are strong ought to bear the infirmities of the weak, and not to please ourselves.' 1 Corinthians 9:22: 'To the weak became I as weak, that I might gain the weak: I am made all things to all men, that I might by all means save some.' I have not written this to condemn my 'perfect' brother, or to call out a reply. He may call one thing perfect sanctification, and I another. If he is 'perfect' and strong, he can bear my weakness. If he wants contention, it will show that he is not perfect, but contentious. I beg of my brother to let me follow on to know the Lord; and God forbid that I should call him back.

I hope he will not boastingly exclude me from the path he would tread. May God sanctify and prepare us for his own use, and deliver us from the wrath to come.

"Yours, in the blessed hope,

"WILLIAM MILLER.

"*Castleton, Vt., Oct.* 12, 1843." [239]

Not only Mr. Miller, but all who were in his confidence, took a decided position against all fanatical extravagances. They never gave them any quarter; while those who regarded them with favor soon arrayed themselves against Mr. Miller and his adherents. Their fanaticism increased; and though opposed by Mr. Miller and his friends, the religious and secular press very generally, but unjustly, connected his name with it; – he being no more responsible for it than Luther and Wesley were for similar manifestations in their day.

CHAPTER 17

Emotions In View Of The Advent Near – Home Of Mr. Miller
– Tour Into Western New York – His Personal Appearance –
Address To All Denominations – Visit To Washington, Etc.

The state of the cause at this time, and the state of mind produced by the belief of the Advent near, was very truthfully and impartially depicted by Rev. Alexander Campbell, President of Bethany College, Va., in the following article, copied from the "Millennial Harbinger."

"As time advances, the doctrine of the Second Advent in 1843 gains new interest, and grasps with a stronger hold the minds of all who assent to its strong probability. This is just what we expected and predicted since first we heard its annunciation. Excitement keeps pace with every new convert, and consequently has not yet reached its proper height. The ardently pious and strongly imaginative proclaimers of the world's immediate end, in their untiring efforts to propagate the opinion in such a community as this, cannot fail to influence thousands, and to inflame their zeal to the highest enthusiasm. What topic more sublime, more soul-subduing, more delightful to the Christian, than that of the Lord's glorious return to judge the world, to reward his friends and punish his enemies? Talk they of sublime themes! Methinks the most sublime of all that earth and time afford are the veriest commonplaces compared with this. [240]

"Many sincere and conscientious spirits are already enrolled amongst its advocates, and some of them are not only sincere, but pure, and noble, and amiable Christians. These are the great apostles of the theory, to whose virtues and excellences the cause is mainly indebted for its comparative success. Its temples are festooned with Christian charity. Its altars are covered with the garlands and wreaths of piety and humanity. Its priests wear the coronal of elevated sanctity, and its votaries are from necessity all more learned in the symbols of prophecy than those who oppose them.

"Everything in society is now favorable to the rapid propagation of the new theory. The prevailing ignorance of the Bible, and especially of prophecy, on the part of many who declaim against 'Millerism,' and the unfortunate essays of learned men in their zeal for old opinions, so far transcending the oracles of reason and the canons of common sense, have contributed no little to advance into public favor the doctrine of 'the Second Advent near.' Amongst these essays may stand first that of Professor Stuart, whose high attainments in biblical learning I highly appreciate. That essay, already trumpeted by a thousand voices, republished in various forms by distinguished preachers and writers from Boston to Cincinnati, – by the Colvers, the Stows, and the Mahans of this land, – has greatly aided 'THE SIGNS OF THE TIMES' and 'THE MIDNIGHT CRIES' of the new school of prophetic expositors.

"But more than any other individual cause have the profane scoffings, falsehoods, and caricatures of the religious and political press, in opposition to the doctrine of the 'Second Advent near,' contributed to confirming the minds of the initiated in the pleasing hope, and to the furnishing of their preachers with new *'signs of the times'* in arguing the certainty of their opinions. If Noah, Daniel, and Job, had reappeared in the person of friend Miller, and uttered the oracles of the Lord, they would have been derided, slandered, misrepresented, and denounced as disturbers of the peace of the world's giddy dance, and troublers of the modern Israel in her one hundred and one fractions of orthodox prescription, just as Mr. Miller and his party have been. [241]

"Another reason of the assurance of the faith in the minds of those who are true believers of the doctrine, is the delightful state of mind into which they feel themselves inducted through the new theory. Every righteous man must feel an exquisite pleasure in the strongly anticipated immediate return of his Lord. What possible event could be hailed with such overwhelming joy as the end of this sin-distracted and convulsed world, and the beginning of a new creation, in which, as Christians, all hope to participate? New heavens, illumined with an unsetting sun of ineffable glory, spangled with stars brighter far than our present sun; a new earth, surrounded with an immortal atmosphere, filled with unfading freshness, sweetness, and beauty, decorated with charms incomparably superior to those of Eden and its ancient Paradise, animated too with the presence of nature's eternal and immortal King and his celestial train, the eternal home of the saints, where 'sin and sorrow, pain and death, are felt and feared no more.' I say, who would not gladly exchange a sin-emaciated face, a shattered constitution, sown thick with the seeds of death, for a spiritual and immortal frame; a shipwrecked earth, filled with unquenchable fires, convulsed with interminable agonies, and covered with floods of water that have washed and drenched its deeply furrowed face with a thousand mountains and valleys, for a new earth never to be trodden by the profane foot of a solitary prodigal, nor marred by the unsanctified touch of a rebel hand, during the ceaseless ages of eternity!

"None on earth are more to be envied than those happy spirits who are wrought up, or have wrought themselves up, to the full persuasion that in one short year, a little less or more, and they shall most certainly realize all this. Methinks to such the year 1843 will pass along with dreams of felicity and sweet antepasts of blessedness, whose remembrance will, in years to come, be as the delightful oasis in a parched desert, – as the vision of a Paul caught away into the celestial Paradise, into the purer climes of the third heavens. And all this, too, without even the parting pang which nature feels when 'shuffling off this mortal coil,' and bidding a long adieu to those we leave behind. For in a moment, in the twinkling of an eye, perhaps during some prayer or song of praise, while in the midst of a monosyllable, [242] one half uttered in time, the other in eternity, – the first accent from a mortal, the second from an immortal tongue, crystallized into a gem in less than time's shortest mark or minutest point, – we have passed the bourn of mortality, and are found dwelling not in houses of clay, founded in the dust, but in a house from heaven, spiritual, incorruptible, immortal, and glorious. And all this, too, I repeat, without the pain of parting from one we love. We cast *not* one 'longing, lingering look behind.' None are left we care anything about. Nature, flesh, and all earth's associations, are forever left without one single feeling that time or sense endear. What a mysterious, delightful, ineffable moment that in which mortality is swallowed up in life; in which we obtain beauty for ashes, joy for mourning, the garment of praise for the spirit of heaviness; in which we part from sin, and sorrow, and woe, and find ourselves at home in the presence of the Lord, in the bosom of his love, surrounded with all the sons of light, with the riches and glory of the New Jerusalem temple, thronged with the great hierarchs and kings of all the dominions of Eternity! Who, of the Christian family, would not rejoice with joy unspeakable and full of glory, that in a few months all this should transpire, and that without the least of all the agonies of death; – perhaps fall asleep some night, and awaken glorified in the presence of the Lord, hearing, with an immortal ear, the last echo of the grave-opening, body-reanimating, soul-transforming sound of the archangel's trumpet!

"No doctrine, then, more cheering than that of 'the Second Advent near;' no opinion produces a more delightful state of mind."

In the interval between Mr. Miller's return from Boston to his home at Low Hampton and the recommencement of his public labors, he was visited by his dearly beloved friend, the late Elder Nathaniel Southard, who wrote as follows of

"THE HOME OF WILLIAM MILLER.

"It was Saturday forenoon when we passed over the rough road, and stopped at a one-storied house, where a post-office [243] is kept. It is the residence of William S., oldest son of Bro. Miller, P. M., at the office, which, for distinction, is called Low Hampton. He was not at home; but one of his little daughters told us the residence of her grandfather was in sight on the hill. Without waiting for her to point it out, I easily recognized it – from previous description – among the good-looking farm-houses in sight. It was not the largest or hand-somest. The back part of it only, which is painted red, could be seen. It is two stories high. The northern front and ends are painted white. On the way we passed the small plain meeting-house of the Baptist church to which Bro. M. belongs.

"At the gate of his hospitable mansion we met a young man in a wagon, with crutches by his side whose round open countenance showed him to be a son of William Miller. He gave us a cordial invitation to enter. Three visitors were already in the house, to whom myself, wife and child, being added, made a number which we feared would be burden-some. We soon found ourselves perfectly at home, though we had never before seen one of the family but its venerable head.

"The next day five other visitors arrived, one of whom was a lady from Iowa, and three from Vergennes. The day was very stormy. We went to the place of worship, and found a congregation consisting of fewer persons than we left at the house. The preacher, Bro. Increase Jones, gave a plain, practical sermon on the text, 'The end of all things is at hand; be ye therefore sober, and watch unto prayer.' In the afternoon we opened the Scriptures, and tried to pursue the apostolic method in speaking of Jesus and the resurrection.

"On our way from the meeting, after referring to the number of guests, we asked Robbins if they usually had as much company.

"'Pretty nigh,' said he; 'I wish I had kept count of the number of visi-tors for the last six months.'

"'Did they come in such numbers when Bro. Miller was sick?' we inquired.

"'It seemed to make but little difference,' he replied.

"We just then passed by the open carriage gate into the spacious enclosure at the west end of the house.

"'It seemed to be the hardest task,' he proceeded, 'to [244] make friends understand that it was not friendly to visit a sick man in such numbers. I have had to stand here and keep people out of the house, and sometimes there were six asking admission at once.'

"As it was, I have no doubt company added weeks to his sickness, and dollars to the doctor's bills. I afterwards learnt that the expenses of his sickness were one hundred dollars.

"Let us try to get a glimpse at his wealth and resources. Twelve years ago he was the owner of about two hundred acres of land, less than half of which was capable of cultivation, yielding a liberal return to hard labor. No one, who knows with what energy, diligence, and firmness, Bro. Miller has prosecuted the labors he seems to have been raised up to perform, will need to be told that he is a man of industrious, temperate, and frugal habits. Such a man, in such a place, with a help meet for him, could not be poor and thriftless. Twenty-five years ago he built his house. Other buildings were erected as they became necessary, but none within the last dozen years, except a bee-house, and small, plain shed, or boiling-house, where food is prepared for his hogs. He showed me his home farm, consisting of ninety-six acres, lying wholly on the south side of the road. There is some common wall upon it; but the moss-grown, weather-beaten stones unanimously contradict the foolish and malicious lies which have been told about its recent origin. He also owns a rough tract of fifty acres, north of the road, and twenty acres of interval a little distance to the east. When he let out his farm to his son, he sold him $500 worth of stock, and has since sold seventy acres of land to his son-in-law. What he has thus realized, and $100 yearly for the use of his farm, have enabled him to meet the expenses of travelling, printing, and giving away books, company, sickness, etc.

"He has brought up eight children, two others having died in early life. His whole family, like Job's, originally consisted of seven sons and three daughters. Four of them are now in the house with him, and two sons are at the West. As a specimen of the fertility of his farm, he showed us a potato weighing two pounds and seven ounces.

"While contemplating this lovely family, and their plain but comfortable dwelling-place, equally free from the marks [245] of wasteful neglect or extravagant expenditure, I saw, never as I saw before, the folly and malignity of those falsehoods which have been so industriously told about them. Look at them.

"A diligent student of the Bible tells us he finds prophetic periods reaching down to the resurrection and the second coming of Christ.

"'Nonsense!' cries one, who must stand at the judgment seat of Christ; 'Mr. Miller is a man of property, and he holds on to it.'

"'But won't you please to look in the Bible, and see the evidence that these periods are just running out?'

"'Humbug!' says another, who must give an account for the manner in which he treats that message from heaven; 'Mr. Miller is building a solid brick wall round his farm.'

"'But will you not consider and discern the signs of the times, which show that the kingdom of heaven is nigh, even at the doors?'

"'It is all a money-making scheme,' says a third, who must soon give up his stewardship; 'Mr. Miller is putting up some large buildings in New Haven, and he has a barrel of jewels in his house, which have been given him where he has preached.'

"The amazing stupidity of these fictions almost hides from view the malice which invented them. But when we look at his wife and daughter, to whom a husband and father's reputation is as the apple of the eye, we begin to feel them as a personal injury, though they are nothing, in this view, in comparison with the public mischief they occasion.

"Bro. Miller's faith remains unwavering. He said he should be happy if he felt as sure of heaven as he did that he had the truth on the prophecies of Daniel.

"His eyesight is improved since his sickness, so that he now uses spectacles which he had laid aside as being too young several years ago. He reads the small Polyglot Bible with the greatest ease. He is a diligent reader of Second Advent papers. After he has received one he seldom lays it aside till he has become acquainted with all its contents. The rest of his reading is nearly confined to the Scriptures. He is able to write freely, and it requires no small share of his time to attend to the numerous letters he receives. [246]

"He starts early next week (Providence permitting) on his way to Rochester, Lockport, and Buffalo, N. Y. It will be necessary for one of his sons to accompany him, as he is not strong enough to travel alone.

"We were interested in seeing his old family Bible, which cost $18.50, and his quarto copy of Cruden's Concordance, which was originally purchased, in 1798, for $8. These two books were almost the only ones he looked at while preparing his lectures. A clergyman once called at his house in his absence, and, being disappointed in not seeing him, wished the privilege of looking at his library. His daughter conducted the visitor into the north-east room, where he has sat so many hours at his ancient desk. Those two books, and no others, lay upon the table. 'That is his library,' said she. The clergyman was amazed. Her remark was strictly true, as far as theological writings were concerned. He never had a commentary in his house, and did not remember reading any work upon the prophecies, except Newton and Faber, about thirty years ago.

"When we spoke to him about the stories in relation to his property in New Haven, he pleasantly remarked that those who believed them could easily satisfy themselves; for he had sold to Bro. McDonald, of Williamsburg, near New York city, all his property, real or personal, out of Low Hampton, for five dollars, and the purchaser had offered to give half of it to any one who would find any.

"Monday afternoon we reluctantly took leave of this peaceful spot, which had been our pleasant home for two days, rejoicing that calumny could there find no truthful basis on which to found its reckless and cruel assertions.

"N. SOUTHARD.

"*Carleton, Vt., October* 23, 1843."

In company with his wife and son George, Mr. Miller started for Rochester, N. Y., on the 9th of November. On his passage down the canal from Whitehall to Albany, by request of the passengers on the boat, he spoke to an attentive audience from Titus 2:13.

From the 12th to the 19th of November, he gave his first course of lectures in the city of Rochester, speaking to full houses on the afternoon and evening of each day. The [247] ground had been previously prepared for him by a course of lectures in June, delivered by Mr. Himes and others, in connection with the "great tent."

Mr. Himes had commenced a paper there, called the "Glad Tidings," and published thirteen numbers of it, which were extensively circulated; and the late Elder Thomas F. Barry, a devoted brother, had remained in that field during the summer. By those instrumentalities quite an interest had been created, and the labors of Mr. Miller there were abundantly blessed.

Receiving a pressing invitation from Rev. Elon Galusha, pastor of the Baptist church, and sixty-eight others, in Lockport, N. Y., to visit that place, he lectured there from the 21st to the 30th of November. The salvation of some souls, and a general expression of interest in the subject of his discourses, were the result of his labors.

From the 2nd to the 10th of December he lectured in Buffalo, N. Y., in the theatre, to a house full of attentive hearers. Writing from that place, on the 4th, he says: "Yesterday I saw the tears of some in the congregation, who, I am informed, were old, hardened infidels."

In compliance with an invitation from Rev. A. Claghorn, pastor of the Baptist church, and twenty-three others, he next lectured in Lewiston, N. Y., from the 11th to the 17th of December. There were many hearers present from Canada, as well as from the American side of the line, who gave him a respectful hearing. Writing respecting this place, Mr. M. says:

> "I was here, as at Rochester and Lockport, challenged to a public debate by a Universalist. I will not contend with them. It would be an admission that they *might* be right, which I cannot for a moment believe. Michael would not contend with the devil. Why? Because he would not admit he could be right. Was he afraid of the devil? No. But he said, 'The Lord rebuke thee, Satan!' And so say I to his ministers."

Being invited to visit Penfield, N. Y., by Rev. David Bernard and the unanimous vote of his church, he lectured in the Baptist meeting-house there, from the 20th to the 27th of December. Some souls professed conversion, and [248] the pastor and a number of his people avowed their faith in the near coming of Christ.

Mr. Miller returned to Rochester on the 29th of December, continued there a few days, gave five discourses, and, on the 3rd of January, 1844, he left for home by the way of Troy. After reaching Low Hampton, he wrote:

> "On Saturday, January 6th, I arrived home, having been absent about eight weeks, and given eighty-five lectures. I have seen a number of infidels converted to God; and more than one hundred have obtained a hope where I have been."

On the 28th of January he again visited Boston, and gave a course of lectures in the Howard-street Tabernacle. This was his ninth visit to Boston, and his seventh regular course of lectures there. On no previous occasion had such crowds been present to hear as were then assembled in that capacious building. On the Sabbath (January 28th), all day and evening, the seats and aisles were filled with as many as could find a place to sit or stand. Many of the young, with the middle-aged, and even men with gray hairs, stood and listened to the story of the coming One, with the evidences of his near approach. Had the Tabernacle been twice its size, it would hardly have held the multitude who sought admittance. The interest continued during his entire course of lectures, which closed on the 4th of February.

On the 5th of February, in company with Mr. Himes, he left for New York city; but the weather was inclement, the boat was delayed in the Sound all the next day by ice, and the passage was uncommonly tedious. Mr. Fowler, the phrenologist, being one of the passengers, to while away the time he gave, by request, a lecture on his science. After the lecture he was blindfolded, and in that state examined quite a number of heads. At the request of the company, Mr. Miller's head was examined. All were eager to hear the opinion of the lecturer. Among other things he said:

> "This man has large benevolence. His object is to do his fellow-beings good. He has great firmness – is a modest man, open, frank, no hypo-crite, good at figures, a man of great mental power, might make a noise in the world, has no personal enemies; if he has enemies, it is not because they know him, but on account of his opinions."

At the close of the examination his blindfold was removed, [249] and he was introduced to Mr. Miller, to the no small amusement of the company.

They arrived in New York on the evening of the 6th of February, 1844, and found a conference assembled in Franklin Hall. Mr. Miller gave two discourses there on the 7th; when, finding the place too small, they adjourned to the Broadway Tabernacle, where he lectured, in the after-noon and evening of the 8th and 9th of February, to crowded assemblies. It was estimated that not less than five thousand persons were present. The audiences were solemn and attentive.

On the 10th of February they went to Philadelphia, and on the 11th Mr. M. commenced a course of lectures in the saloon of the Chi-nese Museum, — closing on the 18th. That immense hall was filled to overflowing.

While laboring here, a friend gave the following description of Mr. Miller's personal appearance:

> "There is a kindness of soul, simplicity, and power, peculiarly original, combined in his manner; and he is affable and attentive to all, without any affectation of superiority. He is of about medium stature, a little corpulent, and, in temperament, a mixture of sanguine and nervous. His intellectual developments are unusually full, and we see in his head great benevolence and firmness, united with a lack of self-esteem. He is wanting in marvelousness, and is naturally skeptical. His countenance is full and round, while there is a peculiar expression in his blue eye, of shrewdness and love. Although about sixty-two years of age, his hair is not gray, but of a light glossy auburn; his voice is full and distinct, and his pronunciation somewhat northern-antique. In his social relations he is gentle and affectionate, and insures the esteem of all with whom he mingles. In giving this charcoal sketch to the public, I have merely sought to correct numerous misstatements, and gratify the honest desire of many distant believers with a faint outline of the character and appearance of the man."

While drawing crowded houses of intelligent and attentive hearers, his name was seldom mentioned in the religious press, except by way of ridicule or denunciation; and many churches, particularly those of his own denomination, were [250] taking disciplinary steps with those who had embraced his views. This called forth from him the following

> "ADDRESS TO BELIEVERS IN CHRIST OF ALL DENOMINATIONS.
>
> "DEAR BRETHREN:- We would ask, in the name of our dear Master, Jesus Christ, by all that is holy, by the fellowship of the saints, and the love of the truth, why you cast us off as if we were heretics? What have we believed, that we have not been commanded to believe by the word of God, which you yourselves allow is the rule and only rule of our faith and practice? What have we done that should call down such virulent denunciations against us from pulpit and press, and give you just cause to exclude us (Adventists) from your churches and fellowship? In the name of all that is dear, all that is holy and good, we call upon some of you to come out and tell us wherein our great sin lies. Have we denied the faith once delivered to the saints? Tell us, we pray you, or, wherein is our fault? If there is an honest man among you, of which we cannot doubt, we shall expect to see your reasons

publicly and honestly avowed; and if we are guilty of heresy or crime, let the Christian community know it, that we may be shunned by all who know and love the truth.

"Is it heterodox to believe that Jesus Christ will come again to this earth, to receive his saints to himself, and to reward all men as their work shall be? If so, then our fathers, and our ministers, our creeds, and our Bibles, have taught us heresy; and from our infancy we have misunderstood our teachers, and misapplied our Bible. Do tell us what mean a class of texts like these John 14:3: 'And if I go and prepare a place for you, I will come again and receive you unto myself: that where I am there ye may be also.' Acts 1:11: 'Which also said, Ye men of Galilee, why stand ye gazing up into heaven? this same Jesus which is taken up from you into heaven, shall so come in like manner as ye have seen him go into heaven.' 1 Peter 1:7 and 13: 'That the trial of your faith, being much more precious than of gold that perisheth, though it may be tried with fire, might be found unto praise, and honor, and glory, at the appearing of Jesus Christ. Wherefore, gird up the [251] loins of your mind, be sober, and hope to the end for the grace that is to be brought unto you at the revelation of Jesus Christ.' Revelation 1:7: "Behold, he cometh with clouds; and every eye shall see him, and they also which pierced him; and all kindreds of the earth shall wail because of him.'

"Does our crime consist in our looking for him and loving his appearing? This, too, we charge upon our fathers and teachers; we have heard, ever since we had consciousness, as our duty explained and enforced, to watch and look, to love and be prepared for his return, that when he comes we may enter into the marriage supper of the Lamb. We also have Christ and the apostles for our example in so doing. Witness Matthew 24:44; 25:13; Mark 13:34-37; Philippians 3:20, 21; 2 Timothy 4:8; Titus 2:13; 2 Peter 3:12; Revelation 14:15.

"Or are we to be severed from our brethren because we believe the prophecies of the Old and New Testament to be the true prophecies of God; or because that we think we can understand them, and see in the history of our world their fulfillment? Are we to be cut off from our connection with your churches because we believe as your ministers have told us we ought to for ages past? Acts 24:14: 'But this I confess unto you, that after the way which they call heresy, so worship I the God of my fathers, believing all things which are written in the law and in the prophets." 26:22: 'Having therefore obtained help of God, I continue unto this day, witnessing both to small and great, saying none other things than those which the prophets and Moses did say should come. King Agrippa, believest thou the prophets?' 1 Timothy

4:14: 'That thou keep this commandment without spot, unrebukable, until the appearing of our Lord Jesus Christ.' Revelation 1:4: 'Blessed is he that readeth, and they that hear the words of this prophecy, and keep those things which are written therein; for the time is at hand.'

"Again, let me inquire: Are we treated as heretics because we believe Christ will come this year? Are we not all commanded to watch? Mark 13:37: "And what I say unto you, I say unto all, Watch.' And I would ask, Is it not our duty to watch this year? If so, will you tell [252] us how a man can watch, and not expect the object for which he watches? If this is the crime, we plead guilty to the charge, and throw ourselves upon the word of God, and the example of our fathers, to justify us in so doing. Ecclesiastes 8:5, 6: 'Whoso keepeth the commandments shall feel no evil thing; and a wise man's heart discerneth both time and judgment; because to every purpose there is time and judgment.' Daniel 12:6, 7: 'And one said to the man clothed in linen, which was upon the waters of the river, How long shall it be to the end of these wonders? And I heard the man clothed in linen, which was upon the waters of the river, when he held up his right hand and his left hand unto heaven, and sware by him that liveth forever, that it shall be for a time, times, and a half; and when he shall have accomplished to scatter the power of the holy people, all these things shall be finished.' 1 Peter 1:9, 13: 'Receiving the end of your faith, even the salvation of your souls. Of which salvation the prophets have inquired and searched diligently, who prophesied of the grace that should come unto you; searching what, or what manner of time, the spirit of Christ which was in them did signify, when it testified beforehand the sufferings of Christ, and the glory that should follow. Unto whom it was revealed, that not unto themselves, but unto us they did minister the things which are now reported unto you by them that have preached the gospel unto you, with the Holy Ghost sent down from heaven: which things the angels desire to look into. Wherefore, gird up the loins of your mind, be sober, and hope to the end for the grace that is to be brought unto you at the revelation of Jesus Christ.'

"Now, if we are wrong, pray show us wherein consists our wrong. Show us from the word of God that we are in error; we have had ridicule enough; that can never convince us that we are in the wrong; the word of God alone can change our views. Our conclusions have been formed deliberately and prayerfully, as we have seen the evidence in the Scriptures; and all reasoning against our views has only served to confirm us in them.

"Or, are you ready to say that our crime consists in examining the Bible for ourselves? We have inquired 'Watchman, what of the night?' we have besought and entreated [253] them to give us any signs of the coming morning, and have waited patiently for an answer; but have waited in vain; have been turned off with some German or French philosophy, or had the book closed in our face, and been insulted for our deep anxiety. We have, therefore, been obliged to study for ourselves; and if we are to be cut off for honestly believing in the exactness of prophetic time, then Scott, and Wesley, and the Newtons, and Mede, Gill, and others, should all be excommunicated for the like offence. We, therefore, once more call upon you to show us our errors; and until this is done, we must continue to believe the Lord will come in this Jewish year. WM. MILLER."

On the 17th of February, Messrs. Miller, Himes, and Elder Josiah Litch, left Philadelphia for Washington city, which they reached on the 20th. On the evening of that day they held their first meeting in the Baptist house, near the Navy-yard. It became so thronged that, on the 26th, they removed to the Apollo Hall, near the President's mansion, where they continued till the 2nd of March.

During these lectures, on the 28th of February, the "Peacemaker," on board of the "Princeton," exploded, killing Colonel Gardiner and Mr. Upshur, the United States Secretary of State, and wounding others. That event added interest and solemnity to the lectures, and caused them to be more fully attended. There were present at the lectures a goodly number of persons belonging to both houses of Congress.

Writing from Washington on the day of that explosion, but before the occurrence, Mr. Miller said:

"They throng us constantly for papers, books, and tracts, which Brother Himes is scattering gratuitously by thousands, containing information on this subject. They send in from this vicinity and from 'old Virginia' for papers and lecturers; but the one-hundredth part of their requests can never be complied with. Never have I been listened to with so deep a feeling, and with such intense interest, for hours."

Mr. Miller gave nineteen lectures in this place, and Messrs. Himes and Litch fifteen.

Calls for them to extend their tour further south came up [254] from Charleston, S. C., Savannah, Geo., Mobile, Ala., and from many other of the larger places in the Southern States. Some of these were very importunate, but previous arrangements prevented a compliance with those requests.

They returned north, held meetings in Baltimore from the 3rd to the 8th of March, and, on the 9th, returned to Philadelphia. There Mr. Miller gave two more discourses on the 10th; on the 11th he lectured in Newark, N. J., in the Free Presbyterian meeting-house; on the 12th he gave one discourse in New York; on the 13th he spoke in Brooklyn and Williams-burg, N. Y., and on the 14th he returned to Low Hampton.

He seems to have kept no minute of his subsequent labors, but closes his note-book, at the termination of this tour, with these words: "Now I have given, since 1832, *three thousand two hundred lectures.*"

CHAPTER 18

The Passing Of The Time – His Position – The Burning Day – Lines On His Disappointment – Confession – Visit Of Elder Litch – Mr. Miller And The Methodist Ministers – Tour To Ohio – Return, Etc.

The vernal equinox of 1844 was the furthest point of time to which Mr. Miller's calculation of the prophetic periods extended. When this time passed, he wrote to Mr. Himes as follows:

"Low Hampton, March 25th, 1844.

"My Dear Brother Himes:- I am now seated at my old desk in my east room, having obtained help of God until the present time. I am still looking for the dear Saviour, the Son of God, from heaven; and for the fulfillment of the promise made to our fathers, and confirmed to them that heard Him, – that he would come again, and would receive us unto himself; gathering together in one body all the family of the first-born in heaven and earth, even in Him. This Paul has told us would be in 'the fullness of time.' – Ephesians 1:9, 10. [255]

"The time, as I have calculated it, is now filled up, and I expect every moment to see the Saviour descend from heaven. I have now nothing to look for but this glorious hope. I am full in the faith that all prophetic chronology, excepting the thousand years of Revelation 20th, is now about full. Whether God designs for me to warn the people of this earth any more, or not, I am at a loss to know. Should time continue longer than I have expected, I mean to be governed by the providence of Him who will never err, in whom I think I have trusted, and have been supported by, during my twelve years of arduous labors, in endeavoring to awaken the churches of God and the Christian community, and to warn my fellow-men of the necessity of an immediate preparation to meet our Judge, in the day of his appearing. I hope that I have cleansed my garments of the blood of souls. I feel that, as far as it was in my power, I have freed myself from all guilt in their condemnation. ...

"I feel almost confident that my labors are about done; and I am, with a deep interest of soul, looking for my blessed and glorious Redeemer, who will be king over all the earth, and God with us forevermore. This, I can truly say, is my chief desire. It is my meditation all the day long. It is my song in the night. It is my faith and hope. It consoles me in sickness, comforts me in tribulation, and gives me patience to endure the scoffs and taunts of the selfish and ungodly. My faith and confidence in God's word are as strong as ever, although Christ has not come in the time I expected. I still believe that the time is not far off, and that God will soon – yes, too soon for the proud and scoffing – justify himself, his word, and the cry which has been given.

"This is the position I have now to take, and what more work I have to do will be done in this manner. I will

"**1.** Prove by Scripture and history that the time is fulfilled.

"**2.** Show the signs completed: and,

"**3.** Present the duty of watching; for 'we know not what hour the Lord may come.'

"If God has anything more for me to do in his vineyard, he will give me strength, open the door, and enable me to do whatever may be his will, for his glory, and for the best [256] good of men. To Him I leave the event. For Him I watch and pray: Come, Lord Jesus, come quickly. Amen! Even so come, Lord Jesus.   WILLIAM MILLER."

On the 2nd of May he wrote as follows:

"To SECOND ADVENT BELIEVERS. ...

"Were I to live my life over again, with the same evidence that I then had, to be honest with God and man I should have to do as I have done. Although opposers said it would not come, they produced no weighty arguments. It was evidently guess-work with them; and I then thought, and do now, that their denial was based more on an unwillingness for the Lord to come than on any arguments leading to such a conclusion.

"I *confess my error*, and acknowledge *my disappointment*; yet I still believe that the day of the Lord is near, even at the door; and I exhort you, my brethren, to be watchful, and not let that day come upon you unawares. The wicked, the proud, and the bigot, will exult over us. I will try to be patient. God will deliver the godly out of temptation, and will reserve the unjust to be punished at Christ's appearing.

"I want you, my brethren, not to be drawn away from the truth. Do not, I pray you, neglect the Scriptures. They are able to make you wise unto eternal life. Let us be careful not to be drawn away from the manner and object of Christ's coming; for the next attach of the adversary will be to induce unbelief respecting these. The manner of Christ's coming has been well discussed. Permit me, then, to address you on the subject of

"THE BURNING DAY.

"'This second epistle, beloved, I now write unto you, in both which I stir up your pure minds by way of remembrance; that ye may be mindful of the words which were spoken before by the holy prophets, and of the commandment of us, the apostles of the Lord and Saviour: knowing this first, that there shall come in the last days scoffers, walking after their own lusts, and saying, Where is the promise of his coming? for since the fathers fell asleep, all things continue as they were from the beginning of the creation. For this they willingly are ignorant of, that by the word of God the heavens were of old, and the earth standing out of the water and in the water; whereby the world that then was, being [257] overflowed with water, perished: but the heavens and the earth, which are now, by the same word are kept in store, reserved unto fire against the day of judgment and perdition of ungodly men.' – 2 Peter 3:1-7.

"This is an important subject; and, on reading it, a number of important queries naturally arise.

"I. *How are we to understand this?*

"II. *What are we to believe will be done when this takes place?*

"III. *When will it take place; at the commencement or end of the one thousand years' reign spoken of in* Revelation 20:6?

"I. *This passage must be understood literally.* 1st. Because there is nothing in the passage to warrant a figurative meaning. 2nd. It is compared to the deluge; and it is universally acknowledged that the antediluvians perished by water. And 3rd. In no place where this burning day is spoken of in Scripture, is it explained to mean a figure. Therefore, I cannot but believe that the earth will be overwhelmed in literal fire.

"II. *What is to be done when this burning takes place?* 1st. Christ comes in power and great glory. 2nd. He takes vengeance on the wicked, consumes their bodies to ashes, melts the elements with fervent heat, and burns up or dissolves the works of men. 3rd. The present governments of earth and the present dispensation of God's grace will pass away, and the new heavens and new earth succeed, wherein the righteous shall dwell forever.

"Those are the prominent events to take place at the consummation spoken of in the word of God. Proof: 'But the day of the Lord will come as a thief in the night; in the which the heavens shall pass away with a great noise, and the elements shall melt with fervent heat, the earth also and the works that are therein shall be burned up. Seeing, then, that all these things shall be dissolved, what manner of persons ought ye to be in all holy conversation and godliness, looking for and hasting unto the coming of the day of God, wherein the heavens being on fire shall be dissolved, and the elements shall melt with fervent heat! Nevertheless, we, according to his promise, look for new heavens and a new earth, wherein dwelleth righteousness.' – 2 Peter

3:10-13. The coming of Christ is here spoken of, the passing [258] away of the heavens, the melting of the elements, the burning up of the works of men, and the new heavens and new earth, as promised.

"Where is that promise? Some say it is in Isaiah 65:17. But that cannot be the original promise to which Peter alludes; it can only be a repetition of the promise to our fathers. 'For the promise that he should be the heir of the world was not to Abraham, or to his seed, through the law, but through the righteousness of faith. For if they which are of the law be heirs, faith is made void, and the promise made of none effect. Because the law worketh wrath; for where no law is, there is no transgression. Therefore it is of faith, that it might be by grace; to the end the promise might be sure to all the seed; not to that only which is of the law, but to that also which is of the faith of Abraham, who is the father of us all.'– Romans 4:13-16. 'For if the inheritance be of the law, it is no more of promise; but God gave it to Abraham by promise... And if ye be Christ's, then are ye Abraham's seed, and heirs according to the promise.'– Galatians 3:18-29. 'For it is written, Rejoice, thou barren that bearest not; break forth and cry, thou that travailest not; for the desolate hath many more children than she which hath an husband.'– Galatians 4:27. Here Paul quotes Isaiah 54:1, and tells us it was written by him; but Isaiah evidently refers us to Abraham's day, and alludes to the history of Ishmael and Isaac, as Paul does in Galatians 4:22-30.

"Peter says: 'Wherein dwelleth righteousness,' *or righteous persons*. This promise Abraham saw afar off. Not the promise that Abraham and his seed should inherit the literal land of Canaan; for that promise was fulfilled. 'And the Lord gave unto Israel all the land which he sware to give unto their fathers; and they possessed it, and dwelt therein. And the Lord gave them rest round about, according to all that he sware unto their fathers; and there stood not a man of all their enemies before them: the Lord delivered all their enemies into their hand. There failed not aught of any good thing which the Lord had spoken unto the house of Israel; all came to pass.' – Joshua 21:43-45. It was a promise that he should be heir of the new [259] earth where the children of the bond woman, *of the earth earthy*, would be cast out.

"If the old land of Canaan is the inheritance, then the old city of Jerusalem must be the sanctuary, and the old Jews must be the heirs, and nothing is true but Judaism. But Isaiah says: 'The former things shall not be remembered, nor come into mind.' This doctrine of the *old land of Canaan* being the inheritance of the saints, and the wicked dwelling on the remainder of the earth, making carnal war with Christ and his immortal saints on the land of Canaan, and the cleansing of the earth by fire, after the saints and Christ have possessed it a thousand years, to me, at least, is neither Scripture nor common sense. I will, therefore, show,

"III. *That the cleansing of the earth by fire will be when Christ comes.* 'Our God shall come, and shall not keep silence: a fire shall devour before him, and it shall be very tempestuous round about him. He shall call to the heavens from above, and to the earth, that he may judge his people. Gather my saints together unto me; those that have made a covenant with me by sacrifice.' – Psalm 50:3-5. In this passage the fire devours 'before him.' He also gathers and judges his people. Verse 6th declares Peter's new heavens and earth, wherein dwelleth righteousness.

"'A fire goeth before him, and burneth up his enemies round about. His lightnings enlightened the world; the earth saw, and trembled. The hills melted like wax at the presence of the Lord, at the presence of the Lord of the whole earth. The heavens declare his righteousness, and all the people see his glory.' – Psalm 97:3-6. Here, as in the last quotation, the fire goeth before him, burns up his enemies, the earth trembles, the hills melt, there is the new heavens, and all the people left see his glorious reign.

"'A fiery stream issued and came forth from before him; thousand thousands ministered unto him, and ten thousand times ten thousand stood before him; the judgment was set, and the books were opened. I beheld then, because of the voice of the great words which the horn spake: I beheld even till the beast was slain, and his body destroyed, and given to the burning flames.' – Daniel 7:10, 11. The fire goes before him; the body of the fourth kingdom, which [260] treads down the sanctuary, the whole earth (see verse 23rd), is destroyed, and given to the burning flame.

"'For behold, the Lord will come with fire, and with his chariots like a whirlwind, to render his anger with fury, and his rebuke with flames of fire. For by fire and by his sword will the Lord plead with all flesh; and the slain of the Lord shall be many. They that sanctify themselves, and purify themselves in the gardens behind one tree in the midst, eating swine's flesh, and the abomination, and the mouse, shall be consumed together, saith the Lord. For I know their works and their thoughts; it shall come, that I will gather all nations and tongues; and they shall come and see my glory.' – Isaiah 66:15-18. God came from Teman, and the Holy One from Mount Paran. His glory covered the heavens, and the earth was full of his praise. And his brightness was as the light; he had horns coming out of his hand; and there was the hiding of his power. Before him went the pestilence, and burning coals went forth at his feet. He stood, and measured the earth; he beheld, and drove asunder the nations; and the everlasting mountains were scattered, the perpetual hills did bow: his ways are everlasting.' – Habakkuk 3:3-6. These passages all harmonize. 'For behold, the day cometh, that shall burn as an oven; and all the proud, yea, and all that do wickedly, shall be stubble; and the day that cometh shall burn them up, saith the Lord of hosts, that it shall leave them neither root nor branch. But unto you that fear my name shall the Sun of righteousness arise with healing in his wings; and ye shall go forth, and grow up as calves of the stall. And ye shall tread down the wicked; for they shall be ashes under the soles of your feet in the day that I shall do this, saith the Lord of hosts.' – Malachi 4:1-3. This text plainly proves that the burning day is when Christ makes up his jewels, when he separates the sheep from the goats, and we discern between the righteous and the wicked; also, that all the proud and all that do wickedly are burned up, and that they are ashes in that day. How can this be if the earth is not destroyed by fire until the thousand years are fulfilled? 'For the wicked live not again until the thousand years are finished.' – Revelation 20:5.

"Again: See Matthew 3:12: 'Whose fan is in his hand, [261] and he will thoroughly purge his floor, and gather his wheat into the garner; but he will burn up the chaff with unquenchable fire.' 'The Son of Man shall send forth his angels, and they shall gather out of his kingdom all things that offend, and them which do iniquity; and shall cast them into a furnace of fire; there shall be wailing and gnashing of teeth. Then shall the righteous shine forth as the sun in the kingdom of their Father. Who hath ears to hear, let him hear.' – *Ib.*, 13:41-43. Here we have the explanation of Christ himself. At his coming he gathers out of the kingdom (the territory or world) all that offend or do iniquity, after which the righteous shine forth in the kingdom – the world cleansed, wherein dwelleth righteous persons.

"John said: 'I indeed baptize you with water; but one mightier than I cometh, the latchet of whose shoes I am not worthy to unloose: he shall baptize you with the Holy Ghost and with fire; whose fan is in his hand, and he will thoroughly purge his floor, and will gather the wheat into his garner; but the chaff he will burn with fire unquench-able.' – Luke 3:16, 17. We may safely conclude, by this passage, that Christ, at his second coming, will immerse the world in fire, and at the same time gather his wheat into his garner. 'But the same day that Lot went out of Sodom, it rained fire and brimstone from heaven, and destroyed them all: even thus shall it be in the day when the Son of Man is revealed.' – Luke 17:29, 30. This text is plain, and shows that, the same day the Son of Man is revealed, he will destroy, by fire from heaven, all the wicked. 'And to you, who are troubled, rest with us, when the Lord Jesus shall be revealed from heaven with his mighty angels, in flaming fire, taking vengeance on them that know not God, and that obey not the gospel of our Lord Jesus Christ; who shall be punished with everlasting destruction from the presence of the Lord, and from the glory of his power; when he shall come to be glorified in his saints, and to be admired in all them that believe (because our testimony among you was believed), in that day.' – 2 Thessalonians 1:7-10. 'And then shall that Wicked be revealed, whom the Lord shall consume with the spirit of his mouth, and shall destroy with the brightness of his coming.' – *Ib.*,2:8. How any one [262] can think to harmonize the Scriptures, and not have the world purified by fire at the coming of Christ, I cannot conceive.

"'Wait on the Lord, and keep his way, and he shall exalt thee to inherit the land; when the wicked are cut off, thou shalt see it.' – Psalm 37:34.

"And now, my brethren, I exhort you not to be led away from plain fundamental truths. Now is the time of danger. Satan has come down, having great power, knowing he hath but a short time. 'Behold, I come quickly; hold that fast which thou hast, that no man take thy crown.' – Revelation 3:11.

"*Low Hampton, May 2*, 1844."

Shortly after this he wrote the following lines respecting his disappointment:

"How tedious and lonesome the hours,
While Jesus, my Saviour, delays!
I have sought him in solitude's bowers,
And looked for him all the long days.

Yet he lingers – I pray tell me why
His chariot no sooner returns?
To see him in clouds of the sky,
My soul with intensity burns.

I long to be with him at home,
My heart swallowed up in his love,
On the fields of New Eden to roam,
And to dwell with my Saviour above."

During the last week of May, the Annual Conference of Adventists was held in the Tabernacle at Boston. Mr. Miller was present, and, at the close of one of the meetings, in accordance with a previous notice, arose, and frankly confessed his mistake in the definite time at which he supposed the prophetic periods would have terminated. The following notice of this confession, written by a hearer, appeared in the Boston Post on the 1st of June following:

> "Father Miller's Confession. – Many people were desirous of hearing what was termed Father Miller's Confession, which, according to rumor, was to be delivered at the Tabernacle on Tuesday evening last, when and where a large concourse assembled, myself among the number, to hear the 'conclusion of the whole matter;' and I confess I was well [263] paid for my time and trouble. I should judge, also, by the appearance of the audience, and the remarks I heard from one or two gentlemen not of Mr. Miller's faith, that a general satisfaction was felt. I never heard him when he was more eloquent or animated, or more happy in communicating his feelings and sentiments to others. Want of time and space will not permit me to give even a mere sketch of his remarks, which occupied more than an hour. He confessed that he had been disappointed, but by no means discouraged or shaken in his faith in God's goodness, or in the entire fulfillment of his word, or in the speedy coming of our Saviour, and the destruction of the world. Although the supposed time had passed, God's time had not passed. 'If the vision tarry, wait for it.' He remained firm in the belief that the end of all things is at hand, even at the door. He spoke with much feeling and effect, and left no doubt of his sincerity.   D."

His disappointment in the passing of the time was great; but it did not at all impair his confidence in God, or affect his usual cheerfulness of disposition. Elder Josiah Litch, who visited him on the 8th of June, at Low Hampton, thus wrote:

> "I found both himself and family well and in fine spirits. Indeed, I have never seen him when he seemed to enjoy himself better than at present. If any evidence of his sincerity in preaching the Advent of Christ in 1843 were wanting, in addition to his arduous and unrequited toil of twelve years, his present humble submission to his disappointment, and the spirit of meekness with which the confession of disappointment is made, is sufficient to satisfy the most incredulous that nothing but a deep conviction of duty to God and man could have moved such a man to such a work. That he is greatly disappointed in

not seeing the Lord within the expected time, must be evident to all who hear him speak; while the tearful eye and subdued voice show from whence flow the words he utters.

"Although disappointed as to time, I never saw him more strong than now in the general correctness of his expositions of Scripture and calculation of prophetic times, and in the faith of our Lord's speedy coming." [264]

In company with his son George and Mr. Himes, Mr. Miller left home on the 21st of July, 1844, for a tour as far west as Cincinnati. They reached Rochester, N. Y., on the 23rd, and on the 24th commenced a series of meetings in a beautiful grove in Scottsville, near that city. Mr. Miller was listened to with unusual interest.

From Rochester they visited Buffalo, N. Y., Toronto, C. W., Lockport, N. Y., Cleveland, Akron, Cincinnati, and other places in Ohio. At this last place he lectured, on the evening of August 19th, to an audience of about four thousand persons, and continued there one week.

They had proposed going further west, but freshets in the rivers in those parts prevented. They returned from Cincinnati, up the Ohio and Muskingum rivers, to McConnellsville, which they reached on the 28th of August, and where Mr. M. delivered five lectures.

On the 2nd of September they left this place by steamboat, down the Muskingum river to Marietta, from thence to take a boat to Pittsburg, on their way to Philadelphia. On board the boat for Marietta they found from thirty to forty Methodist ministers, who were on their way to attend the Methodist Episcopal Conference in that city.

Mr. M. noticed some sly glances from one to another, which seemed to say, "We will have some sport with the old gentleman." He, however, took no notice of them, but went to a retired part of the deck, and commenced reading. Soon a dandy-looking minister walked past him several times, and finally asked him:

"Is your name Miller?"

Mr. M. replied in the affirmative, and kept on reading.

He then asked him if he was the Miller who had prophesied the end of the world.

Mr. M. said he did not prophesy, but supposed that he was the one to whom he referred.

The minister said that he did not believe we could know when the world was to end.

Mr. M., thinking he had a right to his unbelief, made no reply.

The minister then said he did not believe God had revealed the time.

Mr. M. replied, that he could prove by the Bible that God [265] had revealed it; and that, if he was an honest man, he would make him acknowledge it, by asking him a few questions in reference to the Bible, if he would answer them.

The man retired, procured his Bible, and returned with about twenty other ministers, who gathered around him. An elderly one, who looked like an honest man, took his seat in front, on the capstan. All were attention. Mr. M. asked the man to read the first three verses of Daniel 12th.

This he did aloud.

Mr. M. then asked if the *resurrection* was brought to view in those verses.

The man looked at them for a while, and said he did not know that it was.

Mr. M. asked him if he would tell what they did mean.

He said he did not choose to do so.

"O! very well," said Mr. M.; "we have nothing more to say together; for I did not agree to convince you, if you would not answer a few questions."

The elderly minister then asked him why he would not answer.

"Because I do not choose to do so."

"Why," said the old gentleman, "I should have no objection to answering that question. It does refer to the resurrection."

"Well, father," said Mr. M., "I perceive you are an honest man. I will, if you please, ask *you* a few questions."

The old gentleman said he would answer them if he could.

Mr. M. asked him to read the 6th verse – "How long shall it be to the end of these wonders?" – and say what wonders were referred to.

The dandy minister then spoke – "Don't answer that question; he will make a *Millerite* of you."

The elderly minister said he was not afraid of the Bible, let it make what it would of him; and replied, that the "wonders" referred to must mean the resurrection, etc.

"Well," said Mr. M., "is the reply of the one clothed in linen, who sware 'that it should be for a time, times, and an half,' given in answer to the question, how long it will be to the resurrection?"

Here the dandy minister again spoke – "Don't answer that question; for, if you do, he will make a *Millerite* of you." [266]

The other gave him to understand that he was afraid of no result to which an honest investigation of the Scriptures might lead, and that he should answer any questions he chose to. The admission of the dandy minister, that honest answers could not be given to a few simple questions on a portion of Scripture, without making men "Millerites," excited the interest of all to the highest point.

The elderly minister replied, that he thought it must be given in answer to that question.

On hearing the answer, the dandy minister shrunk back, closed his mouth, and interfered no more.

Mr. M. asked who it was that gave this answer.

The other readily replied, that he was undoubtedly the Lord Jesus Christ.

"Well, then," said Mr. M., "if the Lord Jesus Christ, in answer to the question, How long it should be to the resurrection, has sworn with an oath that it shall be for a time, times, and an half, is not the time revealed?"

"But," said the other, "you can't tell what that time, times, and an half mean?"

"I did not agree," said Mr. M., "to do that; our *understanding* of it is another thing. But has not God there revealed the time, and sworn to it with an oath?"

"Yes," said the other, "he has."

"Well, then," said Mr. M., "I have proved all I agreed to."

"Why," said the minister, "I never saw this in this light before. Can you tell what is meant by time, times and an half?"

Mr. M. "I will try. Read, if you please, the 6th verse of Revelation 12."

Min. "'And the woman fled into the wilderness, where she hath a place prepared of God, that they should feed her there a thousand two hundred and three-score days.'"

Mr. M. "Now read the 14th verse."

Min. "'And to the woman were given two wings of a great eagle, that she might fly into the wilderness, into her place, where she is nourished for a time and times and half a time.'"

Mr. M. "Do not those two denote the same period of time?"

Min. "Yes." [267]

Mr. M. "Then must not the time given in answer to the question be the same as the 1260 days?"

The minister acknowledged it must be so.

Mr. M. pointed him to the various places where the same period is presented under different forms, – forty-two months, 1260 days, time, times and half a time, – and showed him how 30 days to a month, and 12 months to a year, would make 3 1/2 years, equal to 1260 days. He then asked him if we might not know that God had revealed the time to the resurrection in days.

He said, yes; but asked if we could know how to reckon them.

Mr. M. pointed him to Daniel 7:25, the time of the continuance of the saints in the hands of the Little Horn, a period of the same length, and asked if that could denote simply 1260 days; "for," said he, "you know that they persecuted the saints more than so many literal days."

This he admitted; but asked, if not literal days, what they were.

Mr. M. showed him that the language was symbolical; that if it had been given in literal time, it would have had a bad effect on past generations, as they would have seen that the judgment could not come in their day, and they might not have lived in continual readiness for it, as they should do. He then referred him to Numbers 14:34 and Ezekiel 4:6, where God has appointed a day for a year; showed him how the 70 weeks were fulfilled in 490 years, – as many years as there were days in 70 weeks, – and showed there were just 1260 years from the time the decree of Justinian went into effect, A. D. 538, to 1798, when the Papacy was subverted by Napoleon.

The minister acknowledged the pertinency of these references, and confessed that the time sworn to by Christ must denote 1260 years.

Mr. M. then showed how the 2300 days and the four great kingdoms, etc., bring us down to the end, and how they must terminate about this time; but confessed that the expected time had gone by. He spoke about an hour, during which the strictest attention was given by those who stood around. Many confessed they never thought that "Millerism" was anything like that. [268]

On arriving at Marietta, Mr. M. was detained a part of the next day in the boat, and the inhabitants came down with the request that he would stop and lecture, offering him the Methodist house. But he was obliged to hasten on, and could not comply with their invitation.

They arrived at Harrisburg, Pa., on Sunday the 8th, and lectured four days in the old Methodist chapel, to good audiences. They then passed on to Middletown, where they remained two days; to Sandersville, where Mr. M. gave one lecture; and to Philadelphia, where they arrived on the 14th of September. On the 16th, Mr. M. commenced his lectures at the Museum Saloon, in Julian street.

On the 19th, Mr. M. reached New York city, and the next day gave a discourse in Franklin Hall. On Sunday, P. M., he preached in the church in Chrystie street, from these words:

> "But this I confess unto thee, that after the way which they call heresy, so worship I the God of my fathers, believing all things that are written in the law and the prophets; and have hope towards God, which they themselves also allow, that there shall be a resurrection of the dead, both of the just and unjust." – Acts 24:14, 15.

He spoke with great ease and clearness respecting the reasons which had fixed his mind on 1843. He acknowledged that there had been a mistake, but expressed his assurance in the near coming of Christ, for which event he entreated all to be in readiness. In the evening, he spoke in the same place, to a crowded and attentive audience, upon the seven last plagues of Revelation 16:15-17, – six of which he believed had been poured out during the last three hundred years.

His health was at this time suffering considerably from the fatigues of the western tour; and, feeling it his duty to rest for a season, he declined the many urgent invitations which were then pressing upon him for lectures elsewhere, and returned to his family at Low Hampton. From that place he wrote as follows:

"September 30, 1844.

"Dear Brother:- I am once more at home, worn down with the fatigue of my journey, my strength so exhausted and my bodily infirmities so great, that I am about concluding I shall never be able again to labor in the vineyard as heretofore. I wish now to remember with gratitude all those who [269] have assisted me in my endeavors to awaken the church and arouse the world to a sense of their awful danger.

"I pray God, my brethren and sisters, that you may receive a reward in this life of an hundred fold, and, in the world to come, eternal life. Many of you have sacrificed much, – your good names, former associations, flattering prospects in life, occupation, and goods; and with me you have received scorn, reproach and scandal from those whom it was our souls' desire to benefit. Yet not one of you *to whom my confidence has ever been given*, has, to my knowledge, murmured or complained. You have cheerfully endured the cross, despised the shame, and with me are looking for and expecting the King in all his glory. This is to me a cause of gratitude to God. May he preserve you unto the end. There have been *deceivers* among us, but God has preserved me from giving them *my confidence* to deceive or betray.

"I found on my arrival here that my brethren had relinquished the meeting-house to a small minority of our church, who separated from us last spring, because the second coming of Christ was there preached – though they claim to be looking for him. Rather than contend with them, our brethren have peaceably relinquished the chapel to them, and will build, if time continues. ...

"William Miller."

CHAPTER 19

For a few months previous to this time, the attention of some had been directed to the tenth day of the seventh month of the current Jewish year, as the probable termination of several prophetic periods. This was not generally [270] received with favor by those who sympathized with Mr. Miller, till a few weeks previous to the time designated, which, on that year, following the reckoning of the Caraite Jews, fell on the 22nd day of October. Mr. Miller had, a year and a half previous, called attention to the seventh month as an important one in the Jewish dispensation; but as late as the date of his last letter (September 30) he had discountenanced the positiveness with which some were then regarding it. On the 6th of October he was first led to favor the expectation which pointed to that month, and thus wrote: "If Christ does not come within twenty or twenty-five days, I shall feel twice the disappointment I did in the spring."

About the same time, also, the belief in the given day was generally received. There were exceptions, but it is the duty of the impartial historian to record the fact, that those who had embraced the views of Mr. Miller, did, with great unanimity, heartily and honestly believe that on a given day they should behold the coming of the King of glory.

The world cannot understand how that could be; and many who professed the name of Christ, have spoken contemptuously of such an expectation. But those who in sincerity love the Saviour, can never feel the least emotion of contempt for such a hope. The effect on those entertaining this belief is thus described by Mr. Miller, in a letter dated October 11, 1844.

> "I think I have never seen among our brethren such *faith* as is manifested in the seventh month. 'He will come,' is the common expression. 'He will not tarry the second time,' is their general reply. There is a forsaking of the world, an unconcern for the wants of life, a general searching of heart, confession of sin, and a deep feeling in

prayer for Christ to come. A preparation of heart to meet him seems to be the labor of their agonizing spirits. There is something in this present waking up different from anything I have ever before seen. There is no great expression of joy: that is, as it were, suppressed for a future occasion, when all heaven and earth will rejoice together with joy unspeakable and full of glory. There is no shouting; that, [271] too, is reserved for the shout from heaven. The singers are silent: they are waiting to join the angelic hosts, the choir from heaven. No arguments are used or needed: all seem convinced that they have the truth. There is no clashing of sentiments: all are of one heart and of one mind. Our meetings are all occupied with prayer, and exhortation to love and obedience. The general expression is, 'Behold, the Bridegroom cometh; go ye out to meet him.' Amen. Even so come, Lord Jesus! WILLIAM MILLER."

The natural heart would be unable to realize that any emotion, but that of fear and dread, could fill the minds of those thus believing. But when the secrets of the great day shall be made known, it will be seen that the coming of Christ was ardently desired by them, and that their hearts were filled with a holy joy, while they were subdued by awe, as standing in the presence of the Governor of the Universe. The state of mind thus produced was a great moral spectacle, upon which those who participated in it will ever look back with pleasure, and without regret.

The next day Mr. Miller wrote again as follows:

"Low Hampton, October 12th, 1844.

"DEAR BROTHER HIMES:- Perhaps you may think me rather too troublesome to write every day; but time is now so short, and the fulfilling of those glories which you have assisted me, more than any other human being, to proclaim, is so near, I cannot help or refrain from congratulating you daily on the glorious prospect we have of soon entering the gates of the beloved city, and of soon harping on the golden harps the everlasting song of hallelujah to the Lamb.

"Yes, my brother, you have borne the shame attached to my name, for some few years past, without a murmur or complaint. I believe it was for Jesus' sake, for we had nothing in common, in a worldly point of view, to prompt *you*, at least, to such an unnatural connection. Our sectarian creeds were at antipodes, our ages very dissimilar, and our habits at a wide difference. You had seen enough, when we became acquainted, to know that your worldly reputation and interest must suffer; and yet you fearlessly left all, launched forth into this glorious cause, – so little understood, [272] so perfectly hated by all the worldly-minded and popular men of our age. This, to me, was a remarkable evidence that God was my helper, and that he would in the end justify us in the work which he must have called us to perform.

"You must bear with me, then, in my folly, if I should seem to boast; for there has been no scene in my life where the hand of God has been more visible than in raising you up to assist me in this work. Had it not been for a few of you, who helped stay up my feeble hands, I must have fainted; but, blessed be the name of God, I am now stronger than ever in faith, and more and more confident that we are within a few days of the crown of glory. I do not expect to see you again in this life, but I do hope to see you soon crowned in glory, and robed in the spotless garment of Christ's righteousness. I expect soon, with you and all true believers and co-workers in this blessed work, to meet around the great white throne, to receive the reward of our sufferings for the name of Jesus. I feel unworthy, and were it not for Christ's worthiness, and the promise of God to save all that believe, I should have no hope. But, blessed be God, his grace and spirit have given me hope, and taught me to believe all things 'which are written in the law and in the prophets.'

"Our meeting last evening was very interesting and solemn. Our brethren came in from adjacent towns. All of our hearts are comforted and faith strengthened that the seventh month begins *to-morrow*. We have two meetings to-day, and we expect the Spirit of God to be with us... Let us all be faithful even to the end. If we faint not we shall reap a rich harvest."

Monday, October 13th, he again wrote:

"Yesterday was a glorious day with us. We commemorated the Lord's supper. Some of those who went out from us came back, and confessed their wrong. ...

"In what a grand and awful time we live.

"Great God, my soul looks up to thine
Eternal purpose still,-
The promise which the word divine
Engages to fulfill. [273]

"I will cut loose from worldly care,
And hope, but never fear;
My daily cry, and nightly prayer,
Is 'Jesus, now appear.'

"Come, Holy God, thy grace to bring,
And rule on David's throne,
While heaven's high arch the echoes ring,
He comes, and all is done.

          "I am, as ever, yours,

             "WILLIAM MILLER."

The phenomenon of a large number of intelligent persons looking for the end of all earthly things was an enigma to mere spectators, and would naturally elicit comment. The following remarks, in the "Middlesex Standard," by a visitor at a camp-meeting held in Derry, N. H., about this time, were conceived in a spirit of candor:

"The Second Advent! – the coming of our Lord in person upon this earth, with signs, and wonders, and terrible judgment! – the heavens rolling together as a scroll! – the elements melting with fervent heat! – the mighty consummation of all things at hand, with its destruction and its triumphs! – the sad wailing of the lost, and the rejoicing songs of the glorified! From this over-swarming hive of industry, – from these crowded treadmills of gain, – here were men and women going out in solemn earnestness to prepare for the dread moment, which they verily suppose is only a few months distant; – to lift up their warning voices in the midst of scoffers and doubters, and to cry aloud to blind priests and to careless churches, 'BEHOLD, THE BRIDEGROOM COMETH!'

"It was one of the most lovely mornings of this loveliest season of the year, – a warm, soft atmosphere, – clear sunshine falling on the city spires and roofs, – the hills of Dracut, quiet and green, in the distance, with their white farm-houses and scattered trees, – around me the continual tread of footsteps hurrying to the toils of the day, – merchants spreading out their wares for the eyes of purchasers, – sounds of hammers, the sharp clink of trowels, the murmur of the great manufactories, subdued by distance. How was it possible, in the midst of so much life, in that sunrise light, and in view of all-abounding beauty, that the idea of 'the death of nature' – the 'baptism of the world in [274] fire' – could take such a practical shape as this? Yet here were sober, intelligent men, gentle and pious women, who, verily believing the end to be close at hand, had left their counting-rooms, and workshops, and household cares, to publish the great tidings, and to startle, if possible, a careless and unbelieving generation into preparation for the day of the Lord, and for that blessed millennium, the restored Paradise; when, renovated and renewed by its fire purgation, the earth shall become, as of old, the 'garden of the Lord,' and the saints alone shall inherit it.

"Very serious and impressive is the fact, that this idea of a radical change in our planet is not only predicted in the Scriptures, but that the earth herself, in her primitive rocks and varying formations, on which is lithographed the history of successive convulsions, darkly prophesies of others to come. The old poet prophets, all the world over, have sung of a renovated world. A vision of it haunted the contemplations of Plato. It is seen in the half-inspired speculations of the old Indian mystics. The Cumaean sibyl saw it in her trances. The apostles and martyrs of our faith looked for it anxiously and hopefully. Gray anchorites in the desert, worn pilgrims to the holy places of Jewish and Christian tradition, prayed for its coming. It inspired the gorgeous vision of Augustine's 'City of God.' In every age since the Christian era, from the caves, and forests, and secluded 'upper chambers' of the times of the first missionaries of the Cross, – from the Gothic temples of the Middle Ages, – from the bleak mountain gorges of the Alps, when the hunted heretics put up their expostulations, 'How long, O Lord, how long!' – down to the present time, and from this Derry camp-ground, has been uttered the prophecy and the prayer for its fulfillment.

"How this great idea manifests itself in the lives of the enthusiasts of the days of Cromwell! Think of Sir Henry Vane, cool, sagacious statesman as he was, waiting with eagerness for the foreshadowings of the millennium, and listening, even in the council-hall, for the blast of the last trumpet! Think of the Fifth Monarchy men, [36] weary with [275] waiting for the long-desired consummation, rushing out, with drawn swords and loaded matchlocks, into the streets of London, to establish at once the reign of King Jesus! Think of the wild enthusiasts of Munster, verily imagining that the millennial reign had commenced in their city! Still later, think of Granville Sharpe, diligently laboring in his vocation of philanthropy, laying plans for the slow but beneficent amelioration of the condition of his countrymen

---

[36] By referring to the Fifth Monarchy men and the men of Munster, he mixes up those who looked for the kingdom of God to be set up *in this world*, and *before* the resurrection, with Millenarians, who look for it in the *immortal state*.

and the world, at the same time maintaining, with the zeal of Father Miller himself, that the earth was just on the point of combustion, and that the millennium would render all his benevolent schemes of no sort of consequence!

"And, after all, is the idea itself a vain one? Shall tomorrow be as to-day? Shall the antagonism of Good and Evil continue as heretofore, forever? Is there no hope that this world-wide prophecy of the human soul, uttered in all climes, in all times, shall be fulfilled? Who shall say it may not be true? Nay, is not its truth proved by its universality? The hope of all honest souls *must* be realized. That through which a distorted, doubtful medium shone even upon the martyr enthusiasts of the French Revolution, – soft gleams of heaven's light rising over the hill of man's passions and crimes, – the glorious ideal of Shelley, who, atheist as he was, through prejudice and early defective education, saw the horizon of the world's future kindling with the light of a better day, – that hope and that faith which constitute, as it were, the world's life, and without which it would be dark and dead, – cannot be in vain."

Thus moralized one who was merely a spectator. Occupying his position, it is easy to conceive the intense interest and pleasure felt by those to whom the near-coming of their Saviour was a welcome reality.

The time immediately preceding the 22nd of October was one of great calmness of mind and of pleasurable expectation on the part of those who regarded that point of time with interest. There was a nearness of approach to God, and a sweetness of communion with him, to which those who experienced it will ever recur with pleasure. During the last ten days, secular business was, for the most part, suspended; and those who looked for the Advent gave themselves to the [276] work of preparation for that event, as they would for death, were they on a bed of sickness, expecting soon to close their eyes on earthly scenes forever.

There were some cases of extravagance, as there have been in all great movements; and it would have been strange had there not been. But the published accounts of these were greatly exaggerated, and hundreds of reports had no foundation in fact. All reports respecting the preparation of ascension robes, etc., and which are still by many believed, were demonstrated over and over again to be false and scandalous. In the investigation of the truth of such, no labor and expense was spared; and it became morally certain that *no instance of the kind anywhere occurred.*

The most culpable incident, which had any foundation in fact, was in Philadelphia. In opposition to the earnest expostulations of Mr. Litch and other judicious persons, a company of about one hundred and fifty, responding to the pretended vision of one C. R. Georgas, on the 21st of October went out on the Darby-street road, about four miles from Market-street bridge, and encamped in a field under two large tents, provided with all needed comforts. The next morning, their faith in Georgas' vision having failed, all but about a dozen returned to the city. A few days later the others returned. That was an act the report of which was greatly exaggerated. It met the emphatic disapproval of Mr. Miller and the Adventists generally, and its folly was promptly confessed by the majority of those who participated in it.

The day passed, and the expectation of the Advent at that time was proved to be premature. The friends were at first quite saddened, but were not disheartened by the passing of the time. This was the *only* specific *day* which was regarded by intelligent Adventists with any positiveness. There were other days named by those whose opinions were received with no favor; but their unauthorized declarations should not be imputed to the body.

The fact that many suspended their business for a few days was censured by opponents; but it was only acting consistently with their faith, opponents being judges. Dr. Dowling, a celebrated Baptist clergyman in New York city, in a review of Mr. Miller, used this strong language: [277]

> "Were this doctrine of Mr. Miller established upon evidence satisfactory to my own mind, I would not rest till I had published in the streets, and proclaimed in the ears of my fellow-townsmen, and especially of my beloved flock, 'The day of the Lord is at hand! Build no more houses! Plant no more fields and gardens! Forsake your shops and farms, and all secular pursuits, and give every moment to preparation for this great event! for in three short years this earth shall be burnt up, and Christ shall come in the clouds, awake the sleeping dead, and call all the living before his dread tribunal.'"

In the first communication received from Mr. Miller after this time, he wrote as follows:

"Low Hampton, November 10th, 1844.

"DEAR BROTHER HIMES:- I have been waiting and looking for the blessed hope, in expectation of realizing the glorious things which God has spoken of Zion. Yes; and, although I have been twice disappointed, I am not yet cast down or discouraged. God has been with me in spirit, and has comforted me. I have now much more evidence that I do believe in God's word. My mind is perfectly calm, and my hope in the coming of Christ is as strong as ever.

"I have done only what, after years of solemn consideration, I felt it my solemn duty to do. If I have erred, it has been on the side of charity, love to my fellow-men, and conviction of duty to God. I could not see that I should harm my fellow-men, even supposing the event should not take place at the time specified; for it is a command of our Saviour to look for it, to watch and be ready. And, if I could by any means, in accordance with God's word, persuade men to believe in a crucified, risen, and coming Saviour, I felt it would have a bearing on the everlasting welfare and happiness of such. I had not a distant thought of disturbing our churches, ministers, or religious editors, or of departing from the best biblical commentaries or rules which had been recommended for the study of the Scriptures. And, even to this day, my opposers have not been able to show wherein I have departed from any rule laid down by our old standard Protestant writers. ...

"Our duty now is to comfort one another with the words [278] of Christ's coming, to strengthen those who are weak among us, to establish the wavering, and to raise up the bowed down, speaking often one to another, and forsaking not the assembling of ourselves together. Let our conversation be in heaven, from whence we look for the Saviour; for the time has now come for us to live by faith, a faith that is tried like gold seven times purified. ...

"Brethren, hold fast; let no man take your crown. I have fixed my mind on another time, and here I mean to stand until God gives me more light, and that is, *to-day, to-day*, and *to-day*, until he comes. Permit me to illustrate this by a parable:

"A certain nobleman, about taking a long journey, called together his servants, gave instructions to every one respecting their work, and commanded them to be faithful in their several occupations; and, at his return, each one was to be rewarded according as his work should be done. He informed them how many days he should be absent, but did not give them the time in the night when he should return; but informed them that, if they would watch, they should know when he was near, even at the door. And he informed them how they might know this: they would first see the lights of his carriage in the distance, and they would hear the rumbling of his carriage-wheels, when they must go out and immediately open for him the portal gates. Whether he should come in the first, second, third, or fourth watch, he would not then inform them; but commanded them to watch.

"After he was gone, many of the servants began to neglect their Master's business, and to form plans for their own amusement; and thus the days appointed for their Master's return were forgotten. The giddy whirl of dissipation filled their mind, time passed rapidly along, and the days had nearly expired, when some of the servants discovered the record of them in the steward's book. This was immediately read in the hearing of all, and created no small excitement among them. Some said the time was not revealed, because the Master said the watch was not known. Others declared that he would never return, but would send his principal servant, when they should have a feasting time to their own liking. Thus were they disputing and wrangling, until the [279] days, according to the best reckoning they could make, had run out, and the night came in which some of them expected him. The porter and a few others determined to watch, while the remainder of the servants were feasting and drinking. The former kept a good look-out; for, at the first watch, they expected their master. They thought that they saw the light, and heard the rumbling of the wheels. They ran among the servants, and cried, 'Behold! the Master cometh.' This made no small stir, and caused many to make preparation for his return. But it proved to be a false alarm. Then the other servants ridiculed the porter and his friends for their *fear*, as *they* called it, and returned to their feasting. The porter and his friends were vigilant until the second watch, when they were again disappointed; and those who had not watched were more vexed than ever. They scoffed and mocked, and turned some of the others out doors. Again they waited for the third watch; and again they were disappointed. The majority of the servants, more angry than ever, now beat and bruise the porter and his friends, and turn them all out of the house, lock the doors, and lay themselves down to sleep. At the fourth watch the Master comes, and finds the porter and a few companions watching, while the doors are barred, and the remainder of the servants are asleep.

"Now let me inquire, Will the Master condemn the porter and his friends for making those false alarms? Will he punish them for disturbing the carousings of their brethren? Which of these two classes of servants will have shown the most love for their Master? Let each one answer these questions, and decide his own case justly. ...

"Yours, as ever, looking, etc.,

William Miller."

On the 18th of November he wrote an article for the Herald on the necessity of exercising patience unto the coming of the Lord. He characterized that as the time of patience, when "ye have need of patience, that, after ye have done the will of God, ye might receive the promise; for yet a little while, and he that shall come will come, and will not tarry." – Hebrews 10:36, 37. Therefore he exhorted them, [280] saying, "Be ye also patient: establish your hearts; for the coming of the Lord draweth nigh." – James 5:8.

There was at that time, certainly, great need of the exercise of patience; for taunting expressions, like "You have not gone up yet!" or "When are you going up, now?" were no uncommon salutation, even from *some* who professed to believe that God *has* "appointed a day in the which he will judge the world;" when the saints *will* "be caught up together to meet the Lord in the air;" and that the elements *will* "melt with fervent heat."

Owing to this state of things, he was led to consider that his work as a public speaker was done; that God, in his providence, had closed the door of his access to the people; and that, consequently, he had nothing more to do in the way of warning sinners to prepare for the coming of Christ, which, he expressed his confidence in the same letter, would not extend beyond that Jewish year.

On the 29th of November, he wrote to Eld. T. E. Jones:

"The disappointment which we have experienced, in my opinion, could never have been foreseen or avoided; and we have been honest men, and believed in the truth of the Bible. I have had time, a few weeks past, to review the whole subject, and, with all the aid of Stuart, Chase, Weeks, Bush, and the whole school of modern writers, I cannot see why we were not right. Taking them altogether, instead of disproving our position, they disprove each other, and confirm me in my views of prophecy.

"But, say you, time has shown us wrong. I am not so certain of that. Suppose that Christ should come before the end of this Jewish year: every honest man would say we were right. And if the world should stand two, or even three years more, it would not, in the least, affect the manner of the prophecy, but the time. One thing I do know, I have preached nothing but what I believed; and God has been with me; his power has been manifested in the work, and much good has been effected; for the people have read the Bible for themselves, and no one can honestly say that he has been deceived by me. My advice has always been for each to study the evidence of his faith for himself."

Four days later he again wrote to the Herald: [281]

"DEAR BRETHREN:- I cannot sit down to write without the reflection that this letter may never reach its destination. Yet I believe in occupying till Christ shall come. Therefore, I still feel it my duty to occasionally drop you a line, to let you know how my soul prospers, and how my faith holds out. As it respects the soul, – I have never enjoyed more calmness of mind, nor more resignation to the holy will of God, and patience of spirit, than I have within a few weeks past. My soul, I think, is stayed on God, and I enjoy peace like a river. For years past, I have often had a spirit of impatience for Christ to come, and have felt grieved in soul because I found in my heart so much of what I called a spirit of fretfulness, and a mind full of impatience. But, I bless God, I have had but little of that recently. I have had great reason to thank God for his abundant goodness in this respect. My *faith* is stronger than ever; and this is somewhat remarkable, when I reflect on the disappointment I have met in my former expectations. But here, too, I see the good hand of God in my strength of faith.

"I believe the ground we have formerly stood upon, as it regards the chronology of prophecy, is the only ground we can take; and if the defect is in human chronology, then no human knowledge is sufficient in this age to rectify it with any degree of certainty; and I see no good that can be accomplished by taking a stand for any future period, with less evidence than we had for 1843-4. For those who would not believe, with all the evidence we then produced, we cannot expect will now believe with much less evidence.

"Again, it is to me almost a demonstration, that God's hand is seen in this thing. Many thousands, to all human appearance, have been made to study the Scriptures by the preaching of the time; and by that means, through faith and the sprinkling of the blood of Christ, have been reconciled to God. And those of us who have been familiar with the fruits and effects of the preaching of this doctrine must acknowledge that He has been with us in so doing, and His wisdom has in a great measure marked out our path, which he has devised for such good as he will accomplish in his own time and manner; as in the case of Nineveh by the preaching of Jonah. If this should be the real state of the [282] case, and we should go on to set other times in the future, we might possibly be found frustrating, or trying to at least, and receive no blessing. I think my brethren will admit that God has been in the work, and he has tried our faith in the best possible manner. ...

"We have erred in many things, and even the second advent brethren were not prepared for the coming of Christ; they had, many of them, left the work of the Lord, and had been doing their own work. The work of the Lord, which he had commanded us to do, was to make the vision plain, to write it on tables, to give the alarm, the midnight cry, and wake up the virgins; and while these things, and these things only, were attended to, our work prospered, and God was with us. And now, my dear brethren, permit me to be plain. I hope all who are worth saving are humble enough to bear my reproof, and I mean to give it with the sincerest of motives, and with the kindest affection of my heart.

"The causes which required God's chastening hand upon us were, in my humble opinion, PRIDE, FANATICISM and SECTARIANISM.

"*Pride* worked in many ways. We ascribed our conquest in argument over our opponents to ourselves. We were seeking the honors or applause of men, more than of God. We were, some of us, seeking to be leaders, instead of being servants; boasting too much of our doing.

"*Fanaticism.* I know our enemies accused us of this before we were guilty; but this did not excuse us for running into it. A thousand expressions were used, without thought or reflection, and I thought sometimes very irreverently, such as 'Bless God,' etc. I was afraid it was done in very many cases to the appearance of outward piety, rather than as the hidden manna of the heart. Sometimes our meetings were distinguished by noise and confusion, and – forgive me, brethren, if I express myself too strongly – it appeared to me more like Babel, than a solemn assembly of penitents bowing in humble reverence before a holy God. I have often obtained more evidence of inward piety from a *kindling eye*, a *wet cheek*, and a *choked utterance*, than from all the noise in Christendom.

"*Sectarianism.* This is always produced by some private opinion of man, rather than by the plain declaration of [283] God's word. For years after I began to proclaim this blessed truth of Christ at the door, I never, if possible to avoid it, even alluded to sectarian principles; and the first objection my Baptist brethren brought against me, was, that I mixed with, and preached unto, all denominations, even to Unitarians, etc. But we have recently, my brethren, been guilty of raising up a sect of our own; for the very things which our fathers did, when they became sects, we have been doing. We have, like them, cried Babylon! Babylon! Babylon! against *all but Adventists*. We have proclaimed and discussed, 'pro et con,' many sectarian dogmas, which have nothing to do with our message. May God forgive us! And now, brethren, we have need of patience, that after we have done the will of God, we may receive the promise.

"Yours as ever,

"William Miller.

"Low Hampton, December 3, 1844."

On the 28th and 29th of December, a conference was held at Low Hampton, N. Y., where Mr. M. spoke of the importance of being found at one's post at the coming of the Master. And, though he thought his work nearly done, yet he should, as he ever had done, follow the leadings of Providence, and he hoped to be found at his post "when the King of kings comes."

An address was then written by Mr. Miller, to those disappointed with him, in which he said:

"We thank God always on your behalf, when we hear, as we already have, that your and our late disappointment has produced in you, and we hope in us also, a deep humiliation and a careful inspection of our hearts. And though we are humbled, and in measure pained, by the jeers of a wicked and perverse generation, we are not terrified nor cast down... You can, all of you, when inquired of for the reasons of your hope, open your Bibles, and with meekness and fear show the inquirer why you hope in the glorious appearing of the great God and our Saviour, Jesus Christ. You need not in a single instance refer the inquirer to your minister, for the reason of your faith... Your creed is the Scriptures; your spelling-book is the Bible; your grammar is the Word indited by the Spirit; your geography [284] respects the promised inheritance of the Holy Land; your astronomy respects the bright starry crown of righteousness; your philosophy is the wisdom which cometh down from God; your bond of union is the love and fellowship of the saints; your teacher is the Holy Ghost; and your professor is the Lord Jesus Christ: your recitation room is your closet; your recitations are heard in your prayers, and your songs fill up your vacations. We speak not of rewards, diplomas, and degrees, for these are reserved in heaven for us, when the dusty walls of this tabernacle shall be dissolved, and we be called home into the new heavens and new earth, to a full fruition of that hope of which we are not ashamed.

"We exhort you, by all the love and fellowship of the saints, to hold fast to this hope. It is warranted by every promise in the word of God. It is secured to you by the two immutable things, – the council and oath of God, in which it is impossible for him to lie. It is ratified and sealed by the death, blood, and resurrection and life of Jesus Christ. You have already had a foretaste of the bliss of this hope, in the seventh month, when every moment you looked for the heavens to open, and reveal unto your gaze the King of Glory. Yes, your whole soul was ravished with a holy joy when you expected to hear the shout of the heavenly host, descending from the Father's glory, to welcome you, a weary pilgrim, to your blessed abode of eternal rest. In that eventful period, where was the world, with all its vain allurements and empty show? It was gone. Had our Saviour then come, no tears would have fallen for a receding world, no sighs would have heaved our breasts for a dissolving earth, with all its pomp, its pleasures, or its praises. All this was then no more to us than a bubble on Niagara's cataract. God's goodness then gave us a slight repast, like Elijah's meat that lasted forty days. And how can you or we give up a hope so full of joy, of holy love, and heavenly anticipation? ...

"But we are taunted with, 'O! you have prolonged your vision again and again, and have failed every time; now, won't you give it up and come back to us? You are not honest if you will not.' When they thus accuse us, have we nothing to say? If we altogether hold our peace, they [285] will be wise in their own conceits, and go and report that they have shut our mouths, so that we could not say a word for ourselves, and thus the cause would be injured. But never fear, brethren; God has told you what to say. Do as he bids you, and he will take care of the consequences. God says, 'Say unto them, the days are at hand, and the effect of every vision.' ...

"We hope that none of us will try to change the chronology of the visions; for they must all fail in our eyes. If any vision should be so construed as to fix on another definite time in the future, we cannot conceive how the Scripture is fulfilled, that 'every vision faileth.' Let us, then, be satisfied in patiently waiting God's time. But let us be careful that we do not lay off our armor, cease our watching, sleep at our post, or be caught in a snare, when the Son of Man shall come. It is better to be ready before the time, and to wait a while, than not to be ready when the time shall come, – to be lost. We exhort you, then, with the Lord's advice, 'Be like men waiting for their Lord, that when he cometh they may open to him immediately.'

"Again we exhort you, brethren, that every one may edify and be edified, that you forsake not the assembling of yourselves together as often as your situation and circumstances shall permit; that we may comfort and console each other in our trials, be ourselves established in the present truth, and our minds be stirred up to remember that our Judge standeth at the door. How can we, who have taken so much delight in the study of the blessed Bible, return to the beggarly elements of vain philosophy and traditions of the fathers? ...

"Again, we exhort you, brethren, to be faithful in business. Let every one labor with his hands in the several callings in which God has placed us, that none of us may be a burden to any, and that we may all of us have wherewith to communicate and do good; for it is more blessed to give than to receive; and that we may none of us give any occasion to our enemies to reproach us with being busy-bodies in other men's matters, or with not providing for our own house. In thus doing, we may put to silence the reproaches of those who are seeking every occasion to destroy the doctrine that we rejoice to believe. We may, while [286] engaged in our several occupations, be fervent in spirit, serving the Lord. If we could not be, it would be evidence that we were not engaged in a proper calling, or that our hearts were not right with God. ...

"We also beseech you, brethren, by the coming of our Lord Jesus Christ, that ye be not led about by every spirit, but try the spirits; for every spirit is not of God, and it is evident that there are now many spirits in the earth. ... There are a few individuals among us teaching that Christ has come, and that we are not mistaken in the *time*, but in the *manner*, of his coming. Let us be careful lest we cease from our watchfulness, and so that day come upon us unawares. Remember that the same Jesus will come in like manner as he was seen to ascend. Every eye shall see him, and we shall see him as he is, and be like him, when that day shall come for which we look; and then the heavens, being on fire, shall be dissolved, and the elements shall melt with fervent heat. ...

"If God means not what he says, to whom shall we go for instruction? Who has been his counsellor, or sat in the council chamber of the Almighty? Man is but grass, the flower whereof fadeth. He is but of yesterday, and his life is a breath. 'Cursed is man who trusteth in man, and maketh flesh his arm, and whose heart departeth from the Lord.' Hold on, then, to the 'Sure Word of Prophecy,' for you will soon reap the fruits of your faith, if you faint not."

On the 16th of January, 1845, after reading a pamphlet[37] which had been sent him, Mr. Miller wrote as follows:

> "I never left off reading any book, save the Bible, with such a deep and heartfelt anxiety to have all Christians, of all denominations, read it, as I have this. I said to myself, If all would candidly read, and honestly compare this with the Word of God, all prejudice and preconceived opinions, which now serve to confuse, divide, and distract the dear family of God on earth, would be removed, and we should see eye to eye on the great and glorious question of the Master's return. Or, at least, all would see the necessity [287] for it, and love and pray for it; and thus our hearts and our prayers would be one.
>
> "I immediately began, in my mind, to devise some plan by which this object could be effected. The first plan which my imagination suggested, was for each one who is already confirmed in the truth of these things, and able, to supply himself with a copy. Then we would each feel bound to go to at least one Christian friend every week, and, by kind and benevolent means, get them to read, digest, and be converted to these glorious truths. I then calculated that when any one was truly converted, he would make another fresh and efficient missionary. I went so far in my imagination as to calculate that one a week for each missionary would be light work; and this, continued in arithmetical progression, to my surprise I found the whole world would be converted to see eye to eye in a very few months.
>
> "What can this mean? said I to myself. Has not the world wisdom enough to have tried this plan? Surely there are thousands now living on the earth wiser and better than myself; why has not the thing been tried and succeeded before?
>
> "I then began to look about for a precedent, and my mind first reverted to Jesus Christ. Surely, said I, he had, when on the earth, more wisdom than all living, for the devising of means; he had all power to accomplish his plans; he had love enough to prompt him to execute it, for he gave his life to redeem lost man; and, if this plan would insure success, he would never fail.
>
> "I therefore reviewed his life. The first act of his ministry was to send out his twelve disciples, and other seventy also, to go two and two into every city in Judea, and into private houses, if possible, to persuade men that the kingdom of God had come nigh unto them. He endued them with power from on high to work miracles, in confirmation of the truth of their proclamation. And what was the effect? We cannot

---

[37] The second number of the "Advent Shield."

exactly tell. We know some things which it did not do. It did not convert many of their political rulers, none of their literati, none of the lawyers or Scribes; not one, as we can learn, of all the priests, and none of the principal sects, believed... Some few [288] years afterwards, the church at Jerusalem tried the same plan. They were driven by persecution from that city, and went everywhere preaching faith, repentance, and the resurrection. They had some better success, yet not in comparison to the number who heard; for Paul says, their sound went out to the ends of the earth. But very few believed. Again, it has been tried in our day. For fifty years the Protestant churches have been sending Bibles, tracts, and publications without number; and is the world converted? No. It has waxed worse and worse. ...

"My visionary scheme was demolished at a blow, and became like Nebuchadnezzar's image, as the chaff of the summer threshing-floor.

"WM. MILLER."

Soon after this, January 29, 1845, by the action of an ecclesiastical council, Mr. Miller and the majority of the church in Low Hampton were virtually separated from the Baptist denomination. The following history of the case was communicated to a Baptist clergyman in western New York, who had written to Mr. Miller for the particulars:

"DEAR BRO. PARSONS:- Your letter, asking for information concerning my exclusion from the Baptist denomination, to which I had belonged for about thirty years, is received. The history of the proceedings against me and my brethren (for the church were excluded with me, or quite a large majority of them) is simply as follows.

"The church, or the majority, had embraced what is called the Advent faith. While some of us believed in the time (1843), there were others who merely believed in the manner of the Advent, and assented to its being near; at the same time, there was a small minority of the church who were opposed both to the manner and time. Yet no labors had been taken on either side while in this situation.

"The church voted that they would support the gospel, or a minister, by taxing themselves equally, according to their ability. Here the first seeds were sown which indicated a division of the church. Two or three of the rich brethren declared they would not submit to the vote of the church, and withdrew their support. The majority of the church then engaged Elder Jones, a Baptist minister. This was in the fall or summer of 1843. In the spring of 1844, the minority [289] engaged Elder Dillaway (a strong opposer of the Advent doctrine after '43), for half of the time, and demanded of the church the meeting-house. But as Elder Jones had been engaged for a year, the meeting-house was not given up until the fall; when the brethren, rather than have any contention, gave it up to Elder D. and his hearers, and held their meetings in a school-house, where the minority had formerly held theirs. On the 29th of January, 1845, the minority called an *ex-parte* council, in a private manner, so that it was not known to the church until the council met. This council, which was constituted on the day above mentioned, consisted of seven ministers and ten lay brethren. Enclosed I send you the doings of the council, and every Baptist can judge who has departed from the usages and customs of the Baptist denomination. We are walking in the ordinances and fellowship as formerly in the church, and think it a small thing to be judged of men.

"Yours, etc.　　　Wm. Miller.

"*Low Hampton, April 27*, 1846."

When the majority of the church found that an *ex-parte* council was in session, they immediately came forward and consented that it should be a *mutual* one. It will be seen that the minority of the church consisted of only five men, about the same number of persons who had been suspended from the church for neglect of covenant obligations, and a number of females who had taken no part in church matters for many years.

The following is the list of charges submitted to the council by the minority against the majority of the church:

Charges.

"The Baptist church in Low Hampton make the following statements, as the grounds of their grievances with the majority of the church, whom they consider as having left the original platform of the Baptist denomination, affording their countenance to doctrines which time has proved to be false, and which have been the occasion of dissension and discord among brethren:

"1st. We are grieved that the brethren claiming to be the church should have employed, in the year 1843, contrary [290] to our expressed wishes, a man of avowed sentiments that the Second Advent of Christ would take place in the year 1843, and whose known purpose was to preach this doctrine.

"2nd. We are grieved that the brethren above named should take up a labor with a number of esteemed brethren and sisters, and, as far as their authority went, to exclude them from the church, because they could not conscientiously attend meetings where doctrines were preached which were so manifestly unscriptural, and of pernicious tendency.

"3rd. We are grieved that a test, not known in the Bible, of Christian character, should be set up by the above-named brethren, namely: A belief in the second coming of Christ in the year 1844, – a test which has been brought to view both private and public.

"4th. We are grieved to hear from the above-named brethren all those churches who do not accord with them in their views, denounced as Babylon, the mother of harlots, etc.; and the ministry calumniated in a most slanderous manner.

"5th. We are grieved to see the above-named brethren countenance a departure from the usages of the Baptist church, and from scriptural examples, in administering the ordinance of baptism to persons without any relation of Christian experience, or other evidence of piety than belief in their peculiar dogmas.

"6th. We are grieved that the above-named brethren should violate their covenant engagements, and adopt a resolution disfellowshipping all those who deserted from them, without taking any previous steps of labor.

"7th. We are grieved that the above-named brethren should take away and withhold from us the church and society books, and communion furniture, and other property belonging to the meeting-house.

"We would further state that the circumstances are a grief to us, inasmuch as they afford evident intimations of a purpose to change the character of this church into that of a Second Advent church, as has been done in many other places, when similar preliminary measures have been adopted.

> "Hezekiah Whittock
> "Seth Peck   } *Committee.*
> "Paulinus Millard

"*Hampton, November* 10, 1844."

[Here follow the names of twenty females, and four males.] [291]

"Report of the Council in the case of the Baptist Church in Hampton.

"In the judgment of the Council -

"**1.** *Resolved,* That the *first* charge has been sustained, and that it is not profitable to the cause of Christ to make the Second Advent of Christ at any definite time the common topic of discussion from the desk.

"**2.** *Resolved,* That the second charge was sustained.

"**3.** *Resolved,* That the third charge was sustained.

"**4.** *Resolved,* That the fourth charge was sustained.

"**5.** *Resolved,* That the fifth charge was sustained.

"**6.** *Resolved,* That the sixth charge was sustained.

"Therefore, we *Resolve,* 1st. That in sustaining the minority in the above charges, we regard them to be the regular Baptist church in Hampton.

"2nd. That we recommend this church to hold itself to receive members of the majority upon suitable confession.

"R. O. Dwyer, Chairman.

"Levi Parmely, Secretary.

"*Hampton, January 29th,* 1845."

MINORITY REPORT

"The minority of the Council would most respectfully protest against the majority of said Council, for the following reasons:

"That the charges exhibited by the minority of the church were not sufficiently proven against the majority; and several of them, if sufficiently proven, imply not in themselves a departure from the Scriptures, nor from the usages of the Baptist denomination. In no case was it proven that the majority of said church took any step towards the minority, that the Bible does not, in our opinion, fully sustain; excepting that the 6th charge was proven, which is for disfellowshipping all those [members of that church] who dissent from them, without any previous steps of labor. But that act was rescinded by the majority of the church, and due notice of it given to the Council before they made their decision known to the public, or the parties, and the church accompanying the vote with a confession that they were wrong and regretted the act. The step, however, upon which the charges were founded against the majority, was not taken [292] until the minority (composed of four or five males only) had restored four or five others who had been excluded from fellowship by the majority, for the neglect of covenant obligations, and agreeably to the usages of the Baptist denomination.

"The 5th charge was for departing from the usages of the denomination, by baptizing persons without any relation of Christian experience, or other evidence. This was not proven to be a church act. The proof was, that the minister, who preached for the majority, baptized a person who insisted upon the administration of the ordinance the same night; but not until the minister, and one other brother at least, were convinced that the candidate was an experienced Christian. This act was justified by the undersigned by Scripture; as, for instance, the case of Lydia and her household, the Jailer and household, Philip and the Eunuch, and also the day of Pentecost, when there were above three thousand baptized. These scriptural examples are believed by the undersigned to be a sufficient warrant for a minister of the gospel, in at least a case of emergency, to baptize, when a candidate urges that he dare not hazard until morning the neglect of a known duty. This baptism has, however, never been sanctioned by any church act of the majority.

"As a further reason for protesting, it was proven that the minority brethren had set up a separate meeting, and, as stated before, had restored, without any confession, we believe, five members of the church, who had been excluded by the majority (and who were the then acknowledged regular Baptist church), for neglect of covenant obligations, and not for a difference of opinion upon the Second Advent, or any other question. Still, the majority of the Council have, with these facts staring them in the face, acknowledged and resolved that the four or five brethren, together with the five brethren and sisters, excluded by the majority for neglect of the covenant obligations, shall be recognized as the regular Baptist church. It is true that the minority have several names of sisters added to their list, some of whom have taken but little part in church matters for many years. Although the Council was called as *ex parte*, yet after assembling it was made a mutual Council.

"The undersigned verily believe that great injustice has [293] been done to the majority for departing from the usages of our denomination, in setting up a separate meeting, and in those four or five brethren pretending to hold church meetings, and restoring members who had been regularly excluded, and which, in fact, is sanctioning the same acts, or worse ones, than those complained of by the minority.

"THOMAS A. SHERWOOD,

"*Member of the Council from the Kingsbury*
"*Baptist Church, Washington Co., N. Y.*"

CHAPTER 20

Results Of The Seventh Month – Discussion Of New Questions – Mr. Miller's Position Respecting Them, Etc.

After this, various questions began to be mooted respecting "the seventh-month movement." Some contended that it was all ordained and ordered of God; and others claimed that it was a work of Satan, to torment God's children by disappointment. The majority of Adventists took the position that the *time* was an error of human judgment; but that preaching the coming of the Saviour in connection with it, where it was attended with love to God, a desire to save men, and a love for Christ's appearing, was attended by the blessing of the Holy Spirit, not because of the *error* in the time, but because of their desire to do the will of God, notwithstanding the erroneous calculation. These did not deem it proper to make God responsible for their mistakes.

Those who ascribed the work specified to the devil soon apostatized, and walked no more with Adventists, some giving up all pretensions to religion. Those who ascribed it all to the Lord, or a majority of such, went into various fanatical views and practices, and imbibed a bitter spirit, which soon made a wide breach between them and those who were willing to admit their own imperfections, and to confess their mistake.

To be consistent, those who ascribed that movement entirely [294] to the Lord had to consider that some event, in connection with the fulfillment of prophecy, *did* transpire at that time. And, as they had taught that Christ would then come, they conceived the idea that he came invisibly, and closed the door of mercy to the sinner – illustrating it by the parable of the Bridegroom's coming and shutting the door, after which the foolish virgins sought admittance in vain. Thus they contended that the work of preaching the gospel was ended.

It was an object of some importance to these to get from Mr. Miller some expression favoring their interpretation. It was known that he held that, for a period previous to the actual coming of Christ, he would cease to intercede for, and the Holy Spirit cease to strive with, sinners; and they were in hopes to convince him that that period had arrived. He was accordingly overwhelmed with letters asking his opinion on that point. To save replying to these, in the Advent Herald of February 12, 1845, he thus referred to the experience of the seventh month:

> "The sympathetic and simultaneous movement on the minds of almost all the Second Advent brethren, and on many others, preceding the tenth day, the rapidity with which that sentiment was received, the general credence that was given to it by nearly all of those who were looking for immediate redemption, the humbling effect it produced on the hearts and conduct of those who believed, – in the abandon- ment of all worldly objects, the sacrifice of earthly goods, and, in many cases, the entire dedication of soul and body to God, – the deep and anxious feelings of heart which many of us felt, – all marked its character. Then, every moment we expected the heavens would open and reveal to us the dear Saviour, with all his shining hosts, and that we should see the graves open, and the loved forms of our relations arise from their dusty beds in immortal bloom and eternal life, and we ourselves pass the sudden change from mortality to immortality, from time to eternity. Then, as we verily thought, we had bid adieu to this world of sin, of misery, and woe, and expected to be ushered into the new heavens and new earth, wherein dwelleth righteousness. O, blissful day! How solemn, yet how interesting! I hope to see another day like this, and to literally realize what I then expected. [295] It was a day long to be remembered, and I cannot account for it on any other principle than to suppose that God's benevolent hand and wisdom were in the movement."

He then recapitulated the arguments which were drawn from the types in reference to the seventh month, showing their plausibility, and proceeded to the second point in the controversy, thus:

> "But you ask why I do not show whether the probation of sinners is ended. I answer, It is a close point, and, if handled at all, it ought to be done very wisely, and with a great deal of humility. I would not grieve, if possible to avoid it, one of Christ's little ones."

He then proceeded to give his views on various Scriptures, from which he argued that, before the end, such a period would transpire, with- out intimating whether he believed it had arrived.

The editors of the Advent Herald, in giving his letter, replied to his arguments, and contended that probation only terminated with the personal coming of Christ. His letter, as published, gave little satisfaction to either party. Both claimed him. To determine his actual position, Prof. N. N. Whiting wrote him, and Mr. Miller replied as follows:

"MY DEAR BROTHER:- Your favor of the 5th was gladly received, and I take this early opportunity to answer your inquiries as far as my memory or knowledge will admit.

"As it respects your first question, whether, in my judgment, 'the time of probation came to an end on the 22nd of October or not,' I answer, my mind was not definite on that day. But the experience and scenes of that month were astounding to me, and my mind was brought to a conclusion that God, by his invisible angels, was separating the two classes of men, the chaff from the wheat. But to say my judgment was fully convinced that it was closed, I must say no. I know it is true that, in answer to a score of letters, making the same inquiries as yourself, in my letter, published in the Herald of February 12, I gave several texts, which, to me, were evidence that, before Christ came, there would be a time when men would seek, knock, and cry, and [296] it would not be opened; for, how sinners could or would knock in the eternal state, I have no means of knowing. The editors of the Herald, knowing more about the controversy which had begun in the ranks of the Adventists than I did or could, in order to prevent the mischief or harm which they supposed my letter might do, attached their notes, which gave the brethren on the other side of the question more reason to suppose I had taken the ground that the door was shut in the seventh month; and they thus claimed me on all the fanciful expositions of the parable of the virgins.

"I have ever been of the opinion that my first and last view of that parable, as given in my lectures, is the true exposition. That parable was never given to show the exact order or time of marriage and shutting of the door; but as an illustration of the kingdom of heaven when these things should transpire, i.e., in its character 'likened unto.' If we strain this parable to make it imply an order in time, we involve ourselves in difficulties with other passages in Scripture, which I have no fair means of extricating myself from, especially those where they are described as asking and begging when it is too late, which, to me, is the very reason I would assign why the door might be shut, yet we be ignorant of the fact.

"With our present light, it would be impossible for any man to prove that the door is shut; it can only be a conjecture, founded upon circumstances in the case. There are two cases which I will mention: one would be the cessation of the operation of the Spirit upon the hearts of the truly pious in laboring and praying for sinners; and the other must be the fearful looking for the fiery indignation, which, I think, according to the Scripture, must seize upon the hearts of those who have willfully rejected Christ. The hypocrite is given over to believe a lie, considering himself safe in his profession; and, consequently, the despair of some, and the perfect recklessness of others, and the restraint of the Holy Spirit being withdrawn from the minds of the impenitent, would immediately produce a time of trouble such as Daniel 12:1 speaks of: 'And at that time shall Michael stand up, the great Prince which standeth for the children of thy people; and there shall be a time of trouble [297] such as never was since there was a nation, even to that same time; and at that time thy people shall be delivered, every one that shall be found written in the book.' These would at least be evidence to my suspicion, if not to my full assurance. It was a fact, for a few days in the seventh month in the circle of my acquaintance, that the reports I heard from every quarter led me to have strong suspicion that we had approached the time which I cannot but believe we must experience before the end. I think at present the evidence is strong against the idea of the door being shut; but those brethren who have adopted the suspicion at least ought to be treated with a great deal of kindness. I do not like much I have seen published and spoken on both sides of the question. It is one of that kind of questions which is calculated to divide warm friends; for it cannot be settled satisfactorily but by time and experience.

"The arguments, in my humble opinion, on both sides, want a great quantity of brotherly love to make them digest easily. I, then, beg and pray my brethren we may let contention alone before it is meddled with. And I now plead with those who have supposed the door to be shut to yield the point to our brethren of the opposite view; for it is evident at present that all the evidence is against its being now shut, if we can believe the reports of our brethren from different parts; and surely my soul will not permit me to doubt their veracity who have been with us as pioneers in the work of calling up the world to this important point of our faith, the second advent of Jesus. Let us be silent at least for two months, if Christ does not come before, and by that time I think we shall obtain more light; and if Christ does come, we shall not wish to be found contending with brethren of a like precious faith on a subject dependent wholly on circumstances in which we may be so likely to err. I do hope my advice will be heeded in this thing, and that we will be patient, and not grieve each other; for the Judge is at the door. ...

"WILLIAM MILLER.

"*Low Hampton, March* 10, 1845."

Soon after this other views were promulgated by those who adhered to the "shut door." Some taught feet-washing [298] and kissing as religious ceremonies; bodily exercises and mesmeric ecstasies were regarded as religious experience; power to discern the spiritual condition of others was claimed, etc. etc.; and they made no scruple in denouncing and consigning to perdition those whom they judged destitute of religion, according to their various standards and tests. Brotherly love gave place to contention and disputation; and the cause had to bear the reproach of those who had thus departed from the position occupied by Mr. Miller and the body.

Writing on the 7th of April, he referred to these things as follows:

"MY DEAR BRO. HIMES:- I should utterly despair of the Second Advent cause, were it not evident, by its past and present history, that God is for us. You know, my dear brother, there was a time when you and I, with a few choice brethren, stood alone. ... We acknowledged our weakness, and claimed no superiority over our fellows. We provoked no one to combat, and made no attack on the prevailing or popular institutions of the day; yet they began to be alarmed. Why? Because, as the people began to hear the foolish reports of our enemies, they became more and more anxious to know what these things meant. ...

"Among the many pious who took sides with us were some of those uneasy, ever-changing, unstable, insubordinate, and self-exalted spirits, who stood ready to jump on and ride into notice and power the moment they saw how the case would go. This kind of spirits have always seized the reins of government, are never satisfied with their present position, and will change every new moon. There are many of this class among us, if not of us, at the present time, who are trying to lead away followers after them.

"This is a peculiar time. The greatest variety of fanciful interpretations of Scripture are now being presented by new luminaries, reflecting their rays of light and heat in every direction. Some of these are wandering stars, and some emit only twilight. I am sick of this everlasting changing; but, my dear brother, we must learn to have patience. If Christ comes this spring, we shall not need it long; and if he comes not, we shall need much more. I am prepared for [299] the worst, and hope for the best. God will not forsake us, unless we forsake him. ...

"'It is a small thing to be judged of man's judgment,' says the apostle; so that you need not fear man. I have often been consigned to perdition, and yet I have a blessed hope. I often think, when I hear a brother judging and condemning another, what an excellent Pope he would make. Therefore, fear them not; for if we judge and condemn our brother, we are making ourselves 'judges of the law, rather than doers of the law.' ...   WM. MILLER.

"*Low Hampton, April 7, 1845.*"

In connection with the great variety of views received by those who adhered to the "Shut Door," there was issued a great variety of papers attempting to sustain them. These, being circulated in every direction, created great confusion, and made it difficult for those not initiated to understand the true position of believers in the Second Advent. This was illustrated by the following anecdote related by Mr. Miller.

The first person in his own parish who fully embraced his views was an old woman, an humble, praying Christian; and she continued steadfast in the faith on the original platform. She was in humble circumstances, and, not being able to take a paper, Mr. Miller sent her his papers when he had read them.

One week he received sixteen different sheets, all purporting to be Advent publications, but the most of them advocating contradictory sentiments. After he had examined them, he sent them to the old woman. It was not long before he had a special message from her, requesting his immediate presence.

He hastened to her house, not knowing but something important was the cause of the summons. On his arrival, she began:

"Have you read all these papers?"

"I have looked them over."

"But are they all Advent papers?"

"They profess to be."

"Well, then," said she, "I am no longer an Adventist. I shall take the old Bible, and stick to that." [300]

"But," said Mr. M., "we have no confidence in one half there is advocated in those papers."

"We!" exclaimed the old lady, "who is *we?*"

"Why," replied Mr. M., "*we* are those who do not fellowship these things."

"Well, but I want to know who *we is.*"

"Why, all of us who stand on the old ground."

"But that an't telling who *we* is. I want to know who *we* is."

"Well," said Mr. Miller, in relating the story, "I was confounded, and was unable to give her any information who *we* were."

In this dilemma it was considered very important, on the part of Mr. Miller and his friends, to define their position, and to ascertain who did sympathize with their views. To determine this, a Mutual Conference was called, to assemble at Albany, N. Y., on the 29th of April, 1845.

CHAPTER 21

*Mutual Conference At Albany – Declaration Of Principles
– Plan Of Operations – Address To The Brethren – Action
Of The Conference Defended By Mr. Miller, Etc.*

On the 23rd of April, Mr. Miller, in company with Mr. Himes, visited Albany, and commenced a course of lectures on the prophecies. Mr. M. spoke with his usual clearness and ability, was in good spirits, and was listened to by a large and respectful audience.

On the 29th, the Conference assembled at 9 A. M., at the "House of Prayer," in Grand street. After singing, and a prayer by Mr. Miller, it was temporarily organized by the choice of Mr. Miller, Chairman, and Mr. Himes, Secretary, who stated the objects for which the Conference had been called, namely, "to consult together respecting the condition and wants of brethren in the several sections of the country; that we may be better enabled to act in concert, and with more efficiency, in the promulgation of Gospel truths."

After the names and residence of members were ascertained, [301] the Conference was fully organized by the choice of Rev. Elon Galusha, of Lockport, N. Y., President, and S. Bliss and O. R. Fassett, Secretaries.

A committee of twelve, consisting of William Miller, Josiah Litch, N. N. Whiting, J. V. Himes, Sylvester Bliss, L. D. Fleming, Erastus Parker, H. Caswell, I. R. Gates, I. H. Shipman, Prosper Powell, and Elon Galusha, were appointed to arrange business for the action of the Conference. While they were thus engaged, the others were profitably occupied in listening to statements of the condition of things in different sections of the country. The committee reported, in part, on the second day, and in full on the third and last day of the session, as follows:

REPORT OF THE COMMITTEE TO THE CONFERENCE

"Your committee, appointed for the purpose of taking into consideration the great principles upon which we can unite and act in advancing the cause of truth, for the edification of the body of Christ, the salvation of souls, and the preparation of man for the near Advent of the Saviour, submit the following report:

"In view of the many conflicting opinions, unscriptural views, leading to unseemly practices, and the sad divisions which have been thereby caused by some professing to be Adventists, we deem it incumbent on us to declare to the world our belief that the Scriptures teach, among others, the following

"IMPORTANT TRUTHS.

"1st. That the heavens and earth which are now, by the word of God, are kept in store, reserved unto fire against the day of judgment and perdition of ungodly men. That the day of the Lord will come as a thief in the night, in the which the heavens shall pass away with a great noise, and the elements shall melt with fervent heat; the earth also, and the works that are therein, shall be burned up. That the Lord will create new heavens and a new earth, wherein righteousness – that is, the righteous – will forever dwell.[38] And that the kingdom and the dominion under the whole [302] heaven shall be given to the people of the saints of the Most High, whose kingdom is an everlasting kingdom, and all dominions shall serve and obey him.[39]

2nd. That there are but two advents or appearings of the Saviour to this earth.[40] That both are personal and visible.[41] That the first took place in the days of Herod,[42] when He was conceived of the Holy Ghost,[43] born of the Virgin Mary,[44] went about doing good,[45] suffered on the cross, the just for the unjust,[46] died,[47] was buried,[48] arose again the third day, the firstfruits of them that slept,[49] and ascended into the

---

[38] 2 Peter 3:7, 10, 13.

[39] Daniel 7:27.

[40] Hebrews 9:28.

[41] Acts 1: 9, 11.

[42] Matthew 2:1.

[43] Matthew 1:18.

[44] Matthew 1:25.

[45] Matthew 11:5.

[46] 1 Peter 3:18.

[47] Luke 23:46.

[48] Luke 23:56.

[49] 1 Corinthians 15:4.

heavens,[50] which must receive him until the times of the restitution of all things, spoken of by the mouth of all the holy prophets.[51] That the second coming or appearing will take place when he shall descend from heaven, at the sounding of the last trump, to give his people rest,[52] being revealed from heaven in flaming fire, taking vengeance on them that know not God, and obey not the Gospel.[53] And that he will judge the quick and the dead at his appearing and kingdom.[54]

3rd. That the second coming or appearing is indicated to be now emphatically nigh, even at the doors,[55] by the chronology of the prophetic periods,[56] the fulfillment of prophecy,[57] and the signs of the times.[58] And that this truth should be preached both to saints and sinners, that the first may rejoice, knowing their redemption draweth nigh,[59] and the last be warned to flee from the wrath to come,[60] before the Master of the house shall rise up and shut to the door.[61]

4th. That the condition of salvation is repentance toward God, and faith in our Lord Jesus Christ.[62] And that those who have repentance and faith will live soberly, and righteously, and godly, in this present world, looking for that blessed hope, and the glorious appearing of the great God and our Saviour Jesus Christ.[63]

---

[50] Luke 24:51.

[51] Acts 3:21.

[52] 1 Thessalonians 4:16, 17; 1 Corinthians 15:52.

[53] 2 Thessalonians 1:7, 8.

[54] 2 Timothy 4:1.

[55] Matthew 24:33.

[56] Daniel 7:25; 8:14; 9:24; 12:7, 11, 12; Revelation 9:10, 15; 11:2, 3; 12:6, 14; 13:5.

[57] Daniel 2d, 7th, 8th, 9th, 11th, and 12th chaps.; Revelation 9th, 11th, 12th, 13th, 14th, and 17th chaps.

[58] Matthew 24:29; Luke 21:25, 26.

[59] Luke 21:28; 1 Thessalonians 4:18.

[60] 2 Corinthians 5:11.

[61] Luke 13:24, 25.

[62] Acts 20:21; Mark 1:15.

[63] Titus 2:11-13.

5th. That there will be a resurrection of the bodies of all [303] the dead,[64] both of the just and the unjust.[65] That those who are Christ's will be raised at his coming.[66] That the rest of the dead will not live again until after a thousand years.[67] And that the saints shall not all sleep, but shall be changed in the twinkling of an eye at the last trump.[68]

"6th. That the only millennium taught in the Word of God is the thousand years which are to intervene between the first resurrection and that of the rest of the dead, as inculcated in the 20th of Revelation.[69] And that the various portions of Scripture which refer to the millennial state are to have their fulfillment after the resurrection of all the saints who sleep in Jesus.[70]

"7th. That the promise, that Abraham should be the heir of the world, was not to him, or to his seed, through the law, but through the righteousness of faith.[71] That they are not all Israel which are of Israel.[72] That there is no difference, under the Gospel dispensation, between Jew and Gentile.[73] That the middle wall of partition that was between them is broken down, no more to be rebuilt.[74] That God will render to every man according to his deeds.[75] That if we are Christ's, then are we Abraham's seed, and heirs according to the promise.[76] And that the only restoration of Israel, yet future, is the restoration of the saints to the earth, created anew, when God shall open the graves of those descendants of Abraham who died in faith, without receiving the promise, with the believing Gentiles who have been grafted in with them into the same olive tree; and shall cause them to come up

---

[64] John 5:28, 29.

[65] Acts 24:15.

[66] 1 Corinthians 15:23.

[67] Revelation 20:5.

[68] 1 Corinthians 15:51, 52.

[69] Revelation 20:2-7.

[70] Isaiah 11; 35:1, 2, 5-10; 65:17-25.

[71] Romans 4:13.

[72] Romans 9:6.

[73] Romans 10:12.

[74] Ephesians 2:14, 15.

[75] Romans 2:6.

[76] Galatians 3:29.

out of their graves, and bring them, with the living, who are changed, into the land of Israel.[77]

"8th. That there is no promise of this world's conversion.[78] That the Horn of Papacy will war with the saints, and prevail against them, until the Ancient of Days shall come, and judgment be given to the saints of the Most High, and the time come that the saints possess the kingdom.[79] That the children of the kingdom, and the children [304] of the wicked one, will continue together until the end of the world, when all things that offend shall be gathered out of the kingdom, and the righteous shall shine forth as the sun in the kingdom of their Father.[80] That the Man of Sin will only be destroyed by the brightness of Christ's coming.[81] And that the nations of those which are saved and redeemed to God by the blood of Christ, out of every kindred, and tongue, and people, and nation, will be made kings and priests unto God, to reign forever on the earth.[82]

"9th. That it is the duty of the ministers of the Word to continue in the work of preaching the Gospel to every creature, even unto the end,[83] calling upon them to repent, in view of the fact that the kingdom of heaven is at hand;[84] that their sins may be blotted out when the times of refreshing shall come from the presence of the Lord.[85]

And, 10th. That the departed saints do not enter their inheritance, or receive their crowns, at death.[86] That they without us cannot be made perfect.[87] That their inheritance, incorruptible and undefiled, and that fadeth not away, is reserved in heaven, ready to be revealed in the last time.[88] That there are laid up for them and us crowns of righteousness, which the Lord, the righteous Judge, shall give at the

---

[77] Ezekiel 37:12; Hebrews 11:12, 13; Romans 11:17; John 5:28, 29.

[78] Matthew 24:14.

[79] Daniel 7:21, 22.

[80] Matthew 13:37-43.

[81] 2 Thessalonians 2:8.

[82] Revelation 5:9, 10; 21:24.

[83] Matthew 28:19, 20.

[84] Revelation 14:7.

[85] Acts 3:19, 20.

[86] Daniel 12:13; Revelation 6:9-11; Romans 8:22, 23.

[87] Hebrews 11:40.

[88] 1 Peter 1:4, 5.

day of Christ to all that love his appearing.[89] That they will only be satisfied when they awake in Christ's likeness.[90] And that, when the Son of Man shall come in his glory, and all the holy angels with him, the King will say to those on his right hand, 'Come, ye blessed of my Father, inherit the kingdom prepared for you from the foundation of the world.'[91] Then they will be equal to the angels, being the children of God and of the resurrection.[92]

"Associated Action.

"We are induced, from present circumstances affecting our spiritual interests, to present, for your consideration, a few ideas touching associated action.

"Order is Heaven's first law. All things emanating from God are constituted on principles of perfect order. [305] The New Testament rules for the government of the Church we regard as binding on the whole brotherhood of Christ. No circumstances can justify us in departing from the usages established by Christ and his Apostles.

"We regard any congregation of believers, who habitually assemble for the worship of God and the due observance of the Gospel ordinances, as a Church of Christ. As such, it is an independent body, accountable only to the great Head of the Church. To all such we recommend a careful examination of the Scriptures, and the adoption of such principles of association and order as are in accordance therewith, that they may enjoy the advantages of that church relation which Christ has instituted.

"Plan of Operations.

"In the midst of our disappointed hopes of seeing the King of Glory, and being made like him, and still finding ourselves in a world of sin, snares, and death, the question forces itself upon us,

"*What now is our work?*

"To us it seems clear that our first work is to make straight paths for our feet, lest that which is lame be turned out of the way. We are in duty bound to give the household meat in due season, and to

---

[89] 2 Timothy 4:3.

[90] Psalm 17:15;

[91] Matthew 25:34.

[92] Luke 20:36.

build ourselves up in our most holy faith. While doing this, we are to continue, in obedience to the great commission, to preach the Gospel to every creature: so long as the love of Christ dwells in us, it will constrain us. We shall not be released, while in our present state, from our obligations to be 'workers, together with God,' in saving those for whom the Redeemer died. It is evident that the duty, which of right devolves on every minister of the Gospel, of proclaiming the hour of God's judgment, is, if performed at all, to be done by those who are convinced of its truth. Shall we continue to do it, or shall it be left undone? And if we continue to work in this peculiar department of the Lord's vineyard, what system of operations shall we adopt for carrying forward our work? On this point we feel that we have need of great wisdom and prudence.

"In sounding the alarm through the length and breadth [306] of the land, and awakening a general interest on the subject of the Lord's speedy coming, and its kindred doctrines, our camp-meetings have been of incalculable importance, and, in many instances, have accomplished much good. But that peculiar work seems to have been performed, and a new aspect presents itself. What we now do must be done more by dint of persevering and determined effort than by moving the masses of community.

"We would, therefore, advise that our mode of operation, in this respect, be varied so as to meet the exigencies of the times, and are of the opinion that our camp-meetings, except in particular cases, where the brethren deem it will advance the cause, should be dispensed with for the present, and our energies expended by visiting the towns and villages, and in some convenient place giving courses of lectures, and holding series of conferences. By this we think our means could be better husbanded, and fewer laborers could carry on the meetings, and thus a wider field be occupied.

"We would also take the liberty of urging the importance of a wider circulation of our books and periodicals. These have been, and may still be, the means of great good to the community; and many may thus yet be reached who have not listened to the public lectures. Especially is it important at the present time to spread widely those which relate particularly to the personal appearing of Christ, the resurrection of the body, the return of the Jews, etc. ...

"Nor can we think ourselves justified in neglecting Sabbath-schools and Bible-class instruction. We would suggest to each congregation the necessity of opening a Sabbath-school for the benefit of at least their own children, and as many more as can be induced to attend. If the beginning is small, perseverance will accomplish the object. ...

"In all our labors we cannot be too deeply impressed with the sentiments of Paul, addressed to Timothy, his son in the gospel. 'The servant of the Lord must not strive, but be gentle toward all men, – apt to teach, patient; in meekness instructing those who oppose themselves, if God peradventure may give them repentance to the acknowledging of the truth, and they may recover themselves out of the snare of the devil, who are taken captive by him at his will.'

"In conclusion, permit us to add the following resolutions: [307]

"*Resolved*, That this Conference, while it sympathizes with every Scripture effort to save men from sin, and prepare them, by grace, for the Kingdom of God, – and while it bids god-speed to the publication of the gospel to every creature in the world, – yet it feels bound, by the most solemn considerations possible, to oppose, to the utmost of its power, that fatal and delusive doctrine of modern days, namely, that the Scripture warrants the belief, or even the hope, that, before the second glorious and personal appearing of Christ, to glorify his saints and renew the earth, the world, or even a majority of it, will be converted to Christ. And, 1st. We deem it *anti-Scriptural*, – opposed to all that class of scriptures which represents the church as in a state of warfare and suffering until her deliverer – Christ – comes, – all those scriptures which declare the coexistence and the mingling of the righteous and wicked, even to the end of the world, – all those passages which represent the continuance of the Man of Sin, the little horn of the fourth beast in Daniel's vision, the great dragon power, etc., as existing till the personal advent of the Saviour, to destroy them that destroy the earth, and to reward his saints. 2nd. We deem it dangerous to the eternal interests of men. It holds out to them the hope that a period more conducive to piety than the present is before them; thus inducing, however unintentionally, the sinner to defer immediate repentance, and encouraging professors to wait for a more favorable opportunity to expend their energies for saving sinners, both at home and abroad. And, finally, its direct influence is to put far off the second advent of the Saviour, and thus lull the world into a state of carelessness with respect to an immediate preparation for the event. There can be no millennium until the first resurrection, the resurrection of the just.

"*Resolved*, That we consider the doctrine of the restoration of the natural Jews, as a nation, either *before* or *after* the second advent of Christ, as heirs and inheritors of the land of Canaan, as subversive of the whole gospel system, by raising up what Christ has broken down – namely, the middle wall of partition between the Jew and Gentile. It contradicts those declarations of the New Testament which assert 'there is no difference between the Jew and the Greek;' that 'the promise that he shall be heir of the world was not [308] to Abraham and his seed through the law, but through the righteousness of faith;' and that 'there is neither Jew nor Gentile, bond nor free, male nor female,' but that, 'if we are Christ's, then are we Abraham's seed, and heirs according to the promise.' For this Judaizing doctrine claims there *is* a difference between the Jew and the Greek; that the children of the flesh *are* accounted for the seed; that there still *is* the distinction of Jew and Gentile; that we *do* henceforth know men after the flesh, etc. We feel bound, therefore, as we value the fundamental principles of the gospel, to enter our most *solemn protest* against all such teachings; and in our public services we will endeavor to meet, in the spirit of love and meekness, this error, and expose its gross absurdity; while, at the same time, we will proclaim to all, both Jew and Gentile, the message found in the commission given by the Great Head of the Church – '*He that believeth and is baptized shall be saved, and he that believeth not shall be damned.*' And 'Whosoever calleth upon the name of the Lord shall be saved.'

"Whereas, in every great religious movement, there have been, among the wise and sober-minded advocates of the truth, others who have risen up, striving about words to no profit, but to the subverting of the hearers; making great pretensions to special illumination; indulging in many evil practices; creeping into houses, and leading captive silly women; laden with sins, led away with divers lusts, ever learning and never able to come to the knowledge of the truth; men of corrupt minds and reprobate concerning the faith, who will not endure sound doctrine, but after their own lusts heap to themselves teachers having itching ears; turning their ears away from the truth, and turning unto fables; and who walk disorderly, working not at all, but are busybodies, for the cause of whom the way of truth is evil spoken of; and, *whereas*, in connection with the doctrine of Christ's near appearing, as in all previous religious movements, some of this class have risen up, calling themselves Adventists, teaching for doctrines that with which we can have no sympathy or fellowship, with many unseemly practices, whereby the word of God has been dishonored, and the doctrine of Christ's appearing brought into contempt; therefore - [309]

"*Resolved,* That we can have no sympathy or fellowship with those things which have only a show of wisdom in will-worship and neglecting of the body, after the commandments and doctrines of men. That we have no fellowship with any of the *new tests* as conditions of salvation, in addition to repentance toward God and faith in our Lord Jesus Christ, and a looking for and loving his appearing. That we have no fellowship for Jewish fables and commandments of men, that turn from the truth, or for any of the distinctive characteristics of modern Judaism. And that the act of promiscuous feet-washing and the salutation kiss, as practiced by some professing Adventists *as religious* ceremonies, sitting on the floor as an act of voluntary humility, shaving the head to humble one's self, and acting like children in understanding, are not only unscriptural, but subversive, if persevered in, of purity and morality.

"And whereas our congregations have suffered greatly from persons who have *called themselves* to the ministry and taught errors, and by smooth words and fair speeches have deceived the hearts of the simple and led them astray; therefore -

"*Resolved*, That we recommend to our brethren to encourage those men only who give evidence that they are called of God to the work; who are of good behavior; who abstain from all appearance of evil; who are vigilant, sober, apt to teach, not greedy of filthy lucre, no brawlers, not covetous; men who will teach the unadulterated word of God, and, by manifestation of the truth, commend themselves to every man's conscience in the sight of God.

"(Signed in behalf of the Committee,)

"William Miller, *Chairman*."

The above, after a full discussion and careful examination, was unanimously adopted; as was also, from the pen of Mr. Miller, the following

Address To The Brethren

"The present state of our faith and hope, with the severe trials which many of us experience, call for much brotherly love, forbearance, patience, and prayer. No cause, be it ever so holy, can exist in this present world, without its attendant [310] evils. Therefore, it becomes necessary for all who are connected with this cause to exercise great charity; for charity covers a multitude of sins.

"The cause we advocate calls upon all men to read the Word of God, and to reason, judge, compare, and digest for themselves. This is certainly right, and is the privilege of all rational members of the community. Yet this very liberty may become a stumbling-block to many, and, without charity, be the means of scattering, dividing, and causing contention among brethren. Human nature is such, that those who are governed by a desire to rule over others will seize the reins, and think all must bow to their decision; while others will think such unfit for the station they assume. James foresaw the evils under which we labor, and gives us a caution in his third chapter, to which we shall do well to take heed. Our present difficulties arise more from the multiplicity of masters and leaders among us (some of whom are governed by carnal motives), than from any want of light. The word of God affords light enough to guide us in all cases, 'that the man of God may be perfect, thoroughly furnished unto every good work.' But among the thousand-and-one expositions of Scripture, which are every day being palmed upon us, some of them, at least, must be wrong. Many of them are so weak and silly that they bring a stigma on the blessed Book, confuse the mind of the inquirer after truth, and divide the children of God.

"To remedy this evil, we must learn to judge men and principles by their fruits, and not be too hasty in receiving the expositions which may be presented by every pretender to wisdom and sanctity. Any exposition of Scripture which conflicts with other texts must be spurious. Any man whose object is to obtain followers must be avoided. Whatever produces envy and strife, brethren, is of the devil; and we must resist his temptations in their beginning. If God has been with us from the commencement of our illumination respecting the hope of His glorious appearing, shall we abandon the truth wherein our souls have been comforted, and our brotherly love established, for fables? We ought to be careful lest we grieve the Holy Spirit. How did we receive this doctrine at first? Was it not by searching the word of God, and a careful comparison of Scripture with Scripture? Yes; our faith did not rest on the word of man. We then [311] required chapter and verse, or we would not believe. Why should we leave our former rule of faith, to follow the vain and changing opinions of men? Some are neglecting the lamp, and seeking to walk by sparks of their own kindling. There is a propensity in many to make all prophecy apply to our time and country. Others have split on this rock. Some of the best writers and commentators have thus erred. They have, in many instances, considered themselves, their sect, or their nation, as the peculiar favorites of Heaven; and have therefore often failed to apply prophecy aright. An Englishman, writing on prophecy, will make the English territory the principal place of action – the Frenchman, France – the German, Germany – and an American, the United States. So is it with all sectarians. When minds are contracted by selfishness and bigotry, they lose sight of the glory of God, and his word, and seek only their own glory. On the other hand, they neglect, if they do not actually reject, such parts of the oracles of God as militate against their views, and rush headlong into error. If we are thus liable to be deceived by the cunning craftiness of men, we ought to be cautious how we are led by every fanciful interpretation of Scripture. Let us then be more wary, and, like the noble Bereans, search the Scriptures daily, to see whether these things are so. Then, if we err, we shall have the consolation that we have made a careful examination of the subject, and that the error was one of the head, and not of the heart. Christians should receive no evidence but the testimony of God as a ground of faith.

"We are commanded to be sober, and hope to the end for that grace which is to be brought unto us at the revelation of Jesus Christ. Our disappointment, as to the time, should have no effect on our hope. We know that Christ has not yet been revealed, and the object of our hope is yet in the future. Therefore, if we believe in God's word, as we profess, we ought to be thankful for the trial of our faith.

"We shall not have to wait long for the glorious appearing of Christ. Therefore, let us lift up our heads and rejoice, knowing that our redemption draweth nigh. We regret to see any impatience manifested among the friends of Jesus. God is now trying our graces. How solemn the thought, that any should lose the crown when near the goal! Let [312] us arise, shake off our dullness, redouble our diligence, let all the world know there is such a grace as Christian perseverance, and let all see that we are truly seeking a better country. Can it be possible, after we have run well for a season, loved the appearing of Jesus, come to a time when we must expect him, and should be ready to cast ourselves into his arms, that we shall go back, or again strike hands with a thoughtless world? May God forbid! Let us then go forward. It is death to go back; to go forward can be no more.

"We are pained to see a disposition to murmur against those who have been pioneers in the war, – who have sacrificed all earthly considerations to support a truth so unpopular as the second advent and personal reign of Jesus Christ.

"Brethren, shun such as cause divisions among very friends. Remember the admonition of James: 'Grudge not one against another, brethren, lest ye be condemned: behold, the Judge standeth at the door.' We see, by this rule, that when a brother loses his fellowship for the saints, he is certainly in darkness. We must be careful not to follow what he may term 'light.' Love for brethren is a test of our interest in Christ, without which all gifts, and works, are like sounding brass, and a tinkling cymbal. Let us cultivate, with peculiar care, this loveliest of all Christian graces, and frown on the man who attempts to cause division. 'Offences must needs come, but woe to that man by whom the offence cometh!' What can we say more, to stir up your pure minds by way of remembrance?

"We would, therefore, recommend more study of the Scriptures, and less writing, and that we be careful not to submit to public inspection mere speculations until they are closely scrutinized by some judicious friend. Thus we shall avoid many errors. We should always be more jealous of ourselves than of others. Self-love is the strongest, most dangerous and deceitful foe that we meet in our Christian warfare. We have arrived at a period of deep interest and peril. It is interesting, because the evidence of the Saviour being at the door is plain, so that no sincere student of prophecy can be at a loss to know that that day, for which all other days were made, is near. How interesting to live in expectation of the day which patriarchs, prophets and apostles, desired to see, but died without the sight! Persecution and death [313] lose their sting, in prospect of the coming Conqueror, who hath all power, and who hath engaged to put all enemies under his feet. We need not murmur; for, in this our day, God will bring to pass this act, this (to the worldly man) strange act, for which all the weary saints, for six thousand years, have lived and prayed. We entreat you to hold fast the confidence, which you have had in the word of God, unto the end. 'Yet a little while, and he that shall come will come, and will not tarry.' 'Here is the patience and the faith of the saints.' 'Be ye also patient; stablish your hearts, for the coming of the Lord draweth nigh.'

"WM. MILLER, *Chairman of Committee.*"

Thus harmoniously terminated a Conference, very fully attended, and congregated under circumstances of peculiar interest, in view of many conflicting opinions, with great forebodings as to the result. The best of feeling prevailed, and great calmness and patience characterized their deliberations. Everything adopted by the Conference was carefully examined in full meeting, and each separate item unanimously received, and then the whole without a dissenting voice.

Mr. Miller, in relating the story of his inability to convince the old lady who "*we*" were, remarked that he went to the Albany Conference with a heavy heart, fearing disunion and conflicting views; but was there cheered and strengthened anew by the unanimity and harmony that prevailed. And he was "rejoiced that so goodly a number had thus united in making known to the world who and what *we* were." He returned to Low Hampton, and the old lady referred to soon had an opportunity to read the doings at Albany. The first time she again saw Mr. Miller, she grasped his hand, and exclaimed:

"I have found out who *we* is; and I shall still be an Adventist, and stand by the old ship."

"And I am glad," said he, in narrating it, "that you have told the world who you are. And if anybody wishes to know where I am, I wish to let them know that I am with you who approve of the doings of that Conference, and have told the world what you are."

The doings of that Conference gave great satisfaction to all of the consistent Adventists, but mortally offended those who [314] had taken new positions, and sought to lead away disciples after them. It was so much misrepresented and opposed that Mr. Miller, a few weeks subsequently, came out, over his own name, in its defense, as follows:

"OBJECTIONS TO ITS DOINGS CONSIDERED.

"DEAR BROTHER HIMES:- I wish to make a few remarks respecting the doings of the Albany Conference.

"While nine-tenths that I have conversed with highly approve of the doings of that Conference, some do not discern clearly the motives which actuated those who there assembled, or understand fully the import of the conclusions arrived at. That some would seek to find fault with the deliberations of those who there represented our brethren in the different sections of the land, we had reason to expect; but all who are sincere inquirers after truth will desire to advance the cause of God by inducing 'brethren to dwell together in unity,' 'endeavoring to keep the unity of the Spirit in the bond of peace,' 'till we come in the unity of the faith, and of the knowledge of the Son of God, unto a perfect man, unto the measure of the stature of the fullness of Christ; that we be no more children, tossed to and fro, and carried about with every wind of doctrine, by the sleight of men, and cunning craftiness, whereby they lie in wait to deceive; but speaking the truth in love, may grow up into him in all things which is the head, even Christ.' Those, therefore, who desire to be set right, if they err at first, on seeing the subject in its true light, will be prompt to plant themselves on the side of truth and righteousness. All others will be expected, of course, to walk in their own ways, and, if possible, draw away followers after them. It is, therefore, my present purpose to answer the objections of all *honest* minds against those proceedings, so that all such may be free from any embarrassment respecting it.

"And, 1st. *What was the cause of the assembling of that Conference?* It need not be replied that it was convened to deliberate respecting, and, if possible, to extricate ourselves from the anarchy and confusion of the 'BABYLON' in which we had so unexpectedly found ourselves. Notice of the proposed convention had been extensively [315] given; all had been invited to be represented there who had the good of the cause at heart; and the brethren came together there from all parts of our land.

"2nd. *The doings of the Conference.* Everything which could not meet the *unanimous* approval of all present was promptly stricken out; and had there been a dissenting voice on the passage of any act, such act would have been promptly reconsidered. The determination was to do nothing but what all, in view of all the circumstances, could fully approve. And it was taken for granted that all who did not meet with that body, or were not represented there, either stood aloof from them from a want of sympathy, or else were willing to acquiesce in the conclusions of those who should there assemble; for if any wished to be identified with those brethren, and feared their deliberations might be actuated by wrong counsels, duty – imperious duty – required that all such should be present to counsel, to advise, and to instruct those who should be in danger of erring in any way from the teachings of the gospel.

"But the Conference assembled; and witness the harmony, the unanimity, the freedom from all contention and strife, – the full discussion and examination to which every act was subjected. In view of all this, will any say that those dear brethren had not the cause of God at heart; that they did not weight well the evils they would remedy, or the means of their removal, or did not desire to act in view of the common good of the children of God? And when those who were absent *fancy* they see difficulties in the results arrived at, as they were not present to hear the reasons advanced, ought they not to be very careful, and cautiously to inquire if they have a full understanding of the exact state of the case, before they throw in a fire-brand to divide and distract the brethren, and thus to defeat the very end for which that Conference assembled?

"3rd. *Objections to the doings of the Conference.* The name 'ADVENTISTS' is objected to as a sectarian name; and it is claimed that, instead of being called an Advent Church, we should be called 'The Church of God.' This is, in my opinion, a misconception of terms. I should oppose our being called, in an associated capacity, a church with *any name*. The Conference at Albany made no provision [316] for calling churches by any distinctive appellation. They merely expressed themselves as regarding 'any congregation of believers who habitually assemble for the worship of God, and the due observance of the gospel ordinances, as *a* church of Christ.' They designed to prefix or affix to it no appellative whatever. To call any denomination *the* Advent Church, *the* Church of God, or any other name, I regard as contrary to the usage of the apostles.

"All true churches are 'churches of God,' 1 Thessalonians 2:14; 'churches of Christ,' 1 Corinthians 11:16; 'churches of the saints,' 1 Corinthians 14:33. They are thus called in the Scriptures; but they are not thus called as distinctive appellations; neither have we the right to choose either of those as a specific term. And if we wished to select either of those terms, by which to be designated, which should we select? The Winebrennarians of Pennsylvania call themselves '*The* Church of God,' as a denominational term. If we were also to be known as such, we should be confounded with them. But we have no right to take a name that belongs generally to the whole family, and apply it exclusively to a branch of the family. If a branch of the family wish for a distinctive appellation, they must apply to themselves a term significant of what they are. But I contend that no name should be applied to the churches as such.

"A church, according to the Scriptures, is a religious assembly, selected and called out of the world, by the doctrine of the gospel, to worship the true God according to his word. *The* church must include all the elect of God, of what nation soever, from the beginning to the end of the world, who make but one body, whereof Jesus Christ is the Head. – Colossians 1:18. 'The church' in any certain place must include all the faithful who are wont to assemble in such place for solemn worship. – Romans 16:5. We thus have in the Scriptures not only 'churches of God,' 'churches of Christ,' and 'churches of the saints,' but we have 'the church at Jerusalem,' Acts 8:1; 'the church which is at Nymphas' house,' Colossians 4:15; 'the church at Babylon,' 1 Peter 5:13; 'the church in the wilderness,' Acts 7:38; 'the church at Antioch,' Acts 13:1; 'the church of Laodicea,' Colossians 4:16; 'the church of Ephesus,' Revelation 2:1; 'the church that is in their house,' Romans 16:5; 'churches [317] of Galatia,' 'of Asia,' 1 Corinthians 16:1, 19; 'churches of Judea,' Galatians 1:22; 'churches of Gentiles,' Romans 16:4; etc. etc. The above are sufficient, to my mind, to establish the position that a church should be simply called a 'church,' so described that its characteristics may be understood. You, therefore, in Boston, have considered yourselves as 'the church at the Tabernacle.'

"Is it asked, Do you repudiate the name of 'Adventists?' I reply, I do, when it is applied to the church, but not when it is applied to those who compose the church. Words are the symbols of ideas. All bodies of men have their peculiarities and characteristics. It is, therefore, necessary to distinguish them as such. Thus God has divided mankind into peoples, kindred, tribes, nations and tongues. Those of the same peculiarities have an affinity for each other, and naturally associate together. All these branches of the race are known by their distinctive names, and all acknowledge the convenience of their being thus known; it enables us to designate those we wish by an intelligible term. Thus the Israelites of old were known as belonging to the tribes of Judah, of Joseph, of Dan, etc., as the case might be. To call men sons of Jacob was sufficient to show that they belonged to the nation; but even then it was found necessary to know their tribe, their family, and their household; and even the different members of the same household must have different names to distinguish one from the other.

"While all Christians in the days of the apostles were known as Christians, yet if they had had no other distinctive appellations, there would have been as much confusion as there would be in a city, if all its inhabitants were known by the name of John and Mary; or as there would be in a family, if there should be twelve children with no individual names, – call one, and all would run; or as it is at the present time, none would regard the call. They would not know which was meant. Therefore, we find the apostles writing, now to the Hebrews, then to the Romans, and again to the Ephesians, and Galatians, etc. etc. If, therefore, it was right for Paul to speak of the 'churches of the Gentiles,' Romans 16:4, it may not be so very wrong for us to speak of the churches of the Adventists, or the churches of the Congregationalists, etc.; while, at the same time, it would be unscriptural [318] to call an association of churches *the* Advent church, *the* Methodist church, etc. etc.

"It is again said that we have no right to be called Adventists, because there are others who believe in the pre-millennial advent; and that to apply it to ourselves is arrogancy. To this I reply, that it cannot be arrogancy if no others claim it but ourselves. We do not claim it belongs to us exclusively. All have a right to it who wish thus to be designated. But those who repudiate the name have surely no right to find fault with our use of it: such can have no claim to it. Neither do we, when we call ourselves Adventists, say that we are the only Adventists, any more than we say, when we call ourselves Americans, that we are the only Americans. It should, however, be understood, that words are entirely arbitrary, and that custom alone establishes their use. Was the term Adventist in use ten years ago? No; it is not in the dictionary; it is a newly-coined word, made by appending an affix to the word Advent. In the use of the word it has been only applied to those of like precious faith with ourselves; and by its use the community understand who, and who alone, are intended. The coiners of the word are entitled to it, and those who associate with them. But let it be distinctly understood, that, at the Albany Conference, the question did not arise whether we should adopt that name. It was already upon us; and the only question that arose respecting it, was whether, when speaking of some fanatics who call themselves Adventists, the word should be permitted to remain in that connection. But, says one, why is that Conference called a 'Conference of Adventists'? It is not so called by vote or direction of the Conference; but as an Adventist is, in accordance with the use of the term, one who believes in the immediate coming of Christ, and as all those who thus assembled professed thus to believe, it was in truth a conference of Adventists. What's in a name?

'The rose would smell the *same*,
If called by *any* name.'

"**2.** Another objection to that body is, that they told the world some things which they believed the Scriptures teach, and some things which they believed they do not teach. Let us look at this objection. Has not a man a right to tell the [319] world what he does or does not believe? O, yes, certainly. Then have not five, or ten, or fifty men the same privilege? Most certainly. Then, wherein, pray, is the objection? O, says one, it looks too much like a creed; and I object to all creeds, either *oral* or *written*. But what do you mean by a creed? If you mean by it a test of Christian character, I agree with you; and the Conference expressly voted that they had 'no fellowship with any of the *new tests*, as conditions of salvation, in addition to repentance towards God, and faith in our Lord Jesus Christ, and a looking for and loving his appearing.' But if you mean that a man or body of men have no right to speak or write what they believe, I must dissent from you. The objector replies, We want nothing short of the entire Scriptures for our creed; that alone is sufficient. And that alone is sufficient for me. But while I receive the entire word of God according to my understanding of its teachings, and while different men draw different and opposite conclusions respecting its teachings, have I no right to inform the world what I conceive to be the truth it inculcates?

"To say that I believe the Bible, and that alone, is to say the same that all denominations say. It is, therefore, meaningless as far as any distinctive idea is conveyed; it is truth in general, meaning nothing in particular. And with that view, why should we stand aloof from all others who claim to believe the same? Theodore Parker, the rationalist, claims to stand on that ground; and yet his constructions of Scripture are so *anti*-scriptural, that even the Unitarians repudiate him. Can there then be no line of demarcation between what we believe to be the truths and errors which are alike claimed to be based upon the word of God? Have we no right to tell the world which of opposite doctrines we believe are therein contained? If not, we have surely no right to disfellowship Theodore Parker and his adherents; and nothing can be rejected, and nothing received. And if so, those who told us to come out of Babylon, because the churches rejected their creed, which was their understanding of the Scriptures, did wrong.

"I wish here to say, that, in proclaiming the coming of Christ to the world, nothing was further from my thoughts than to form a separate, distinct body of Christians. It never [320] came into my heart; I thought to benefit all. But, by a combination of circumstances within and without, over which we had no control, we find ourselves as we are. We have been called out of the churches, and thrust out of the churches. The churches have refused to fellowship us; and what shall we do? We cannot go back, and give up our blessed hope. And all we can do is to find what the gospel teaches, and act accordingly.

"The fact is, there is no man living without his distinct creed; for a creed is nothing more or less than (*credo*) a belief. When a man makes his belief, or a body of men make their belief, the test of other men's salvation, they act as bigots; they usurp God's prerogative. But when he or they allow to others the same liberty of thought and speech that they ask for themselves, making them only responsible to their Maker, they do not transgress the 'golden rule.'

"What a man believes is his creed. The creed of the infidel is, 'I believe in all unbelief.' The creed of another is, 'I believe we have no right to write out our belief.' Another's creed is, 'I do not believe in any creed, except the New Testament.' And the creed of another is, 'I believe we have the right to write out and undeceive the world as to our understanding of scriptural teachings.' Now shall the man whose creed is, 'I believe we have no right to have an *oral* or written creed' (belief), make that creed the standard to which all men must submit? If he does, he is himself a bigot. A man who thus believes, has no right to speak or write; for, if he speaks what he believes, he has an 'oral creed,' and if he writes what he believes, he has a '*written* creed.' If, therefore, he speaks or writes, he puts forth his creed, unless he speaks or writes what he does *not believe*; and then he is a hypocrite. A man who thus believes, can write for no periodical; he can preach no sermon; every thought he gives utterance to is a violation of *his* creed; it is a departure from it, or in confliction with it. And while thus continually violating his *own* creed, he has surely no right to oblige all others to submit to it.

"Those who cry the loudest against creeds, and disclaim the strongest, are the very men who require others to submit to their *ipse dixit*. They require the largest liberty for themselves, and allow the least to others. And if others are not [321] ready to comply with their fancies, ever varying as they are, they are ready to consign them to perdition. For shame on such absurd inconsistencies!

"The aim of all our writings has been to show the church and the world what we believe to be the great truths the Bible inculcates. We have had a right so to do. These truths have had a mighty influence on the community. To bring discredit on them, and thus to weaken our labors, the adversary has connected with them, in the mind of the public, various odious extravagances. When we, therefore, set ourselves up as teachers, all have a right to demand of us what we believe, and what we teach. Says the apostle, '*So* we preached, and *so* ye believed.' We must, therefore, be ever ready to tell *how* we believe, *what* we believe, and *why* we believe. If, therefore, we have no fellowship with any of the abominations so rife among us, we have the right to tell it to the world. And if a large company of 'like precious faith' have the same views on these points, they have an equal right to unite in thus proclaiming it to the world. Those who have sympathy with those things, or who will unite with none who avow to the world their belief, have the same privilege to dissent from them. And if any prefer to stand alone, rather than to unite with a body who do not act in every respect in accordance with their individual creed, who seek to get up a party that do, let it be so understood, that all may act accordingly and understandingly.

"But what has the Albany Conference done? Why, it has committed the crime of informing the world of some of the important truths which the members of it believe the Bible inculcates, with the reasons therefor; and some things which they believe are not therein contained! No Advent lecturers or writers can consistently object to that; for in so doing they would condemn themselves. 'Thou, therefore, which teachest another, teachest thou not thyself?' 'Thou that abhorrest idols, dost thou commit sacrilege?'

"**3.** Another objects to the doings of that Conference because they recommended organization. Indeed! And what did they recommend? Why, they recommended to all 'a careful examination of the Scriptures, and the adoption of such principles of association and order as are in accordance therewith, that they may enjoy the advantages of that church [322] relation which Christ has instituted.' It is left to each church to judge of their own association for themselves. Those who would object to this would surely object to the recommendation of the Scriptures as a rule of faith and practice. Those who would object to this would have objected had they recommended all to fear God and give glory to Him.

"**4.** Another objection is, that they passed *resolutions* expressive of their sense of truth and duty. This is a great sin, truly. It is said, a resolution can prove nothing; and that it would be absurd to resolve that light is light, or that God reigns. That may all be; and yet it may be perfectly proper to resolve that we will walk in the light, or that we will submit to the rule of God. Every soul does this at conversion; and what may be done individually may certainly be done collectively. To bring forward, as an absurdity, the use of a thing to which it is never applied, as an argument against its being applied to other uses, is to set up a man of straw which cannot stand alone, and, in knocking it down, take to one's self the credit of having overturned an immutable principle, of which it was only an effigy. Resolutions serve the two-fold purpose of showing our true position to the public, and of nerving up our hearts in defense of such position.

"**5.** Another objection is, that they have expressed themselves with regard to the intermediate state of the dead, respecting which there is a difference of opinion among Adventists. To this I reply, that that question did not arise at the Conference. No allusion was made to it either in their doings or speeches. They expressed, what all Adventists believe, that the time of the entrance of departed saints into their inheritance is at the resurrection. But the question, whether the intermediate state of the dead is a conscious or an unconscious one, was not even mooted there. This shows the necessity of great cautiousness in stating objections against what is not perfectly understood.

"**6.** Another objection is, that the proceedings 'look like doing something in the future;' 'seem like aiming at something which we shall not approve.' Well, as those are not objections to what was there done, and are only fears of what may be done, arising out of the jealousy of the human heart, I shall not spend any time in replying to them; for all magnanimous [323] minds are content with pointing to actual transgressions, and never allude to future fancied ones, unless they are very desirous of finding something to find fault with, in accordance with their pre-judgment.

"The above are all the objections I recollect to have heard or seen advanced against the doings of the Albany Conference; and those have been by a very few. I am happy to see that the doings there give such general satisfaction. What weight such objections are entitled to, all must judge of for themselves. It must be evident, that unless we come out of the BABYLON into which we have been thrust, God will not bless us.

"The question then comes home to each one of our hearts, Shall we continue in the anarchy in which we have been, or shall we take gospel measures to restore gospel order, that, at the Master's coming, we may be approved of Him? It must be evident to all, that without union we can do nothing; and if there are no 'important truths' in which we are united, all can see that there can be no union among us. 'How can two walk together except they be agreed?' We can only unite on those points in which there is union. The great doctrine which has called us out is the nearness of Christ's Advent. To persuade men to repent, in view of the coming King, we should all be willing to lay aside the unessentials of our belief, which are at variance with such union.

"All union consists in a sacrifice of individual prepossessions for the common good. Those who love the peace of Zion more than they do their private opinions will be prompt thus to unite. Those who love self more than they do the general good will contend for their own selfish ends. Any doctrine, however plausible to the human mind, which tends to divide true Christians, cannot be of God. We cannot be the disciples of Christ, unless we love one another, and faithfully labor to keep the unity of the Spirit in the bond of peace. And, therefore, those who seek to produce disorder and confusion, contrary to the doctrine of Christ, cannot be true friends of the cause.

"The union that prevailed at the Albany Conference was what should ever characterize the children of God. They laid aside their prejudices, and acted for the general good; and the Adventists, as a body, approve of their doings. [324] What, then, shall we think of the efforts of any who seek to undermine the counsels which there prevailed? Shall we not look upon them as endeavoring to divide the children of God? Shall individuals set up their own individual creed as the criterion to which a united and harmonious body shall come?

"Let all ponder these things well. We live in an awfully dangerous moment of time, when we are beset with foes without and foes within. Let us, therefore, take heed to our ways, to all our thoughts, and to all our doings. Let us have no enemies in disguise among us, professing to be friends. Let all who have no fellowship with the principles we inculcate, manifest it. But let all who are willing to contend earnestly for the faith once delivered to the saints not be afraid to tell the world what they believe the Scriptures teach, and fight manfully the good fight, for they will soon win the race. Yours in the blessed hope,

"WILLIAM MILLER.

"*Boston, May 27, 1845.*"

The doings of that Conference were unanimously ratified by the annual Conferences subsequently held, in that year, in New York, and in Boston; and the "important truths" there inculcated were often unanimously reaffirmed, so that they have become the settled principles of those known as Adventists. Others, dissenting from them, but agreeing in unimportant particulars, and yet claiming to be Adventists, are not recognized as such by Adventists.

By the date of the foregoing article it will be seen that Mr. Miller was in Boston, where he arrived on Saturday, May 24th, to attend the annual Conference there of the week following. That commenced on Monday, May 26th, when Mr. M. discoursed from Revelation 6:17, – "For the great day of his wrath is come; and who shall be able to stand?" He made a personal and practical application of this event, and presented the evidence of its probable nearness.

During the Conference, he spoke feelingly of the passing of the time. He remarked that,

> "Ere this, he had been in hopes of meeting all present in the heavenly kingdom. But, if we love the Lord Jesus Christ, however much we may be disappointed, we shall not forget Christ's coming. God may [325] see fit to disappoint us, sometimes, for our good. We may not see the wisdom and fullness of the whole of God's plan; but he never tries us but for our profit. Therefore, we should not be disheartened or cast down. Every disappointment only made him more strong in the belief of the certainty of the nearness of Christ's appearing.

"I had," he said,

> "denied the Bible for twelve years. I used to read it to see how curiously men would act, and contradict each other. But, suddenly, I

became more solemn; its truth began to dawn upon my mind; and I was in great darkness for six months. I saw that I was a poor sinner; but I was soon enabled to love Jesus Christ, and have continued to love him even till the present time. I saw that, if the Bible was true, Christ was the only Saviour of men. I then began to study more fully the Scriptures, – determined to study, text by text, till I was fully satisfied as to their import. In comparing Scripture with Scripture, such a light broke in upon my mind as I had never before seen. I was about two years in going through with the Bible, in this manner; and I found it a perfect piece of order and beauty. And, though I have been greatly disappointed, yet I have never ceased to love and regard the authority of the Scriptures.

"Brethren, we must keep humble. I sometimes tremble when I see individuals endeavoring to exalt themselves, and denounce others who do not see just as they do. Be careful not to err in favor of self. Be careful to avoid self-righteousness. I have noticed that those who have left the Second Advent cause are the very ones for whom I used to tremble, in view of their arrogancy and self-righteousness. We must not look to ourselves, but must look alone to God. We must cling to our Heavenly Father's arm, that we may hold fast our confidence even unto the end. The word of God teaches us that we are to be guided alone by Him. Had our brethren, who have apostatized, thus looked to Him, they would never have fallen into the awful errors into which they have been led. I love those brethren, but I tremble for their errors. O, let us depend wholly on God, that we may be preserved also from departing from the rectitude of our faith! And may we all be enabled to live out the prayer, 'Not my will, O God, but thine be done.'" [326]

It was at this Conference that he narrated the story of the old lady, whose anxiety to know who "*we* is" was so happily allayed by the doings at Albany.

CHAPTER 22

*His Apology And Defense – Definiteness Of Prophetic Time
– Erroneous Views Connected With The Doctrine, Etc.*

After the Boston Conference, Mr. Miller accompanied Mr. Himes to Portland, Me., where he gave discourses in the afternoon and evening of Sunday, June 1st, to crowded audiences. Many of those present, doubtless, were drawn to hear him by motives of curiosity, because of the disappointment in time. The necessity of patience and of watchfulness were subjects on which he discoursed.

He returned to Boston, and from thence went to a camp-meeting at Champlain, N. Y., on the 10th of June. After this he returned home, in the enjoyment of good general health, but somewhat afflicted by boils.

As the author of a movement which had resulted in disappointment, and, in some respects, disaster, Mr. Miller deemed it proper that he should make a personal statement to the Christian public, show the motives that had actuated him, and disavow any sympathy with the extremes into which some had gone, contrary to his earnest remonstrances. His growing infirmities made him shrink from the labor of writing, and caused him to desire an amanuensis. For this purpose the writer of this visited him, in the month of July, 1845, and Mr. Miller dictated his "Apology and Defence," a tract of thirty-six pages, which was published by Mr. Himes, in Boston.

It was addressed "To all who love the Lord Jesus Christ in sincerity," and commenced with:

> "As all men are responsible to the community for the sentiments they may promulgate, the public have a right to expect from me a candid statement in reference to my disappointment [327] in not realizing the advent of Christ in A. D. 1843-4, which I had confidently believed. I have, therefore, considered it not presumptuous in me to lay before the Christian public a retrospective view of the whole question, the motives that actuated me, and the reasons by which I was guided."

He then proceeded to narrate his early history, and gave an account of his "deistical opinions," his "first religious impressions," his "connection with the army," his "removal to Low Hampton," his "determination to understand the Scriptures," his "manner of studying the Bible," the "results arrived at," and his subsequent labors; all of which have been noticed at greater length in the foregoing pages. He then summed up his labors as follows:

> "From the commencement of that publication, I was overwhelmed with invitations to labor in various places, with which I complied as far as my health and time would allow. I labored extensively in all the New England and Middle States, in Ohio, Michigan, Maryland, the District of Columbia, and in Canada East and West, giving about four thousand lectures in something like five hundred different towns.
>
> "I should think that about two hundred ministers embraced my views, in all the different parts of the United States and Canada; and that there have been about five hundred public lecturers. In all the sections of country where I labored, – not only in the towns I visited, but in those in their vicinity, – there were more or less that embraced the doctrine of the Advent. In some places only a very few, and in other places there have been a large number.
>
> "In nearly a thousand places Advent congregations have been raised up, numbering, as near as I can estimate, some fifty thousand believers. On recalling to mind the several places of my labors, I can reckon up about six thousand instances of conversion from nature's darkness to God's marvelous light, the result of my personal labors alone; and I should judge the number to be much greater. Of this number I can recall to mind about seven hundred, who were, previously to their attending my lectures, infidels; and their number may have been twice as great. Happy results have also followed from the labors of my brethren, [328] many of whom I would like to mention here, if my limits would permit.
>
> "In all my labors I never had the desire or thought to establish any separate interest from that of existing denominations, or to benefit one at the expense of another. I thought to benefit all. Supposing that all Christians would rejoice in the prospect of Christ's coming, and that those who could not see as I did would not love any the less those who should embrace this doctrine, I did not conceive there would ever be any necessity for separate meetings. My whole object was a desire to convert souls to God, to notify the world of a coming judgment, and to induce my fellowmen to make that preparation of heart which will enable them to meet their God in peace. The great majority of those who were converted under my labors united with the various existing churches. When individuals came to me to inquire respecting

their duty, I always told them to go where they would feel at home; and I never favored any one denomination in my advice to such.

"But my brethren began to complain that they were not fed by their ministers, and wanted expository preaching. I told them it was their duty to interest their ministers in the prophecies; but, if they could not receive the teachings under which they sat, they must act in accordance with their own sense of duty. They then began to complain that they had not liberty in the churches to present their views freely, or to exhort their brethren to prepare for the judgment. Those in the neighborhood of Advent preaching felt that, when they could listen to these glorious truths, it was their privilege so to do. For this many of them were treated coldly. Some came out of their churches, and some were expelled. Where the blame lay it is not necessary here to inquire; there was, doubtless, wrong on both sides. The result was that a feeling of opposition arose, on the part of many of the ministers and churches that did not embrace these views, against those who were looking for the blessed hope and the glorious appearing of the great God and our Saviour Jesus Christ."

He then spoke of various points as follows: [329]

"DEFINITENESS OF PROPHETIC TIME.

"I had never been positive as to any particular *day* for the Lord's appearing, believing that no man could know the day and hour. In all my published lectures will be seen, on the title-page, 'about the year 1843.' In all my oral lectures I invariably told my audiences that the periods would terminate in 1843 *if* there were no mistakes in my calculation; but that I could not say the end might not come even before that time, and they should be continually prepared. In 1842, some of my brethren preached, with great positiveness, the exact year, and censured me for putting in an IF. The public press had also published that I had fixed upon a definite day, the 23rd of April, for the Lord's advent. Therefore, in December of that year, as I could see no error in my reckoning, I published my belief, that, some time between March 21, 1843, and March 21, 1844, the Lord would come. Some had their minds fixed on particular days; but I could see no evidence for such, unless the types of the Mosaic law pointed to the Feast of Tabernacles.

"During the year 1843, the most violent denunciations were heaped upon me, and those associated with me, by the press and some pulpits. Our motives were assailed, our principles misrepresented, and our characters traduced. Time passed on, and the 21st of March, 1844, went by without our witnessing the appearing of the Lord. Our disappointment was great, and many walked no more with us.

"Previously to this, in the fall of 1843, some of my brethren began to call the churches Babylon, and to urge that it was the duty of Adventists to come out of them. With this I was much grieved, as not only the effect was very bad, but I regarded it as a perversion of the word of God, a wresting of Scripture. But the practice spread extensively; and, from that time, the churches, as might have been expected, were closed against us. It prejudiced many against us, and created a deep feeling of hostility between Adventists and those who did not embrace the doctrine; so that most of the Adventists were separated from their respective churches. This was a result which I never desired [330] nor expected; but it was brought about by unforeseen circumstances. We could, then, only act in accordance with the position in which we were thus placed.

"On the passing of my published time, I frankly acknowledged my disappointment in reference to the exact period; but my faith was unchanged in any essential feature. I, therefore, continued my labors, principally at the West, during the summer of 1844, until 'the seventh-month movement,' as it is called. I had no participation in this, only as I wrote a letter, eighteen months previously, presenting the observances under the Mosaic law which pointed to that month as a probable time when the Advent might be expected. This was written because some were looking to definite days in the *Spring*. I had, however, no expectation that so unwarranted a use would be made of those types that any should regard a belief in such mere inferential evidence a test of salvation. I, therefore, had no fellowship with that movement until about two or three weeks previous to the 22nd of October, when, seeing it had obtained such prevalence, and considering it was at a probable point of time, I was persuaded that it was a work of God, and felt that, if it should pass by, I should be more disappointed than I was in my first published time.

"But that time passed, and I was again disappointed. The movement was of such a character that, for a time, it was very mysterious to me; and the results following it were so unaccountable that I supposed our work might be completed, and that a few weeks only might elapse between that time and the appearing of Christ. However that might be, I regarded my own work as completed, and that what was to be done for the extension of these views must be done by younger brethren, except an occasional discourse from myself."

In conclusion, he considered the

"ERRONEOUS VIEWS CONNECTED WITH THE DOCTRINE.

"As time has progressed, I have been pained to see many errors which have been embraced, in different sections of the country, by some who have labored in connection with myself; errors which I cannot countenance, and of which I wish to [331] speak freely, although I may lose the fellowship of some for faithfully doing my duty.

"I have been pained to see a spirit of sectarianism and bigotry, in some sections, which disfellowships everything that does not square with the narrow prejudices of individual minds. There is a tendency to exalt individual opinions as a standard for all to submit to; a disposition to place the results of individual investigation upon a level with solemn conclusions to which the great body of brethren have arrived. This is very wrong; for, while we are in this world, we are so short-sighted that we should never regard our conclusions as infallible, should bear with the imperfections of others, and receive those that are weak in the faith, but not to doubtful disputations.

"Some have an inclination to indulge in harsh and denunciatory remarks against all who do not agree with them. We are all liable to err; but we should avoid thus giving occasion of offence. We should instruct with meekness those that oppose themselves, and avoid foolish and unlearned questions, that gender strifes.

"There may be causes operating on the minds of others, of which we know nothing, that influence them contrary to the truth, as we have received it. We should, therefore, in all our intercourse with those we deem in error, treat them with kindness and affection, and show them that we would do them good, and not evil, if God, peradventure, will give them repentance to the acknowledging of the truth, and that they may recover themselves out of the snare of the devil, who are taken captive by him at his will.

"Some are prone to indulge in a spirit of uneasiness and disorder, and looseness with regard to church government and doctrine. In all the essential doctrines of the Bible, as they have been held by the pious of the church in all ages, were given to the saints, and for which we are commanded earnestly to contend, I have never seen any reason to change my faith. Jesus I regard as my all-sufficient Saviour, by whose merits alone I can be saved. No being but Him, 'whose goings forth were of old from everlasting,' who should take upon himself our nature, and bear our sins in his own body, could make an atonement, on the efficacy of which I should dare to rely. The Bible speaks as plainly [332] of my Saviour's divinity as it does of his humanity. He is, therefore, Emanuel, God with us. The Bible tells us plainly what the Saviour is. That should satisfy us, without venturing beyond the Bible to say what he is not.

"It is in the use of terms not found in the Scriptures that disputations arise. For instance, the difference between the Calvinist and Arminian I often thus explain: Both are in the same dilemma. They are like a company of men in the lower story of a house when the tide is entering, and from which there is no escape only by a rope by which they may be drawn up. All endeavor to lay hold of the rope. The one is continually afraid he has not hold of the right rope; if he was sure he had the right rope he would have no fears. The other has no fear but he has hold of the right rope; he is continually afraid his rope will break. Now both are equally fearful they may perchance not escape. Their fears arise from different causes. How foolish it is, then, for them to begin to quarrel with each other, because the one supposes the rope may break, and the other that it is the wrong rope!

"Now I have found Christians among those who believed that they were born again, but might fall away; and among those that believed that, if they were ever born again, they should certainly persevere. The difference between them I regard as a mere matter of education; both have their fears, and both believe that those only who persevere unto the end will be saved. I, therefore, look on men as bigots who quarrel with others and deny that those are Christians who cannot see just as they do.

"Some are disposed to lay a stress on the seventh-month movement which is not warranted by the Word. There was then a dedication of heart, in view of the Lord's coming, that was well pleasing in the sight of God. Desire for the Lord's coming and a preparation for that event are acceptable to Him. But, because we then ardently desired his coming and sought that preparation that was necessary, it does not follow that our expectations were then realized. For we were certainly disappointed. We expected the personal coming of Christ at that time; and now to contend that we were not mistaken is dishonest. We should never be ashamed frankly to confess all our errors. [333]

"I have no confidence in any of the new theories that grew out of that movement, namely, that Christ then came as the Bridegroom, that the door of mercy was closed, that there is no salvation for sinners, that the seventh trumpet then sounded, or that it was a fulfillment of prophecy in any sense. The spirit of fanaticism which resulted from it, in some places leading to extravagance and excess, I regard as of the same nature as that which retarded the Reformation in Germany, and the same as have been connected with every religious movement since the first advent. The truth is not responsible for such devices of Satan to destroy it. I have never taught a neglect of any of the duties of life, which make us good parents, children, neighbors, or citizens. I have ever inculcated a faithful performance of all those duties, enjoining good works with faith and repentance. Those who have taught the neglect of these, instead of acting with me, or being my followers, as they are called, have departed from my counsels, and acted in opposition to my uniform teachings; men have crept in unawares, who have given heed to seducing spirits and doctrines of devils, teaching lies in hypocrisy, denying any personal existence of Christ, forbidding to marry, and commanding to abstain from certain kinds of food, denying the right to pray for sinners, and commanding to violate our social duties, etc. With such things I have no sympathy.

"The doctrine of annihilation and the soul's unconsciousness in death has been connected in the minds of some with the doctrine of the Advent. With this there is no necessary connection. This its advocates acknowledge. The doctrine of the Advent was the faith of the primitive church; while the doctrine of annihilation was no part of their faith. It evidently arises from a mistaken use of Bible terms, and a stress on words not warranted by parallel Scriptures. The fact that no trace of this doctrine is found among the ancient Jews, except the Sadducees, who were reproved for not believing in angels, spirits, and the resurrection, shows that none of the pious of that nation attached a meaning to the words of the Old Testament that would sustain such a doctrine. And the fact that no trace of such a belief is found among the early Christians, shows that those who sat under the teachings of the apostles and martyrs gathered no such [334] doctrine from their instructions. Therefore, when such a doctrine is taught, a meaning must be attached to words that they would not bear at the time the Scriptures were written. To get the correct understanding of Scripture, we must use words as they were used at that time.

"The translators of the Bible had no faith in such a doctrine; therefore they attached no such meaning to the language they used in rendering the original as is attached to the words of the texts by those who quote them to maintain that doctrine. All the arguments in its favor rest on a certain meaning attached to such words as perish, destroy, death, etc. But when we find that the old world, being only overflowed with water, perished; and that when our Saviour told the Jews to destroy the temple of his body, and in three days he would raise it up (John 2:19), he did not mean that his body should cease to be a body during those three days; we see that such words do not necessarily convey a meaning that proves that doctrine. In fact, one evangelist uses the word *destroy*, – 'Wilt thou destroy us before the time?' – where another does the word *torment*, – 'Wilt thou torment us before the time?' Compare Mark 1:24 and Matthew 8:29. God said that in the flood he would destroy man with the earth (Genesis 6:13), but the earth did not cease to be. Therefore we learn that these words cannot set aside the declarations that the wicked shall go away into everlasting punishment, etc.

"If the word death implies that there can be no part of the man then conscious, it would follow that, when Christ died, there could be no part of Him that was conscious; and if there could be no part of Christ conscious after his body was dead, there could have been no part of Christ conscious before he was born of Mary. Death, therefore, can only apply to the body. But that doctrine, carried out, must lead to a denial of the divinity of Christ; and we find that in all past history, in the different periods when it has come up for a time, it has been connected with that and other heresies.

"The calling of all churches, that do not embrace the doctrine of the advent, Babylon, I before remarked was the means of our not being listened to with candor; and, also, that I regarded it as a perversion of Scripture. This I think [335] all will see who compare Revelation 14 and 18, and observe the chronology of the fall of Babylon.

"Revelation 14:6, 7, represents an angel flying in the midst of heaven, proclaiming the hour of God's judgment as having come. This proclamation must, of course, continue until Christ shall actually come to judge the quick and dead at his appearing and kingdom. In the 8th verse, another angel follows, crying, 'Babylon is fallen;' but, as the first continues till Christ comes, this cannot follow till Christ comes. But, on turning to Revelation 18:1, 2, we find that the angel that follows, crying 'Babylon is fallen,' is one that comes down from heaven, having great power, and lightens the earth with his glory. This angel that follows must therefore be the Lord Jesus Christ descending from heaven to take the kingdom; and when he takes to himself his great power to reign, Satan is no longer the God of this world. It may then be well said, Babylon is fallen; *i.e.*, it has lost the supremacy; Christ has taken that. But while it has fallen, it is not destroyed; before that can be done the saints must be taken out, that they may not partake of the consequences of her sins, nor receive of her plagues, which shall be poured out when Great Babylon shall come in remembrance before God, to give unto her the cup of the wine of the fierceness of his wrath. When the angel has cried 'the hour of his judgment come,' and the angel has come down from heaven, declaring the fall of Babylon, then, in Revelation 14:9-12, another angel follows, pronouncing the fate of the worshippers of the beast, which they are to experience when the cup is poured upon them; then, in v. 13, a voice is heard from heaven, declaring those who died in the Lord blessed from thenceforth. The time has then come when the dead are to be raised; and this must synchronize with the voice from heaven in Revelation 18:4, saying, 'Come out of her, my people.' To come, is to go in the direction of the invitation. It must, therefore, be the invitation, from where Christ will then have come, to meet him in the air.

"In Revelation 14:14-16, Christ is symbolized as seated on a cloud; the cry is given to reap the earth, and the earth is reaped; the saints are caught up to meet the Lord in the air. Then, in verses 17-20, the vine of the earth is reaped [336] and cast into the wine-press of God's wrath; Babylon is thus destroyed.

"Thus we have a harmonious view of those Scriptures. If this is the correct application, to apply them differently is to pervert them. And if it is, then everything, of whatever name, that is conformed to this world, that loves this world more than the kingdom of God, must have its portion with it; it is Babylonish.

"The 'woman,' or mystical Babylon, I regard as the fallen church, that ruled by means of the kings of the earth; and all churches that have the papal spirit of *formality* or *persecution* are partaking of her abominations. But it does not therefore follow that there can be no churches that love the Lord in sincerity.

"Intimately connected with the construction which has been given to this portion of God's word is a notion respecting the writing out of our belief. It is said by some to be Babylon to be associated together, to write out a synopsis of our belief, or to subscribe our names to our opinions. I am never afraid to put my name to whatever I may believe; and I can find no text of Scripture that forbids it. When the Jews went up from the Babylonian captivity, they made a sure covenant, and wrote it, and the princes, Levites, and priests, sealed unto it. – Nehemiah 9:38.

"With regard to the association of the church, her practice has varied in different ages, according to the circumstances in which she has been placed. When all thought alike, or understood the Bible alike, there was no necessity for an expression of opinion respecting its meaning. But when heresy crept in, it was necessary to guard the meaning of Scripture, by expressing, in plain and unequivocal language, our understanding of it. It is because the early Christians did this that we are enabled to ascertain the understanding which the primitive church had of the faith once delivered to the saints. When this has not been done, the history of the church shows that error has spread with the greatest rapidity. For instance, Theodore Parker, among the Unitarians, celebrated for his transcendentalism, takes ground that his brethren have not the right to disfellowship him on account of his constructions of Scripture; and, as they have heretofore denied the right of the church to express [337] its belief, they must, on their own ground, fellowship him with all his infidel sentiments; for the dispute between them respects only interpretations of Scripture. To guard against such evils, I am in favor, where erroneous views prevail, of expressing my understanding of the Word in such plain terms that all may be able to compare my views with the Bible, and see whether I make a faithful application of it. And if the world wishes to see, in short, the peculiar characteristics of my faith, and of those who associate with me, I see no harm in giving, as did the Mutual Conference of Adventists at Albany, a synopsis of the views in which we can unite and act, and which, among others, we believe the Bible teaches.

"I have thus given a plain and simple statement of the manner of my arriving at the views I have inculcated, with a history of my course up to the present time. That I have been mistaken in the time, I freely confess; and I have no desire to defend my course any further than I have been actuated by pure motives, and it has resulted to God's glory. My mistakes and errors God, I trust, will forgive. I cannot, however, reproach myself for having preached definite time; for, as I believe that whatsoever was written aforetime was written for our learning, the prophetic periods are as much a subject of investigation as any other portion of the Word.

"I, therefore, still feel that it was my duty to present all the evidence that was apparent to my mind; and were I now in the same circumstances, I should be compelled to act as I have done. I should not, however, have so done, had I seen that the time would pass by; but not knowing that it would, I feel even now more satisfaction in having warned my fellow-men than I should feel, were I conscious that I had believed them in danger and had not raised my voice. How keen would have been my regret, had I refrained to present what in my soul I believed to be truth, and the result had proved that souls must perish through my neglect! I cannot, therefore, censure myself for having conscientiously performed what I believed to be my duty.

"But while I frankly acknowledge my disappointment in the exact time, I wish to inquire whether my teachings have been thereby materially affected. My view of exact time [338] depended entirely upon the accuracy of chronology; of this I had no absolute demonstration; but as no evidence was presented to invalidate it, I deemed it my duty to rely on it as certain, until it should be disproved. Besides,

I not only rested on received chronology, but I selected the earliest dates in the circle of a few years on which chronologers have relied for the date of the events from which to reckon, because I believed them to be best sustained, and because I wished to have my eye on the earliest time at which the Lord might be expected. Other chronologers had assigned later dates for the events from which I reckoned; and if they are correct we are only brought into the circle of a few years, during which we may rationally look for the Lord's appearing. As the prophetic periods, counting from the dates from which I have reckoned, have not brought us to the end, and as I cannot tell the exact time that chronology may vary from my calculations, I can only live in continual expectation of the event. I am persuaded that I cannot be far out of the way, and I believe that God will still justify my preaching to the world.

"With respect to other features of my views, I can see no reason to change my belief. We are living under the last form of the divided fourth kingdom, which brings us to the end. The prophecies which were to be fulfilled previous to the end have been so far fulfilled that I find nothing in them to delay the Lord's coming. The signs of the times thicken on every hand; and the prophetic periods must certainly, I think, have brought us into the neighborhood of the event.

"There is not a point in my belief in which I am not sustained by some one of the numerous writers who have opposed my views. Prof. Bush, the most gentlemanly of my opponents, admits that I am correct in the time, with the exception of the precise day or year; and this is all for which I contend. That the 70 weeks are 490 years, and the 1260 and 2300 days are so many years, are admitted by Messrs. Bush, Hinton, and Jarvis. That the 2300 days and 70 weeks commence at the same time, Prof. Bush does not deny. And Dr. Jarvis admits that the former carry us to the resurrection and judgment. Prof. Bush, Dr. Jarvis, Mr. Hinton and Mr. Morris, admit that the legs of iron and [339] fourth beast are Rome, and that the little horn of Daniel 7th is Papacy, while Dr. Jarvis and Mr. Hinton admit that the exceeding great horn of Daniel 8th is Rome. The literal resurrection of the body, the end of the world, and a personal coming of Christ, have not been questioned by several who have written against me.

"Thus there is not a point for which I have contended that has not been admitted by some of those who have written to disprove my opinions. I have candidly weighed the objections advanced against these views; but I have seen no arguments that were sustained by the Scriptures that, in my opinion, invalidated my position. I cannot, therefore, conscientiously refrain from looking for my Lord, or from exhorting my fellow-men, as I have opportunity, to be in readiness for that great event. For my indiscretions and errors I ask pardon; and all who have spoken evil of men without cause I freely forgive. My labors are principally ended. I shall leave to my younger brethren the task of contending for the truth. Many years I toiled alone; God has now raised up those who will fill my place. I shall not cease to pray for the spread of truth.

"In conclusion, suffer a word of exhortation. You, my brethren, who are called by the name of Christ, will you not examine the Scriptures respecting the nearness of the Advent? The great and good of all ages have had their minds directed to about this period of time, and a multitude are impressed with the solemn conviction that these are emphatically the last days. Is not a question of such moment worthy of your consideration? I do not ask you to embrace an opinion of mine; but I ask you to weigh well the evidence contained in the Bible. If I am in any error, I desire to see it, and I should certainly renounce it; but do look at the question, and, in view of the teachings of the inspired Word, decide for eternity.

"What shall I say to my unconverted friends? I have faithfully exhorted you these many years to believe in Christ; you have excused yourselves. What can I say more? Will not all the considerations that are presented in the Scriptures of truth move your hearts to lay down the weapons of your rebellion? You have no lease of your lives, and, if the Lord should not come, your eyes may be [340] soon closed in death. Why will you not improve the present moment, and flee from the wrath to come? Go to Christ, I beseech you; lay hold on the promise of God, trust in his grace, and he will cleanse you by his blood.

"I would exhort my Advent brethren to study the Word diligently. Let no man spoil you through philosophy and vain deceit. Avoid everything that shall cause offence. Let your lives be models of goodness and propriety. Let the adversary get no advantage over you. We have been disappointed; but disappointments will work for our good, if we make the right use of them. Be faithful. Be vigilant. Exhort with all long-suffering and patience. Let your conversation be in heaven, from whence you look for the blessed hope. Avoid unnecessary controversy and questions that gender strifes. Be not many masters; all are not competent to advise and direct. God will raise up those to whom he will commit the direction of his cause. Be humble, be watchful, be patient, be persevering. And may the God of peace sanctify you wholly, and preserve you blameless unto the glorious appearing of the great God and our Saviour Jesus Christ!   WILLIAM MILLER.

"*Low Hampton, August* 1, 1845."

CHAPTER 23

The Value Of Faith – Unfinished Letter – Visit To New York City,
Philadelphia, Etc. – Address To The Public – Visit To Canada, Etc.

In the month of September Mr. Miller attended conferences in Addison and Bristol, Vt., and lectured in each place. He then took a journey into Connecticut, and visited Hartford, attended a camp-meeting in Newington, near Hartford, and one at Square Pond, in Tolland county. He then visited Middletown. He was much pleased with his journey, and returned home refreshed.

After this, in connection with Elder A. Hale, he lectured, in November in the State of Vermont, at Waterbury, Morristown, [341] Stowe, Waitesfield and Burlington. Besides at these places, he seems to have labored but little during the remainder of the year. He occasionally communicated articles for the Advent Herald, giving expositions of Scripture, etc.; but the approaching infirmities of age admonished him that his labors were nearly ended. On the 11th of December, he wrote:

> "I am much troubled with my old complaint. Bless the Lord, I hope to be with him soon," etc.

On Christmas Day he communicated the following:

> ### "THE VALUE OF FAITH.
>
> "BROTHER HIMES:- I send you a few of my Christmas thoughts, in verse; they are the simple effusions of my heart, and can claim no merit beyond a medium of expressing my joys and sorrows. Was the dear Saviour born 1847 years ago to-night? Some think he was. Did the angels sing the Christmas chant, 'Peace on earth and good will to men,' 1847 years ago? If I could know this fact I would believe that, before another Christmas, I should hear, as did the shepherds in Judea, the same voices, chanting 'Glory on earth! Hallelujah! The King of Glory comes to dwell with men below!' This would be glory; the thought that it may be so fills me with joy unspeakable. I hope it is true. I do believe the Bible; if that's not true, there's nothing true on earth.

"Faith looks, the heavens resplendent shine;
Its opening portals bring to view
Things past and present, age and time,
God's vast creation, old and new.
Look up, my soul! why grovel here,
When glories such in heaven appear?

"See on yon throne, in dazzling white,
The Son of Man with God is crowned, –
Diffusing gracious heat and light
To myriad living creatures round!
Come, O my Faith! look up and see –
This man, Christ Jesus, died for thee!

"Upon his brow, once crowned with thorns,
Grace now sits smiling – how divine!
And whispers 'peace,' amidst the storms
That rack this troubled breast of mine.
Faith hears the word, and doth impart
Sweet consolation to my heart. [342]

"When weak, the tempter me assails,
And draws my love from Christ astray;
He speaks in love, no promise fails,
'Come back, my child, I am the way.'
Faith forsakes all these worldly charms,
And brings my soul back to his arms.

"When, filled with doubts, for sins I mourn,
And Satan's darts upon me fall, –
When, full of tears, my heart is torn,
And longs for help, on Him I call;
'Fear not,' He says, and Faith relies
On promises which he supplies.

"When Death, the tyrant, claims his due,
And threatens to devour his prey,
It fills my soul with dread to view
The cold, dark tomb, and mouldering clay;

Faith hears His voice say, 'Soul, come home!
The battle's fought, the victory won!

"If war and famine fill the land,
And pestilence and flame should be, –
Robbers and thieves join hand in hand,
Scoffers and mobs should all agree, –
These would be evidence for faith:
I credit what my Master saith.

"Go, then, ye skeptics, laugh and sneer;
Your time for sport will soon be o'er;
The Judge himself will soon appear,
And your vain boasts be heard no more.
Faith sees the end, and weeps for you,
Repent and love, – believe him too.

"If those, who once companions were
In my lone pilgrimage below,
Should leave me, and become a snare
To draw me to the pit of woe,
Faith bids me fly from earthly rest,
And cast my burthen on his breast.

"Faith hears the word Jehovah speaks,
Faith sees the way that Jesus trod, –
Faith, by the Spirit, praying seeks
The truth by faith that leads to God.
By Faith we tread this thorny grove,
Through Faith and Hope, to Christ above.

"WILLIAM MILLER.

"*Low Hampton, Dec. 25, 1845.*"

He left, among his MSS., the following fragment, which was probably commenced as a New Year's communication to those addressed: [343]

"Low Hampton, Dec. 1845.

"To the dear brethren who love the appearing of our dear and precious Saviour Jesus Christ:

"Let me address you in love, with the affection of one who has been often refreshed by your readiness to hear, believe, and obey the truth, and has taken sweet counsel with many of you in the house of God, – where our faith has been more and more established by the word of his grace, – where our prayers were mingled at the same altar, and have arisen in the same cloud of incense to the mercy-seat of our Redeemer, – where our hearts burned with the same love and gratitude to God for the good and glorious news of the near approach of the King of kings, – where our songs of praise and hallelujahs to the Lamb, in unison and sweet harmony, cheered our drooping spirits, while, like strangers and pilgrims, we expected soon – yes, very soon – to reach the long-sought and promised rest; – where heart mingled with heart, soul with soul, and love with love, holy, heavenly and divine, uniting us in the oneness of gospel truth; – where prejudice and party names were dissipated like the midnight fogs by the morning sun, – and where, may I not say, we learned the first practical lesson of gospel union!

"Were we wrong then? If so, then wrong will give a love as holy as angels breathe, and pure as the water of life. Who was our Master then? – Jesus Christ, who was at the door. Who claimed preeminence above his fellows then? None. Like little children, we sucked the honeyed flower and ate the naked truth. The *Bible!* – a precious book! The Bible! – no treasure on the earth was prized like that! We knew our friends and brethren by this Book of books. If we met a stranger, and in his pocket, hand, or heart, we found a Bible, we called him brother; and even the infidel would call him opprobrious names which they had affixed to us.

"That looked and seemed like the apostolic age. But O, how short! The spirits of the dark abyss were moved to spoil, if possible, this holy, happy union of gospel love. The base and sordid hypocrites from east to west began to foam and fret; the bigots all began to scowl and sneer; the world began to rage. The man-made wisdom and worldly greatness of the earth began to shake the drowsy spirits of their titled champions, and they arose to combat – what? – a [344] Bible doctrine, a long-acknowledged truth, a part of all their creeds from ages framed! Scoffs and ridicule, for a season, flew, thick as hailstones, in every direction. But this mode of warfare only caused the valiant soldiers of the Advent banner to buckle on their armor strong and firm, and tread the myriads of this army in the dust; and thus, through God, we conquered valiantly.

"The war was changed. The mighty heads of human creeds came forth, – some clad in mitred crowns and surpliced gowns, in college robes and doctors' caps, in presidential chairs and professors' seats, – with their retainers, serfs and allies, to shout the victory before the battle was won. Those who saw this mighty host can but remember what a cloud of dust was raised. A cry went forth like the war-whoop of the native Americans. The earth trembled; the heavens shook. Some of these champions were armed with a weapon forged by the pagan Vulcan, and polished by German ingenuity, and supposed, by their followers, to be as invincible as the club of Hercules. The multitude looked to see the little Advent band demolished at a blow. Many who had made up their minds, on the first opportunity which might look favorable to them, to unite their interest with the little flock, hearing the dreadful din made by this heterogeneous mass, through fear fled, and joined the ranks of the approaching foe. Many who had been lingering around the camp for the loaves and fishes, now forsook them, and became deserters and informers in the enemy's camp. Nevertheless, the little band had a goodly number of valiant souls, who had taken a bird's-eye view of the approaching army, had concluded to entrench themselves behind the enemy's own castle, built of human creeds, and called, by themselves, the Temple of Orthodoxy.

"This temple had a number of pillars, built, as was supposed, of true Grecian and Italian marble. One of these pillars was named the pillar of *judgment*; another, the *personal coming*; a third, the *resurrection*; the fourth, the *kingdom of God*; the fifth, the *reign of the saints*; the sixth was the *end of the world*; and the seventh, the *burning day*; with others of less importance.

"Other pillars had been erected long since the temple was first built, and these were made of hay, wood and [345] stubble, and were plastered and painted in imitation of marble, so that they were called by the vulgar the *new marble pillars*, and were considered a part of the original temple. One of these modern pillars was named '*conversion of the world*.' This pillar stood by the side of another called '*theological schools*,' and both together supported one of the main arches of the modern part of the building. On the right stood '*temporal millennium*,' and in its neighborhood was '*Jews' return*.' Scattered in every direction were smaller and insignificant ones, reared up by private individuals, – negative pillars, which bore no weight, yet served to confuse and perplex the worshippers. These were such as '*no heaven*,' '*no hell*,' '*no consciousness after death*,' '*no judgment in the future*,' '*no resurrection*,' '*no punishment*,' '*no spirit*,' '*no future existence of* the *wicked*,' 'no personal Christ,' 'no personal coming,' 'no kingdom, only in men's hearts,' etc.

"In this temple the battle begun. In a few moments the imitation pillars and paper walls were prostrate in the dust; and many noble warriors were overthrown, and lay in confused masses among the heaps of broken columns and paper rubbish which had been profusely scattered in the field. During this battle the little band of Adventists had stood their ground behind the marble pillars, which for ages have stood the shocks of war, although the champions of the attacking foe tried their weapons on these ancient columns. One attacked the 'resurrection' pillar, and would have demolished it even with the ground, had his strength been equal to His who reared the same in ancient days. Others tried to demolish the pillar of 'prophetic chronology;' but this stood the strokes of many a daring and presumptuous warrior, and is" ...

It was left thus unfinished, – something, probably, having interrupted its completion.

On the 13th of January he again wrote:

"Dear Brother Himes:- I am yet in this land of toil, where sin has spoiled all the blessings and enjoyments of earth, which were appointed by our beneficent Creator for the best good of his creatures, and which, had it not [346] been for sin, would have led us to reverence and adore that Being who had produced, by his power, this earth and all its appurtenances, and placed in it man – rational, intelligent, social man – to enjoy this vast and wondrous piece of mechanism.

"Perhaps we are unable rightly to appreciate the blessings which were placed within the reach of man at his creation, when 'the sons of God shouted for joy.' Yet I think that we do realize some of the evils which man is heir to by reason of 'sin, and death by sin,' which have entered the world. How manifest it is, at the present day, that all the influences of the pit are inciting men to crime, bringing in their trail consequences ten-fold more dreadful than those entailed upon us by the sin of our first parents! If there were one spark of philanthropy existing in the world, methinks it must bleed at beholding the rapid increase of evil within the last few years.

"I confess that to me it would be but a dismal and appalling prospect in the future, did not a ray of light beam forth from the Word of God, that there should be a glorious and final renovation of all things! This 'exceeding great and precious promise,' to the man of God, is the only hope that cheers him in his weary pilgrimage. Every means that the wisdom of man could devise for the melioration of the condition of man has failed; ministers of the gospel have been sent into every land; Bibles have been scattered broadcast in the earth, translated into almost every tongue, and placed in the hands of the poor, 'without money and without price;' schools of every grade, from the college to the common, have sprung up, in which have been developed the highest mental qualities of man; societies have been multiplied, for the moral improvement of our race, – to Christianize the heathen, – to reform the inebriate, – to break the bonds of the enslaved, – to liberate the debtor, – to stop the horrid practice of legal murder, – to promote peace among nations, – to protect the orphan, – to clothe the naked, – to feed the hungry, – to nurse the sick, and even to bury the dead. These, and many other noble and benevolent enterprises, have been formed within the present century. But how much good have they accomplished? That great good has been done, cannot be denied. But it is [347] likewise true, that evil has predominated in a far greater ratio than at any former period.

"When I look back to the period when we began to publish the news of a coming Saviour, I think it the happiest time of my life. How were our hearts refreshed by the readiness of the dear brethren in Christ to hear, believe, and obey, the simple gospel of the kingdom! With what delight have I, in company with many of the dear, anxious children of God, read and re-read the Scriptures, searched diligently and compared the prophets, Jesus Christ, and his apostles, to see if these things were so! What glorious light I have often seen in that holy book while thus engaged! And with what joy have I taken sweet communion with kindred hearts in the house of God, where our faith was more and more established by the word of His grace; where our prayers were mingled at the same altar, and arose together, as incense, to the mercy-seat of our Redeemer, for a preparation to meet the coming glories, which we then expected shortly to realize; where our hearts burned with love and gratitude to God for the good news of the near approach of the King of kings; where our songs of praise and hallelujahs to the Lamb cheered our drooping spirits, and prepared us more vigorously to pursue our weary pilgrimage to the land of promise, which, from evidence to us conclusive, and which I am not ashamed of, we soon expect to reach!

"Then, heart beat in unison with heart, soul mingled with soul, and love, holy, heavenly, divine, united us in that oneness of gospel truth, and prejudice and party were dissipated from our thoughts like midnight darkness, or the morning mists by the rising sun. This was a time of love, a time of faith, working by love and purifying the heart. It was this hope, 'the blessed hope,' that made us purify ourselves from our sectarian prejudices and bigotry.

"I have often thought that we then enjoyed a foretaste of the love and fellowship of the saints in light. Why is it not so now? The reason is as obvious as the sun at noonday. We have been drawn from our *first principles* by wicked and designing men, who have crept in among us and drawn us into parties, to follow men instead of God, and to form new tests instead of the Bible. Some of our lecturers [348] first began the confusion, by declaring an unholy crusade against the sects, which brought in men of blood instead of men of peace. True, after the manner of men, the sects had provoked us to the course we took by all the wicked arts and misrepresentation of our views and motives that human and satanic agency could invent, – by slanders, ridicule, and wresting the Word of God from the meaning which had long been laid down in their own creeds, and departing from those rules by which their fathers, for centuries, had applied mystic Babylon to the church of Rome. We were not called, in my humble opinion, to engage in so universal a war. I think we have, in this, 'left our first principles,' which were, to preach the blessed hope, and beseech men to be ready for the 'glorious appearing of the great God and our Saviour Jesus Christ,' without personal or denominational considerations. While we pursued this course, God blessed us in our work. We were commanded by the Word to be patient, sober, to judge not, not to be high-minded, but to fear, and, by so doing, manifest the same spirit that was in Christ. What have been the fruits of this departure from the plain line of duty? Surely they have not been love, peace, and joy, such as we formerly experienced, when we believed in our hearts that Christ was at the door. On the contrary, it has, in many instances, separated those who had been knit together in the closest friendship, fomented jealousies, produced 'lo heres, and lo theres!' while some have blasphemously arrogated to themselves names and titles which belong to Christ. With such I have no sympathy, – no fellowship. I will refer them to Christ's words, Revelation 3:3: – 'Remember, therefore, how thou hast received and heard, and hold fast and repent. If, therefore, thou shalt not watch, I will come on thee as a thief, and thou shalt not know what hour I will come upon thee.'

"The glorious appearing of Christ is my only hope; to this I cling, – it is my anchor; and all who look for and love his appearing are my brothers and sisters, and with such I have fellowship in the Lord, and exhort them to watch. WILLIAM MILLER.

"*Low Hampton, January* 13, 1846."

On the 11th of March, 1846, in company with Messrs. [349] Himes and Apollos Hale, Mr. M. lectured at Glenn's Falls, N. Y. It does not appear that he visited any other place till about the time of the Annual Conference, which met in New York city on the 12th of May.

His bodily infirmities rendered it unsafe for him to journey without the attendance of some one to render him all needful assistance; therefore he arranged with Elder Henry Buckley, of Hampton, N. Y., to accompany him to New York city.

They left home on Saturday, the 9th of May, and proceeded as far as Lansingburg, N. Y. On the Sabbath he went to Middletown, N. Y., where he preached twice, returning, after service, to Lansingburg. On Monday, the 11th, they proceeded to New York city. He took part in the debates and preaching of the Conference, and, though feeble, seemed to enjoy the meetings.

After its adjournment, they visited Philadelphia. On Sunday, the 17th, he preached in the morning and evening to large and attentive congregations. The next day he visited his former acquaintances, and, on the 19th, he left for Providence, R. I. There they attended a meeting of the friends, which continued four days, and to which Mr. M. preached four discourses, with his usual interest. On the 25th he visited North Scituate, R. I., and gave two discourses. On the 26th he preached twice in North Attleboro', Mass., and, on the 27th, arrived in Boston. The Annual Conference was adjourned from New York to meet there, and commenced on the day previous. He again took part in its debates, but spent most of his time in visiting friends and acquaintances in the vicinity. They visited Westminster, Mass., where Mr. M. preached on the 3rd of June; and, on the 5th, he arrived home, much fatigued with his journey, but in good health and spirits.

On the 24th of June, in company with Elder Buckley, Mr. M. visited Cranbury Creek, N. Y., where he preached seven discourses in four days. No other place being open for the meetings, they were held in a large barn, owned by Judge Gilbert. It was comfortably furnished with seats, and accommodated very respectable congregations, composed of the more intelligent and pious portion of the community. Mr. M.'s discourses there were spoken of by those present as logical and interesting. [350]

During the warm months he attempted no public labors; and his pen, even, seems to have lain idle. The next communication received from him was published in the Advent Herald of September 9, 1846, as follows:

"ADDRESS TO THE PUBLIC.

"DEAR READER:- Permit me to address you once more, by calling your attention to the great events which the word of God declares are soon to come to pass, that I may faithfully perform my duty; and that you may be able to answer, in that way which will be satisfactory to your own soul, in the day when God shall judge the secret thoughts of men by Jesus Christ.

"In my former communications to you on this subject, – which is near my heart, fills my soul at times with indescribable joy and consolation, and is big with the hope of soon, very soon, coming into possession of immortality and eternal life, – I readily confess I was misled in my calculations; not by the word of God, nor by the established principles of interpretation I adopted, but by the authorities which I followed in history and chronology, and which have been generally considered worthy of the fullest confidence. And I fear many of you have been blinded to your own interest, which may be of eternal consequences to you, by hasty expressions of full confidence in these authors, before I had carefully and more extensively examined the subject to which I had, in the simplicity of my heart, called your candid and serious attention.

"The testimony of historians, as to the dates of events, cannot affect the testimony of the word of God, that, at certain periods from these events, his promises shall be fulfilled. They may fail, but his word cannot fail. I confess I have been thus mistaken as to the definite time; but what of that? Will you or any man dare to take the ground that, because Mr. Miller or any other man made a mistake, the word of God is not true? No, no. There would be nothing in that worthy of being called an argument.

"But, above all things else, I was deceived in the number and character of those who, without study, argument, or reason, rejected the (to me at least) glorious news of the coming Saviour. Neither did I suppose that a man or woman [351] could have been found on the habitable earth, who loved the Lord Jesus Christ and believed the

Bible, that would reject the Second Advent or the redemption of the body; the final salvation of the soul, or the inheritance of eternal life, at the appearing of Jesus Christ. Yet facts warrant me to say, I find more than one-half who profess Christianity denying one or more of these fundamental pillars of the Christian hope.

"I am thankful to God, although much and sorely disappointed, that I never pretended to be divinely inspired, but always directed you to the same source from which I obtained all the information I then had and now possess on this glorious and heart-cheering subject. Let me, then, exhort you, kind reader, by the value of truth, by the worth of your own soul, and the love of life everlasting, to examine your Bible on the coming of Christ, the redemption of the body, the salvation of your soul, and the everlasting inheritance. Lay by all prejudice, all opinions not founded on the plain and clear declarations of God's word; keep close to that rule which will thoroughly furnish you, and make you perfect in every good work; examine for yourselves; let no man deceive you in these days of deception, when the devil has come, deceiving, if possible, the very elect. Now is the time for you to exercise the 'sober second thought;' a good time for you to come over on the side of truth, to choose the good, and refuse the evil. I beseech you do not say, 'Nay, I will not examine!' Do not say, 'I am well enough off, and I have got the truth!' Perhaps you have; if so, it will not hurt you to reexamine, for every reexamination only makes the truth the brighter, our evidence more clear, and our love for the truth more fervent; it helps to establish our faith and hope, and keeps us from wavering.

"And now, dear reader, let me propose a few questions, in view of what I have said, for you to answer to God and your own soul; and I pray you not to trifle with them, or one of them, if you can find a plain Scripture text which authorizes the question. And I beg of you delay not to answer every question which may or can be answered; and let your answers be such as you will be willing to meet before the throne of God in the day of judgment, to which day [352] I appeal in thus addressing you. I append a text to every question, to show you they are scriptural:

"**1.** Will Christ appear the second time? Hebrews 9:28.

"**2.** Will he come himself? 1 Thessalonians 4:16.

"**3.** Who will see him? 1 John 3:2; Revelation 1:7.

"**4.** Who will not be ashamed before him at his coming? 1 John 2:28; 4:17.

"**5.** What will Christ come to do? 1 Thessalonians 1:7-10; Hebrews 1:10-12; Revelation 21:5.

"**6.** When Christ comes will there be a resurrection, and of whom? 1 Corinthians 15:23; 1 Thessalonians 4:14-18.

"**7.** Where is Christ now? Acts 1:11; 3:21.

"**8.** At what time will Christ be sent again to earth? Acts 3:20, 21.

"**9.** When may we know he is near, even at the door? Matthew 24:30, 33.

"**10.** Has any one of the signs been seen which are given by our Lord in Matthew 24:29; Mark 13:24, 25, or Luke 21:25, 26; or by Paul in 1 Timothy 4:1-3; also 2 Timothy 3:1-9; or by Peter in 2 Peter 3:3, 4, by any one living in this generation?

"**11.** When is the day of redemption? Ephesians 4:30; Luke 21:28.

"**12.** When shall our bodies be redeemed? Romans 8:23.

"**13.** When shall our souls be saved? 1 Peter 1:7-13.

"**14.** When shall the righteous inherit eternal life? Mark 10:17; Matthew 19:29; 25:46.

"**15.** What is the earnest of that inheritance? Ephesians 1:13, 14; 2 Corinthians 1:22; 5:4, 5.

"**16.** If we are to receive all this when Christ appears, and not until then, can you blame any Christian for loving his appearing? 2 Timothy 4:8.

"**17.** And, if you were commanded to watch for him, and these blessings were promised when he comes, would you not look with intense interest until his coming?

"**18.** And, if you were commanded to watch, would you watch without expecting him? Luke 12:35-40.

"**19.** And, if he did not come when you expected, would [353] you not be disappointed in some proportion to your love for his appearing?

"Remember this is the situation of your Advent friends; this is our experience. And may God help you to love, watch, and expect the dear Saviour until he shall come.

"WILLIAM MILLER."

On the 4th of September, in view of many contradictory opinions afloat, he proffered the following advice:

"When we write to a brother to complain of some of his opinions, let us consider of it three days before we write; pray God nine times to direct us before we take up the pen; read it in the room of our brother three times before we send it; seal it only when we love him for being God-like; send it when we would delight to be the bearer; while it is going, think with what tears of joy he will devour its contents; and remember to pay postage."

On the 8th of September Mr. M. commenced a tour into Canada. He went by way of Lake Champlain to Burlington, Vt., where he preached, in the evening of that day. There he met Elder Buckley, who accompanied him on his tour. From this place they went to Essex, Vt., where Mr. M. gave two discourses. On the 12th, they commenced a two days' meeting in Cambridge, Vt., where there was a good attendance. On Tuesday, the 15th, they commenced a meeting in Montgomery, Vt., which continued over the following Sabbath, Mr. Miller generally preaching twice a day.

While at this place he was taken with a severe pain in one of his toes. He was soon relieved of that, when the pain commenced in his left shoulder. He then desired to return home, but was persuaded to continue his journey. On the 22nd, he gave two discourses in South Troy, Vt. The meeting was held in a large hall which had formerly been used for a ball-room. While he was preaching in the evening, the windows were pelted with eggs, clubs, and stones, thrown by some "rude fellows of the baser sort," who were outside of the building. Some of their missiles entered the room. One stone, about the size of a hen's egg, struck the desk in front of Mr. Miller, where he was speaking. He paused, and, with emphasis, asked, very composedly: [354]

> "Is this Vermont, the state which boasts of its freedom, of its republicanism? Shame on Vermont!"

The audience were somewhat agitated; but he requested them to be quiet, and proceeded with his discourse. No one was injured, and good evidently resulted from the interruption; for it aroused the old gentleman's energy, and gave additional interest to the remainder of the sermon.

On Thursday, the 24th of September, they commenced a Conference at Derby Line, Vt., which continued four days. The pain in Mr. M.'s shoulder had increased considerably, and resulted in a tumor of considerable size, which was much inflamed. Yet he preached six times, with a good degree of vigor.

On Monday, the 28th, a widowed sister of Mr. M., living in Canada, having met him at Derby Line, he left with her for her residence in Hatley. He was there confined about three weeks with the tumor on his shoulder, which was very painful, affecting his neck and head, and discharged freely for many days. In consequence of this indisposition, he was unable to fulfill several appointments, which he had made in that region, much to the disappointment of the inhabitants.

As soon as he was able to ride, they started for Low Hampton; but the weather and roads made the travelling very tedious. On his way home he spent a Sabbath, and preached a discourse of two hours' duration, at Rickford, Vt., which left him so weak that it was with difficulty he could walk. On arriving at Fairfield, Vt., they spent a night, and Mr. M. preached in the evening. They arrived at Low Hampton after an absence of about nine weeks, during which he had been treated with great kindness and respect wherever he visited, – with the exception of the incident at Montgomery.

"My tour into Canada," he wrote soon after his return, "would have been pleasant and agreeable to me, had it not been for sickness, which confined me to the house."

On the 27th of November following, he wrote to Elder Buckley, who accompanied him on the above journey:

> "I cannot tell you what I have done since you were here, but I can tell you what I have not done.
>
> "1st. I have not done with vanity. It is as natural as my breath; and if I ever cease from vain and trifling conversation [355] in this world, you must place me in society which I have no regard for, – either to love or to hate, – where I could be a hypocrite without any drawback. For I have often noticed, when I am alone and with no one to converse with, that I am not tempted to speak words of vanity. This is the reason why I choose to be alone much of my time. In my opinion, this accounts for the ascetic lives of the early Christians. What think you – is it not best for me to become a hermit?
>
> "2nd. I have not done with *pain*. I have been troubled with head-ache, teeth-ache, bones-ache, and heart-ache, since you left; but much more of the *last* ache, when I think of so many of my once dearly beloved brethren, who have, since our disappointment, gone into fanaticism of every kind, and left the first principles of the glorious appearing

of the great God and our Saviour, Jesus Christ. And now, can you blame me for desiring a hermitage, away from these evil tidings and shameful acts of our friends in this time of severe trial?

"3rd. I have not done with corruption. My swelling discharges a little every day, and I see myself falling to corruption daily. It may be that I am corrupting others who may be brought into contact with me, – for instance, the fanatics. If they never had heard of 'Millerism,' they would have been sober, worldly-seeking, church-loving, and sectarian-building men and women to this day; and they would have been respected as much as other church members are by the rich and popular worldlings. Yes, yes; so says the world; and you know that what the world says must be true. This is, in these modern times, the best evidence. If, then, I had been a recluse, instead of running at large, it might have saved the world a great deal of trouble, and the church the knowledge of a great deal of corruption.

"4th. I have done no good thing. I can prove this by every writer, Christian and political, editors, doctors of divinity, professors and ministers of all denominations, – from the Roman Catholic to the Mormon, – save only a few despised Adventists, who, in the eyes of the world, are as much below the Mormons, as Christ was below Barabbas in the Jews' estimation.

"'But,' say you, 'you say you have done no good [356] thing. Was it not a good thing to tell us, who love Christ's appearing, that he was near to come? Was it not a good thing to read the Bible to us, and show by history its fulfillment and truth? Was it not a good thing to warn sinners of their danger, which might lead them to repentance and a preparation for the judgment? Was it not a good thing to preach the kingdom of heaven at hand and the judgment? Was it not a good thing to preach the resurrection of these bodies, the inheritance of the saints, and the reign of Christ and his people on the earth made new forever? Was it not a good thing to comfort the saints with the words of his coming, and to stir them up to a remembrance of the things which Christ, the prophets, and apostles, have spoken concerning his coming? And have not you done all this?'

"No, no.

"'Who has then?'

"I answer, it was the grace of God which worked in me of his own good pleasure both to will and to do.

"Since I have been preaching this hour, I will give you my text, 2 Corinthians 12:11, last clause: '*Though I be nothing.*' And now, lastly, the improvement.

"1st. You may learn, by my subject, that I am nothing – like the clay in the hands of the potter.

"2nd. You may learn, if any good has been done, that God has done it by his grace; and if any evil, it is a chastisement for disobedience; for 'shall there be evil in a city, and the Lord hath not done it?'– Amos 3:6.

"3rd. We may learn, by the effect of any work, whether it be of God. If wicked men, and proud, selfish, popular professors join hand in hand to oppose you, you may be sure that God is in the work.

"4th. You may learn, by my subject, that I am not well of my disease. Nor do I expect to be till Christ comes; for which event I look with a great interest and desire.

"Yours,   WM. MILLER."

Having desired a visit from Elder Himes, who had spent the summer in Great Britain, and having received intelligence that such a visit would have to be deferred till the January following, he wrote him, on the 7th of December, 1846, after expressing his regrets for the delay, as follows: [357]

"I feel lonesome; yet I have great reason to bless God, and to take courage. I also rejoice that, with all the departures from the faith which has cheered the people of God in every age, you, and those connected with you in conducting the Advent Herald, have remained steadfast. In this, I have abundant reason to thank my Heavenly Father. Amidst my severe disappointments and trials, God has given me a few faithful companions who have not been shaken from the truth, nor been turned unto fables and new theories of men, by the cunning craftiness of those who lie in wait to deceive. Yes, my brother, if you will continue to hold up the truth as you have done thus far, God will bless you; and when the Master comes, be it sooner or later, he will say to you, 'Well done, good and faithful servant, enter thou into the joy of thy Lord.'

"If this should be the last letter you receive from old Brother Miller (which may be the case), remember it has been his earnest desire, and the last wish of his heart, that you might be preserved from imbibing those views so derogatory to the Word of God; – the return of the carnal Jew, – a millennium before the coming of Christ, – probation after the Advent, – sinners or sin and death dwelling in the new earth, – regeneration for resurrection, – unconscious state of the dead, – annihilation of the soul, etc. All these views, with many others of a like character, I have no faith in, nor fellowship for. I therefore feel that it is my duty, and my present infirmities admonish me that it is one of my last, to affectionately, yet earnestly, warn my dear brethren against these dangerous errors and practices. Examine the Word of God, and judge of their fruits. Follow no man, or men, unless they have the spirit of Christ, which is not a spirit that manifests itself in a love of self.

"My health is very poor. I never expect to see many of my dear brethren again in the flesh; and perhaps, before you come, I may be with Christ in spirit, and my body under the cold clods of the valley. I have often wondered why God had so long spared me, and suffered death to rob us of so many more useful than myself.

"WILLIAM MILLER."

With the exception of an occasional article for the press, [358] Mr. Miller made no public effort during the winter. His health would not permit. As the time approached for the usual Annual Meeting in New York city in May, 1847, he made arrangements to be present; but his health was not sufficient. In writing of his inability to be present, under date of May 6th, 1847, he said:

"I cannot charge myself with any corrupt motive in promoting the Second Advent doctrine. If I have any regret, it is because I have done so little, and because I have been so inefficient. I have lacked in zeal more than I have lacked in faith. I believed, and do still, in this glorious and Bible doctrine of the second coming of our dear Redeemer, and of his everlasting kingdom or reign in paradise restored.

"I fear that I shall not be able to attend at Boston."

His health was, however, so much improved, that, with Elder Buckley, his companion in travel of the previous year, he left home on the 20th of May, and arrived in Boston on the 22nd, three days before the Conference commenced.

The day following was Sunday, and he preached two discourses, in the afternoon and evening, at the Saloon, at No. 9 Milk street, where the Adventists then worshipped. On Monday evening he preached, in the same place, on the resurrection of the body. He took part in the discussions of the Conference during the week, preached once on the following Sabbath, and on Monday left for home, where he arrived on Tuesday, June 1st. This was his last visit to Massachusetts.

CHAPTER 24

Dream – Loss Of Sight – Events In Europe – Health Declines – Expression Of Sympathy By The New York Conference – His Reply – Letters Of Elders Kimball And Robinson

ON the 15th of September, 1847, he was present at a tent-meeting at Basin Harbor, in Ferrisburg, Vt., which continued four days. In a letter written on the 27th of the same month, he makes the following reference to it: [359]

"DEAR BROTHER HIMES:- I cannot refrain from writing a few words to you, to let you know how my soul and body prosper since our tent-meeting at Basin Harbor.

"That was to me a profitable time. It seemed like former times, when the truth cut to the heart all who heard. The preaching was plain, powerful, and convincing. The prayer-meetings were humble, devotional, and penitent, and very properly conducted. No uproar, confusion, or fanaticism, which disturb the mind, and leave a bad savor upon the hearts of the fastidious. The conferences were perfect love-feasts, and the songs such as the poet describes:

'My willing soul would stay
In such a frame as this;
And sit and sing herself away
To everlasting bliss.'

I never expect to enjoy another such a feast of tabernacles in the flesh. God was with us. Praise his holy name.

"You have a real helper in Brother Hutchinson. I am thankful to God for you, Brother Himes, for you need just such a companion. God bless you both, and prosper you in your work of preaching the kingdom of heaven at hand, which is the everlasting gospel, and the best news ever heard by man.

"This gospel I am not ashamed of, although it is the cross-bearing gospel of the present day. I was edified, instructed, and encouraged. Yes, I am more than all that; I am strengthened to await God's appointed time with patience and hope, knowing shortly, if we faint not, we shall receive an abundant admittance into the kingdom of God. ...

"There are some things, which I call non-essential, that are gravely discussed by some among us, as though life and death depended on them, and are by many made test questions of fellowship, termed 'the questions of the age,' etc. I mean by 'non-essential things' those questions which have no practical bearing on our present life. For instance, suppose one good brother is pleased to believe that the saints, after the resurrection, will have two wings, another four, and a third that they will have six, while the fourth argues for none at all. If this was continually debated, how long before there would be four parties, especially if one began to [360] boast over the other. This, every man in his right mind would say, was of no consequence to us in this life, – whether they had two, four, or six wings, or none at all. So to me is the question of the annihilation of the wicked; it has no manner of use to me in this life. And I, for one, am determined, God being my helper, not to belong to that class in the world to come.

"I do not wonder that the world calls us insane; for I must confess it looks like insanity to me, to see religious, candid men, spend their time and talents on questions of so little consequence to us here or hereafter."

Because of his position in opposition to certain theories, the advocates of them, who wished to sustain them by his influence, towards the close of his life represented that he was controlled in his opinions by Mr. Himes. In a published letter to him, dated October 26th, 1847, he says:

"It has been charged, by some, that I have been influenced in my course by you and others. Such is not the case. I would say to all, that I have never been dictated to by Bro. Himes; nor has he, to my knowledge, ever tried to direct me. But these things do not affect me. I am able to bear all that my enemies can heap upon me, if the Lord helps me."

As his infirmities increased and strength diminished, he was very much pained by the irregularities, extravagances, and strange notions practiced or entertained by those who had departed from his teachings and counsels. That subject so much occupied his waking thoughts, that it was not singular if his sleeping hours were affected by the same.

He, no more than others, placed any reliance on dreams; yet the comfort he derived from one, about the middle of November, caused him afterwards to write it out for publication. In a letter, written three weeks subsequently, he thus relates it:

"DEAR BRO. HIMES:- I am yet in the land of the living, and under the trials of this inconstant world. I am confident that I cannot bear the trials, perplexities, and evils, to which we are all subject, more or less, as I once could; whether it is owing to my age, infirmities, or for the [361] want of my former activity, I cannot tell; perhaps all these things may operate on my mind as causes to produce impatience, uneasiness, and the like; to avoid which, and to retain and possess an equilibrium of temper, I have had to use all the powers of my body and mind. I have often found it a hard contest on my part to overcome these evils, or bear up under them, with the fortitude and courage of a soldier of the cross. I find more need of grace as I progress in my journey towards the saints' inheritance.

"About three weeks since, owing, as I suppose, to a discovery, which I thought I had made, that some brethren, whom I had loved in the gospel with a deep and intense interest, had become alienated from me, as well as from each other, and were trying to supplant and injure the characters, usefulness, influence, and abilities of other brethren and myself, and had become like the obscene fowls of the air who live only on carcasses and putrid flesh; it seemed to me that I should be obliged to give up all confidence in men, and all love for them; so that, like David, I had no Jonathan left, and like him could say, 'I shall fall one day by the hand of Saul.' While in this deplorable state of mind, when I was about to believe in the total depravity of all men, and that all profession of religion was nothing but hypocrisy, I received comfort and consolation from the following, which may pass for

"A Dream.

"I dreamed that God, by an unseen hand, sent me a curiously wrought casket, about ten inches long by six square, made of ebony and pearls curiously inlaid. To the casket there was a key attached. I immediately took the key and opened the casket, when, to my wonder and surprise, I found it filled with all sorts and sizes of jewels, diamonds, precious stones, and gold and silver coin of every dimension and value, beautifully arranged in their several places in the casket; and thus arranged, they reflected a light and glory equaled only by the sun.

"I thought it was my duty not to enjoy this wonderful sight alone, although my heart was overjoyed at the brilliancy, beauty, and value of its contents. I therefore placed it on a centre-table in my room, and gave out word that all [362] who had a desire might come and see the most glorious and brilliant sight ever seen by man in this life.

"The people began to come in, at first few in number, but increasing to a crowd. When they first looked into the casket they would wonder and shout for joy. But when the spectators increased every one would begin to trouble the jewels, taking them out of the casket and scattering them on the table.

"I began to think the owner would require the casket and jewels again at my hand; and if I suffered them to be scattered, I could never place them in their places in the casket again as before; and felt I should never be able to meet the accountability, for it would be immense. I then began to plead with the people not to handle them, nor take them out of the casket; but the more I plead, the more they scattered; – and now they seemed to scatter them all over the room, on the floor, and on every piece of furniture in the room.

"I then saw that among the genuine jewels and coin they had scattered an innumerable quantity of spurious jewels and counterfeit coin. I was highly incensed at their base conduct and ingratitude, and reproved and reproached them for it; but the more I reproved the more they scattered the spurious jewels and false coin among the genuine.

"I then became vexed in my very soul, and began to use physical force to push them out of the room; but while I was pushing out one, three more would enter, and bring in dirt, and shavings, and sand, and all manner of rubbish, until they covered every one of the true jewels, diamonds, and coins, which were all excluded from sight. They also tore in pieces my casket, and scattered it among the rubbish. I thought no man regarded my sorrow or my anger. I became wholly discouraged and disheartened, and sat down and wept.

"While I was thus weeping and mourning for my great loss and accountability, I remembered God, and earnestly prayed that he would send me help.

"Immediately the door opened, and a man entered the room, when the people all left it; and he, having a dirtbrush in his hand, opened the windows, and began to brush the dust and rubbish from the room. [363]

"I cried to him to forbear, for there were some precious jewels scattered among the rubbish.

"He told me to 'fear not,' for he would 'take care of them.'

"Then, while he brushed, the dust and rubbish, false jewels and counterfeit coin, all rose and went out of the windows like a cloud, and the wind carried them away. In the bustle I closed my eyes for a moment; when I opened them, the rubbish was all gone. The precious jewels, the diamonds, the gold and silver coins, lay scattered in profusion all over the room.

"He then placed on the table a casket, much larger and more beautiful than the former, and gathered up the jewels, the diamonds, the coins, by the handful, and cast them into the casket, till not one was left, – although some of the diamonds were not bigger than the point of a pin.

"He then called upon me to 'come and see.'

"I looked into the casket, but my eyes were dazzled with the sight. They shone with ten times their former glory. I thought they had been scoured in the sand by the feet of those wicked persons who had scattered and trod them in the dust. They were arranged in beautiful order in the casket, every one in its place, without any visible pains of the man who cast them in. I shouted with very joy, and that shout awoke me.

"The effect of this on my mind has been extremely consoling and happy. Write to me the interpretation, and receive my love for you and yours.

"WM. MILLER.

"*Low Hampton, December* 3, 1847."

On the publication of the above, it was generally regarded as a dream of his *waking* hours; but he subsequently assured his biographer that it was what it purported to be – a dream. He received many letters, inquiring if it *was* actually a dream; but his usual reply was, "I so stated it; did you doubt my veracity?"

In response to his request, "Write me the interpretation," many attempted to solve the enigma, to explain which no Daniel was needed. Without professing any skill in the "interpreting of dreams," the "showing hard sentences [364] and dissolving doubts," Mr. M. acquiesced in the following interpretation.

"The 'casket' was the volume of God's truth, – his whole revealed Word.

"The 'jewels, diamonds, precious stones,' etc., were the *doctrines* of the Bible, which, each sparkling and bright like precious gems, glittered in the casket as they were unfolded to view.

"The scattering of these gems was the sad havoc which the unstable, and those turned about by every wind of doctrine, made with certain portions of revealed truth; preaching for doctrines the imaginings of their own hearts, and placing precious doctrines of God's grace and providence among the rubbish, dirt, shavings, and sand, of the great apostasy; wresting them to their own destruction.

"While Mr. Miller expostulated with one class of these errorists, three more would arise in other places, until it was difficult to convince the people who 'we were.'[93]

"The restoration of the jewels to their place was the ushering in of the kingdom of God, when each diamond truth will be separated from

---

[93] See p. 301.

the dust and mist with which the ignorance, unbelief, or depravity of man has encumbered it, to shine in the Saviour's diadem."

Among the interpretations communicated to him, though not expressing his own views, the two following are deemed worthy of preservation for their poetic merit.

"To Mr. William Miller.

"Thoughts Suggested by Reading Your Letter Containing the Dream.

"Bright was the gift to thy hand once given,
Sparkling with gems, for thy crown in heaven;
More precious the jewels glittering there
Than Ethiop's topaz, or sapphires fair,
Than the coral branch, or pearls most fine,
Or the golden coin from fair Ophir's mine:
'T were souls that were gathered, and washed in light,
Streaming from heaven, transcendently bright.
And yet, weary pilgrim, thy gift's pure ray
Seemed dimmed, even lost, in the rough, dark way;
Its beautiful brilliance was hid in dust,
Its gold seemed cankered, and eaten with rust;
Lost! lost! seemed the once sparkling diadem,
And scattered and trodden each costly gem. [365]
Was thy heart then stricken, poor weary one?
Seemed there nothing to light thee, – no star, no sun, –
To find the rich gift that thy God had given,
As a token to thee of thy peace with heaven?
Ah yes! at that moment of anguish most deep,
Israel's God did not slumber nor sleep:
He knows of each tear, and lists to each sigh;
Angels are sent from their bright home on high,
To guard and to keep thee in all thy ways,
And to pour on thy soul the heaven-lit rays.

"Thy jewels are gathered, – the false ones are flown;
The chaff and the dust to the winds are strewn,
Thy casket is glowing with rubies most rare,
The pearls are the purest, the diamonds fair:

O! bright is the light of each shining gem
That burns in that glorious diadem.
On! on! brave old pilgrim, thy task soon is done, –
Thy struggles soon ended, thy victory won."

Mrs. L. H. Smith

"To Father Miller.

"Aged saint, why weepest thou?
Christ is at the fountain still,
Whence the healing streams do flow,
Powerful yet to pardon ill;

"Every jewel in his crown,
Washed and purified from stain,
Brighter far than diamonds found,
Polished by the art of man.

"Beauteous settings! not one lost,
Every tribe and nation here,
Through the anguish of the cross,
Rich in glory shall appear.

"Now, amidst the mines of earth,
Lost in darkness, sin, despair,
Where's the glory of their birth?
Where's the holy and the fair?

"When, upon thy ravished sight,
God's own city rose to view,
With its gates and pillars bright,
Sea of glass, and glory too -

"Quick to wondering sinners thou
Gladly saidst, 'The Lord is nigh;'
Aged servant, rest thee now,
For thy record is on high.

"If, about thy pathway strewed,
Dust and gems promiscuous lie,
Saint, look up, thy Lord doth know
Every gem thy sight would spy. [366]

And when Jesus comes to winnow
Wheat from chaff, – the saint from sinner, –
All thy jewels will be there,

In his diadem most fair;
Not a saint will then be lost,
Purchased by the Saviour's cross.
Joyful, then, wilt thou behold
Casket fair, and burnished gold,
Precious stones and coins most rare; –
All, all, *all* will then be there!
Hold thee on a little space,
For thy Master, face to face,
Will sweetly say, "Come, dwell with me,
From the dust of death set free."
Every pain that now afflicts thee,
Every ill that now besets thee,
All will vanish in the light
Of thy casket second sight."

Mrs. C. A. Ludlow.

Towards the last of January, 1848, Mr. Miller was attacked with a dimness of sight, which deprived him of his usual privilege of reading and writing, which, through life, had been to him a source of great enjoyment. His health, otherwise, continued as good as could be expected, in his gradually declining age.

With the loss of his sight, he had to depend on others to read to him, and to write the letters which he dictated. He desired the continuance of letters from his correspondents, but requested them to excuse him from replying.

The hope of soon meeting them where the lame man shall leap as an hart, the tongue of the dumb sing, the blind receive their sight, and the deaf hear, and the belief in the nearness of that day, was a great consolation to him under his accumulating infirmities. His loss of sight was communicated by his son, Wm. S. Miller, Esq., in a letter dated February 10th, about two weeks after his attack.

On the 7th of March, a letter, from a daughter-in-law of Mr. Miller, stated that his general health was then better, but that he had been unable to read a word for seven weeks anterior to the preceding Sabbath. On that day, his son Robbins took the glass from the spy-glass, and held it to his eye, so that he read a few words. She added:-

"His eyes are not sore: the physician whom he has consulted says the retina is affected. Father bears his affliction well. I have never heard him murmur, nor say that it was [367] hard. I think that he feels somewhat 'cast down, but not forsaken.'"

Appended to the above letter, Mr. Miller wrote, without being able to see a word:

"God bless you, bless you all, and save you, is my prayer.

"WM. MILLER."

After this his general health was some improved, so that he was able to be about and to busy himself with light work. He was able to distinguish one object from another, and could often recognize his friends and acquaintances; but, with the best glasses he could get, he could not so distinguish letters as to read words. He sometimes attempted to write without seeing the letters that he traced. In an unfinished letter of this kind, dated April 10, 1848, he says:

"The stone has commenced its breaking process, and, ere the governments held by the ten kings shall be totally overthrown, the kingdom of God will come. The accounts from Europe prove to my mind that the work is now begun, and the saints may lift their heads and look up; for their redemption draweth nigh. Be of good cheer. Be not faithless, but believing. We shall soon see Him for whom we have looked with such anxiety, and waited for with patience. I believe and rejoice."

On the 14th of September, 1848, he wrote to Mr. Himes:

"Permit me to write a few words, although you may not be able to read them. Yet it may fill up a lonesome hour or two of many a wearisome day to think I have indited some of my thoughts to my old brother traveller. It would, indeed, be a sad and melancholy time with me were it not for the 'blessed hope' of soon seeing Jesus. In this I flatter myself that I cannot be mistaken. And although my natural vision is dark, yet my mind's vision is lit up with a bright and glorious prospect of the future. ...

"WM. MILLER."

Among his papers he left an unfinished letter, dated Jan. 1, 1849, as follows: [368]

"DEAR BRO. HIMES:- I wish you a happy new year. And I hope it may bring to you a happy eternity; or, at least, as much more evidence of its near approach as the past year has given. Take courage, brother soldier; the battle is almost won. We shall not long be disappointed. God began this work, this strange work; and, in a short time, he will accomplish his purpose in the earth. Sheshach is now drinking the cup of his fury."

The form of the letters and direction of the lines in the above writing gave too plain an indication that the pen was not guided by the eye.

Mr. Miller had watched the European events of the year 1848 with a good deal of interest, as one revolution succeeded another. The following letter, written while the Pope was in exile, and before the reaction in the several governments was developed, gives the view which he then took of those events:

"Low Hampton, February 13, 1849.

"BROTHER HIMES:- Permit me to drop you a few thoughts on the historical facts of the last year, compared with the prophecies in the word of God. The little horn of the 7th and 8th chapters of Daniel, the man of sin of the 2nd chapter of 2nd Thessalonians, the latter part of the beast and the image-beast of the 13th chapter of Revelation, are evidently prophecies concerning the Popes of Rome. The reasons which are conclusive to me are, 1st. These characters are represented as having great power, blood-thirsty, cruel, and blasphemous, making war against the saints, and prospering until the Ancient of Days shall come, or until the end of the indignation, or the appearing of the Son of Man. The time of his rule, when given, is the same; the consumption and destruction at his end is the same; the means of that destruction are represented to be, not by the power of men, but of God. Daniel represents that his dominion shall be taken away, and his body reserved to the burning flame. He also represents that he shall be broken without hand, and destroyed in the indignation of God's wrath. Paul represents that he shall be consumed by the spirit of God's mouth, and destroyed by the brightness of his coming. John represents his consumption as being by the sword that proceedeth [369] out of the mouth of God, with which he smites the nations, and casts the beast alive into a lake of fire burning with brimstone. – Revelation 19:15, 20. Therefore, the character, acts, chronology, consumption, and destruction of the little horn, the man of sin, and the beast, in these three prophecies, synchronize to a charm. Daniel represents him as making war against the saints, and prevailing until the Ancient of Days came, and judgment was given to the saints of the Most High, and they possessed the kingdom. The first thing Daniel saw previous to the coming of the Ancient of Days was, that the thrones were cast down.

"Now for the historical facts. The Popes of Rome have declared and made war, as predicted, for more than twelve centuries; so that, in the beginning of last year, he had prospered, and established dioceses and parishes in every land and continent on the habitable globe. His legates and ministers were known and recognized in all cabinets of the world. His subjects are scattered into every land in Christendom; acknowledged to be the supreme head of the church by almost every kingdom and government on the earth; lauded and extolled by the citizens of Protestant as well as Catholic countries; he was called the Apostle of Liberty, the Reformer of the Age, and worshipped, if not deified, by congregated citizens in many of our cities and principal towns: no emperor, king, or potentate, so popular as Pius IX. Thus stood matters in the beginning of the year 1848. In one short year many of the Catholic governments of Europe have been revolutionized, and lost a part, if not all, the power they possessed in the beginning of the year. Pope Pius IX has lost his supremacy and civil power, and become a refugee from his own government, and can neither make nor declare war. How was he deprived of his secular power and his dominion taken from him? I answer, evidently by the providence and power of God, as predicted. No kingdom at war with him, no ambitious Bonaparte to dethrone him, no collected armies to fight him, no organized force to oppose him. In one hour, as it were, he fell by his own arts, perhaps through fear – of what, we can hardly account for.

"What ailed thee, O thou potentate of kings? Didst thou discover on the walls of the Vatican the hand-writing of Belshazzar, 'Mene, mene, tekel'? or did a few plebeians [370] of Rome, collected as a mob around thy palace-gate, make the infallible head of the church, the vicar of God, truly afraid? Where was thy faith in the great promise, that the 'gates of hell shall not prevail against it'? or was it the power of Him who had declared by his prophet that you should be broken without hand, or consumed by the spirit of his mouth? Where were those millions who considered thy word more sacred than the Word of God, and idolized thee as a god on earth? Where were all those that, a few months before, were shouting paeans to thy glory? Could not the adoration of the world calm thy fears? Had thy popular name no talisman, and thy pride no helper? No, no. It was the God of heaven that smote thee. It was the spirit of the Most High that made thee afraid. It was the word of Him that dwelt in the bush that made thee cower. It was the pen of the prophet that told thy fate. You fled in the dark watches of the same night, disguised as a livery-servant, from the walls of that palace which had for ages sent out mandates for kings and laws for the world, and became a refugee in a neighboring kingdom, a resident in a small village on the shores of the Mediterranean. And well do your friends talk of purchasing some small island in that sea for your asylum, or a small farm on its borders for your cultivation! But, hark ye! the prophet's pen has further described your fate. Not only is your dominion to be taken away, but your body is to be given to the burning flame. You are not only to be broken without hand, but destroyed in the indignation, consumed by the spirit of his mouth, and destroyed by the brightness of Christ's coming.

"We live in a moment of awful consequences to the world, at a point when the fate of the universe will be decided forever.

"WM. MILLER."

About the last of April, 1849, his health began to decline more rapidly. This being communicated by Mr. Miller's son to Mr. Himes, and received by him at New York during the session of the Annual Conference there on the 10th of May, 1849, he stated to the Conference the intelligence, and moved that they convey to Mr. M. an expression of sympathy. The following resolution was immediately drawn up [371] by the president, and unanimously adopted by a rising vote:

"Advent Conference, New York, May 10, 1849.

"Whereas our beloved Brother William Miller has been called to endure a great fight of afflictions; and as God has been pleased, after employing him in advancing the cause of truth, to lay his hand on him, and suspend his labors; therefore,

"Resolved, That we deeply sympathize with our brother in his sorrows, and assure him that our love to him is steadfast, and that he has our earnest prayers that 'these light afflictions, which are but for a moment, may work out for him a far more exceeding and eternal weight of glory;' and that we hope, ere long, we may meet with him and all the saints in the new heavens and earth, where there will be no more sighing, sorrow, or death.

"(Signed,)   NATHAN N. WHITING, *President.*

"SYLVESTER BLISS,   }
                      Secretaries."
"O. R. FASSETT,   }

Mr. Miller received the above on the 12th of May, by the hand of his biographer. On entering his room, he was reclining on a lounge. At the mention of his name, he immediately arose, and recognized the messenger. He was much affected with the expression of sympathy sent by the Conference, and returned the following reply, which was received by the Conference at Boston, to which place it had adjourned, where it was entered on its minutes, May 29th, 1849:

"Low Hampton, May 12th, 1849.

"To my beloved brethren in Christ, assembled in conference, and to the saints scattered abroad. Grace be unto you, and peace, from God our Father and the Lord Jesus Christ:

"I give thanks to God for your kind remembrance of me, as expressed in the resolution of the 10th of May inst., in your late meeting at New York city, and forwarded to me by the hand of Bro. Bliss. I have not ceased to make mention of you always in my prayers, that you might walk together worthy of your high calling in Christ Jesus, that you may be filled with the knowledge of his will, in all wisdom [372] and spiritual understanding, being fruitful in every good work, and increasing in the knowledge of God. I feel myself greatly revived by your expression of sympathy, and trust that you will never have occasion to feel that it has been misplaced.

"My multiplied and increasing infirmities admonish me that the time of my departure is drawing nigh. My earthly labors have ceased, and I now await the Master's call, to be ready at his appearing, or, if it so please him, for the little while his coming may be delayed, to depart and be with Christ, which is far better than to abide in the flesh. I feel that I have but little choice, whether I shall be continued in life till that event, or my spirit be gathered to the spirits of just men made perfect. However God may be pleased to deal with me, I am sustained by the blessed assurance, that, whether I wake or sleep, I shall be present with the Lord.

"I daily have you all in grateful remembrance; and rejoice that so many of you continue steadfast in the faith once delivered to the saints, looking for that blessed hope and the glorious appearing of the great God, even of our Saviour Jesus Christ. I pray God that your faith may fail not, and that you may continue working together in harmony, building up one another in the most holy faith, and, by your blameless lives and godly conversation, commending this gospel of Christ to the hearts and consciences of dying men.

"I have but little hope, in my present weakness and infirmities, of seeing the faces of many of you in the flesh. Permit me, therefore, to exhort you not to be ashamed of the doctrine of the kingdom of Christ, nor of acknowledging on all proper occasions your confidence in the nearness of his coming.

"My belief is unshaken in the correctness of the conclusions I have arrived at and maintained during the last twenty years. I see no reason to question the evidence on which rest the fundamental principles of our faith. I cannot avoid the belief that this earth is to be restored to its Eden state, and become the eternal residence of the saints; that Christ is to come personally, to reign on the earth; that he will redeem us from death, and ransom us from the power of the grave; that he will change our vile bodies into the likeness of his glorified body, and destroy those who destroy the [373] earth; and that at his coming will be the restoration of all things spoken of by the mouth of all the holy prophets since the world began, the establishment of the new heavens and new earth, the resurrection of the righteous, and the change of the living wicked from the earth, – whose resurrection will not transpire till after one thousand years.

"The evidences of Christ's coming are continually thickening; it hasteneth greatly, and should this earthly house of my tabernacle be dissolved, my hope is still strong that I shall shortly meet him in the air. The political clouds in the Eastern horizon indicate to me the near approach of the battle of the Lord God Almighty, the destruction of the kingdoms of the earth, and the establishment of the kingdom of God. We may not know the precise time, but I entreat of you all to be prepared for the approaching crisis.

"Grudge not one against another, brethren. Be patient, for the coming of the Lord draweth nigh. Be not many masters, but let each one do the work which God has fitted him for. Avoid vain janglings and questions which gender strife. Keep constantly in view the great question of the coming of the Lord, – the hope of which purifieth the heart, and tends to the unity of the whole body of believers. If you do this, you will do well, and will each seek the other's good in preference to his own, and thus become living epistles, known and read of all men.

"In unity of effort will be your only strength. Therefore I recommend your meeting often in conference, as you have done, to consult with and encourage each other, in these times of trial and temptation. Be not turned away from your great work by friends or foes; but let each one occupy the talent intrusted to him – each working in his appropriate field of labor. Be charitable to all, and not indulge in harsh and bitter denunciations against those who are not enabled to see with you. Cultivate that spirit of good will towards all men, which shall fit you to be instrumental, in the hands of God, of saving some; and be less interested to advance the prosperity of party or sect, than to extend the cause of truth. Above all, keep close to the word of God. And, finally, brethren, farewell. Be perfect, be of good cheer, be of one mind, live in peace; and the God of love and peace shall be with you. WM. MILLER." [374]

He was at this time somewhat disposed to melancholy, but while the writer was with him, which was two days, he partook of his food with the family, and ate with considerable relish, – which was, they stated, what he had not done before for several weeks. He never doubted his acceptance through the blood of Jesus, but rather shrank from the expected sufferings attending the dissolution of the body. Still he was willing to endure all that for the sake of the prospect beyond. In a letter written at this date, he said:

"If the meeting with one kindred spirit is so cheering to a sick man here, what must be the joy of our greeting in the other world! The thought of death is a chilling one; but a meeting with the kindred spirits who are with Christ waiting for the consummation of his kingdom reconciles me to the idea of passing through the dark valley."

In November, 1849, Elder L. Kimball, who had had the charge of the church in Low Hampton, took his leave of that people. He writes:

"Agreeably to Bro. Miller's urgent request, we held the evening meeting [of the first Sunday in Nov.] at his house. He said he wanted to hear me preach once more. He also desired the singers to attend. After assembling, he called me to his room, and gave me for a text, 'And when they had seen the brethren, they comforted them and departed,' Acts 16:40. He was drawn, in his easy-chair, from his room to the kitchen, where he remained till the close of the services. He was unable to take any part, but expressed himself gratified, and wished that he could have said a few words to the brethren and friends present. It was to me a solemn season."

About the 1st of December, Elder D. I. Robinson visited him. He writes:

"Such was the state of the roads that I did not arrive there till sunset. His house stood in sight of the stage-road to Rutland, so that it was a subject for observation to all the passengers in the stage. It was pointed out to me by one of them, who lived in an adjoining village. It was to me a fruitful subject, as I beheld, for the first time, both beauty and sublimity in the cultivated vale and snow-capped, venerable mountains in the vicinity. I thought how appropriate, – how like the hills and vales of Judea, [375] where Amos and other shepherds, and former servants of the Most High lived, were called, and sent to warn mankind!

"As I approached across the farm, I passed the grove where he had meditated, wept and prayed, and entered the house of the aged, worn-out, sick and dying servant of God, who had been so scorned by the world. I felt favored of God. I was welcomed in the simple, hearty, easy style of a Vermont Christian farmer's family. That pleasant, beaming countenance of his wife, and the hearty shake of the hand, told me I was at home; and the kettle of homony, just taken from the fire, was at once prophetic of my supper. And all the members of the family, intelligent, modest and cordial, made me feel how really glad they were of the call, and to hear from those abroad.

"I was quickly invited into the 'east room,' where 'Father Miller' greeted me, though he could not see so as to know me; but, when told, recollected distinctly. He was much changed, and yet so changed as to leave all the good outlines of former acquaintance behind. His sufferings, through the summer and fall, had been very great. He was much swollen by dropsy. His strength and sight were much diminished. His venerable white locks were few and thin, and his flesh was like that of a child. But his voice was full, his memory good, his intellect strikingly strong and clear, and his patience and resignation were remarkable. He asked of my welfare, and of the friends; and said he was never so strong in his mind that we were right as now. He was sure it could not be long before the coming of the Lord. He wished him to come soon; but, if not, to be taken himself to the Lord."

He was drawn to the table in his chair, and ate supper with the family, probably for the last time. Elder R. left the next morning, between four and five o'clock; but Mr. Miller was awake, and arose to take an affectionate leave of him. [376]

CHAPTER 25

*His Last Sickness And Death – Funeral – Letter
Of Condolence To Surviving Friends*

For several months he had been confined mostly to his room. During a part of the time he had been confined to his bed, lounge, or easy-chair; and he suffered excruciating pain, which he endured with Christian patience. During his greatest sufferings he solaced himself by quotations of numerous passages of Scripture, and favorite hymns of Watts and others, expressive of the hope and joy of the redeemed.

He had watched all the occurrences in Europe with great interest; but, giving up the idea of seeing the Saviour before his death, he had arranged all his business, and waited for the summons when he might "depart and be with Christ."

On the 13th of December he had one of the most severe attacks of pain which he was called to endure. It was then thought he would not survive till the next morning, and Elder Himes was immediately telegraphed for, at the request of Mr. M. Mr. Himes wrote:

> "On my arrival, early in the morning of the 17th, he had obtained some relief, and was quite comfortable. On entering his room, he immediately recognized my voice, and, on approaching his bed-side, he was able to distinguish my features, though his eyes were dim. He grasped my hand, and held it for some time, exclaiming, with much earnestness, and in a tone of affection:
>
> "'Is this Elder Himes? – Is it Elder Himes? – O, is it Elder Himes? I am glad to see you!'
>
> "'Then you do know me, Father Miller, do you?'
>
> "'O yes; I understand, – I know what is passing.'
>
> "He was then silent for a few moments, apparently in a deep study. Presently he introduced the subject of my connection with the Advent cause, and spoke of my responsibility; expressed much anxiety about the cause, and alluded to his own departure. I assured him that he had [377] faithfully discharged his duty, was clear from the blood of all men, and could now leave this matter in the hands of God; and, so far as I was concerned, I hoped for grace to enable me to be faithful in

the ministry I had received. He seemed to assent, and fell into a doze, – being weak, and unable to converse longer than a few moments at a time. Presently he said:

"'Elder Himes has come; – I love Elder Himes.'

"He then spoke on the subject of the 'Spirit of adoption,' which we have now, and of the final adoption, for which we look *at* the second coming of the blessed Saviour. Last evening he said to Bro. Bosworth:

"'Tell them (the brethren) we are right. The coming of the Lord draweth nigh; but they must be patient, and wait for him.'

"His mind is still clear and strong on the subject of the conscious intermediate state. He believes that when he shall be absent from the body he will be present with the Lord. He expects that his flesh will slumber in the ground till Jesus comes and bids it rise, when he will be perfected. He never looked for the crown at death, but at the time when Jesus should come in his glory. The intermediate state is not that for which he longs most (though, with the apostle, he thinks that it is 'better' than this state of toil and sorrow), but the final, the glorified state, when the body shall be redeemed, and made like unto the glorious body of Christ, is the subject of this hope.

"For some weeks past his mind dwelt much on the subjects of the judgment, the 'adoption,' and the new heavens and earth. The following hymns very much interested him. He repeated them over and over, and requested his children to sing them. He seemed to be greatly comforted in hearing the hymn by Dr. Watts -

"'There is a land of pure delight,
Where saints immortal reign;
Infinite day excludes the night,
And pleasures banish pain,' etc.

"He was also very fond of hearing -

"'In the midst of temptation, and sorrow, and strife,
And evils unnumbered, of this bitter life, [378]
I look to a blessed earth, free from all care,
The kingdom of Jesus, and long to be there.
Long to be there, long to be there,
The kingdom of Jesus, and long to be there,' etc.

"Such views of the future glory tended to mitigate the pains of his body, which, at times, were violent.

"'Happy the spirit released from its clay,'

was one of the hymns in which he was deeply interested during the last four weeks of his life. It was sung by his children, and those who visited him, repeatedly, at his request. It enraptured his soul during his last hours, when he seemed to be absent, conversing with God and heaven. He often repeated -

"'Victory! victory! shouting in death!'

"The closing scene finally came. On the 20th of December, in the morning, it was manifest to all that he must soon depart. During the morning he made no particular conversation, but would break forth in expressions like the following:

"'Mighty to save!' 'O, I long to be there!' 'Victory! victory!' 'Shouting in death!' etc.

"He finally sunk down into an easy sleeping or dozing state. Occasionally he roused up, and opened his eyes, but was not able to speak, though perfectly rational, and knew us all. He continued to breathe shorter and shorter, till five minutes past three o'clock, P. M., when he calmly and sweetly gave his last breath. The silver cord was loosed, the golden bowl was broken at the fountain, and the wheel broken at the cistern; the dust was left to return to the dust as it was, and the spirit returned to God who gave it. Peacefully and happily he died, with his wife, children and friends about his bed! I closed his eyes, while all other eyes were filled with tears. It was a solemn scene. While the wife and children and friends were weeping the loss of a beloved relative, *I* was there to weep the loss of a father in Israel.

"The funeral service was attended on Sunday, December 23rd. The Advent chapel in Low Hampton being too small to accommodate the family, friends and citizens, who were [379] desirous of attending, Mr. Shaw, pastor of the Congregational church in Fairhaven, kindly offered the use of his large and commodious house. It had been Mr. Miller's request that the funeral service should be held in the Advent chapel; but, this being found impossible, the family decided to have a short service at their residence, to bury the body, and then to proceed to the Congregational house, for the performance of the more public service.

"The relatives of the deceased, and a large number of his neighbors and others, assembled at the house at 10 A. M. I read the following portions of Scripture, namely, 1 Thessalonians 4:13-18; Philippians 3:20, 21; Colossians 3:1-3. The choir from the Fairhaven church then sung the hymn commencing with -

"'Unveil thy bosom, faithful tomb.'

After a prayer, those present took leave of the corpse, and the procession – formed under the direction of Dr. Smith, of Castleton – proceeded to the old family burying-ground, about half a mile distant. The body being lowered into the tomb, the following hymn was sung by the choir:

"'Happy the spirit released from its clay,' etc.

"With a last, lingering look, we turned from the tomb, and proceeded with the numerous friends to the meeting-house, to attend the more public service. About one hundred sleighs followed in the procession.

"On arriving at the house, I found it densely filled with people, with the exception of seats reserved for the family, and those who had formed the procession. The service was commenced by singing the hymn in the *Harp*, beginning with -

"'How blest the righteous when he dies.'

Mr. Shaw, pastor of the church, read the 90th psalm, and addressed the throne of grace; after which the hymn -

"'Why do we mourn departed friends?'

was sung. I gave a discourse from Acts 26:6-8: 'And now I stand, and am judged respecting the hope of the promise made by God to our fathers; to which promise our [380] twelve tribes, earnestly serving God day and night, hope to attain; respecting which hope, King Agrippa, I am accused by the Jews. What! is it judged an incredible thing with you, that God should raise the dead?' With a narration of the prominent events in the history of the deceased, and a brief synopsis of his views, the speaker presented the hope of the promise of God to the fathers, to be consummated at the coming of the Lord. The services lasted three hours, and were concluded with the hymn -

"'They sleep in Jesus, and are blessed.'

The audience were attentive and interested to the close.

"J. V. Himes."

Mr. Miller left a wife, six sons, and two daughters.

At the Annual Conference, held in New York, in May following, by a unanimous vote, the following letter of condolence, prepared by a committee appointed for that purpose, was addressed to the relatives of the deceased:

"In Conference, New York, May 8th, 1850.

"*To Mrs. Lucy Miller, her children, and other relatives.*

"AFFLICTED FRIENDS:- Since our last meeting, you have been called to mourn the death of a beloved husband, a tender parent, and an affectionate friend. In your bereavement we truly sympathize. In your loss we also have lost a friend and brother. But we mourn our loss in view of higher considerations. We regard him as a man called of God to a most important work; and as a man greatly blessed in the successful performance of that work. The unsullied integrity of his life was crowned by a peaceful and hopeful death. The deep sense of gratitude we feel to God for the benefits conferred on us, through his instrumentality, we trust will find a response in many Christian hearts. Through the divine blessing on his teaching, our attention has been directed to a more faithful study of the Scriptures, to clearer, more harmonious and correct views of divine truth. We have thus been led to rejoice in hope of the glory to be revealed at the appearing of Christ. We fondly [381] hoped that he might have been spared till our expectations were realized. He has passed away. May we remember that our obligations are increased by the truth which he taught. May we be prepared for a reunion with him and all the redeemed in that day. Our sincere and united prayer is, that the grace which sustained him under his severe trials, and in the closing scene, may support you in your bereavement, and in all the afflictions of the present state, and secure to you the enjoyment of the glorious future. Tendering to your acceptance this expression of our sympathy and condolence, we remain your affectionate brethren in the faith once delivered to the saints.

"(Signed,) N. N. WHITING, *President.*

"O. R. FASSETT,
"S. BLISS, } *Secretaries.*"

The death of Mr. Miller was very generally noticed by the religious and secular press, many of whom spoke in just terms of his honesty and ability. Other papers connected with his memory extravagances with which he had no sympathy and never participated in. But he has gone into His presence who will right all wrongs, reverse all unjust conclusions, and mete out to each one his just measure, according to the deeds done in the body. He died in the confident expectation of departing to be with Christ, and of shortly participating in the glories of the first resurrection.

A friend, Mrs. L. H. Smith, communicated the following lines

"ON THE DEATH OF MR. MILLER.

"Has our noble old soldier resigned his last breath?
On the battle-field's front has he yielded to death?
Is that glorious armor now low in the dust?
Are its splendor and brightness now marr'd by earth's rust?
Must we bear him away, 'midst the darkness and gloom
That shroud and pavilion the gates of the tomb?
But stand for a moment, ye who bear up the bier,
Let us give one last tribute – the fast rising tear;
Let us look on that brow, with its broad, high expanse;
Let us gaze on the veiled eye, once bright in its glance;
And that marble lip's curl. – O! how lifeless and still!
How the touch of that hand brings a soul-thrilling chill!
Yet, a halo of glory seems shrouding that form,
That has past the dread tempest of life's closing storm: [382]

It was left by the spirit that upwards has fled,
Surrounding with radiance the form that is dead;
Like a beautiful star that's departed from heaven,
But has left gleams of light in the spot where 't was given;
Or a sparkling diamond in a casket fair,
Though removed, yet its brilliance seems lingering there.
But, bear onward, bear onward the course to its sod;
Tread softly, for you're bearing the servant of God.
But where are the laurels, the bright wreaths of fame,
And the heralds announcing his deeds and his name?
Where the gorgeous procession, the splendid array,
With earth's glorious trappings, its pomp, its display?
Him you bear has been noble in deed and in word;
Mankind he has served, with his life, with his sword.
But that sword was the Spirit's – his armor was given

From the arsenal kept in the high courts of heaven.
But – bear onward, bear onward the corse to its sod;
Tread softly, for you're bearing the servant of God.

"Farewell to thee, pilgrim; to earth thou didst come,
Like the star of the morning, precursing the sun.
In our moral horizon, when darkness was deep,
When the world seemed all wrapped in a lethargic sleep,
When the mantle of death hung round like a pall,
And his sceptre of strength seemed to wave o'er it all;
Then the light of thy spirit gleamed forth like a star
On the beautiful hope of the land that's afar;
Then the gems of God's word were brought forth from the mine,
And the key of that casket of glories was thine;
And then on thy spirit the rich light was poured,
Of the beauty of earth, with its Eden restored,
Never more to know aught of a withering bloom,
Never more on its bosom to bear up a tomb;
But, to crown all these glories, that time must *soon* bring
The hope of God's people – our conquering King.

"Farewell to thee, pilgrim; no green wreaths we twine,
In token of honor for deeds like to thine.
From the hand of the Master that bright gift must be,
That can bring aught of glory or honor to thee.
Rest there, beloved sleeper, 'neath the snow-curtained bed;
Soon the mandate shall echo – 'Come forth, all ye dead!' –
Through the caverns of earth where God's people may be,
And to depths of the coral groves, under the sea.
Ye who bear him now rest. – Lower the corse 'neath the sod;
Farewell to thee, thou faithful, true servant of God."

The remains of William Miller repose in the Low Hampton Cemetery, a short distance east of his late residence. The family have marked the spot by a neat monument, the pattern of and inscriptions on which are given on the page following. [383]

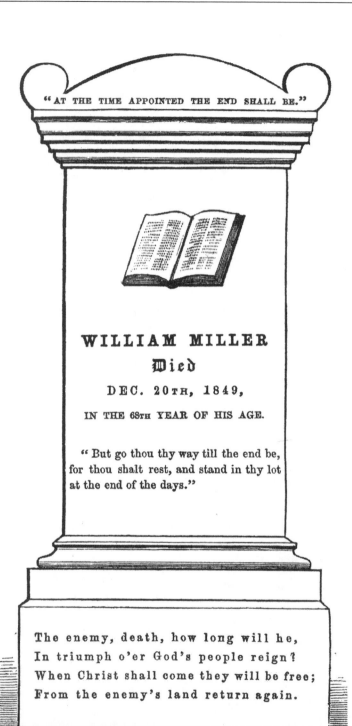

"AT THE TIME APPOINTED THE END SHALL BE."

WILLIAM MILLER
Died

DEC. 20TH, 1849,

IN THE 68TH YEAR OF HIS AGE.

"But go thou thy way till the end be,
for thou shalt rest, and stand in thy lot
at the end of the days."

The enemy, death, how long will he,
In triumph o'er God's people reign?
When Christ shall come they will be free;
From the enemy's land return again.

CHAPTER 26

Extracts From Mr. Miller's Writings – The Times And Its Duties
– The Kingdom Of God – A Scene Of The Last Day, Etc.

MR. MILLER'S published writings comprise his Sixteen Lectures on the Prophecies, his Life and Views, of about three hundred pages each, and a number of pamphlets, tracts, etc., comprising reviews of his reviewers, expositions of Scripture, etc.

Dr. Jarvis remarked that he had "often been edified by his excellent and pious observations on the necessity of being in readiness to meet our Judge." – *Sermons*, p. 58. He instanced the lecture "on the Times and its Duties," and that "on the Parable of The Ten Virgins." A portion of the latter has already been given; the remainder of the book is devoted to the former, and a few other selections.

"THE TIMES AND ITS DUTIES.

"'The night is far spent, the day is at hand: let us therefore cast off the works of darkness, and let us put on the armor of light.' – Romans 13:12.

"THE apostle in the context exhorts his Roman brethren to good works, to a holy life in conformity with the law, – the royal law, which teaches us to love God with all our heart, and our neighbor as ourselves. He then gives the text as one of the most prominent reasons why we should conform to the requisitions of the law: because the *night* is far spent, and the *day* is at hand.

"I shall, therefore, in explaining the text,

"I. SHOW WHAT THE APOSTLE MEANS BY 'NIGHT AND DAY.'

"II. SHOW THE PROPRIETY OF HIS ADMONITION, 'CAST OFF THE WORKS OF DARKNESS.'

"III. ATTEND TO HIS EXHORTATION, 'LET US PUT ON THE ARMOR OF LIGHT.'

"I. EXPLAIN THE TERMS NIGHT AND DAY.

"Night and day are used in this passage to illustrate a [385] moral or spiritual idea, which the apostle wished to communicate to his brethren at Rome, and through them to us. 1. *Night*, in the natural world, is that portion of time in which the face of the natural sun is hid from us, or that part of our earth on which we dwell, in accordance with certain infallible laws of nature, such as light and the vivifying influence of the sun, or the revolution of our earth upon its axis. 2. *Night* in the moral world is like night in the natural. God is the fountain of all light, life, and holiness, and without his vivifying influence we are left to grope our way in moral darkness. We cannot see things clearly, but we stumble upon the dark mountains of infidelity and doubt. This great Sun of light, life, and holiness, is governed by as immutable laws as the natural sun, yes, and ten thousand times stronger, and more stable; because natural laws may change; 'heaven and earth may pass away,' but not one jot or tittle of his word or law shall ever fail. One of these unchangeable laws is, that God cannot look upon sin with the least allowance. Witness the withdrawal of his countenance from Adam in the garden when he sinned, and the beginning of the night spoken of in our text. Adam, like the natural world, turned from God, and all was darkness. He broke the holy law, – 'thou shalt not sin,' – and he and all his posterity became involved in a moral night, with only now and then some glimmering star, – some Abel, Enoch, Noah, some patriarchs and prophets, – or a changing moon, – the church, – to shed a glimmer upon this moral night, that may haply lead us to a blessed hope of the glorious appearing of the Son of Man. The ancient prophets and apostles all prophesied of the glory that should follow; these were stars in the night of moral darkness. The church, which Christ in his flesh set up in the world, has sometimes, like the moon at its stated seasons, shown her full round face, and has given strong evidence that there was a *sun*, although hid from the immediate view of the world, and that she looked, by faith at least, upon the glorious Sun of Righteousness. At other times she has been veiled in a cloud of smoke, or error, which rose from the bottomless pit. Sometimes she has been made gory by the persecutions which have assailed her; for the faithful have waded through trials, changes, afflictions, and death. Yet one thing have they all shown by these things, that this is not [386] their continuing city; but that they seek one to come, whose builder and maker is God. But the apostle says in our text that this *night* (of moral darkness) is far spent, and the day is at hand; which brings us to consider,

"Second, what we may understand the apostle as meaning by *Day*. Natural day flows immediately from light, or the great luminary of the heavens, the sun. Just so the moral day. Wherever God by his immediate presence dwells, and light, life and righteousness are enjoyed, there is *day*. The gospel is sometimes compared to the sun and light, and where and when that is enjoyed, it is sometimes called *day*, as in Zechariah 14:7, 8; Psalm 95:7. 'To-day, if ye will hear his voice, harden not your hearts.' – Hebrews 3:7.

"But that the apostle did not mean this gospel day, is evident from the text immediately preceding: '*For now is our salvation nearer than when we believed.*' '*For the night is far spent,*' etc.; strongly expressing it to be future. Now if it meant the gospel day, why did the apostle call the time in which he wrote *night*? Surely, if ever the gospel shone in our world, it was in the apostles' days. Then, before the antichristian beast, and the smoke out of the bottomless pit, arose on the earth, and darkened the sun, and filled the world with corrupt sentiments, and the minds of men with heretical principles, – before the obnoxious vapors of the doctrine of devils filled the moral *air*, and the moon was turned to blood, and the stars fell to the earth, – this day must have been, or we must look for it in the future.

"That the apostle does not mean the gospel day, is evident, also, from the fact that he gives instructions to the Roman Christians how to obtain the gospel armor, which was to be as light to them during this night of moral darkness; for if it had been day their armor of light would be of no more use than a candle at noon.

"Again. The day spoken of cannot mean death; for death is nowhere in Scripture called *day*, but the reverse. 'The night cometh, when no man can work.' – John 9:4. Then I know not what day the apostle alludes to, unless he has reference to the great day when 'Christ shall come in the clouds of heaven with power and great glory.' That this day is what the apostle meant, is evident, – 1. Because it is a day of salvation, as he says in the context – 'For now [387] is our salvation nearer than when we believed,' and 'he comes the second time without sin unto salvation.' Again, 'I pray God your whole spirit and soul and body be preserved blameless unto the coming of our Lord Jesus Christ.' 'To the end he may stablish your hearts unblamable in holiness before God, even our Father, at the coming of our Lord Jesus Christ with all his saints.' It is evident that he means this day, also, because the Sun of Righteousness will then live and dwell on the earth, and he shall be the light thereof. See Malachi 4:2: 'But unto you that fear my name, shall the Sun of Righteousness arise with healing in his wings, and ye shall go forth and grow up as calves in the stall. And ye shall tread down the wicked; for they shall be ashes under the soles of your feet, in the day that I shall do this, saith the Lord of hosts.' Again, in Psalm 68:18: 'Thou hast ascended on high, thou hast led captivity captive: thou hast received gifts for men, yea, for the rebellious also, that the Lord God might dwell among them.' Zechariah 2:10: 'Sing and rejoice, O daughter of Zion: for lo, I come, and I will dwell in the midst of thee, saith the Lord, and many nations shall be joined to the Lord in that *day*, and shall be my people; and I will dwell in the midst of thee.' Again, Revelation 21:3: 'And I heard a great voice out of heaven, saying, Behold, the tabernacle of God is with men, and he will dwell with them, and they shall be his people, and God himself shall be with them, and be their God.' This is the *day*, my brethren, which the apostle Paul alludes to in our text; and if he could say, eighteen hundred years ago, 'The night is far spent, the day is at hand,' surely, my brethren, we may say now he standeth at the door. And I do most solemnly believe that the day of the Lord is near, yes, very near. 'Let us, therefore, cast off the works of darkness.' This brings us to our second head, – to show,

"II. THE PROPRIETY OF THE ADMONITION, 'CAST OFF THE WORKS OF DARKNESS.'

"What, then, is meant by works of darkness? In the first place, it is an abhorrence of light, for fear our sins will be brought to light, or made manifest. 'We love darkness rather than light, because our deeds are evil.' These characters may be known by their anxiety to destroy the main principles of the word of God. Sin, in their view, is nothing [388] more than a misfortune; salvation is only the good deeds of man; Christ is only a man that set good examples; atonement is only the forgiveness of our Adamic sin; and punishment is only the evils of life! They always are very uneasy, and often angry, if future punishment is mentioned. And we may know they are wrong; 'for anger rests only in the bosom of fools.'

"Again, there is another class who work the works of darkness. These are those who are ignorant of the righteousness of God, and go about (as the apostle says) to establish their own righteousness. These may be known by their complainings. Nobody is right but themselves; they are always justifying their own ways and condemning others; they will ever be framing some plausible excuse for neglect of any duty, and condemning others for the merest trifle. They are strange characters. You may preach to them of their crimes, and they will give it to their neighbor; you may admonish them, and they regard it not. They are so completely shrouded in their mantle of selfishness that nothing makes any impression upon them. Preach law, they have kept it; preach gospel, they need it not; preach duty, they will throw in your face a host of excuses. Their coat of mail is like the hide of Leviathan, – no arrow can pierce it; and I have thought that nothing but the trump of God will ever awake them. Well did Christ say to such characters, 'O generation of vipers, how can ye escape the damnation of hell?'

"There is another class, whom the apostle calls 'worldly-minded sinners,' who 'work the works of darkness.' These may be known by their anxiety for the world, and their disregard for all the means of salvation. Visit them, and their whole mind is on the world; they can talk freely and flippantly of their farms, their silver, their cattle, and sheep; but not one word about salvation. They can go into a long detail of their plans to gain property; but talk to them of the plan of salvation, and it will be very insipid and dry. The week is spent in hoarding up treasures, and the Sabbath in counting their silver and casting their accounts. They never visit the house of God without some worldly motive in view. They search their accounts oftener than their Bibles; they study more how to obtain the world than eternal life. [389] In one word, they are glued to the present evil world; and, when the day shall come, they will, with the rich man, lift up their eyes, being in torment.

"There is still another class, and they are those who seek for the honors of this world more than to honor God, having men's persons in admiration. In their works of darkness you may discover them; they are deceitful; their words are smooth as oil, and with their lips they use deceit. They flatter but to destroy; they deceive but to betray; they pretend to be friendly to all, yet are friends only to themselves. They never talk plainly or open-heartedly, brutal ways wound in private. There is no meanness which they will not stoop to do, to obtain their end. Solomon says, 'He that knoweth and dissembleth with his lips, and layeth up deceit within him, when he speaketh fair believe him not, for there are seven abominations in his heart. Whose hatred is covered by deceit, his wickedness shall be showed before the whole congregation.' 'But the fearful and unbelieving, and the abominable, and murderers, and whoremongers, and sorcerers, and idolaters, and all liars, shall have their part in the lake which burneth with fire and brimstone; which is the second death.' – Revelation 21:8. If these things are so, then surely the apostle has done well to admonish us to 'put off these works of darkness;' and O! my hearers, we should do well, yes, we should be wise, and that, too, for ourselves, to obey the injunction of the apostle; 'for the *night* is far spent, the *day* is at hand, when every man's works will be tried so as by fire.'

"III. WE WILL NOW EXAMINE THE APOSTLE'S EXHORTATION, 'LET US PUT ON THE ARMOR OF LIGHT.'

"The Christian, in this night of darkness and error, is compared to a soldier on guard in the night, and in time of war; and how apt and instructing is the allusion! In the night, on guard, a soldier must have his armor all on; he must not lie down; he must keep awake, not sleep, stand at his post; he must watch the approach of the enemy, hail the approach of a friend, understand the use of his armor, have in readiness the watchwords of the camp; and he will watch for the dawn of the morning with as much anxiety as a bride for the return of the bridegroom. Just so with a Christian in this night of moral darkness. He is called to [390] watch, and to have on the armor of light. He must stand up, and, having done all, must stand. He, too, must keep awake, as says the prophet Isaiah 51:17: 'Awake, awake, stand up, O Jerusalem.' He must not sleep, as Paul says, 1 Thessalonians 5:6: 'Therefore let us not sleep, as do others; but let us watch and be sober.' He must watch his enemies both outward and inward; he must hail and rejoice over one sinner that repenteth; he must learn and understand the use of his spiritual armor; he must be ready with the word at all times, so that he may give the reason of his hope with meekness and fear. And, if he is a good soldier of Christ, he will watch for the dawn of the morning when the Captain of his salvation shall come the second time without sin unto salvation; when his enemies will all be slain, and the shout of victory be heard by all the righteous dead, and the last loud blast of the trump of God shall proclaim universal peace in the kingdom of Christ.

"Then how happy will that soldier of the cross be whom, when his Lord comes, he shall find with his whole armor of light on! So doing, 'stand, therefore, having your loins girt about with truth.' The truth will make you free. It will strengthen you to combat error; it is all-powerful, for God is truth, and He hath all power in heaven and earth. You will never be afraid that your cause will not prevail; for truth is mighty and will prevail. You will never want to use carnal weapons, for the holiness of truth will forbid the thought; and that man who resorts to carnal weapons to support his cause, may depend upon it he is not on *truth*.

"And having on the breastplate of righteousness.' This, too, is the armor of God, prepared for us by Christ himself. This righteousness will give us confidence, that we shall not be afraid to front all enemies, even death itself, knowing that in him and by his robe we shall be justified from all things wherein the law could not justify; for we, being weak in the flesh, could not justify ourselves by the works of the law; but Christ becoming the end of the law for righteousness to every one that believeth, we, therefore, may have confidence, who have fled for refuge, to lay hold on the hope set before us; and such need not be ashamed before him at his coming.

"'And your feet shod with the preparation of the gospel [391] of peace.' This teaches us that we must walk after the example of John, who prepared a people made ready for the Lord, and Christ, who fulfilled all righteousness. How necessary, my brethren, that our walk be found according to the examples of Christ and the apostles, that our feet may be shod with the gospel of peace, that we may be ready to enter in through the gate into the city!

"'Above all, taking the shield of faith, wherewith ye shall be able to quench the fiery darts of the wicked.' This is an important part of the armor. *Faith* is able to carry us through all the trials of life. By faith we receive and enjoy all the rich promises of God. By faith we live upon his Word, as the children of Israel lived on manna in the wilderness. By faith we please God; by faith we believe in the day spoken of in our text; and through faith we shall be able to subdue kingdoms, work righteousness, obtain promises, stop the mouths of lions, quench the violence of fire; in one word, come off conquerors through Him who hath loved us.

"'And take the helmet of salvation.' This is our hope, and the evidence of this can be obtained only by our diligence in the calling, and by our love for the Author of our salvation. How do we know that we are in a state of salvation? Answer. By our hope. And how do we know our hope is a good one? By its being founded on the grace of God, and not on our works. Then the speaker, say you, has contradicted himself, for he has just told us that hope was obtained by our diligence, and that part suited his belief exactly. You have mistaken me; I did not say our hope was obtained by our diligence, but the evidence of its being a good one. Will not smoke ascend, and will not water run down? If you have a good hope, you have a good heart, and from that heart will proceed good fruits.

"Again: 'The sword of the Spirit, which is the Word of God.' This, being our only rule of life, and the only means of trying the spirits, may be truly compared to a sword, for it cuts off all false rules, doctrines, spirits, and leaves nothing but 'thus saith the Lord.' And here, again, we may try ourselves. In every trial do we fly to the Word of God for direction? Do we square our lives by its rules? Is this Word our law-book, our directory? And, like David, can we say, 'How love I thy law?' [392]

"'Praying always with all prayer, and supplication in the Spirit, and watching thereunto with all perseverance and supplication for all saints.' These constitute the whole armor of light, or of God, as the apostle calls it in Ephesians 6:13. Here, again, is another rule to try ourselves by. Is prayer a solemn, an interesting, and soul-reviving duty? Do we, in trials, in afflictions, in joy and sorrow, in light and darkness, in coldness and warmth, find peace, comfort, consolation, and reconciliation, in this duty? Or do we pray to be seen of men, or to stop the gnawings of a guilty conscience? Or do we neglect this weapon altogether? Let God and our own consciences decide, and let us decide quickly and justly, for the 'day is at hand which will try every man's work, whether it be good or evil.' – 'Let us, then, put on the whole armor of light.'

"Improvement.

"**1.** By our subject we learn that the night of sin, error, darkness, and every evil work, is almost spent.

"**2.** The day is near when all these things will be brought to light, and every evil work will receive a just recompense of reward.

"**3.** We are admonished to cast off the works of darkness. And,

"**4.** We are exhorted to put on the armor of light."

"The Kingdom Of God.

"'And in the days of these kings shall the God of heaven set up a kingdom which shall never be destroyed; and the kingdom shall not be left to other people, but it shall break in pieces and consume all these kingdoms, and it shall stand forever.' – Daniel 2:44.

"Much has been said and written on this by different commentators. Different sects and partisans have seized this text, and applied it to their sect, and proved, as they verily believe, that their sect is the true kingdom of God, which will stand forever.

"The Catholics say it was set up in the days of the Roman Caesars, and thus claim for the Pope St. Peter's chair and [393] the kingdom: that to the Bishop of Rome were the keys of this kingdom given at the demise of St. Peter, and that the popes have been the successor and earthly head of this kingdom ever since. The Baptist writers, many of them, say the same, and claim a descent from the apostles for the Baptist church, – making the church what the Catholics do the Pope, – and try to show a regular succession of the church, as the Catholics do their popes. They also claim believers' baptism *(immersion)* as an initiatory rite into the kingdom, and that none are citizens of this kingdom until they comply with this requisition. The Episcopalians, or some of them, claim this same kingdom to have been set up in the days of the kings of England; and, therefore, the kings or queens of England are the accredited head of the episcopacy, and rulers over the visible church. The Presbyterians say it was set up in the days of Luther, among the German kings; the Quakers, in the days of Fox; the Methodists, in the days of Wesley; the Shakers, in the days of Ann Lee; and the Mormons, by Joseph Smith.

"All writers seem determined to have an earthly kingdom, and an earthly head to that kingdom. 1 Corinthians 3:3, 4: 'For ye are yet carnal; for whereas there is among you envying, and strife, and divisions, are ye not carnal, and walk as men? For while one saith, I am of Paul; and another, I am of Apollos; are ye not carnal?' Or, as is properly said by James (James 3:14-16): 'But if ye have bitter envying and strife in your hearts, glory not; and lie not against the truth. This wisdom descendeth not from above, but is earthly, sensual, devilish. For where envying and strife is, there is confusion, and every evil work.'

"And now permit me to show that this kingdom is neither 'earthly, sensual, nor devilish;' but I shall show -

"I. What It Is;
"II. Whose It Is;
"III. When It Is; and,
"IV. Where It Is.

"I. What It Is. It is heavenly; for the God of heaven sets it up, that is, exalts it. It is evidently a holy kingdom, for the will of God is to be done in it as in heaven. Luke 11:2: 'And he said unto them, when ye pray, say, Our Father which art in heaven, hallowed be thy name: Thy [394] kingdom come. Thy will be done, as in heaven, so in earth.'

"It is a righteous kingdom. See Romans 14:17: 'For the kingdom of God is not meat and drink, but righteousness, and peace, and joy, in the Holy Ghost.'

"It is an everlasting kingdom, – 'shall stand forever,' says our text. Psalm 145:12, 13: 'To make known to the sons of men his mighty acts, and the glorious majesty of his kingdom. Thy kingdom is an everlasting kingdom, and thy dominion endureth throughout all generations.' Daniel 7:14, 27: 'And there was given him dominion and glory, and a kingdom, that all people, nations, and languages, should serve him; his dominion is an everlasting dominion, which shall not pass away, and his kingdom that which shall not be destroyed.' 'And the kingdom and dominion, and the greatness of the kingdom under the whole heaven, shall be given to the people of the saints of the Most High, whose kingdom is an everlasting kingdom, and all dominions shall serve and obey him.' Hebrews 12:28: 'Wherefore, we receiving a kingdom which cannot be moved, let us have grace, whereby we may serve God acceptably, with reverence and godly fear.' 2 Peter 1:11: 'For so an entrance shall be ministered unto you abundantly into the everlasting kingdom of our Lord and Saviour Jesus Christ.' Revelation 11:15: 'And the seventh angel sounded; and there were great voices in heaven, saying, The kingdoms of this world are become the kingdoms of our Lord, and of his Christ, and he shall reign forever and ever.' Revelation 22:5: 'And there shall be no night there; and they need no candle, neither light of the sun, for the Lord God giveth them light: and they shall reign for ever and ever.'

"As there cannot be two kingdoms, and both stand forever, we must naturally suppose, by the texts which I have quoted, that it must be a glorified kingdom; and, indeed, the last text quoted proves it to be in the New Jerusalem state. See, also, Psalm 24:7-10: 'Lift up your heads, O ye gates, and be ye lift up, ye everlasting doors, and the King of glory shall come in. Who is this King of glory? The Lord strong and mighty, the Lord mighty in battle... Who is this King of glory? The Lord of hosts, he is the King of glory.' Psalm 145:10, 11: 'All thy works [395] shall praise thee, O Lord; and thy saints shall bless thee. They shall speak of the glory of thy kingdom, and talk of thy power.' Isaiah 2:10, 19, 21: 'Enter into the rock and hide thee in the dust, for fear of the Lord, and for the glory of his majesty. And they shall go into the holes of the rocks, and into the caves of the earth, for fear of the Lord, and for the glory of his majesty, when he ariseth to shake terribly the earth. To go into the clefts of the rocks, and into the tops of the rugged rocks, for fear of the Lord, and for the glory of his majesty, when he ariseth to shake terribly the earth.' Isaiah 4:2-5: 'In that day shall the branch of the Lord be beautiful and glorious, and the fruit of the earth shall be excellent and comely for them that are escaped of Israel. And it shall come to pass, that he that is left in Zion, and he that remaineth in Jerusalem, shall be called holy, even every one that is written among the living in Jerusalem; when the Lord shall have washed away the filth of the daughters of Zion, and shall have purged the blood of Jerusalem from the midst thereof, by the spirit of judgment, and by the spirit of burning. And the Lord will create upon every dwelling-place of mount Zion, and upon her assemblies, a cloud and smoke by day, and the shining of a flaming fire by night; for upon all the glory shall be a defense.' Isaiah 24:23: 'Then the moon shall be confounded, and the sun ashamed, when the Lord of hosts shall reign in mount Zion and in Jerusalem, and before his ancients gloriously.' 1 Thessalonians 2:12: 'That ye would walk worthy of God, who hath called you unto his kingdom and glory.'

"If it is a glorified and an eternal kingdom, it cannot be an earthly or mortal kingdom. It is an immortal one. Christ says, John 18:36: 'My kingdom is not of this world: if my kingdom were of this world, then would my servants fight that I should not be delivered to the Jews; but now is my kingdom not from hence.' It cannot be an earthly kingdom. And again, 1 Corinthians 15:50: 'Now this I say, brethren, that flesh and blood cannot inherit the kingdom of God; neither doth corruption inherit incorruption.' If this be true, it cannot be in a mortal state. But I will prove it immortal. Matthew 8:11, 12: 'And I say unto you, that [396] many shall come from the east and west, and shall sit down with Abraham, and Isaac, and Jacob, in the kingdom of heaven; but the children of the kingdom shall be cast out into outer darkness; there shall be weeping and gnashing of teeth.' Luke 13:28, 29: 'There shall be weeping and gnashing of teeth, when ye shall see Abraham, and Isaac, and Jacob, and all the prophets, in the kingdom of God, and you yourselves thrust out. And they shall come from the east, and from the west, from the north, and from the south, and shall sit down in the kingdom of God.'

"This can never be in a mortal state; for Abraham, Isaac and Jacob, together with all the prophets, have passed from the mortal state. Then we may well conclude that the kingdom spoken of in our text is a heavenly kingdom, holy, righteous, and everlasting; an eternal kingdom, where the subjects of the kingdom will shine as the sun, and all the heirs be glorified, and corruption be changed into incorruption, and the mortal to immortal. Then death will be swallowed up in victory.

"How foolish and ridiculous is the idea that 'it shall not be left to other people,' if the subjects are not immortal! If deaths and births continue as now, in one hundred years death would conquer the whole kingdom, and in process of time would change every subject from those who received it at the beginning, to their descendants; and in the fullness of time, according to the temporal millennial doctrine, the devil will be let loose, and conquer a large number of children, which have been literally born in the kingdom, the number of whom is as the sand of the sea-shore, and transplant them out of the eternal and everlasting kingdom of God into the kingdom of the devil, and there excite them to make war against their sires in the beloved city. [1] If our learned men can reason no better than this, I would advise them to go where they can get a little common sense, before they undertake to teach people who know their right hand from the left. And were it not for the influence they obtain by newspaper puffs, for which the editors make them pay well, they would obtain no more influence than their writings deserve. But let us now inquire concerning this kingdom. [397]

"II. Whose It Is.

"**1.** I answer, it is God's kingdom. Acts 14:22: 'Confirming the souls of the disciples, and exhorting them to continue in the faith, and that we must through much tribulation enter into the kingdom of God.' 2 Thessalonians 1:5: 'Which is a manifest token of the righteous judgment of God, that ye may be counted worthy of the kingdom of God, for which ye also suffer.' Both of these show that the kingdom of God was not then come; but believers were exhorted to be faithful, and endure sufferings and tribulation, that they might be counted worthy to obtain the kingdom of God when it should come. Therefore, none will pretend that a temporal millennium is here alluded to, or that the gospel church is here meant; for these brethren were already counted worthy to belong to the church.

"Again, Luke 14:15: 'And when one of them that sat at meat with him heard these things, he said unto him, Blessed is he that shall eat bread in the kingdom of God.' Now, I ask, is every one blessed who eats bread in the church, or in the gospel day? If so, what can the text mean (Luke 13:26): 'Then shall ye begin to say, We have eaten and drunk in thy presence, and thou hast taught in our streets?' Every unbiased mind must see at once that the kingdom of God, of which our text speaks, is not temporal, but eternal; not earthly, but heavenly.

"**2.** It is a kingdom given unto Jesus Christ, the Son of Man, when he leaves the mediatorial seat, gives up the redeemed church to God the Father, and the mediatorship becomes subject to God. Christ having performed all the work which the Father gave him to do as Mediator, the mediatorial kingdom, or kingdom of grace, is given up, and the kingdom of God set up; and Christ then sits on the throne of his father David, having put down all enemies, and all authority and power, against his rightful reign on earth; having dashed the kingdoms to pieces like a potter's vessel, burned up the wicked, cleansed the earth, and raised the saints. Then the kingdoms of this world become the kingdom of our Lord and of his Christ, and he shall

---

[1] See "Dowling's Reply to Miller," pp. 217, 218.

reign for ever and ever. Then Jesus will be God blessed for evermore; and his kingdom will fill the whole earth and his [398] tabernacle will be with men, and he will dwell with them, and be their God, and they shall be his people.

"Now you will ask for my proof. This is right; and in my soul I wish you would be as particular with all who preach the gospel, and demand their evidences. We should have less error in our world, and more truth.

"First: see Daniel 7:13, 14: 'I saw in the night visions; and behold, one like the Son of Man came with the clouds of heaven, and came to the Ancient of Days, and they brought him near before him. And there was given him dominion, and glory, and a kingdom, that all people, nations and languages, should serve him: his dominion is an everlasting dominion, which shall not pass away, and his kingdom that which shall not be destroyed.' This proves the kingdom to be given to the Son of Man.

"Second: see 1 Corinthians 15:23-28: 'But every man in his own order: Christ the first fruits; afterward they that are Christ's at his coming. Then cometh the end, when he shall have delivered up the kingdom to God, even the Father; when he shall have put down all rule, and all authority and power. For he must reign till he hath put all enemies under his feet. The last enemy that shall be destroyed is death. For he hath put all things under his feet. But when he saith, all things are put under him, it is manifest that he is excepted which did put all things under him. And when all things shall be subdued unto him, then shall the Son also himself be subject unto him that put all things under him, that God may be all in all.' Also, Psalm 2:9: 'Thou shalt break them with a rod of iron; thou shalt dash them in pieces like a potter's vessel.' Psalm 5:3, 6: 'My voice shalt thou hear in the morning, O Lord; in the morning will I direct my prayer unto thee, and will look up. Thou shalt destroy them that speak leasing; the Lord will abhor the bloody and deceitful man.' 2 Peter 3:10: 'But the day of the Lord will come as a thief in the night; in the which the heavens shall pass away with a great noise, and the elements shall melt with fervent heat; the earth, also, and the works that are therein, shall be burnt up.' Also, verse 13: 'Nevertheless, we, according to his promise, look for new heavens, and a new earth, wherein dwelleth righteousness.' Revelation 11:15: 'And the [399] seventh angel sounded; and there were great voices in heaven, saying, The kingdoms of this world are become the kingdom of our Lord, and of his Christ, and he shall reign for ever and ever.' Psalm 47:2, 9: 'For the Lord most high is terrible; he is a great King over all the earth.' 'For God is the King of all the earth: sing ye praises with understanding.' Zechariah 14:9:

'And the Lord shall be King over all the earth; in that day shall there be one Lord, and his name one.' Romans 9:5: 'Whose are the fathers, and of whom, as concerning the flesh, Christ came, who is over all, God blessed forever. Amen.' Revelation 21:3: 'And I heard a great voice out of heaven, saying, Behold, the tabernacle of God is with men, and he will dwell with them, and they shall be his people, and God himself shall be with them, and be their God.' These texts prove the remainder of what I have stated above. We may further inquire, To whom is the kingdom given?

"Third: I answer, it is given to the saints. See Daniel 7:21, 22, 27: 'I beheld, and the same horn made war with the saints, and prevailed against them; until the Ancient of Days came, and judgment was given to the saints of the Most High; and the time came that the saints possessed the kingdom.' 'And the kingdom and dominion, and the greatness of the kingdom under the whole heaven, shall be given to the people of the saints of the Most High, whose kingdom is an everlasting kingdom, and all dominions shall serve and obey him.' Luke 12:32: 'Fear not, little flock, for it is your Father's good pleasure to give you the kingdom.' Matthew 25:34: 'Then shall the King say unto them on his right hand, Come, ye blessed of my Father, inherit the kingdom prepared for you from the foundation of the world.' James 2:5: 'Hearken, my beloved brethren; hath not God chosen the poor of this world, rich in faith, and heirs of the kingdom which he hath promised to them that love him?' 2 Peter 1:11: 'For so an entrance shall be ministered unto you abundantly into the everlasting kingdom of our Lord and Saviour Jesus Christ.' These texts prove abundantly that the saints are to possess and inherit the kingdom; and that it is the everlasting kingdom of Jesus Christ.

"III. I will now show WHEN IT IS they will enter this [400] kingdom and inherit it forever. Not in this present world; for in this world they are to suffer persecution; also, they are strangers and pilgrims in this world. 2 Timothy 3:12: 'Yea, and all that will live godly in Jesus Christ shall suffer persecution.' 1 Peter 2:11: 'Whereas angels, which are greater in power and might, bring not railing accusation against them before the Lord.' Hebrews 11:13, 14: 'These all died in faith, not having received the promises, but having seen them afar off, and were persuaded of them, and embraced them, and confessed that they were strangers and pilgrims on the earth. For they that say such things, declare plainly that they seek a country.' Also, verse 16: 'But now they desire a better country, that is, an heavenly; wherefore God is not ashamed to be called their God; for He hath prepared for them a city.'

"But it is at the coming of Christ with power and great glory, when he shall come in the clouds and in his kingdom. See Daniel 7:13, 14: 'I saw in the night visions; and, behold, one like the Son of Man came with the clouds of heaven, and came to the Ancient of Days, and they brought him near before him. And there was given him dominion, and glory, and a kingdom, that all people, nations, and languages, should serve him: his dominion is an everlasting dominion, which shall not pass away, and his kingdom that which shall not be destroyed.' Matthew 25:31-34: 'When the Son of Man shall come in his glory, and all the holy angels with him, then shall he sit upon the throne of his glory. And before him shall be gathered all nations; and he shall separate them one from the other, as a shepherd divideth his sheep from the goats. And he shall set the sheep on his right hand, but the goats on the left. Then shall the King say unto them on his right hand, Come, ye blessed of my Father, inherit the kingdom prepared for you from the foundation of the world.' 1 Thessalonians 2:12: 'That ye would walk worthy of God, who hath called you unto his kingdom and glory.' 1 Thessalonians 3:13: 'To the end he may stablish your hearts unblamable in holiness before God, even our Father, at the coming of our Lord Jesus Christ with all his saints.' 2 Timothy 4:1: 'I charge thee therefore before God, and the Lord Jesus Christ, who shall judge the quick and the dead at his appearing and his kingdom.' [401] Also, verse 8: 'Henceforth there is laid up for me a crown of righteousness, which the Lord the righteous Judge shall give me at that day; and not to me only, but unto all them also that love his appearing.'

"It will be after the resurrection; for when Christ comes he will reward his saints with his kingdom, as we have proved. Matthew 16:27: 'For the Son of Man shall come in the glory of his Father, with his angels; and then he shall reward every man according to his works.' Then the kingdom of God is not yet set up? No. But our text tells us it will be set up in the days of those kings. What kings? I answer: the ten toes, of which he had just been speaking, are a representation of ten kingdoms, into which the iron, or fourth kingdom, should be divided. Compare Daniel 2:41, 42, with Daniel 7:23, 24: 'And whereas thou sawest the feet and toes, part of potter's clay and part iron, the kingdom shall be divided, but there shall be in it of the strength of the iron, forasmuch as thou sawest the iron mixed with clay. And as the toes of the feet were part of iron and part of clay, so the kingdom shall be partly strong, and partly broken.' 'Thus he said, The fourth beast shall be the fourth kingdom upon earth, which shall be diverse from all kingdoms, and shall devour the whole earth, and shall tread it down and break it in pieces. And the ten horns out of this kingdom are ten kings that shall arise: and another shall arise after them: and he shall be diverse from the first, and he shall subdue three kings.'

"Then our text more than implies that these ten kings are to be in existence until Christ shall come and dash them to pieces, and they be destroyed by the brightness of his coming. 2 Thessalonians 2:8: 'And then shall that Wicked be revealed, whom the Lord shall consume with the spirit of his mouth, and shall destroy with the brightness of his coming.' Also, Daniel 2:45: 'Forasmuch as thou sawest that the stone was cut out of the mountain without hands, and that it brake in pieces the iron, the brass, the clay, the silver, and the gold; the great God hath made known to the king what shall come to pass hereafter: and the dream is certain and the interpretation thereof sure.' These passages are as simple and as plain as words can make them. And I am bold to say, that no one will, or can, consistently with common sense, deny [402] that these ten toes do denote ten kings; and I have never yet seen any but scoffers, skeptics or infidels, who would deny it. If these ten toes do represent ten kings or kingdoms, as all good expositors do admit, there can hardly be a shadow of a doubt but we are on the very close of the kingdoms; for they have now existed more than 1300 years, and this is a greater proportion than other parts of the image have borne with reference to time. And had we no other rule, we ought to be near our watch-tower night and day, lest he, Christ, come and find us sleeping.

"IV. I will now show WHERE THIS KINGDOM IS TO BE. And, 1. It is to be under the whole heaven. See Daniel 7:27. Philippians 2:9, 10: 'Wherefore God also hath highly exalted him, and given him a name which is above every name; that at the name of Jesus every knee should bow, of things in heaven, and things in earth, and things under the earth.' 2. It is to be on the earth. Psalm 2:8: 'Ask of me, and I shall give thee the heathen for thine inheritance, and the uttermost parts of the earth for thy possession.' Also, 25:13: 'His soul shall dwell at ease, and his seed shall inherit the earth.' 37:9: 'For evil-doers shall be cut off: but those that wait upon the Lord, they shall inherit the earth.' Verse 11: 'But the meek shall inherit the earth; and shall delight themselves in the abundance of peace.' Also, verse 22: 'For such as be blessed of him shall inherit the earth; and they that be cursed of him shall be cut off.' Isaiah 60:21: 'Thy people also shall be all righteous; they shall inherit the land forever, the branch of my planting, the work of my hands, that I may be glorified.' Revelation 5:10: 'And hast made us unto our God kings and priests; and we shall reign on the earth.' 3.

It will be called a new earth. Isaiah 65:17: 'For behold, I create new heavens, and a new earth: and the former shall not be remembered, nor come into mind.' Isaiah 66:22: 'For, as the new heavens and the new earth which I will make shall remain before me, saith the Lord, so shall your seed and your name remain.' 2 Peter 3:13: 'Nevertheless, we, according to his promise, look for new heavens and a new earth, wherein dwelleth righteousness.' Revelation 21:1: 'And I saw a new heaven and a new earth: for the first heaven and the first earth were passed away, and [403] there was no more sea.' Also, verse 5: 'And he that sat upon the throne said, Behold, I make all things new. And he said unto me, Write; for these words are true and faithful.'

"By the proof thus adduced we see that the kingdom spoken of in our text is not earthly; for the kingdoms of the earth are broken to pieces and carried away, and no place found for them. It is not sensual, – man ruling over man, or tyrannizing over his fellow; but each will do as he would have others do unto him, and each will love his neighbor as himself. It is not to be wondered at, then, that a rich man cannot easily enter this kingdom, nor one who lords it over his fellow; for the meek only can inherit it. This, too, shows why kings, captains, and mighty men are destroyed in the great battle of God Almighty; for those spirits and principles cannot exist in the kingdom of God. We learn, too, by this view, why the earth is cleansed by fire; for the proud and all that do wickedly must be consumed out of it. See Matthew 13:41, 42: 'The Son of Man shall send forth his angels, and they shall gather out of his kingdom all things that offend, and them which do iniquity; and shall cast them into a furnace of fire; there shall be wailing and gnashing of teeth.' This, too, accounts for the scoffers in these last days; for they well know, if the kingdom is to be a righteous one, they themselves can have no part in it. We also learn by this why some of our doctors of divinity and professors, some of our reverends and clergy, some of our editors and Christian teachers, as they wish to be called, are so strongly opposed to this doctrine. They know, if Christ should come, he would not regard their high-sounding titles nor their dogmatical teachings; they know that the great aim of some has been to seek honors of men and worldly profits, and their trade is in danger. The spiritual reign and conversion of the world has been their hobby, and they hug to the foolish idea of converting the world to their dogmas and faith by means of money and sectarian missionaries. As well may they undertake to dip the ocean dry with a fireman's bucket as to convert the world with their sectarian motives and party creeds. How can men be so ignorant as not to see that every convert only makes the rent worse, and every [404] year divisions and subdivisions increase? Can a kingdom thus torn and divided stand for 'millions of years,' – as one of the sectarian editors lately proclaimed, – and our dear Saviour be correct, Matthew 12:25: 'And Jesus knew their thoughts, and said unto them, Every kingdom divided against itself is brought to desolation; and every city or house divided against itself shall not stand'? We know they cannot be true.

"Every discerning mind knows that, at the present time, the Roman church are making two proselytes to the Protestants' one; and all must agree that, of those converted by Protestants, one-half, or nearly so, are mere nominal professors. Well may we say, 'millions of years' must pass away before our world could be converted. But I ask, what man of common sense, who has read and believes his Bible, can for a moment believe that 'millions of years' must intervene before Christ will come? How different did the apostle Peter preach from this! 1 Peter 4:7: 'But the end of all things is at hand; be ye, therefore, sober, and watch unto prayer.' Also Christ, Revelation 22:12: 'And behold, I come quickly; and my reward is with me, to give every man according as his work shall be.' And 20: 'He which testifieth these things saith, 'Surely I come, quickly; Amen. Even so, come, Lord Jesus.' Likewise James 5:8, 9: 'Be ye also patient; establish your hearts; for the coming of the Lord draweth nigh. Grudge not one against another, brethren, lest ye be condemned; behold, the Judge standeth before the door.'

"Much more Scripture might be produced to show we are on the end of the world. Yet the Scripture is fulfilling to the very letter by those scoffers of the present day, who say, 'Where is the promise of his coming?' and, also, who 'say in their hearts, My Lord delayeth his coming.' And some of them are so awfully daring as to publish openly and boldly to the world that he will not come this 'million of years yet.' Strange infatuation! It is time for all who sincerely love our Lord to awake from their slumbers, trim their lamps, and be ready; for the Bridegroom is at the door. Why will you be so backward in believing God's word? Can you not discern the signs of the times?

"I beseech you, O sinner! do not hear to those who [405] will deceive you. Look for yourselves; read, study, and consider for yourselves. You may depend upon it, every important movement of the nations, of the church, of sects, and societies, of the world, denotes the end of all things at hand. A few more days to be numbered, and time will be no more. Regard not those teachers, who are crying peace and safety, when sudden destruction cometh; that say, 'My Lord delayeth his coming.' Be warned by one who feels for your souls. I ask not for your honors, nor for your money; let them perish with the world. I ask you to escape for your life, your eternal life. O save, save your soul! Think of that world which will never end, of that state which will never be changed. Think, my dear friend, of your own good; buy the truth, buy oil, buy wine and milk, without money and without price. Come, ye poor, take hold of the riches which can never perish; eat, O! eat and drink of that food which can never cloy, which, if a man eat of, he shall live forever. Come, ye sick, here is health for you; ye lame, you will find strength; yes, weary ones may find rest, and captives go free. The bars of the prison-house will be broken, and the shackles of the slaves will be unloosed. Captain Jesus is knocking at the door; King Immanuel will soon come in."

A Scene Of The Last Day

"The supposed reflections of a sinner, witnessing the solemn events which immediately precede and follow the second advent of our Lord Jesus Christ and the conflagration of the world."

"'Ah! what means that noise? Can that be thunder? Too long, too loud and shrill; more like a thousand trumpets sounding an onset. It shakes the earth ... See, see, it reels! How dreadful! how strange! .. Another phenomenon to frighten poor, ignorant fanatics. I will not be afraid. Let Nature play her fantastic gambols. My soul's too brave to shake, too big to be afraid. When the stars fell [406] like hailstones I stood unmoved, and laughed at others' fears. They passed away, and all was calm again. It was one of nature's freaks. So oft of late has nature played her tricks, methinks 't is natural. There was a time when superstition reigned. The world would then have said – ah, yes, and believed it, too – that these denoted war, bloodshed, and great convulsions among men; but now the world has become more wise; they are not fools and cowards, as our forefathers. ... Hark! another sound, more long, more loud, more dreadful still! Rock, rock! the world is rocking men, like babes, to sleep. I will not yet be scared. This may be natural. The wind is pent up in the bowels of the earth, and, in seeking vent, makes all this uproar. These noises in the earth and roarings of the sea, which have of late made timid mortals shake, by this philosophy are all accounted for. I am not shaken yet. Nature will work her own cure; and, while these Christian fools are trembling under their vain imaginations of these sights and signs of the great last day, I stand un ... A third great blast – a shout, a cry! What means this wild roar? I'll go and see. ...

"... 'Ah! I thought it so. Aurora borealis!' *[Speaking to the multitude.]* 'Ye fools and cowards all! why do you make ado about this so common sight? Have you not often seen, within a few years past, the heavens almost as brilliant as now, – what the vulgar illiterate called "fire, and blood, and pillars of smoke;" and then it passed away, and nothing was left but to ridicule each other's fears? And so now; this will soon pass a---

"... 'But it increases. See, see, how brilliant! The very clouds are bright with glory. It rolls and gathers to the zenith. ... Hark! hark! another sound, more deep; a fourth, more loud and long; a second shout! 't is like the human voice; it is the wind, the electric fluid in the air. See, see! the heavens do shake! the clouds, the light, the air, are trembling yet. ... And yet the light rolls on, the cloud grows brighter, and the rays diverge from yonder point. An eye! an eye! how like the All-seeing Eye! I will not tremble yet. These coward souls shall never see me sha----. What! yet another crack! How deafening to the ear! Another shout! ... Sure, [407] that was a shout of men; I hear them still. The mountains shake and tremble on their base; the hills move to and fro; the compass-needle has forsaken the pole, and leaps towards the zenith point. The sea has fled its bounds, and rivers backward in their channels run. What can this mean? Is nature in a fit? ... The light! the light! it still approaches nearer to the earth – and brighter, too; it dazzles my weak sight. Is it a comet, or some other orb, that has strayed from its track, and, by the laws of gravitation, is approaching to our earth? Now for the laws of nature here's a struggle! and if that other law, repulsion, does not repel its force and drive it back, then surely this poor, dark, sublunary globe must be drowned in a sphere of fire; and where will mortals ... Another sound! a dreadful blast, a hundred-fold more loud than former trumpets! This shakes my soul; my courage, too, has fled. What but a Gabriel's trump could give such sounds – so loud, so long, so clear? ... Look! see! the sun has veiled his face; all nature heaves a groan, one deep-drawn sigh, and all is still as death. ...

"'The clouds – those vivid clouds, so full of fire – are driven apart by this last blast, and, rolling up themselves, stand back aghast. And, O, my soul, what do I see? A great white throne, and One upon it. His garment is whiter than the driven snow, and the hair of his head is like the pure wool. See fiery flames issuing from his throne, rolling down the vault of heaven like wheels of burning fire. Before him are thousands and thousands of thousands of winged seraphim, ready to obey his will. See Gabriel, the great archangel, raising his golden trump to his mouth. The last great trumpet sounds, – one heavenly shout, – and in a moment every angel flies, each different ways, in rays of light, to this affrighted globe. The earth now heaves a throb for the last time, and in this last great throe her bowels burst, and from her spring a thousand thousand, and ten thousand times ten thousand immortal beings into active life. And then those few who had looked on the scene with patient hope, were suddenly transformed, from age to youth, from mortal to immortal; and thus they stood, a bright and shining band, all clothed in white, like the bright throne which yet appeared in heaven. [408]

"'While I stood gazing on this heavenly band, I saw the winged seraphs, who had come from the great white throne when the seventh trumpet sounded, standing among them. "All hail!" they cried, "ye blood-washed throng – arise, and meet your Saviour in the middle air." They clapped their wings, and the next moment all the air was full of the bright seraphs and their train of immortals whom I late had seen spring from the earth. I saw them pass through the long vista of the parted cloud, and stand before the throne. Then I beheld one, like the sons of men, came on a cloud, whose rays of brightness filled the upper vault with radiant streams of light, more brilliant than a thousand suns. He came before the throne, and then I heard the shout of the celestial host, which filled the upper regions with a sound that echoed down to earth, and made the dark spirits in the pit of woe shriek out in lamentations of dread despair. It was a shout of victory. A thousand harps were tuned, and soon the heavenly choir sang hallelujah to the Lamb of God. Thrice they repeated the grand chorus, and thrice with shouts of these young immortals did the arch of heaven echo back to earth this shout of victory; when suddenly the cloud, which late had parted to give this view to earth, rolled up the vault of heaven its dark and sable mass from the horizon, until it closed from view the great white throne, and Him that sat upon it, and wrapt this globe in darkness, such as covered Egypt when Moses stretched his rod over the land of Pharaoh.

"'The air now became stagnated with heat; while the dismal howlings of those human beings who were left upon the earth, and the horrid yells of the damned spirits, who seemed to have been driven from the middle air by the cloud which shut down its impenetrable veil upon the world, filled my soul with horror not easily described. I thought myself in the dark pit of hell, which I had often made a ridicule of in former days. But soon a flash of lightning showed me that I was still on earth, and then a peal of thunder, which shook the globe to its very centre, and made this earth to tremble like a poplar leaf; while flash after flash of vivid lightning made darkness visible, and roar after roar of the approaching thunder made horror still more horrible. The air, if air it could be called, became impregnated with a sulphureous flame, that [409] choked the lungs of man and beast, and seemed to hush in silence those dismal yells and moans of wretched mortals in this wreck of matter. I asked death to rid my suffering frame from torture; but, ah! death now denied me aid. I now remembered all the warnings of my former days, and these enhanced my pain. I remembered, too, the Scriptures, which spoke of this great burning day, which I had treated as a fiction to frighten weak and silly mortals. I saw, and now believed – but O, too late! – that all that God had promised had been, was now, and would be, literally fulfilled. My conscience now spoke terror to my soul. I now began to repent; but O, it came too late! I cried for mercy; but where was mercy now? When last the heaven was open, and I had seen the Judge upon his throne, Mercy had veiled herself; and when the immortal band had left the earth, I saw her leave the globe, and wing her way up to the throne of God; and, as she left the world, I heard her voice proclaim, "It is finished." I knew her work was done; and yet my tongue cried mercy! I saw, when the flash of lightnings gave me chance to see, a thousand damned forms of demons, grinning out horrible delight. I heard, between each roar of thunder, their tauntings and horrible imprecations.

"'The heat became severe; combustibles began to burn; when suddenly the heavens began to rain a shower of hailstones. I fled for shelter to a shelving rock, and there secure I lay. The air became more clear and cool. I now could see the inhabitants left on earth flying for shelter in every direction; some wounded by the hail, and with their horrid oaths crying for help to their more fortunate companions. But there was no regard for others' woes – each one sought shelter for himself. The hail increased, until nothing but rocks and caverns of the earth could stand before it. The buildings, temples, and proud palaces of kings were all demolished, and lay a heap of ruins. The forest trees and groves were scattered upon the plain; and nothing stood the storm, of all the works of man. The face of the earth was covered over with ice, as though a hundred winters had reigned predominant. The eye could rest on nothing but one wide waste of frozen heaps of hail, with now and then a solitary human being wandering among the ruins of the once [410] inhabited cities, half chilled to death, seeking for shelter, or to satisfy a craving appetite, cursing and blaspheming the God of heaven for the plague of the hail.

"'The storm had ceased. The sun had appeared behind the broken clouds, far in the west, with now and then a faint and sickly ray, that made the desolation still more desolate. The beasts that were upon the face of the earth were all slain, except a few who had burrowed in the earth. The fowls of the heavens were scattered over the earth among the slain; and of all the feathered tribe there was nothing left but scattered carcasses. Bodies of human beings were underneath the ruins in every place, some dashed in pieces, some without heads, and some whose limbs were severed from their trunks, and in every form that death could prey upon the human frame. Some, still in life, though wounded, filled up the dismal scene with moans, and groans, and shrieks of wild despair.

"'The cloud, which but recently had covered the earth with darkness, and had discharged its contents of massy balls of ice upon the world, now rolled its broken columns to the east. The sun was sinking in the western horizon, as if it hid itself from this vast desolation. And when the cloud rolled half way down the eastern sky, there opened to the view another sight, – more grand there could not be, – a city! Its walls were great and high. The foundation appeared to be the great white cloud, on which the throne was placed when first I saw the light. This city lay four square upon the cloud. The height, the length, the breadth appeared equal. The walls were made of jasper, more pure than gold that is seven times purified. It shone more brilliant than crystal. Twelve manner of precious stones garnished the wall. Each several stone outshone his fellow; and yet the polish of the stone was such that each reflected back the rays his fellow gave, and, thus commingled, formed one general mass of rays of light and glory, increasing with every reflection twelve-fold, and thus increasing, for aught that I can tell, to infinity. Twelve gates I saw – three on every side. These gates were made of pearls; each pearl a gate, and every gate a pearl more brilliant than a sun. All the streets were gold, so highly polished that they shone as it were transparent glass. I saw no temple there; but I beheld such glory as [411] my eyes never saw before. It was the Great I Am, Lord God Almighty, and the Lamb of God, that filled the city with such rays of light, that if the sun, and moon, and stars had all combined, they would not have compared with it, any more than the small glow-worm could with the sun in his meridian glory. I wonder how I did behold such rays of glory, and yet they dazzled not. But yet, I now bethink myself, while I stood gazing, this thought was whispered, as I imagined, to my mind – "All this you have lost for your rejection of the Lamb, you see, the light of yonder city!"

"'At this my soul was filled with horror, and madness seized my brain. I cried to the rocks to hide me from the view of him whom I had thus rejected. But rocks were deaf. I then fled to the mountains, and called on them to fall upon me, and hide me in the bowels of the earth, or crush me into non-existence. But mountains had no pity on a wretch like me. I turned my eyes away, that I might not behold the sight again; but still the view was plain. I shut my eyes, determined to shut out this hateful vision; but, O, the form was printed on my brain in lines of livid fire! Which way I turned, the city lay before me. I saw, or thought I saw, the glory, harmony, and happiness of the citizens; and every view added rancor, enmity, and envy to my soul. I gnashed my teeth with pain; I raved and roared like a wild maniac; and yet my reason told me I was sane, – these things were real. I cursed and swore, – blasphemed the God of heaven; yet every oath returned upon me, and was like a dagger piercing to my heart. I called on death to rid me of my pain: but death obeyed not. I thought of suicide, to rid myself of self; but then eternity – O dreadful thought! – would rush upon my brain, and fill my mind with horror inconceivable. I tried to hope that things would change, or use would reconcile me to my lot; but hope had fled, and this I saw forever! No hope of change for better; for all that hope of change that I had ever had, I treated with disdain, – yea, worse, with ridicule and contempt. I saw the very nature of the holy law required my banishment forever. And all the time of probation which I had formerly enjoyed, I saw was on this express condition, – to be prepared to meet this very time, when holiness and sin, happiness and misery, would be forever [412] separated; when he that is filthy would be filthy still, and he that is holy would be holy still. I knew that God himself had told us this; but yet I listened not. Filled with my own vain thoughts and vainer lusts, I trampled on the commands, warnings, and invitations of the God of heaven, – and here end all my hopes! Ah! could I hope to be happy, on the condition of being holy too, I would cast it from me: for in my very soul I abhor, I hate the very name of holiness. I should be willing to be happy; but to love others as I do myself, – and then to love that God supreme above all others, and even above myself, – I will not, cannot, shall not, here submit.

"'While my mind thus passed from bad to worse, and every avenue of the heart was filled with evil passions, I saw the city still drew nearer to the earth; and from its rays had poured such a flood of light and heat upon the earth, that the hail melted, and the streams and fountains of water dried up. The tops of mountains soon began to burn; the rocks began to melt, and, with their lava, filled up the streams and vales below. This was not like the former heat which I had recently experienced before the storm of hail; no sulphureous smell, no suffocating heat, like that. It was a flame more pure, – a searching, cleansing, penetrating flame of fire, – that searched in every nook and corner of the world, and pierced the very bowels of the globe; that penetrated every crevice, crack, and cavern of the earth, and then descended to the bottom of the deep, the sea, and thus destroyed all that had life, and all on which the curse of sin was found. The monuments of man, that long had stood the shocks of ages, now mouldered down to dust. The works of art, the "proud-capt towers and gorgeous palaces," and all the modern pageantry of pride and show, were by this flame to ashes turned. The cities, villages, and towns, which once had filled the world with human beings, and all the seats of science, where man had long been taught the ancient fables and the vain philosophy of the former generations, and also learned the more modern customs and fashions of the day, to lord it over others, who had not thus been blessed, as they supposed, with this great ray of light, this mortal-cast, man-made wisdom, – these all did melt away, and not an eye could see or finger point where once [413] they stood. The battlements of war, – the pride of kings, defense of nations, and the boast of warriors, – which longer yet had stood the ravages of time, and now, for ages back, had claimed the name and title which mortals give, "impregnable," – who, from their gaping sides, had poured at times such showers of missiles upon the approaching foe, that many a gallant ship, with all her crew, had found a berth beneath the watery wave, or scattered in fragments into the middle air, and many a brave and fearless hostile band had left their bones to whiten on the plain; – these, too, had sunk beneath this powerful flame, and there was not a fragment left to tell where once they stood.

"'I saw the cloisters of the Roman monks, and the dark cells of the nuns, which long had kept from view the secret crimes and midnight revels of their murderous, cruel, lustful inmates; – I saw the dark-walled chamber of the Inquisition, filled with its means of torture, that had, in ages past, drenched all its walls in blood, now hung, in solemn mockery, with images of Christ, with likenesses of angels, and pictures of the Virgin Mary, blasphemously called "the mother of God;" – all were consumed by this pervading flame. I then beheld it approaching where I stood. My flesh began to quiver on my bones, my hair rose up on end, and all within me was suddenly turned into corruption. I felt the flame when first it struck my person; it seemed to pierce through all the joints and marrow of my frame, dividing soul and body. I shrieked with pain, and, for a moment, I was all unconscious. The next moment I found myself a spirit, and saw the mass, of which my body lately was composed, a heap of ashes; and, although my spirit yet retained a form like that which I had dropped, yet half the pain was gone, and a moment I seemed to live again for pleasure. But the next moment, turning from the loathsome lump of ashes, I saw the flame, and in it saw the form of the Most Holy. I fled as on the wings of the wind, and skimmed the surface of the earth, if possible to escape the sight of that All-seeing Eye; and, as I flew, I soon found many thousands more unhappy spirits like myself, seeking for the same object. We fled together, and every moment added to our numbers scores of these unhappy beings; but still the same most holy flame pursued, until we found no [414] place on earth could hide us from his view. We then launched forth into the lower air, and sunk, and sunk, and sunk, until we came to this dark gulf; and here we found this pit, where light can never enter; and, glad to find a place where holiness will never enter, we plunged in here. And when we left the light, and sunk into this dark and dismal place of wretchedness and woe, we found ourselves enclosed on every side in chains of darkness, that all the demons and spirits of the damned can never break, until He who shut us up will please to let us loose again. And then we know there is another place, which lies far beneath this dark and dismal pit, that, if he conquers then, will be our last abode, – A Lake Of Fire And Brimstone.'"

"A Vision Of Death.

"I saw, – whether asleep or awake, I cannot tell, but this I know: I saw the dark and dismal door of Death. It was narrow as the grave; and only one could enter at a time, and tread its winding steep. Yet thousand passed the door. At its threshold, all left their earthly idols. Some cast a wishful look, as they pushed forward, and shrieked. Some lingered trembling, and some rushed forward regardless of the consequences. There were seen all ages, all ranks, and all conditions, passing towards the door.

"I saw the drunkard quaff his bowl of poison, burst open the door of death, and stagger in. I heard a curse, a groan, a fall, a hollow, dismal sound, and all was silent as the tomb.

"Next came a voluptuary. He laughed, he danced, and leaped the fearful leap. The door closed on him. I heard a trembling cry. Spectators shuddered and turned their eyes away, and nothing more was seen.

"A selfish miser came, loaded down with bags of gold. His head was white with care. His look was fearful with despair. Envy was his only attendant. He staggered to the door, laid down his gold, and wept. A dismal cloud [415] enveloped him. A laugh was heard. And, when the cloud was gone, gold, miser, – all had disappeared.

"There came a man of honor. On his brow wreaths of victory were twined. His step was stately. At his nod many bowed and fawned. He, too, must pass the gate. He touched the secret spring. The door wide open flew. Darkness enveloped him. The multitude shrank back, to follow some other leader. And nothing now was seen, save a few dried leaves of laurel.

"There came a giddy youth. His eye was sparkling. His step was light. Many a jocund story hung upon his lips. While looking on the world, he backward ran against the door, and fell. I heard a piteous moan, a distant shriek, and silence reigned again.

"I saw one other come. Hope sat upon his brow. He smiled and wept; but, with a forward look, he traced the path, while in his hand he held a little Book, and often read. I saw he had a glass that penetrated the dark abyss, and left a ray behind. I heard him sing. 'T was not a song of earth, but soft and sweet like the melodious sounds of distant music on a summer's eve. He passed the door of death; and, like the setting sun, whose rays have chased the flying clouds away, he passed to rise more glorious on the morrow."

"ON JEREMIAH'S LAMENTATION.

"How doth the City, once so full of fame,
Now silent sit and mourn her widowed name!
She, that was great among the nations far,
When kings and princes brought their gold to her!
She weepeth sore. The midnight hears her moan –
Her tears fast flowing, as she sits alone.
Her friends are foes. To fill her general doom,
Her lovers, children, sink into the tomb.
Judah afflicted is, a slave of old;
She's gone a captive, – to a servant sold.
Her people, scattered through a heathen land,
No rescue have they from the spoiler's hand.
O Zion! mourn thy state, because there's none
To spread thy feasts, or call thy children home.
Thy temple's empty; all thy teachers sigh

In bitterness, to hear thy maidens cry: [416]
'The Lord Jehovah hath this wonder wrought,
For her transgressions are these judgments brought'

Zion's fair daughters, all their beauty fled!
Her princes fallen! all her heroes dead!
Jerusalem once great, how changed the scene!
Her sorrows double, make her anguish keen,
When recollection calls her mercies o'er, –
The pleasant things she had in days of yore.
Her foes approach; her people all are slain;
She cries for help, – alas! she cries in vain.
Behold the envious! how he taunting says:
'Where are your Sabbaths and your solemn days?'
The nations that have known and heard her fame
Despise her now and publish all her shame.
Her downcast look, her end, her bitter sigh,
Are not regarded. No Deliverer's nigh.

Behold, O Lord, how her afflictions grow!
Her enemies have magnified them too.
There walk the plunderer's and the murderer's band,
No place so sacred can their rage command.
Her people sigh for bread; they seek in vain
Their pleasant things for meat. They cry again:
'Look down, O Lord! consider all my ways;
How vile am I, how sinful all my days!
Ah! what is that to you who pass me by?
Does any sorrow with my sorrow vie?
The Lord in judgment hath afflicted me;
From his fierce anger whither shall I flee?
In every path my feet have found a snare.
If I return, it's desolation there.
And my transgression, like a yoke, is bound
Upon my neck. My crimes are twisted round.
My strength is weakness. Lord, how can I rise,
Delivered over to my sins a prize?
The Lord hath trodden, by a mighty host,

My old and young men, humbled in the dust.
For these I weep; my tears are streaming fast;
No comfort near, nor desolation past.
In vain I spread my hands; for there is none
To comfort me or bring my children home.
The Lord commands; in terror I am bound,
And all my foes encompass me around.
O righteous Sovereign! lo, how just thy cause!
For I've rebelled and trampled on thy laws.
Hear, all ye people, and my woes behold;
My virgins captured, and my young men sold.
I call my lovers, once my hope and pride;
But they despise me, and my sighs deride.
My priests and elders, while they seek for bread,
Give up the ghost, and slumber with the dead.
Behold, O Lord, in me is sore distress,
My heart is troubled, and I find no rest; [417]

Abroad the sword, at home is naught but death,
I sigh, a rebel, with my every breath.
There's none to comfort, though they hear me sigh
"The Lord has done it all," they gladly cry.

Behold the day the Lord has called his own,
When they, like me, shall come before his throne.
There all their sins and wickedness shall be,
And do to them as Thou hast done to me.

For my transgressions and my soul's complaint
My sighs are many, and my heart is faint.'"

―――――――

"ON TIME.

"YOU ask me, sir, to tell the cause
Why nature changes in her laws;
And why, in youth, time lags so slow,
But flies so swift as old we grow.

"I'll tell thee, friend. Lay not the blame,
Nor call old time 'a fickle dame.'
She heeds you not, nor will she stay,
To stop your progress or decay.

"When you were young, like other boys,
You sought anticipated joys;
And when for future years you pined,
You thought not of those left behind.

"You watched for years, for weeks, and days
To come, to bring your wished-for plays;
And, with our future good in view,
Time lags behind to me and you.

"We measure not by running sands,
Nor by the clock's revolving hands;
But think old time must run and fly,
To bring our wished-for objects nigh.

"But, when we to the object come,
We think old time must cease to run,
And be obedient to our need:
To walk or fly, as we shall speed.

"So the vain youth, to imitate
Follies and vices of the great,
Longs for the day of liberty,
When he from guardians may be free. [418]

"Old time revolves at slowest pace
When we're most eager for the race.
In youth or age, in hope or fear,
He walks or runs, till death draws near."

A Fragment. – An Allegory.

"There was a certain prince of royal blood. His father was one of
the most powerful monarchs in the world, and every way qualified to
rule over the people of his inheritance. He bid fair not only to rule

in justice and equity, but to exalt his subjects to an honorable station and to great glory.

"This prince, whose name we shall call Emanor, was brought up at his Father's court, where he was taught all the principles of truth and righteousness. He was early taught to learn obedience to his Father's will; and was never known to be disobedient to a single command, or to break one of those righteous principles by which his Father's subjects were governed. Emanor learnt the first great lesson, self-command, which only can teach men to command others. He suffered much, that he might have pity on those who suffered. He was tempted often by foreign courtiers, who visited his Father's court, to follow the vanities and follies of other courts; but was always able to resist the temptation, and expose their false reasoning to their own shame and confusion. He was, therefore, able to succor others that were tempted. He lived on the most simple fare, was frugal and plain in his dress, and economical in his expenses, that he might make the poor richer. He was affable and free in his manners, that he might encourage the poor and needy, the weak and afflicted, to apply to him for succor or help. He was meek and humble in his intercourse with his fellowmen, that, by his practice, he might teach others those virtues which were greatly admired and rewarded at his Father's court.

"We must not forget to mention that Emanor was pious. His was not that ostentatious piety which says, 'Stand by thyself' – 'I am more holy than thou;' nor that sectarian piety which denounces all that will not 'follow us.' No, my [419] kind reader, he had not that dogmatical piety which lords it over fellow-worshippers, and says, 'This you must do, and that you may leave undone; you must support this improvement, that institution, or join such a social compact, or we can have no fellowship with you as Christians. You must forbear to eat or drink any of the good things of life, if your masters say forbear.' Neither had he that proud, scholastic piety, which knows no greater depths than the wisdom of man, supported by vain philosophy, and has no higher motive than self-aggrandizement at the expense of others. No, his piety was that of the heart, founded on the first grand principle of his Father's kingdom, namely, to 'love God with all the heart, and our neighbor as ourselves.' It manifested itself in his constant, daily submission to the commands and dealings of God, and in diligently inquiring after and relieving the wants of his fellow-creatures. 'He went about doing good.' No ostentation, no self-aggrandizement was in his religion, but a pure, holy flame of love to God and man. His person was perfect, his form comely, his soul pure. This was the character, and such the qualifications of Emanor, the Prince of whom I have been speaking.

"In addition to what I have related, he was a great Captain, a mighty Conqueror, and a Prince of peace. In the wars which his Father waged with the most potent enemies of his government, he came off conqueror, and more than conqueror, over some of the most stubborn and rebellious subjects that any government was ever troubled with. He carried the olive branch of peace into the enemies' camp; and, although he was treated with indignity, scorn, and hatred, was reviled, mocked, spit upon, was smitten, bruised, wounded, and torn, slandered, defamed, and cast out, yet he ceased not to cry, Peace, and to proclaim, Pardon to the chief of the rebels, on condition of their throwing down the weapons of their rebellion, and returning to the allegiance of their lawful and righteous Sovereign. And, when they refused even these conditions, he brought them of his Father, paid the utmost farthing for their release, and then followed them, day after day, with kind invitations, with soft words, and great and rich promises, until his own spirit was kindled in their hearts, and they yielded to the 'power of his word;' for 'never did man speak as he spake.' And then he [420] adopted them as joint heirs with himself in his Father's kingdom. This, surely, you will say, is more than being conqueror. He not only destroyed their weapons of warfare and humbled their proud hearts, but he destroyed the enmity of their minds, and made them willing and obedient subjects to his Father's government. He produced in their very souls a hungering and thirsting after the constitution and laws of the kingdom which they had formerly attempted in vain to destroy. He likewise, by his power, goodness, and love, begot in each of these rebels a spirit of emulation to be like their young Prince, to think like him of his Father's glory, to act like him, to 'do to others as they would have others do to them,' and to be like him, – perfect in all their ways, as the King himself was perfect. Their chief object was to glorify their beloved Prince, by obedience to his laws and require-ments, as he glorified his Father, and obeyed his laws and requests.

"Here the reader must acknowledge that we have a pattern worthy of all love, imitation, and adoration. All rational minds must admit that it could not be properly called idolatry to adore and worship so perfect, powerful, and excellent a Being as this. And these rebels were in the habit of calling him their 'Master,' 'Saviour,' 'Creator,' 'Lord God,' 'the Holy One,' 'the First and the Last,' 'the only true God,' etc. The unreconciled rebels complained loudly and bitterly of those who were reconciled, for their idolatry and submission to the dear Prince in whom they had received such innumerable blessings;

but this complaint only went to prove the unreconciled state of heart which they possessed against this Prince of princes. It has always been noticed that, when any of these complainers have been truly humbled and reconciled to this Prince and his Father's government, they have become idolaters equally with their brethren, and have acknowledged him a God in human form.

"The King, the Father of Emanor, having designed to procure a bride for the Prince, his son, made a general proclamation in his empire, and sent forth a herald to publish even to the ends of the earth this his design, and fixing to his decree some of the following conditions:

"1st. The damsel who would aspire to this great honor must believe in this proclamation, and place implicit confidence [421] in the word, power, and goodness of the Prince; her faith must be tried by all the means the wisdom of the Prince could devise, to know whether it was pure and would endure to the end; and this was to be known by her obedience to the commands of her Lord and Prince."…

This sketch is, of course, incomplete. It is a subject of regret that he did not proceed to describe the trials of the church, the manner in which God led her, to prove her and try her, and fit her for the exalted position to which she is destined, when she shall be presented to the Father, without spot or blemish, at the marriage supper of the Lamb.

"The Day Of The Lord.

"'Ye, brethren, are not in darkness that that Day should overtake you as a thief. Ye are all the children of light, and the children of the day: we are not of the night, nor of the darkness.' – 1 Thessalonians 5:4, 5.

"This passage of Scripture is one of many that come to us in this time of trial with a blessed promise that, if we are what we should be, we shall know something respecting the coming of the day of the Lord.

"Many tell us it is no matter whether we know anything on this subject, and that, if we remain in ignorance of it, we shall be safe. But the apostle, in the context, shows us the consequences of that day coming on us as a thief: 'For yourselves know perfectly, that the day of the Lord so cometh as a thief in the night. For when they shall say, Peace and safety; then sudden destruction cometh upon them, as travail upon a woman with child; and they shall not escape.'

"He cannot mean by this that that day will steal in upon us, and we not be looking for it. It is only those who say, Peace and safety, – who say the day is not coming, – who are thus overtaken, as a thief comes unawares and spoils his neighbor of his goods.

"How blessed the thought – the Day of To-morrow!
When Glory's bright Sun shall banish all sorrow;
When the trials of life shall be over; and never
Draw us from our love, for ever and ever. [422]

"I long for the day! The night has been dreary.
To tarry and pray, the flesh becomes weary.
I long for the voice, God's servants awaking,
That soon shall announce that that day is breaking.

"O, then shall our eyes refrain from all weeping,
And our eyelids no more shall be heavy with sleeping,
When death is disarmed of his trident of terror,
And sin has no charms for ever and ever.

"Let weary ones sing! How can they be fearful?
Since Christ is our King, our hearts will be cheerful
I long for the day, 'mid this wreck of commotion,
To land me safe home in eternity's ocean." [423]

———————

Adventist Pioneer Library

For more information, visit:
www.APLib.org

or write to:
apl@netbox.com

Made in the USA
Las Vegas, NV
27 January 2024

84974767R00230